# A Slice of History
# & A Piece of Pie

Nancy Pickering Thomas

# A Slice of History & A Piece of Pie

## Recipes and Remembrance

**A Cookbook of Family Favorites from Early Estes Park**

*Estes Park Friends & Foundation, Inc. Press*
2014

2014 © Estes Park Museum Friends & Foundation, Inc. Press
200 Fourth Street, Estes Park, Colorado 80517

Printed in the United States of America

The paper used in this publication meets the minimum requirements of the American National Standard for Information Sciences—Permanence of Paper for Printed Library Materials.
ANSI Z39.48-1992

LCCN: 2013940202

ISBN: 978-0-98477-808-9

First Edition

Front cover photograph by Doug and Penny Fox, Elaine Downing, and Dave Albee. Back cover photographs (*clockwise from top*): courtesy of the Estes Park Museum; courtesy of the National Park Service; courtesy of the Carnegie Library for Local History, Boulder, Colorado.

Text and cover design by Pratt Brothers Composition

To the memory of Estes Park's pioneer women whose recipes can be found here, and to cooks then and now who, following their fine example, continue to prepare good things to eat in this lovely place.

*Ethel Steere Mills, of Crags Lodge, with her daughter Eleanor Ann, c. 1910.*
**Photo courtesy of the National Park Service**

# Contents

*Preface* | **ix**

*Introduction* | **xi**

*Acknowledgments* | **xix**

**Chapter 1.** Kitchen Realities and Rituals in Historic Estes Park | **1**

**Chapter 2.** Homesteaders and Old Settlers | **19**

**Chapter 3.** Early Estes Park Resorts and Inns | **83**

**Chapter 4.** Estes Park Villagers | **183**

**Chapter 5.** Cottager Communities | **299**

*Bibliography of Estes Park Cookbooks* | **375**

*Appendix A* | **379**

*Appendix B* | **383**

*References* | **387**

*Name and Subject Index* | **391**

*Recipe Index* | **401**

# Preface

This is an important book. A culinary delight, to be sure, it brings together in one place the earliest and most loved recipes of many of those who have made the Estes Valley and its nearby places their home. The recipes themselves are, of course, intrinsically interesting both in their variety and their creativity. Modest and unpretentious for the most part, they reflect a way of life that most of us have come to associate with Estes Park. Good food is valued here, as a part of good living. And it has been that way since the beginning.

However, *A Slice of History & A Piece of Pie* is a good deal more. Thanks to the painstaking original research of Nancy Thomas and her associates, what we have here is a major new contribution to the history of Estes Park. By carefully contextualizing these little-known and in most cases long-lost recipes with the lives of their creators, the author has given them a human dimension that few community cookbooks even attempt. The result is an invaluable and most interesting social history of the Estes region that will be of great value to those of us who delight in knowing as much as we can about the lives of those who have come before and prepared the way.

The effort that has gone into producing this book—including the careful selection of vintage photographs and illustrations—is clearly enormous and will be greatly appreciated by all those who read and use it. Congratulations on a good job—well done. You have produced a book destined to become a classic.

*James H. Pickering*
*Historian Laureate, Town of Estes Park*

# Introduction

*"... the recipes include those of the best cooks in Estes Park."*
— *Trail Talk*, 1920

*A Slice of History & A Piece of Pie* is an effort to reclaim the experience of the first generations of Estes Park families by considering their foodways—defined as "the eating habits and culinary practices" of people in a particular geographical area or historical epoch. Part history, part cookery, the book owes its inspiration and a number of its oldest recipes to cookbooks published in the town of Estes Park in the early decades of the twentieth century. The first edition of the *Tried and True Recipe Book*, published by Chapter AV of PEO in 1920,[1] and revised and republished in 1925 and in 1985, has been invaluable as a resource for identifying or confirming early Estes Park families as well as providing access to their recipes.[2]

Given that the *Tried and True Recipe Book* included the recipes of pioneer Estes families, we can assume that it was among the first cookbooks, if not *the* first, published in Estes Park. That its appearance was an exciting event in the Village was palpable in the *Estes Park Trail's* enthusiastic announcement of its publication:

> At last Estes Park is to have a cookbook all its own, with recipes specially adapted to this altitude. The women of the Estes Park chapter of the PEO have scoured Estes Park in search of the most tempting

*The town of Estes Park, c. 1907.*

Clatworthy photo, courtesy of Cheryl Pennington

*and practical recipes available, and the results are published in their "Tried and True Recipes."... The cookbooks are bound attractively in white oil cloth, and the recipes include those of the best cooks in Estes Park. No one who has found it difficult to cook in this high altitude can afford to be without this new recipe book, and the best culinary artists will find helpful hints within its pages.*[3]

A second important resource has been the *High Altitude Cook Book*, published by the Estes Park Ladies Aid Society about 1936. Although there were some few families referenced in both works, most are unique to one or the other. To a certain extent, the later work documents an influx of new families that began in the 1920s as well as the passing away of the pioneers of '75, so many of whom were gone by the 1930s.

These two cookbooks, as well as others published locally[4] during the town's history, attest to the continuous and enduring interest

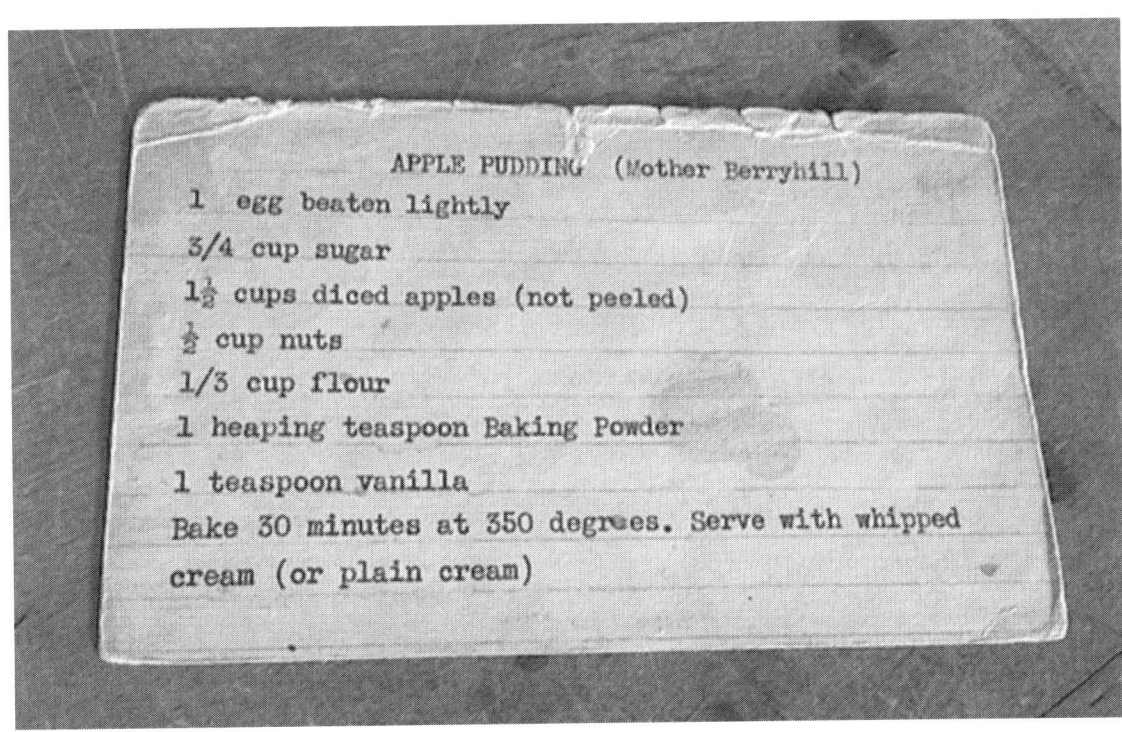

*An original card from the Berryhill family's recipe collection.*
Artifact courtesy of the Berryhill family

over time, that local women have taken in enlarging their personal repertoire of recipes and in learning, through access to the recipes of others, how friends and neighbors cope with the inevitability of meal preparation. Then too, the careful labeling of each recipe with the name of its donor documents a pride in the gifting of something personal and valued, without thought of personal gain. In a very real sense it is this act of sharing that makes most vintage cookbooks of enduring social interest. In addition, because the cookbooks represent the charitable aspirations of a group of community women, they can be seen as part of a nineteenth-century tradition, grounded in post–Civil War efforts to alleviate the suffering of war widows and orphans, of using recipe books as philanthropically-driven fundraising projects. That this tradition is alive and well in the twenty-first century is undeniable.

Beginning in the 1950s, perhaps in response to popular demand, community cookbooks produced in Estes Park began to include signature dishes from some of the major restaurants and lodges in and around the Estes Valley. In one such, *A Treasury of Famous*

*Recipes from Estes Park, Colorado*, restaurant recipes were highlighted by being gathered in a special section. By donating signature recipes in this way, commercial interests joined hands with families in the promotion of community goals and the common good.

Where possible, this current work has sought original, previously unpublished recipes from the families and businesses that were a part of the early history of Estes Park. Where it was not possible to obtain these, we have mined earlier Estes Park cookbooks and searched back issues of *Trail Talk,* the *Estes Park Trail,* and the *Estes Park Trail-Gazette*. Collecting recipes in this way has made it possible to ensure the survival of locally created dishes from hard-to-find resources long out of print. Our aim throughout has been to preserve the integrity of the original recipes and the voices of their authors. To that end, recipes and any explanatory details appear exactly as they came to us; no effort has been made to standardize measurements, abbreviations, nor vocabulary, nor to amplify the authors' original descriptions of their cooking processes.

*A Slice of History & A Piece of Pie* is organized into chapters that provide a historical and familial context for the recipes presented. Within each and where possible, we have used chronology in determining the order of stories and recipes. In chapter 1, "Kitchen Realities and Rituals in Historic Estes Park," readers are invited to consider the recipe ingredients and cooking techniques for what they reveal about local history, cultural traditions, and changing trends, as well as the historical context that conditioned the procurement, preservation, and preparation of foodstuffs from the 1870s to the 1950s.

In chapter 2, "Homesteaders and Old Settlers," readers will find historical vignettes of the earliest days in Estes Park, in Isabella Bird's account of her adventures in high-country cooking, and recipes from Joel and Patsey Estes and the "pioneers of '75" (e.g., the Spragues, the Fergusons, the Jameses, and the MacGregors).

Recipes for dishes that sustained nineteenth- and early twentieth-century visitors to Longs Peak Inn, Stead's Ranch and Hotel, Sprague's Lodge, the Crags, and more are brought together in chapter 3, "Early Estes Park Resorts and Inns."

In chapter 4, "Estes Park Villagers," readers will find recipes of families who operated iconic restaurants, cafés, and watering holes downtown, and of the merchants who for decades provided goods and services for locals and tourists: the Macdonalds, the Gooches, the Byxbes, the Clatworthys, the Burgesses, the Seybolds, and the Herzogs, to name just a few. Recipes and stories from landmark restaurants in the nearby villages of Glen Haven, Meeker Park, and Allenspark have been included as well.

In the early years, most Estes "residents" were "seasonals," who retreated to lower altitudes and more temperate climates during the winter months. Over time, as more and more people chose Estes Park as their permanent home, the distinction between seasonal "cottagers" and permanent residents became more well-defined. By the 1920s, little communities had sprung up in Moraine (Willow) Park, on Prospect Mountain, in the Tahosa Valley, and along Fish Creek, for example, populated by those who came to the mountains for temporary relief of respiratory problems or to escape the summer's heat and humidity at home. The stories and recipes of some families for whom Estes Park became a second home can be found in chapter 5, "Estes Valley Cottagers." In hosting family and friends in their summer cabins, these flatlanders often fostered in their youngest guests a lifelong love of the Rockies, anchored in childhood memories of annual trips to hike, fish, and ride along the very same trails, streams, and lakes that continue to lure today's visitors.

To assist readers, citations and commentary for information in the text are included in a Notes section at the end of each chapter. The cookbook also contains two indexes. One is an alphabetical list of names, institutions, and topics found in the text, captions, and notes. The other provides alphabetical access to all the recipes that the cookbook contains. A bibliography lists some of the cookbooks produced in Estes Park through the years. There are also two appendices. Appendix A features nineteenth-century recipes for dishes that Isabella Bird prepared at the Evanses' ranch during the winter of 1873. Appendix B provides additional recipes created by Bob Burgess and served at the Plantation Restaurant in the 1950s and 1960s.

While the Estes Park Museum Friends & Foundation, Inc. Press is proud to have been able to bring together recipes for dishes and desserts prepared, consumed, and enjoyed in and around Estes Park since early times, we acknowledge the fact that the families and establishments featured are representative rather than

*Two women share a picnic lunch in this photo by Fred Payne Clatworthy, c. 1904.*

Clatworthy photo courtesy of Cheryl Pennington

definitive — and that there are many more early Estes families and stories to be told than it has been possible to include in a single book. If time and interest permit, perhaps there will be future cookbooks that will make available other interesting Estes Park recipes and stories.

As with other publications and activities undertaken by the Friends Press, all proceeds from the sale of *A Slice of History & A Piece of Pie* are used to advance the mission of the Estes Park Museum Friends & Foundation, Inc.: to ensure that the Estes Park Museum is the premier local history museum in Colorado.

*Nancy P. Thomas*

# Notes

1. PEO established a chapter in Estes Park in 1918.

2. The contemporary members of Chapter AV of PEO have graciously allowed us to reproduce recipes from their original cookbook. Permission to use recipes previously published in other Estes Park cookbooks has been obtained from the families or descendents of original donors whenever possible.

3. *Trail Talk* (August 13, 1920).

4. The titles of locally produced cookbooks that we have been able to locate so far are included in a bibliography that appears on pages 375–378. There are no doubt others. Because cookbooks are most often considered ephemera, libraries do not, as a general rule, acquire or archive those that are produced locally.

# Acknowledgements

The creation of *A Slice of History & A Piece of Pie* has required many months and many hands. We are especially grateful to longtime Estes Park residents and cookbook committee members Marty Yochum Casey, Verlene Thorp, Alma Hix, and Penny Fox, who so generously expended time and effort to identify families, restaurants, and businesses to include, to obtain and organize the recipes, to find and scan photographs, and to attend to all the many details that have brought this project to a successful completion. Special thanks go as well to those, including Verlene Thorp, Jane Wright, and the late Jerry Miller, for their assistance with the research and to Pat Pickering, Charlie Wright, and others, who volunteered to try some of these recipes. We are also indebted to Bobbie Heistercamp and Dave Tanton for the inclusion of postcards from their personal collections and to Cheryl Pennington for generously allowing us to reproduce a number of original photographs by Fred Clatworthy. Then too, we want to acknowledge the staff of the Estes Park Museum, Derek Fortini, Alicia Mittelman, and Bryon Hoerner; Archivist and Geologist Tim Burchett at Rocky Mountain National Park; and the archives staff of Estes Valley Public Library, all of whom provided assistance with historical details, resources, and photos. We are also grateful to the AV chapter of PEO and the Eta Omega chapter of Epsilon Sigma Alpha for allowing us the use of recipes from their original cookbooks. The Estes Park History Rescue Project has been of particular value in making available online some early Estes newspapers. Thanks are also due to our fellow board members of the Estes Park Museum Friends & Foundation, Inc. We could not have completed our tasks without your enthusiasm, your encouragement, and your support. Board members Verlene Thorp and Jan Swaney deserve special thanks for proofreading the text. Finally to the institutions, individuals, and families who contributed recipes, photos, and stories—we express our thanks for your generosity and for your patience.

# A Slice of History
& A Piece of Pie

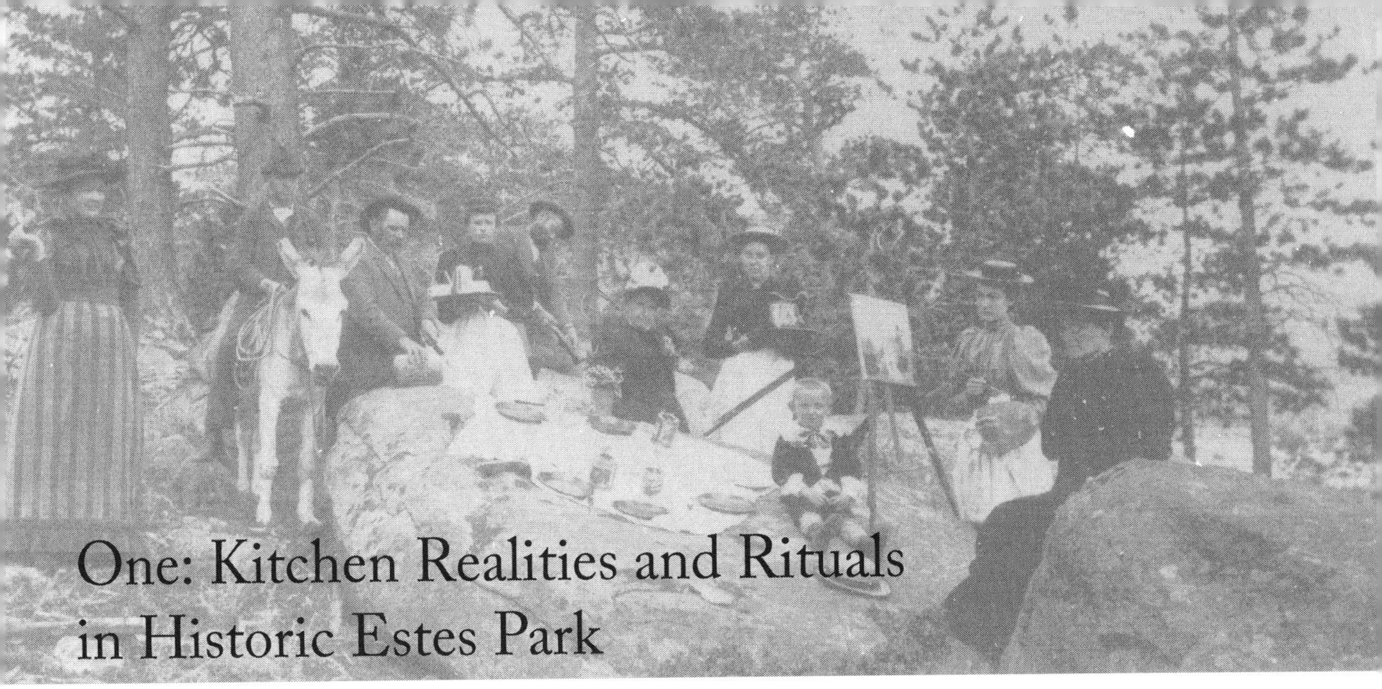

# One: Kitchen Realities and Rituals in Historic Estes Park

*"Tell me what you eat, and I'll tell you who you are."*
—Brillat-Savarin[1]

Estes Park has been a favorite destination for generations of vacationers, and the Village, its surrounding community, and nearby Rocky Mountain National Park have received considerable attention from historians, travel writers, and hiking enthusiasts for well over a century. First-generation pioneers, ranchers, innkeepers, and entrepreneurs have also been the subject of research interest, but thus far no effort has been made to tell the more personal stories of Estes Park and its founders from the vantage point of their kitchens.

As the title suggests, *A Slice of History & A Piece of Pie: Recipes and Remembrance—A Cookbook of Family Favorites from Early Estes Park* provides an entrée into the experiences of families who have chosen Estes Park as their home. Taken together, family stories and foodways, as reflected in family recipes, serve as a historical text that in many instances reveals the cultural roots of pioneers and homesteaders. Because the care and feeding of tourists was such a common practice so early in Estes Park history, high-country cooking has had both a private/domestic/familial dimension and a public/com-

mercial one. *A Slice of History & A Piece of Pie* reflects this duality, in the inclusion of recipes from families who ran resorts, restaurants, and businesses, as well as from Estes' cottager communities. While they hardly constitute "the world in a teacup," early recipes provide insights into cooking preferences and practices in one mountain village and how these changed over time. As such they serve as tangible links between contemporary times and an Estes Park that has all but passed into history.

## Early Estes Park Cookbooks

Our own research into vintage recipes began with those that first appeared in the *Tried and True Recipe Book*, published by the PEO chapter in Estes Park in 1920, and the *High Altitude Cook Book*, published by the Ladies Aid Society in 1936. Embedded in these recipes, and in others retrieved from early Estes newspapers and from the recipe collections of the descendents of early cooks, is information related to the availability, preservation, and accessibility of specific kinds of food items as well as food preferences of particular families. In many cases, the recipes also reveal something about the cooking acumen of their "inventors."

Immediately apparent in an examination of the oldest recipes is the lack of specifics related to technique and process—that is, a description of how ingredients are put together and how the actual "cooking" is to proceed. In addition, some recipes describe measurements and processes metaphorically rather than numerically—"butter the size of an egg," "a teacupful of flour"—or not at all ("enough flour to make a firm dough") ("bake til done in a quick oven"). It is easy to see that the latter approach assumes a good deal of experience on the part of the cook and the ability to put ingredients together by look, feel, and taste.

Contemporary practices in recipe writing, which often involve a listing of ingredients followed by specific details regarding cooking processes, were an innovation of the late nineteenth century.[2] As homemaking tasks came increasingly to be viewed as "domestic science," advocates moved to standardize measures in terms of, for example, an eight-ounce/forty-eight level-teaspoon "cup," and to include detailed directions on oven temperatures and cooking times.

This revolution in the way that people began to think and talk about cooking was spearheaded by Fannie Merritt Farmer (1857–1915) and others who opened cooking schools in Boston in the 1880s and 1890s to provide instruction on new methods, techniques, and nutrition. That these practices transformed cooking from a homely activity, predicated on a sort of family apprenticeship model, to a scientific process that could and should be formally taught, has been considered by many as a watershed moment in the history of American cookery.

## Estes Park Kitchens in the Early Days

By most contemporary American standards, early Estes Park cooks prepared dinners for their families and their guests under relatively primitive conditions. Although by the turn of the twentieth century, little high-country cooking was still taking place over an open hearth, preparing three meals a day on wood- or coal-burning stoves or ranges was both time-consuming and complex. The cook was required not only to clean out the ashes from the previous day each morning and lay the new fire using twigs and kindling, but also to trim the damper and adjust the flue. The latter activities made it possible to establish and maintain the temperatures required for stove-top cooking and oven baking and roasting. While some ranges were relatively simple affairs, others were elaborate entities with reservoirs for heating water, warming cabinets, and multiple ovens.

From the details provided in early recipes, one can see that most pioneer kitchens offered few amenities, with cooks dependent on basic utensils: an iron skillet, a tea kettle and coffee pot, ceramic crocks and mixing bowls, a rolling pin, an egg beater, and wooden spoons. Those who had access to potato ricers, cherry pitters, food grinders, apple corers, and other nineteenth-century, labor-saving innovations no doubt considered themselves lucky indeed. Of course, the cook's ingenuity often resulted in the creation of labor-saving devices. At her cabin in Moraine Park, May Brevard Scott outfitted a tin pail with crank-turned paddles as a way to create an effective bread-kneading "machine."[3]

*The wood-burning range in the kitchen of the Macdonald/Cobb cabin at the Estes Park Museum. The cabin dates from 1910.*
**Artifacts courtesy of the Estes Park Museum**

Gaining access to potable water posed a number of challenges for many early Estes Park residents. Very few had the advantage of water piped directly into kitchen sinks. More often, water for drinking and household use had to be hauled from a well or a creek, sometimes located at some distance from the house or cabin. This situation increased the time and effort required for the completion of the most mundane household tasks, cooking included.

## Procuring Comestibles

While by the 1920s multiple grocery stores in the Village would have provided access to dressed meats, fresh vegetables in season, and canned goods of all kinds, cooks in earlier generations relied on a self-sufficiency model, producing fruits and vegetables in the kitchen garden, obtaining meat by raising one's own livestock, or relying on a neighbor's. And, while family cooks could certainly count on an abundance of local fish and wild game to supplement homegrown victuals, the tasks related to the preparation of these resources were both labor-intensive and cumbersome.

The processing of ordinary meats, which today generally takes place out of our conscious awareness and long before it appears in the refrigerated cases of the local supermarket, was a fact of daily life for many in the nineteenth century, and usually the responsibility of the cook. Fresh game and beef had to be skinned, gutted, and butchered, and then preserved by smoking. Poultry had to be killed and then dressed, a process that involved plucking, gutting, and trussing. All of these tasks added greatly to the complexity of preparing even the simplest meals. Perhaps for this reason cooking processes for high-country cooks in the early days appear most often to include baking, roasting, and stewing, which would have required, in most cases, less continuous oversight.

When one reviews the ingredients used across vintage recipes, it is clear that most cooks had access to a relatively static set of pantry staples. Dairy products were apparently widely and easily available and were a part of many early recipes. The careful distinction made between "sweet" and "sour" milk no doubt points not only to taste preferences but also to the difficulty of keeping perishable items fresh in the absence of refrigeration. Butter and lard most often constituted shortenings in recipes recorded before 1920, while by the 1930s, oleomargarine and solid shortenings began to appear in recipes more regularly. Types of flour for breads, rolls, and cookies in the early recipes included white, whole wheat, cornmeal, and graham; rye flour was used much less often. Sorghum or molasses and sugar were the sweeteners called for in vintage recipes; honey was not. Given the frequency of their

use in recipes from cakes to salad dressings, access to eggs seems to have been widespread and unproblematic.

Other staples that appear as ingredients in early recipes were spices (cinnamon, ginger) and flavorings (vanilla, lemon extract). In addition, recipes indicate frequent use of dried fruits such as raisins, dates, and figs. Not only do these have long shelf lives but also they are suggestive of Scotch-Irish and English family foodways, a heritage that typified so many early Estes Park pioneers. The popularity of steamed puddings may be an indication of these same cultural traditions.

At the outset, standard pantry items (e.g., flour, cornmeal, sugar, spices) would have been available in bulk. In the waning years of the nineteenth century, however, the processing of food grew as a commercial enterprise, so that over the course of the next three decades, pre-packaging of staples in smaller quantities and marketed under specific brand names became more common. By the 1920s, Jell-o, Knox Gelatin, Karo Syrup, Eagle Brand Condensed Milk, and Snowdrift (shortening) were specified in a number of recipes, indicating how successful and widespread the practice of commercial branding had become.

Although early cookbooks include recipes across the range of menu items, the preponderance of sweet items is striking. That desserts were an important course of family and resort dinners is evinced in the number and variety of recipes for these "end-of-the meal" dishes. Cakes, which may well have posed the greatest challenge to bakers living at 7,500 feet and above, were also among the most numerous early cookbook entries—enduring markers of their status as special-occasion foods celebrating birthdays, weddings, and other family milestones. In addition, the abundance of recipes for breads and cookies certainly points to the fact that commercial bakeries were few and far between.[4] There were aids for the home baker, however, as commercially prepared yeast, baking soda, and baking powder were among the first processed food items, and available from the 1870s on.

Beginning at the turn of the twentieth century, growth of the Village and improvements in technology combined to improve the "food situation" in Estes Park. For example, the July 16, 1908 edition of the *Mountaineer* proudly announced the opening of a new dairy in Moraine Park, where Charles Lowery Reed, the owner of "a good bunch of fine cows" was "ready to supply milk to all."[5] The

*Branded baking powder, baking chocolate, and spices, all of which were available in commercially produced packaging in the last decades of the nineteenth century, are indicative of the evolution that occurred in food processing as a result of the Industrial Revolution.*
**Artifacts courtesy of the Estes Park Museum**

following week, the same paper announced the availability at F. C. Adams Bakery of "Bread, cakes, pastry. All kind of bakery goods. Fresh vegetables in season. Soft Drinks."[6] There was even a kind of "home delivery" of groceries through local peddlers who brought wagonloads of fresh vegetables to Moraine Park and other smaller settlements and communities in and around town. In the Scott family's memoir, *The Scottage: A Medley*, Dorothy Carnine Scott recalled that during their summers in Moraine Park, the family "got our fresh vegetables from a huckster who used to drive around to the summer cabins in a wagon at least once a week, sometimes twice. It was always a thrill when he came and oh! What goodies he had."[7]

Chapter One: Kitchen Realities and Rituals in Historic Estes Park

*Before electric refrigerators were introduced in the 1930s, perishable foods were often kept in iceboxes like this one. Lined with zinc or tin, iceboxes were cooled by storing a large chunk of ice (harvested during the winter months and kept in local ice houses or barns) in a container in the top, with the food arranged on shelves in the cabinet below.*

**Artifacts courtesy of the Estes Park Museum**

## Preserving Perishables in the High Country

Preservation of foods was an important issue for high-country families from early days and continuing, in some cases, beyond the first decades of the new century. While during Estes Park's long winter months frigid temperatures made it difficult to open a cask of butter or to retrieve molasses from a keg, and buttermilk could survive in a churn for weeks without spoiling,[8] the return of warmer weather required pioneer families to rely on root cellars, "caves," and "spring houses" to keep eggs, dairy, and meat fresh. Even so, many homemakers were forced to "sleep with the ham"[9] (e.g., bring pork products, such as bacon and ham, into the house) in order to prevent bears from coming down from their lairs at night and raiding outside storage places. As noted earlier, the consistent use of sour milk in recipes may well be indicative of difficulties encountered in keeping dairy products fresh.

Perhaps nothing was more important to Estes Park's earliest cooks than the coming of electricity to the Estes Village, thanks to the construction (1909) of a hydroelectric plant by Freelan Oscar Stanley (1849–1940). Where electricity was available, high-country kitchens eventually came to include electrified iceboxes, waffle irons, toasters, hot plates, and other labor-saving devices; larger operations could afford large-scale refrigeration, electrified churns, and the like.

Commercial canning, which was introduced in the United States as early as the 1830s, was, by the 1870s, a reliable way to supply basic commodities not available locally. In early Estes Park cookbooks canned products frequently appear as ingredients in family recipes from succotash to salmon loaf. Canned pineapple, which became available in the 1890s, was a feature of many of the early recipes, perhaps evidence of its novelty at the time.

## High-Altitude Cookery

While many of the kitchen realities that framed early Estes Park food preparation might have been considered a normal part of nineteenth-century domestic life, cooks also had to contend with the altitude. Water boils at a lower temperature at high altitudes,[10] resulting in cooking times longer than those experienced at sea level. Higher altitudes also alter the chemical interaction between sugar and fat, which makes the reproduction of recipes that work perfectly elsewhere impossible to duplicate in the mountains. Indeed, then as now, "first-generation" cooks in each family were eventually compelled to create new recipes or adapt old family favorites to ensure culinary success at

altitudes of 7,000 feet and above. It is probably not a coincidence that the two earliest cookbooks published in Estes Park advertised the fact that the recipes they contained had been adjusted to take mountain altitudes into account.

## Kitchen Help

Although most early Estes families lacked kitchen help beyond that provided by family members, there were a few exceptions. The family of Colorado's twenty-third governor, William Ellery Sweet, for example, arrived at the family's summer home near Fish Creek, with a maid, a cook, a chauffeur, and the children's nurse in tow. Freelan and Flora Stanley brought their maid, Minnie Lundberg (1865–1958), with them from Denver during their first summers at their rented cabin, Rockside. Once the Stanleys had completed their summer home, located on what is now Wonderview Avenue, Minnie kept house and cooked for them every summer until Mr. Stanley's death in 1940. Fred and Jessie Sanders and the Steiner family, cottagers in the Tahosa Valley, also relied on family cooks to prepare meals on a daily basis. In these cases, it fell to the long-suffering cooks to make altitude adjustments in family recipes and adapt to the reduced amenities available in mountain kitchens. Freda Songer's delicious Longs Peak Cake is a testament to the ability of "seasonal" cooks to manage this expertly.

## Dining Inside and Out

Any effort to understand cooking history and foodways in the mountain communities of the Estes Valley must also consider dining options and patterns. Of course, practically from the beginning, homesteaders and settlers offered hospitality to high-country visitors with meals provided on an informal basis. Later, dining facilities became a central focus of Estes Park resorts, with meals available on the American Plan[11] as a formal part of resort packages. As will be seen in chapter 3, which features recipes from early resorts and inns, these were outfitted with dining rooms of varying degrees of sophistication and elegance, with the cooking managed most often by the owner's wife. While in many cases breakfasts and lunches might have been informally served, dinners tended to be more formal affairs.

*In this undated photo, Alberta Sprague (standing fifth from left) oversees ice cream making at her family's resort hotel.*

**Photo courtesy of the National Park Service**

At the same time, family cooks had many opportunities to demonstrate their culinary skills in a wide variety of social events, many of which were enthusiastically described in the local newspapers. The Estes Park Woman's Club, founded in 1912, had a powerful impact on both the cultural and social life of the town; still, it was but one example among many of local clubs and organizations that occasioned social events. In fact, by the early years of the twentieth century, church suppers, community dinners, birthday parties, club luncheons, dinner dances, costume parties, weddings, and receptions were regular events, all of which mandated the serving of some sort of refreshments.

*As waiting diners relax nearby, Abner Sprague, with help from an unidentified woman, assumes cooking responsibilities at a picnic lunch, c. 1890s.*

Photo courtesy of the National Park Service

In homage, one suspects, to the delights of the scenery and the lure of special places in the forests and mountains and moraines of the Estes Valley, eating outside was a gustatory exercise enjoyed by almost everyone from early days on. A tradition that no doubt began with the arrival of the firstcomers who lived in tents and prepared meals over an open fire, picnicking in the mountains is one of the most enduring of Estes Park traditions. While some alfresco meals have become the stuff of legend—think here of the winter picnic shared by the homesteaders Esther Burnell (later the wife of Enos Mills) and her friend Katherine Garetson on Christmas Day, 1916—others have gone unmarked and un-remarked, an ordinary part of everyone's summer experience. Sometimes picnic fare was prepared in advance at home and brought along as a culmination to a day's outing; at other times picnics were cookouts with food prepared as well as consumed in the open air.

*Young people gather around a campfire to roast marshmallows at a community party in Estes Park (no date).*

**Photo courtesy of the Estes Park Museum**

The importance that early Estes Park residents attached to these events is evident in their newsworthiness. For example, the July 9, 1908 edition of the *Mountaineer* reported that

> *Mr. and Mrs. Richard H. Tallant entertained a picnic party at their home in Devils Gulch on 4 July 1908. Dinner was served among the trees, and the day was spent free from the noises that so often mar the pleasure of people who love quiet.*

Picnics were also important and well-attended events in cottage communities and at resorts. Angelo Scott, the son of Iola, Kansas newspaper editor Charles F. Scott, described family picnics in Moraine Park. "The food," he recalled in *The Scottage*,

> *was always wonderful—bacon frizzled over a little fire, perhaps some trout, fried potatoes, and the like. Or perhaps just cold stuff, topped off for the kids with the special treat of date nut butter or brown sugar sandwiches.*[12]

*Diners at the Chalets' "picnic park" are entertained by a pair of western singers.*

Postcard courtesy of the Bobbie Heistercamp Collection

The *Estes Park Trail* reported on an outing sponsored by The Stanley Hotel that sought to link outdoor eating with wildlife viewing. This particular event, during the summer of 1912, was hosted by none other than Flora Stanley herself:

> *Mrs. Stanley and Mrs. Lamborn entertained 16 guests from The Stanley Hotel with a fish fry and picnic at Horseshoe Park last Friday. The day was perfect, and some of the more venturesome ones climbed to upper Horseshoe Falls. On the return trip to Estes Park, the first automobile load had a fine view of a band of ten mountain sheep at Sheep Lake. The occupants of the second automobile saw them partway up the mountain leaping from rock to rock, and the last of the party caught just a glimpse of them as they walked serenely around the top of the hill, apparently in single file.[13]*

Another resort-sponsored picnic, this one arranged for Elkhorn Lodge visitors that same summer, featured a horseback ride to Gem Lake and a campfire. No doubt planned by Eleanor Hondius, the Elkhorn's proprietor, hostess, and chief cook, the meal was also described in the paper:

> *The plentiful lunch that was prepared was divided into packages, and was carried safely with the exception of the breakage of one egg, the remains of which still adhere to the slicker of one of the young ladies. The early arrivals at the lake had a fire burning briskly when the laggards put in their appearance, and as is usual and customary, the original site did not suit the late arrivals, so they started a rival fire in a secluded nook. The majority ruling, the coffee pot was transferred to the new fire, and all proceeded as per the usual schedule of picnics.*[14]

While initially lodges and resorts may have staged alfresco lunches and dinners on an ad hoc basis, as the years passed most incorporated picnics, fish fries, and chuckwagon dinners as regular features of their resorts' gustatory repertoire. The Chalets set up a permanent natural-rock grill and "a picnic park" for weekly outdoor dinners and provided cowboy entertainment as well. In another example, longtime Estes resident and Seasonal Ranger Jay Grooters provided a description of similar dinners held weekly at the McGraw Ranch:

> *Thursday evening . . . we'd walk up the meadow to the steak fry grounds, again by the stream. There we'd find the coffee brewing in the huge pot, the beans were cooking, and the corn was simmering. When everyone had arrived, they'd start cooking the tenderloin pieces, and the results were the most tasty meal you could possibly imagine.*[15]

That these same resorts continued to provide indoor dining for the less adventurous, complete with white linen tablecloths, cloth napkins, and fresh flowers, is a testimony to the flexibility, stamina, and desire to fulfill a wide range of guest expectations on the part of these high-country hosts.

## Invitation

An early (c. 1935) brochure prepared for visitors to Rocky Mountain National Park urged them to leave the comfort of their cars and engage the natural setting firsthand:

> *To try to see the Estes Park region thoroly by automobile is much like trying to tour Venice on a bicycle. The Park is justly proud of its scenic highways, but most of its glories lie hidden in valleys and canyons, or*

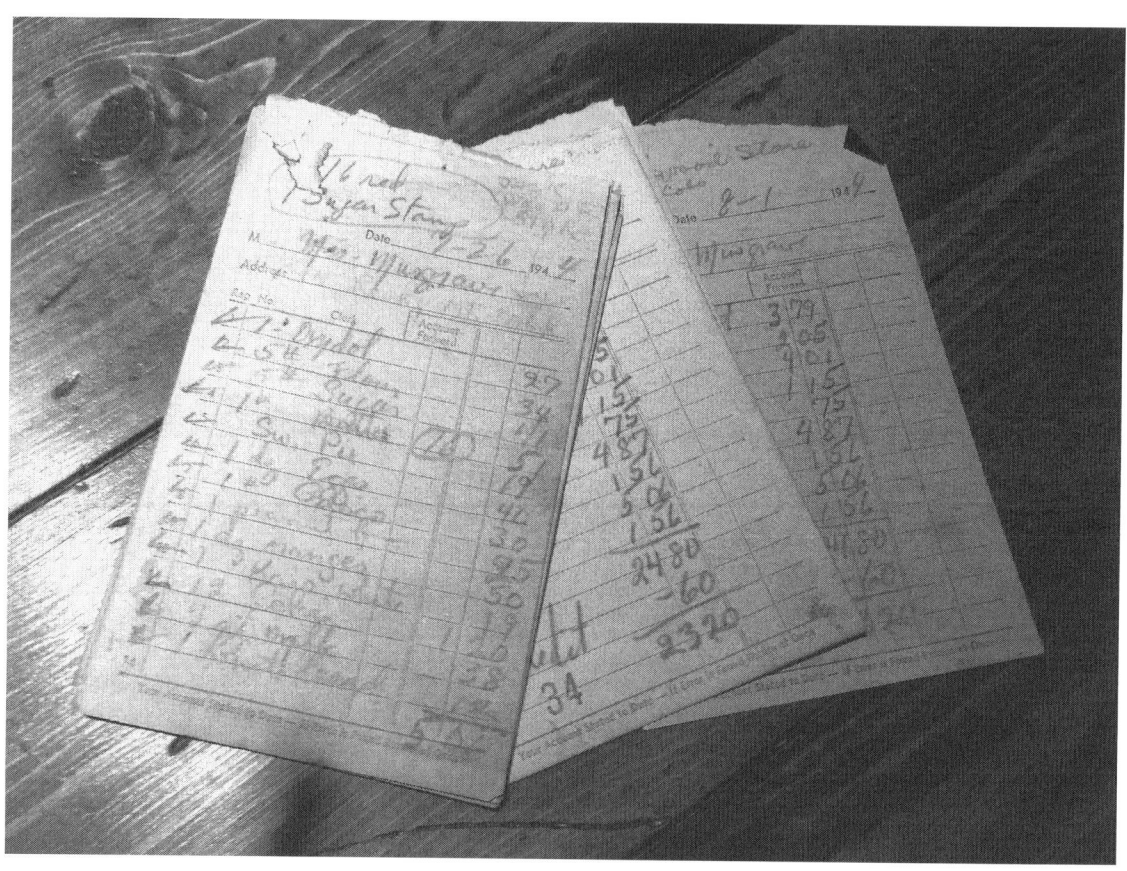

*Purchases a Mrs. Musgrave made in July 1944 indicate how far the food industry had evolved since the turn of the century, not only in terms of standard measures but branded products as well.*

**Artifacts courtesy of Marcia Taylor**

*along the timbered slopes, or on the majestic heights above the timberline. All these are yours to enjoy—if you will.*

It is in this same vein that we offer to readers of *A Slice of History & A Piece of Pie* a chance to relive the experience of Estes Park's earliest residents and visitors through the recipes that they have left for us. In the words of the visitors' brochure quoted above, "All these are yours to enjoy—*if you will.*"

Our hope is that readers will find the text enlightening and the family stories compelling. But it is perhaps in and through preparing these vintage recipes themselves that readers can engage most personally in the history of early Estes Park.

# Notes

1. Jean Anthelme Brillat-Savarin (1755–1826) was a French epicure.
2. Social reformers during this same period began to direct women's attention to nutrition and dietary issues and healthier eating patterns for everyone in the family, just as they aimed to improve the condition and educational opportunities for women and children in society.
3. Dorothy Scott Gibbs (personal communication, 2012).
4. A singular lack of recipes with alcohol as an ingredient until after the 1940s may say more about Prohibition restrictions and Women's Christian Temperance Union (WCTU) sentiments among the cooks than personal taste, for, occasionally, wine glasses were used as "cup" measures in recipes recorded prior to that time.
5. It is worth noting that Mary and "Young Bill" White, the children of William Allen White who summered in the family's Moraine Park cabin, refused to drink the milk from local cows as the sagebrush on which the cows tended to graze flavored the milk unpleasantly. D. Ferrel Atkins (personal communication, September, 2003).
6. *Mountaineer* (July 30, 1908).
7. Emerson Lynn, Carruth Scott, Angelo Scott, Dorothy Carnine Scott, and William Lindsey White, *The Scottage*, A Medley (unpublished manuscript, n.d.), p. 22.
8. Isabella L. Bird. *A Lady's Life in the Rocky Mountains*. (New York: G. P. Putnam's Sons, 1888), p. 245.
9. Anita F. Pickering, quoting Jessie M. Sanders. (Personal communication, 2000.)
10. At an altitude of 7,500 feet, for example, water boils at 198° F not 212°.
11. With American Plan accommodations, room rates included three meals a day. European Plan accommodations did not include meals.
12. E. Lynn, et al., *The Scottage*, p. 26.
13. *Estes Park Trail* (August 17, 1912).
14. *Estes Park Trail* (July 20, 1912).
15. Jay Grooters (personal communication, 2013).

# Chapter Two. Homesteaders and Old Settlers

As with most histories, the first "stories" of any locality generally constitute accounts of those families intrigued enough by the promise of adventure and courageous enough to brave the elements to create new lives in the wilderness. More often than not, it was the *pater familias* who identified the settling place for the family and the *mater familias* whose job it was to create a home, often under the most primitive and unforgiving conditions. So too in Estes Park, the initial settlers and homesteaders carved out lives in this beautiful place against all odds, as we might think today, with the women working alongside the men in building the community. In bringing to the Rocky Mountains their cultural traditions and their dedication to family life, these wives and mothers were true pioneers in every meaning of the word and deserve recognition along with their husbands for the contributions they made to the economic and social development of early Estes Park. One thinks here of Areanna Sprague Chapman, Alberta Morrison Sprague, Eleanor Estes James Hondius, Alma Sanborn Bond, Louise Jesser Griffith, Josephine Cheney Hall, Hannah McLean McCreery, and Sara Armstrong Wiest, among others, whose recipes and family stories appear in this chapter.

The first white "comers" to the Estes Valley were Joel Estes and his family, who were followed shortly thereafter by the Griff Evanses, the Horace Fergusons, the Alexander MacGregors, the

*Members of the Chapman and Sprague families pose in a steam car in front of their log home in Moraine Park in this undated photograph. Front seat from left: Charles A. Chapman, his mother Areanna Sprague Chapman, and an unidentified woman. Back seat from left: Areanna's son Alson Chapman Jr. and Aeranna's mother, Mary Margaret Wolaver Sprague.*

Photo courtesy of the Estes Park Museum

Abner Spragues, the William McCreerys, and the William Jameses. While homesteaders most certainly, many of these newcomers soon abandoned their original plans for making their livings and turned instead to innkeeping,[1] or, like the MacGregors, expanded their ranching activities to accommodate summer guests. Abner Sprague himself described this turnabout. "The hotel business was forced on us," he would later write.

> *We came here for small ranch operations, but guests and visitors became so numerous, at first wanting eggs, milk, and other provisions, then wanting lodging, and finally demanding full accommodations, that we had to go into the hotel business or go bankrupt from keeping free company.*[2]

*Sarah Estes (1842–1911), daughter of Joel S. and Martha Ann Stollings Estes, accompanied her parents and her brother Milton and his family to Estes Park in 1861.*

Photo courtesy of the Estes Park Museum

## The Golden Pioneers: Joel and Patsey Estes

The first cabin in Estes Park was built by Joel Estes and his son Milton in the fall of 1859, soon after father and son had happened upon the beautiful valley that would, in time, bear their name. "We had a little world all to ourselves," Milton would later write. "There was no end of the game, for great bands of elk, big flocks of mountain sheep and deer were everywhere."[3] The following year a larger cabin was constructed on the site to house Joel, his wife Patsey,[4] and the couple's six children. Located at the junction of Fish Creek and the road to Lyons, the Joel Estes homestead was later enlarged to accommodate Milton and his wife, Mary Louise Fleming Estes, and their children. Milton's third son, Charles Francis Estes, was born at the homestead in 1865, the first Caucasian child born in the Estes Valley.

Life for the Estes family was, of necessity, a simple affair. Water for cooking and other household uses had to be carried from the creek nearby. Cooking tasks were accomplished over an open hearth, and most meals consisted of wild game supplemented by home-baked breads. That these efforts were appreciated is apparent in Milton's somewhat idealized description:

> *The women of our families, my mother, sister and wife, cheerfully shared with us the rugged life of the pioneer. With Dutch-ovens, iron kettles hanging over open fireplaces, they cooked food that could not be surpassed. No modern methods could equal the splendid meals of wild game, hot biscuits, berries, cream, etc. that they prepared.*[5]

Twice a year, the family would travel to Denver to purchase supplies not available locally and to bring back the mail.

## Beaver Tail

In *The Golden Pioneer*, the biography she wrote about her famous ancestor Joel Estes, Colleen Estes Cassell (1999) reports on a visit John T. Prewett made to the Estes family in April 1864. In his account, Prewett described for the *Rocky Mountain News* (File 101–103) his trip into the mountains and the memorable meal he was served in the Estes home. "We each of us took a rifle and started out early in the morning," Prewett wrote of his journey from the ranch of Benjamin A. Franklin, located at the mouth of the St. Vrain Canyon, to the Estes homestead:

> *We had a hard day's ride to make a distance of about thirty-five miles. It was a very rough road, mostly trails. Estes had made a road to get in with two wagons. We got in somewhat after dark. He had big fires made in the fireplaces. It was cold in there, and he had a Beaver tail supper.... We had sent him word we were coming and he was wonderfully pleased to see us. The woman [presumably Patsey] had*

*hot biscuits and plenty of good coffee, and we enjoyed a fine supper. However I didn't enjoy the beaver tail as much as he thought I did.*

Quoting from David H. Coyner's *Lost Trappers*, first published in 1847, Cassell provides some details of how Patsey and Joel might have handled the preparation of the main course. According to Coyner,

*The flesh of the beaver was prized by Indians. It was occasionally eaten by the trappers, but in general was too musky to be relished. The tail, however, was invariably saved along with the pelt as "medicine" for camp. The tail, a foot long, flat and thick and scaly, the trapper boiled in his kettle, or transfixed with a stick and placed before the fire with the scales on. When the heat of the fire strikes through so as to roast it, large blisters rise on the surface, which are very easily removed. The tail is then perfectly white, and very delicious.*[6]

# Griff and Jane Evans and Isabella Bird

*"Eat as much as you can, it'll do you good."*
—Griff Evans to Isabella Bird

The Estes family's sojourn in Colorado was relatively brief. Finding the climate insalubrious to successful ranching, Joel, Milton, and their families decamped in 1866, selling out to a Welshman named Griffith J. Evans and his wife, Jane Owen Evans, who arrived the following year. The genial Evans turned out to be a model host, and soon visitors were coming to his ranch on a regular basis to enjoy the coolness of the mountains and the activities afforded both hunters and hikers.

While no recipes from the Evans family have apparently survived, we do know a good deal about culinary life and times on the Evans ranch thanks to the wonderful letters Isabella Lucy Bird (1831–1904) wrote home to her sister Henrietta (Henny) during Bird's visit to the Evans Ranch in 1873. In describing the ranch to her sister, Bird wrote that its primary cabin was unchinked but contained a boarded floor; and a huge stone fireplace that could accommodate pine logs "half as large as I am"; "a round table, two rocking chairs, a carpet covered backwoods couch"; and Indian artifacts, with guns arranged in each corner.[7]

By the time of Bird's stay with them, the Evanses had greatly improved Patsey Estes' kitchen through the addition of "a great American cookstove," of which Bird would make immediate use. Commenting on the housekeeping and culinary talents of her hosts, she proclaimed Jane "most industrious" and Griff "a capital cook" and a "generally 'jolly fellow.'"[8] As for the Evans' children, Bird declared them "beautifully brought up."[9]

Although best remembered as an intrepid, globetrotting adventuress and travel writer, Bird was also a prideful and accomplished cook, who not only described the ranch's primitive kitchen in some detail but also her own cooking adventures in it. Indeed, when not out exploring the mountains around Estes Park, including an ascent of Longs Peak in the company of a local desperado, Rocky Mountain Jim Nugent, Bird was energetically producing meals of astonishing complexity considering the paucity of ingredients on hand. "Food is the great difficulty," she wrote in November 1873. "Of 30 cows only one remains and it does not give enough milk for drinking. The only meat is some pickled pork very salty and the

*Griff and Jane Owen Evans arrived in Estes Park in 1867. Together, they were the parents of seven children. The last one was a daughter they named Isabella, after the Evans' most famous house guest, the intrepid world traveler Isabella Lucy Bird.*

**Photo courtesy of the Evans family**

hens only lay less than an egg a day." In spite of that, she continued, "Yesterday morning I made some rolls and made the last bread into a bread and butter pudding."[10] At the time, the Evans women had decamped to lower altitudes for the winter, and Bird was left to handle not only cooking at the ranch but also the housekeeping. Of the days that followed, Bird wrote,

*This has been a day of manual labour. We did not breakfast till 9:30. Then they went out and I never got done till one. I cleaned the parlour and the kitchen washed up baked and then made 4lbs of sweet biscuits and baked them after which I had to clean all my tins and pans and do my own room and haul water.*[11]

Wintry temperatures also made cooking difficult, but the energetic Isabella continued to make the best of it.

*After washing up I made a 4lb spiced gingerbread cake, which is a wonderful success. But oh what a day it was getting a cask of butter open in the milk house, getting molasses from a keg so cold as to be torpid, assembling everything. I found some buttermilk which had stood a fortnight in the churn and raised the cake with this and soda. Then I baked 3 loaves of bread.*[12]

And on Thanksgiving Day, she made a "wonderful" pudding:

*I had saved eggs and cream for it and dried and stoned cherries took the place of currents. I made a very rich custard sauce for it and having some essence of lemon flavoured it. They all said it was "splendid." They have eaten my 4 lb cake in 2 days and hint that they would like another.*[13]

Later, that same weekend, she prepared "two roly poly puddings, made with molasses for supper which require boiling attended to." She concluded:

*How easy cooking must be when you have all the appliances. We have only a kettle, a frying pan and a 6 gallon brass pan and use a cup for a rolling pin. I cooked some trout which looked and were perfectly delicious, rolling them in coarse cornmeal and frying them.*[14]

In these brief accounts, the indomitable Miss Bird has provided a remarkably detailed view of nineteenth-century mountain housekeeping and cookery and marked her own ability to create an array of entrees, side dishes, breads, and desserts using only, as she says, a kettle, a skillet, a brass pan, and a tea cup.[15]

*The MacGregor family in front of their home in the Black Canyon in 1893. From left: George, Donald, Halbert, Alexander, and Clara.*
Photo courtesy of the National Park Service

## The MacGregor Family

Maria Clara Heeney (1852–1901), a Wisconsin-born artist who had been educated at the Chicago Academy of Design (later the Chicago Art Institute), traveled to Denver in 1872 on a sketching trip and stayed on to set up a studio where she taught drawing and painting. Shortly thereafter, Clara met and fell in love with Alexander Quiner MacGregor (1846–1896), a newspaperman, also from Wisconsin, who had moved to Colorado two years before. After their marriage, which took place in Wisconsin in 1873, the couple returned to Colorado and homesteaded in the Black Canyon near present-day Estes Park.

Clara and Alexander continued to winter in Denver, coming to the mountains in the summer to take active roles in running their ranch. Clara maintained high levels of activity during the summer months, for not only did she plan, prepare, and serve meals for her husband and three boys, but she also kept up with her painting, served as Estes Park's postmistress for a year (1876–77), and ran the

*Maria Clara Heeney and Alexander Quiner MacGregor homesteaded near Estes Park in 1873.*

**Photo courtesy of the National Park Service**

ranch store. Clara's interests in food preparation and homemaking apparently date from an early age, for in 1865 she wrote her own cookbook, which also included recipes for "medicinal cures" for a variety of ailments.

Alexander and Clara had three children: George H. (1875–1959), Donald (1878–1950), and Halbert P. (1887–1962). Donald married Minnie Maude Koontz (1872–1950) in 1903, and as the new mistress of the ranch it fell to her to tend the large ranch garden and

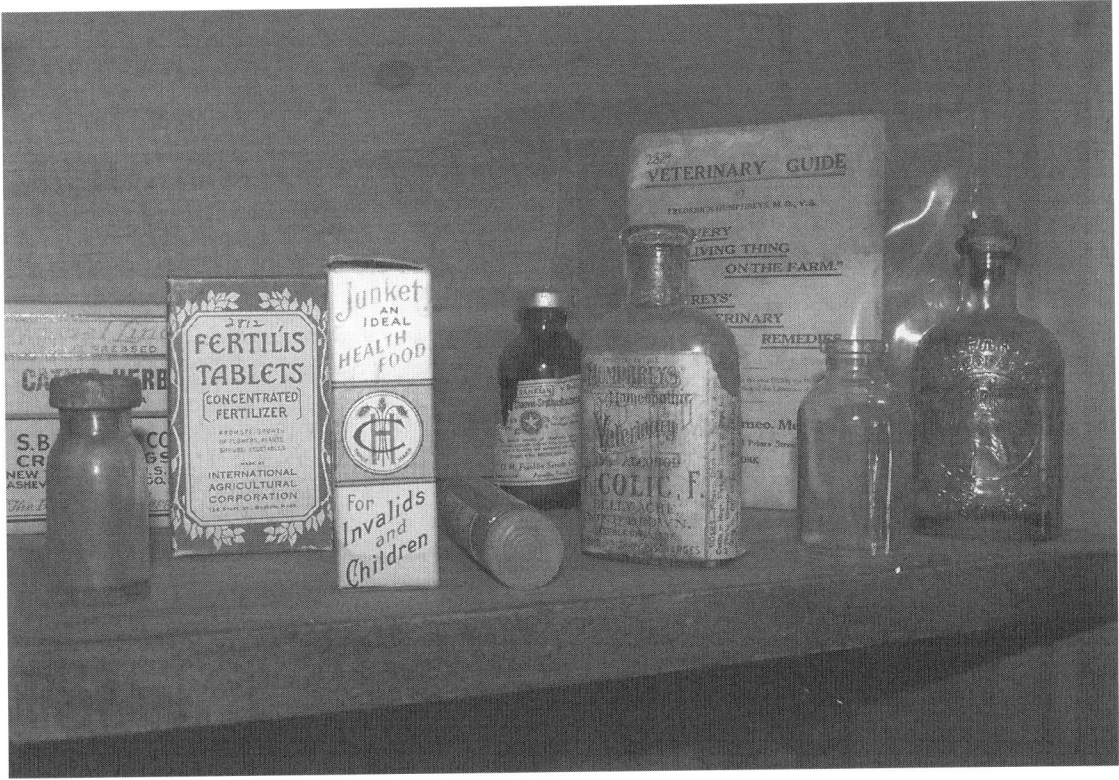

*Doctoring animals and people on the ranch was part of Maude MacGregor's responsibility.*

**Artifacts courtesy of the MacGregor Ranch**

its dairy herd, flock of chickens, and herd of cattle. In addition, Maude handled the selling of meat, dairy products, and produce and kept the records.

Thanks to her efforts the MacGregor Ranch was able to provide vegetables, milk and butter, fresh eggs, and fresh beef and poultry for the tables of many local families. Maude baked bread, rolls, cakes, and pies on a daily basis as well. Somehow she also found time to participate in community life as a member of the Estes Park Woman's Club from 1913 until 1921.

As with so many other first families in the Estes Valley, the MacGregors eventually found themselves renting out tents and cabins to summer visitors who stopped at the ranch seeking accommodations. And so it was that each of the MacGregor women often prepared meals for these guests, as well as for the ranch hands that helped in running a large and complex ranching operation.

*Donald MacGregor's wife Minnie Maude participated actively in the running of the MacGregor Ranch.*

**Photo courtesy of the National Park Service**

Upon the deaths of Donald and Maude in 1950, their holdings passed to their only child, Muriel Lurilla MacGregor (1904–1970), an attorney who managed operations at the ranch until her own death twenty years later. Thanks to Muriel's efforts, the ranch continues to thrive, managed by the Muriel L. MacGregor Charitable Trust, as a living history museum.

The following recipes, published here with the permission of the MacGregor Trust, were taken from Clara and Maude MacGregor's handwritten recipe books.

*Clara and her daughter-in-law Minnie Maude kept track of favorite recipes and homemaking tips in handwritten notebooks, now carefully preserved at the MacGregor Ranch.*

**Artifacts courtesy of the MacGregor Ranch**

## Dressing for Goose or Duck
*(Clara Heeney MacGregor) (Minnie Maude Koontz MacGregor)*

2 cups chopped prunes
2 cups finely chopped apples
2 cups bread crumbs
1 teaspoon salt
1/4 cup cold water

Allow 20 minutes to the pound for roasting.

Chapter Two: Homesteaders and Old Settlers

## Macaroni and Cheese

*(Clara Heeney MacGregor) (Minnie Maude Koontz MacGregor)*

1 cup macaroni
2 cups milk
1/2 teaspoon salt
1/2 cup grated cheese
2 tablespoons flour

Cook the macaroni in salted water 20 minutes, then drain.
Mix flour, salt and cheese.
Place macaroni in a buttered baking dish, then cheese; repeat, last layer cheese. Pour milk over enough to cover top. Bake 45 minutes in a moderate oven.

## Roast Brisket or Veal

*(Clara Heeney MacGregor) (Minnie Maude Koontz MacGregor)*

Select brisket or shoulder of veal, 5 or 6 pounds. Have bone removed, soak. Stuff and press into shape, dress with flour, sprinkle with salt and pepper. Put thin slices of pork over top and also a layer in bottom of pan.

Allow 20 minutes to the pound for baking, remove bacon from top 30 minutes before done, then brown top.

### *Stuffing*

Melt 4 tablespoons butter. Add 1 cup cracker crumbs, stir until thoroughly mixed. Add 1 teaspoon finely chopped parsley, 1/4 teaspoon pepper, 1 onion cut fine and if desired, 1 cup mushrooms. If mixture seems dry, add 1/4 to 1/2 cup water, mix well.

# The McCreery Family

Estes Park has been home to six generations of the McCreery family, beginning with William H. McCreery (1839–1926) and his wife Martha Marshall (1843–1900), who homesteaded in the Estes Valley in 1874 and built a cabin along the Fall River as a summer retreat. An ordained minister from Pennsylvania, Reverend McCreery founded the First United Presbyterian Church and a school in the nearby town of Loveland, Colorado, where the family maintained a winter home. He also managed real estate and insurance businesses in Loveland and later, from 1882–1887, served there as first superintendent of the Larimer County schools.

In 1911 Leon Worthington Tresnor (1859–1936), a carpenter and contractor from Fort Collins, built William and Martha a house they called the Sun Shine Inn on land north of Estes Park. The McCreerys soon expanded their holdings into a ranch and dairy farm, which was known for the quality of the cottage cheese, butter, and buttermilk that the family delivered to a number of local families.[16]

William and Martha had three children–two daughters, Mabel (1873–1938) and Ida (1875–1941), and a son, Elbert L. (1877–1955). Elbert graduated from Monmouth College in Illinois and from 1922 to 1927 taught at the Moody Bible Institute of Chicago. He also served as dean of the Bible Institute of Los Angeles from 1929 to 1937. A missionary as well as a scholar, Elbert traveled to Africa in 1906 to minister in the Sudan. While there, he created written alphabets for two of the Sudanese languages and a grammar for one of them, as well as a translation of the Bible's Book of John.

It was in Africa that Elbert met Hannah Caroline McLean (1884–1948), the first unmarried female Presbyterian missionary to be sent there. The couple was married in 1909 in Alexandria, Egypt, and returned to Colorado four year later over concerns about Hannah's health.[17] Hannah and Elbert were the parents of seven children: three daughters, Ruth Elberta (1915–2010), Martha (1918–2012), and Anna (b. 1921); and four sons, John (1911–1993), William M. (1912–1999), Samuel (1913–1974), and Robert (b. 1925).

With such a large family to feed, Hannah McCreery must have been an accomplished cook, especially as she did not use written recipes; instead, she relied on memory and instinct to guide her culinary endeavors. Her descendents reported:

*Hannah Caroline McLean served in Africa as a Presbyterian missionary before her marriage to Elbert McCreery in 1909.*
**Photo courtesy of Linda McCreery**

*On Sunday mornings, Hannah would get up at 6:00 a.m., put a roast, potatoes, and vegetables in a roaster, and put them in the oven before church. When they came home, they had the roast for Sunday dinner (noon) and then they used the leftovers for stew all week.*

## Steamed Suet Pudding for Christmas

*(Hannah Caroline McLean McCreery)*

1 scant cup of Suet finely chopped and salted
1 cup Raisins, chopped
1/2 teaspoon Cinnamon
1 scant cup of Sugar
1 1/2 cup Buttermilk or Sour Milk
2 teaspoons soda
2 scant cups of Flour

Steam 3-4 hours in a well-greased mold.

*Anna Belle [(1912–2010), wife of William M. McCreery] used a small pail-like pan with wire handle with a cone in it like an angel food cake pan. She would pick it up by the handle with a hot pad when taking it out of the steamer pan.*

Serve with Nutmeg Sauce.

### *Nutmeg Sauce*
*(Hannah Caroline McLean McCreery)*

Mix together-1 cup Sugar and 1 tablespoon cornstarch. Pour 3/4 C boiling water over above mixture and stir in a piece of butter the size of an egg. Flavor with Nutmeg. Boil until mixture begins to thicken.

## McCreery Family Salad Dressing
Combine equal parts of Catsup, Oil, Sugar and Vinegar

# Chocolate Cake
*(Maggie Jane Sloan Bay)*

*"I made this chocolate cake almost every Saturday-growing up for Sunday dinner after church. It is from my great grandmother, Maggie Jane (Sloan) Bay, from Glasgow, Scotland."*

**—Linda McCreery**

Makes 2-9" square layer pans or 1 large loaf pan.

Stir into bowl until soft: 3/4 C butter and 1 C minus 2 Tablespoons milk

Stir together into butter: 2 cups flour, 2 cups sugar, 1 teasp salt, 2/3 cup cocoa, 1 teasp soda

Add 1 cup milk. Beat vigorously 300 strokes by hand.

Stir in 3/4 teasp baking powder, 1/4th cup milk, 3 eggs, 1 teasp vanilla.

Beat as before—300 strokes by hand.

Put into pans and bake at 350 for 30 to 35 minutes. Frost with chocolate frosting or fluffy white frosting.

*Guests at the Elkhorn Lodge, c. 1885, pose amidst stacks of the resort's trademark antlers.*

Photo courtesy of the National Park Service

## The James and Hondius Families

Among the earliest settlers in the Estes Valley was William Edwin James (1842–1895), a farmer turned shopkeeper from upstate New York. Seeking a new start in the West after the panic of 1873, William filed on a homestead in 1875. When his wife, Ella McCabe James (1843–1917), and their three little boys, Homer, Charles, and Howard,[18] arrived in Estes Park in 1876, she found the sod-roofed homestead cabin too cramped and primitive to serve as a permanent residence for herself and a growing family. For this reason, William sought to purchase property at the upper end of the Black Canyon as the site for a ranch. However, the MacGregor family, who had extensive holdings in the area, objected to his claim as an infringement on their property. To reconcile the conflict, Reverend William H. McCreery stepped in and agreed to swap his own homestead, purchased two years before on the Fall River and close to the Village, for the James' homestead further along Devils Gulch. This solved the problem. Four years later, William

*Dining room at Elkhorn Lodge, c. 1955. Linen, crystal, and silver table settings at mid-century were in marked contrast with the Lodge's otherwise casual, western atmosphere. Menus offering the choices for breakfast, lunch, and dinner each day were prepared in advance and distributed to diners each morning.*

Postcard courtesy of the Bobbie Heistercamp Collection

and Ella welcomed their fourth child and only daughter, Eleanor Estes (1880–1968), to their new home, built on land that had been William McCreery's initial homestead.[19]

As was the case with so many "old settlers," the James family soon expanded their commercial activities beyond their ranching operation by renting guest rooms to summer visitors, offering accommodation first in tents, later in tent cabins,[20] then in log cottages, and finally in lodge rooms.

Catering to the tourist trade proved so profitable that William soon abandoned ranching altogether, even remodeling the original farmhouse to accommodate additional visitors. A new "main lodge" building was added in 1900 and expanded seven years later, so that by 1912 the Elkhorn Lodge, as it came to be known, could house and feed 180 paying guests.

William and Ella James turned out to be a talented and popular innkeeping team. Indeed, while William was long remembered

*Eleanor James Hondius, (front row, fourth from right) and her husband, Pieter Hondius (back row, third from left), pose with members of the Hondius family.*

**Photo courtesy of the Estes Park Museum**

as a gracious host with a special fondness for the children of his summer visitors, it was Ella who "looked after the comforts of the guests and provided good things for the inner man."[21]

Unfortunately, William died in 1895, and Ella was left to run the Lodge with the help of Homer (1866–1958), Howard (1874–1928),[22] and Eleanor (1880–1968). With Ella's passing in 1917, Eleanor, who had married the Dutch immigrant and rancher Pieter Hondius (1864–1934) in 1903, eventually took over management of the lodge and its dining room. Among the most famous of items on the "good table"[23] at the Elkhorn in those years was the "unforgettable and sinfully delicious"[24] Welsh Rarebit, a staple item on Sunday evenings, while fish fries, which were held on Tuesdays, became

*Elkhorn Lodge menu and specially designed china greeted the Lodge's guests.*
**Artifacts courtesy of the Estes Park Museum**

"one of the features of the park and add[ed] materially to the popularity of the hotel."[25] In her *Memoirs*, Eleanor described in some detail the taffy parties that were a regular feature of the summer season:

> *Every once in a while the guests would beg me to make some taffy, and I remember one taffy pull when I buttered the plates for 65 guests, and filled them with taffy. When it had cooled enough to be pulled, they were all called in. Never have I seen a worse conglomeration of taffy. Some of it was white as they pulled it, some of it was sticky. But most of it disappeared, for every little while each taffy puller would take a bite. Whatever was left was cut into little pieces and distributed among the guests.*[26]

At the end of the summer, Eleanor and her staff would throw a Harvest Moon party. At 11:00 p.m.

> [t]wo long tables were brought from the dining room and placed at either end of the living room. One table held chafing dishes of lobster Newberg and creamed mushrooms; platters of fried chicken, sliced ham, roast beef, and tongue; all sorts of salads, olives, preserves, and pickles. The other table had on it a little keg of cider sitting in a pan of ice, doughnuts, pumpkin pie with whipped cream, mince pie, cream puffs, and several different kinds of cake.[27]

Truly her mother's daughter, Eleanor managed to juggle her work at the Elkhorn with her roles as wife and mother, even finding time to play the organ at church services and at community functions. In addition, her efforts to join with other prominent women in Estes Park to improve roads and trails in and around the valley led ultimately to the organization of the Estes Park Woman's Club, of which she was a founding and prominent member. In her *Memoirs*, Eleanor also mentioned a literary club for both men and women that she helped to organize.

Both Eleanor and her sister-in-law Jennie L. James, Homer's wife, were members of Chapter AV of the PEO sisterhood.

## Elkhorn Lodge Welsh Rarebit

*(Eleanor Estes James Hondius)*

1 lb. cheece (cut into small cubes)
1 tablespoonful of butter
1 egg
1/2 glass milk
2 Tablespoons Worcester sauce
1 tsp mustard (dry)
1/2 teaspoonful salt
Tabasco or red pepper to taste

Put butter in double boiler and when melted add cheese, when melted add rest of ingredients slowly. Stir well until smooth, then pour over toast or crackers.

## Molasses Taffy
*(Eleanor Estes James Hondius)*

2 cups New Orleans molasses
4 cups granulated sugar
1/2 lb. butter
2 cups light-colored Karo
1 tablespoonful vinegar

Cook slowly until taffy becomes brittle when dropped into cold water. Taffy must not be so soft that it will stick to the teeth or so hard it is difficult to chew. If too soft when cut, roll in powdered sugar. When done, remove from the stove, add 1/2 teaspoonful soda, stir well, pour into well-buttered pans and, when cool enough, pull with the fingers and not palm of hand.

## Chop-Suey
*(Eleanor Estes James Hondius)*

1/2 pound fresh pork, veal, or chicken (diced)
1 cup finely chopped celery or cabbage
1 cup finely chopped onions
3 tablespoonfuls Oriental Show You Sauce[28]
1 tablespoonful brown sugar
1/2 tablespoon lard

Begin to cook rice needed. Melt lard and fry meat in it until tender. Add Vegetables, a pinch of salt and sugar and cook for ten minutes. Thicken slightly with flour.

## Fig Delight (Sugared Figs and Whipped Cream)
*(Eleanor Estes James Hondius)*

1 pound dried figs
3/4 cup sugar

Chop figs until fine, sugar, put into stew pan, add a little water, stew until tender and cool. Fill sherbet glasses half full and fill the balance of the glass with whipped cream. The cream should have sugar to sweeten and a little vanilla to flavor. Serve Cold.

*Howard James and unidentified child enjoy the view from the running board of Howard's touring car at the Elkhorn Lodge.*
Photo courtesy of the Estes Park Museum

## Dutch Apple Fritters
*(Eleanor Estes James Hondius)*

Two cakes Fleishmann yeast. Make light batter of flour, milk, salt and add the yeast cakes, which have been dissolved in warm water. Allow to raise until the batter is light. Pare several tart apples and core and cut in slices across the apple. Have ready a kettle of hot lard. When batter is light, dip slice of apple into batter and cook in fat until a light brown. When cold sprinkle well with powdered sugar.

## Parker House Rolls
*(Jennie L. James)*

Dissolve one cake of compressed yeast in 1 pint of milk, scalded and cooled. Add 4 tablespoonfuls melted butter or lard, 2 tablespoonfuls sugar, 1 1/2 pints flour; beat until perfectly smooth. Let rise until light, then add 1 teaspoonful salt and 1/1/2 pints flour. Knead well and let rise until double in bulk. Roll out 1/4 inch thick, brush with butter, cut with cookie cutter, crease through the center and fold over. Let rise until light. Bake about fifteen minutes in a hot oven.

*Members of the Sprague and Chapman families pose for the camera as they picnic together in this humorously staged (undated) photo. Alberta Sprague stands (far left) with a dinner bell; Abner (third from left) cuts a loaf of bread.*

Photo courtesy of the National Park Service

## The Sprague and Chapman Families

Of the homesteading families in early Estes Park, the Spragues and Chapmans are among the best remembered. While Abner Sprague was initially drawn to Willow Park (now Moraine Park) by the ranching opportunities it appeared to offer, from an early date he and members of his extended family turned their hands to innkeeping, founding not one but two of the most popular early resorts: Sprague's House (1878), which was destined to became Stead's Ranch in 1902, and Sprague's Lodge (1914), located in Glacier Basin. Abner was quick to credit the culinary talents of his mother and his wife in making each of these enterprises a success.

Abner Erwin Sprague was born in Illinois in March 1850, the son of Thomas (1821–1882) and Mary Margaret Wolaver Sprague (1831–1917). Thomas's parents had moved their family from New York to the Chicago area in 1844. At first a sea captain on the Great

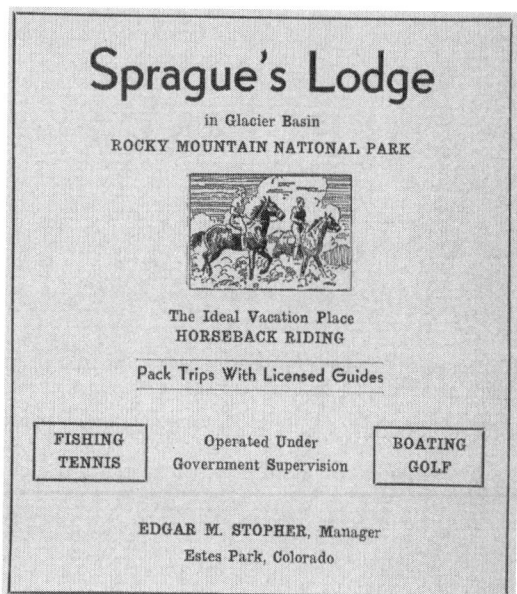

Lakes, Thomas turned to farming soon after his engagement to Mary. Hoping to improve his economic prospects and provide for his growing family, Thomas decided to go west to Iowa, where he secured a homestead, built a log house, and put in a crop. When this venture too did not prove a success, Thomas left his family, which by then included Abner's younger siblings, Areanna (Arah) and Fred, for the gold fields newly discovered in the Colorado Territory. After four years, during which time Mary had taken the children back to her family in Illinois, in 1864 Thomas purchased a farm in the valley of the Big Thompson river, and moved the family to Colorado.[29]

As the eldest child, Abner (1850–1943), of course, helped his family on the farm and also worked for others in the area as a farm laborer. However, being a young man of diverse abilities and extraordinary flexibility, he soon began exploring the mountains of the Front Range. Falling in love with the area around Estes Park, he staked out a claim for himself in Willow Park with the intention of ranching. The following year, he persuaded his parents, sister, and brother to follow his example, which they all did. At one time the Spragues' combined homesteads extended to 900 acres.[30] This venture was initially successful, and Thomas soon added a dairy herd to his own beef cattle operation.

In the closing decades of the nineteenth century, it did not take long for passing hikers to discover the ample and tasty chicken dinners[31] available from the kitchen of Mary Wolaver Sprague. Irresistible as well were the treats of spring water, fresh milk, and homemade ice cream available from the family's springhouse, which, according to one contemporary observer, was kept in a state of "scrupulous neatness."[32] Writing later in his life, Abner would sum up their situation in this way:

> It never entered our minds when we settled in the Park that the region would attract others as it did us. Enjoying and loving the region as we did, we should have realized that other lovers of the out-of-doors would come to enjoy our streams, mountains, and forests, and soon our isolated lives would come to an end.[33]

46   Chapter Two: Homesteaders and Old Settlers

*Abner and Alberta Sprague (seated center) with Areanna (front left) and her sons. Abner's mother, Mary Margaret Wolaver Sprague (seated, far right) was a talented cook in her own right and an asset to Sprague's Lodge in the early days.*

Photo courtesy of the National Park Service.

Certainly Mary's "loving kindness" and her reputation for excellence in preparing, serving, and pricing food had everything to do with the little hotel's growing popularity. And the Spragues, father and son, were justly proud of their wife and mother. In his autobiography, Abner wrote:

*On baking days, I would prepare a bed of coals and the Dutch oven. When the dough was ready, I would watch the baking. If one has never tasted the bread my Mother bakes in a tight Dutch oven, they have missed the best-tasting bread that was ever baked.*[34]

Hoping to capitalize on the opportunity and the increase in his income by providing services to summer visitors, Thomas began by expanding his original homestead building to include a new kitchen and guest rooms. He also added a number of primitive log cabins.

About 1876, Areanna Sprague married Alson Chapman (1851–1889) and moved with him to New York, where their first child, Lena, was born in 1878. Two sons followed: Charles A. (1879–1951) and Alson Jr. (1890). Areanna was widowed at the age of thirty-eight when Alson Sr. died, leaving her to raise their three small children alone. She had little choice but to move home to Colorado and rejoin her mother, brothers, and sister-in-law in Moraine Park, where she and her sons would eventually assist Abner, Alberta, and Mary in their innkeeping activities. As Pedersen notes in *Those Castles of Wood*, "[t]he Sprague, Morrison, and Stopher families were closely knit, loved and trusted one another, and worked together in a viable collaborative partnership."[35]

After Thomas' death in 1882,[36] Mary Sprague stepped in to run the ranch as well as the kitchen; with the help of her sons Abner and Fred, the Hotel continued to offer guided fishing, hunting, and climbing trips, and horseback riding, as well as carriage rides, dances, lawn games, and picnics. Mary, now known affectionately as Grandma Sprague, also served as postmistress for Willow Park, a job that she would eventually pass on to her daughter, Areanna Sprague Chapman.

In 1888, Abner, a thirty-eight-year-old bachelor, met and married Mary Alberta Morrison of Hickman, Nebraska. Later, Abner would describe his bride as "the romance of my life" and "the luckiest thing that ever happened to me."[37] Alberta "Bert" (1867–1949) was one of nine children and the daughter of a man whom Abner met while working as a surveyor for the Missouri Pacific Railroad in Nebraska. While Abner was away, Fred, with the assistance of his sister Areanna, continued to operate Sprague's Hotel. Areanna was entrepreneurial in her own right, eventually renting out summer cottages and running a small general store and post office to serve the growing Willow Park community.

By 1902 Sprague's ranch had grown in size and popularity to the point that Abner felt compelled to take on a partner. Given his propensity for choosing from among his relatives, it was perhaps not surprising that he invited James D. Stead, a Chicago dairyman who had married his mother's niece—his cousin Eudora Mary Wolaver (1859–1931)—to join him in owning and running the Hotel.

Although the two men seemed to get along well in their shared enterprise, their wives did not. In an effort to avoid a potential

*Mary Alberta Morrison Sprague and Abner Sprague (n.d.). They were a devoted couple, and their marriage was a long and happy one.*
**Photo courtesy of the National Park Service.**

conflict between "Dora" and Bert, the ranch duties of the two women were to be kept entirely separate, with Dora running the housekeeping side of ranch management while Bert ruled the kitchen. Even so, Dora proved to be so "opinionated and overbearing" that daily life became decidedly unpleasant for everyone. To put an end to this, the Spragues sold out to the Steads and moved to Loveland, where Abner took up work as the county surveyor.

Abner seems to have enjoyed his work in Loveland, but he and Bert missed the mountains. Thus in 1908, the couple decided to

*Sprague's Lodge pottery and original advertising card for "Sprague House" in Willow (now Moraine) Park. Thomas E. Sprague, Abner's father, was the resort's first proprietor.*

**Artifacts courtesy of the Estes Park Museum**

build a summer cottage in Glacier Basin, and asked Bert's younger sister Mabel[38] and her husband John Samuel Stopher (1877–1909), who were also living in Loveland at the time, to join in the project. A summer home was soon built to be shared by the two families, but it was not long before the Spragues decided to move back to the mountains on a permanent basis. This they did in 1910, with Mabel and her two children, Alberta and Edgar, Mabel's husband John having died tragically just before the birth of his only son the previous year.

Once the decision had been made to re-enter the innkeeping business, the families' joint cabin was enlarged as Sprague's Lodge,

*The dining room at Spragues Hotel, about 1925.*
Postcard courtesy of the Bobbie Heistercamp Collection

and additional cabins were built to provide ample room for a substantial number of summer guests. Abner even built and stocked a trout pond. "Mr. Sprague is very proud of his kitchen," an article in the paper acknowledged. "He specializes in trout dinners, the charge is $1.50."[39] At the same time, Abner stepped in to help Mabel raise her little ones, and her son Edgar M. Stopher came to regard him as the father he had lost.

Although they lived some little way from the Village, it should be noted that both Abner and Bert were active contributors to the civic and social development of the Estes Park community. As early as 1895, Abner was chairing the Estes Park Protective and Improvement Association (EPPIA), a group dedicated to the improvement of roads and ranching, fire prevention, and wildlife protection. Alberta was a member of Chapter AV of PEO, and joined the Estes Park Woman's Club soon after its founding in 1912; in 1926–1927, she found time to serve a term as its president. A major personality in her own right (Frederick Chapin named

Chapter Two: Homesteaders and Old Settlers

*Elizabeth "Libby" Buchanan Chapman, Areanna's daughter-in-law (standing), at the Moraine Park Post Office in 1905.*
Photo courtesy of the National Park Service

the lovely water falls off the trail to Mills Lake "Alberta Falls" in her honor), Bert Sprague was an avid hiker as well as an extraordinarily good cook, and she was as well known in the Village for her culinary skills as she was among guests at Sprague's Lodge.⁴⁰ She also played the organ and sang for a variety of club and community functions. Both Abner and Alberta were beloved by their contemporaries, if the number and tenor of the newspaper accounts documenting their activities can be taken as evidence of the fact.

While Sprague's Lodge at Glacier Basin never grew to the size of Stead's Ranch, it was a great favorite of summer guests who aimed at a more intimate mountain experience than was available in the larger resorts. In 1932, the National Park Service bought out the Spragues but allowed them to sign on as concessionaires for a period that eventually extended twenty-five years. Seven years later, Edgar Stopher bought the lease from his aunt and uncle, expanding the lodge to accommodate eighty-five guests, and operating the resort until 1957. The NPS quickly removed the buildings, so that by 1960 the only remaining structure was the stable. Neither Alberta nor Abner lived to see the destruction of their beloved Lodge, Abner having died in 1943 and Alberta six years later.

## White Bread
*(Mary Alberta Morrison Sprague)*

1 2/3 C. liquid  4 tsp. sugar  3 tsp. salt
2 tbs. shortening  1 cake compressed yeast

Add crumbled yeast to liquid that has been scalded and cooled, then add sugar, salt, and shortening. Add flour (4 to 5 cups) and knead until you have a smooth texture. Put into a greased bowl and cover until it is twice its size in bulk (about 45 minutes). Knead and return to rise about the same time or bulk, then divide in two parts for loaves. When almost twice the size put into the oven and bake 45 to 60 minutes at 350 degrees.

## Bread Jug or Soft Yeast
*(Mary Alberta Morrison Sprague)*

One pint loose or 1 cup pressed hops in a pan with a pint of hot water and steep 10 minutes. Pare and slice 8 medium-sized potatoes and drain hop water over them, adding 1 quart of hot water, and cook until potatoes are done. Put through a ricer or colander and add enough water to make 2 quarts, and allow to cool until luke-warm. Add 1/4 cup sugar, 1 tablespoonful salt and 2 good yeast cakes that have been previously soaked in warm water. Keep in a warm place for several hours, or until foamy and light. Put in a cool place and use for raised bread.

## Twin Mountain Muffins
*(Mary Alberta Morrison Sprague)*

1/4 cup softened butter  1/4 cup sugar  1 egg  3/4 cups milk
3 level teaspoonfuls  2 cups flour
   baking powder

Cream butter and sugar and add beaten egg; add a part of the flour and baking powder and then milk, and continue until all is used. Bake in buttered muffin tins from one-quarter to one-half an hour.

## Swiss White Soup

*(Mary Alberta Morrison Sprague)*

Three pints of chicken or veal broth, beat 3 eggs well, add 2 tablespoons flour and 1 cup milk. Pour this through a sieve into the boiling soup, add salt and pepper to taste.

## Orange Marmalade

*(Mary Alberta Morrison Sprague)*

3 oranges
1 lemon and juice of 1 lemon
16 glasses of water
8 cups sugar

Slice oranges and 1 lemon very thin and cut in small lengths. Squeeze in juice of the other lemon, add water and set away for 24 hours. Put on fire and boil until peel is tender. Set off and add sugar. Stir while sugar dissolves and set away 24 hours. Third day boil until it jellies. This recipe makes about 9 glasses.

## Soft Ginger Bread

*(Mary Alberta Morrison Sprague)*

1 cup sugar
1 cup molasses
1 teaspoonful soda
3 eggs
1 cup butter or lard
4 cups flour
1 teaspoonful each ginger, cinnamon and cloves

Mix all the ingredients together and add 1 cup of boiling water.

## Hard Ginger Bread
*(Areanna Sprague Chapman)*

Rub 1 teacup butter into 1 quart of sifted flour; add 1 tablespoonful ginger, 1 wine glass of water in which 1 teaspoonful soda is dissolved, 1 pint molasses. Sifted flour enough to make a stiff dough. Mix all together well. Roll it out thin and bake on buttered tins. You may brush over the cake sugar syrup when you put it in the oven.

## Molasses Drop Cookies
*(Mabel Morrison Stopher)*

2/3 cup brown sugar
2/3 cup lard
2 eggs
1 cup sweet milk
1 cup syrup
1 teaspoonful each cinnamon, cloves, salt, and soda

Mix lard, sugar and eggs, beat well; then add syrup, milk, spices, soda and flour. Drop in small spoonfuls on buttered tins. Bake in quick oven. An icing may be put on before removing from the pans consisting of sugar moistened with water.

*Mary Margaret Grim Griffith and her husband Albin, pictured in an old family photo with their children and grandchildren, homesteaded in Estes Park at the turn of the last century.*

Photo courtesy of the Griffith family

## The Griffith Family

Albin and Mary Margaret Grim Griffith and their family played active roles in many aspects of village life in Estes Park from the 1890s through the 1960s. A minister in the United Brethren Church of Christ, Albin (1858–1946) served as a pastor and circuit-riding preacher in the Front Range communities of Loveland and Fort Collins. In 1890, he retired from active ministry and moved with Margaret (1858–1917) and their three children, sons John Nolan (1884–1946) and Dan Braxton (1882–1969), and daughter Oma Katherine (1886–1969), to a homestead site near the Fergusons' Highlands resort. Two additional children, Nellie (1894–1918) and Mary Lois (1896–1968), were born to the couple during the following decade.

In 1907, Albin and his sons built a sawmill at Bierstadt Lake, on land they had leased from the National Park Service in order to harvest dead trees killed in a fire seven years before. Two years later the Griffiths started a lumber yard "on the Moraine Park road."[41] It was the Griffiths who supplied the lumber for Freelan Oscar Stanley's grand, neo-Georgian hotel, which opened in 1909.

*Albin Griffith atop a log wagon at his sawmill.*
Photo courtesy of the Griffith family

Busy as he was with these enterprises, Albin still found time and energy to "spell" Rev. Elkanah Lamb in the pulpit of the Presbyterian Church of Estes Park from time to time. A community booster as well as a jack-of-all trades in his later years, Albin also leased cottages to tourists and raised hogs and vegetables for the local market.[42]

Albin and Margaret's sons, John and Dan, established their own families in Estes Park and made many contributions to town life over the next nine decades. In 1906, John married Estes Park-born Virginia Cleave (1885–1936), daughter of John and Margaret May Cleave, the couple whose original homestead property at the confluence of the Fall and Big Thompson Rivers became the site for the town of Estes Park. Seven years later, Dan married Louise Ellen Jesser (1891–1990), the daughter of Russian immigrants. For a wedding present, Dan presented his bride with a .22-caliber rifle, which she used to hunt varmints![43]

The Griffiths' youngest child, Mary Lois (1896–1968), was educated at Colorado State Teachers College (now the University

*Dan and Louise Ellen Jesser Griffith on their wedding day, Oct. 2, 1913.*
Photo courtesy of the Estes Park Museum

of Northern Colorado) in Greeley and taught art and music in the Estes Park schools. She was an active member of Chapter AV of PEO (serving as state president of the organization in 1955), Eastern Star, and the Community Church of the Rockies in Estes Park. In addition, she helped her sister-in-law Louise run the family-owned Rockmount Cottages, assisted her father at the lumberyard, and kept house for him after Margaret's death in 1917.

## Sweet Milk Doughnuts
*(Louise Ellen Jesser Griffith)*

1 egg, 1 cup sugar, 1 cup sweet milk, 2 teaspoons baking powder, butter size of egg, dash of nutmeg may be added if desired, flour Makes eight doughnuts.

---

## 12-Day Chunk Pickles
*(Louise Ellen Jesser Griffith)*

Select medium-sized cucumbers and allow to stand for 3 days in brine (one cup of salt to one gallon of water). Then drain and let stand 3 days in cold water. On the seventh day cut in chunks as you prefer, and cook in weak vinegar until tender. Let stand 3 days and then drain.

Make a syrup of:

3 lbs. sugar, 1 pint vinegar, 1/2 tsp whole cloves, 1 stick cinnamon, 1 tablespoon mustard seed, 1/2 tsp whole allspice. Pour hot syrup over pickles for 3 days and seal on third day.

---

## Fudge
*(Louise Ellen Jesser Griffith)*

2 squares chocolate
1 cup milk
2 cups sugar
1 teaspoon butter
1/2 cup walnuts
1 teaspoon vanilla

Boil chocolate and milk until thick like gravy, add sugar and continue boiling until it forms a soft ball when dropped in cold water, remove from stove, and add flavoring and butter. When cool beat until thick and creamy, add walnuts and put in shallow pan to cool. Do not stir after sugar has been added.

## Raisin Drop Cookies
*(Louise Ellen Jesser Griffith)*

Cream thoroughly 1/2 cup shortening with 1 cup sugar (granulated or brown); add 1 egg well beaten, 1/3 cup milk, 1 1/2 cups rolled oats, 1 cup seedless raisins, and 1/2 cup chopped walnuts if you like. Add to this mixture 1 1/2 cups sifted flour—sifted again with 1/2 teaspoon each of salt and soda, and 1 teaspoon each cinnamon, nutmeg and ginger. Drop from spoon on well greased pan, about 3 inches apart. Bake in moderate oven about 15 minutes.

## Suet Pudding
*(Louise Ellen Jesser Griffith)*

2/3 Cup molasses
1 1/3 Cup milk
1 tsp Soda
2 eggs
3 Cups flour
1/2 C ground suet
1 Cup Raisins
1 Cup dates or currants

1/2 recipe for 8 people

Steam 2 hours - 1 hour for 1/2 of recipe.

## Hard Sauce
*(Louise Ellen Jesser Griffith)*

1/2 C. Butter or Oleo
2 C. powdered sugar
1/2 tsp vanilla
Yield - one cup

## Corn Bread
*(Louise Ellen Jesser Griffith)*

1 egg
1 teaspoonful soda
2 cups white corn meal
1/2 cup sour milk
1 cup sour cream

Bake in a moderate oven.

## Chocolate Cake
*(Mary Lois Griffith)*

Cook 1/2 cup milk and 2 squares of chocolate until smooth and thick. Let cool.

1/2 cup butter creamed. Add 1 1/2 cups sugar—less 4 level tbsp.— and cream. Add 3 egg yolks and cooked chocolate. Add 1/2 cup milk, 2 1/2 cups flour (sifted), 1 tsp vanilla, 1 tsp soda dissolved in 1/8 cup milk. Fold in egg whites. Start in cool oven, increase heat gradually.

### *Chocolate Fudge Frosting*
Cook 2 squares chocolate and cup of milk until thick. Stir in 2 cups sugar. Cook without stirring until it forms a soft ball in water. Add tbsp. butter, 1 tsp. vanilla, cool. Beat. Nuts may be added.

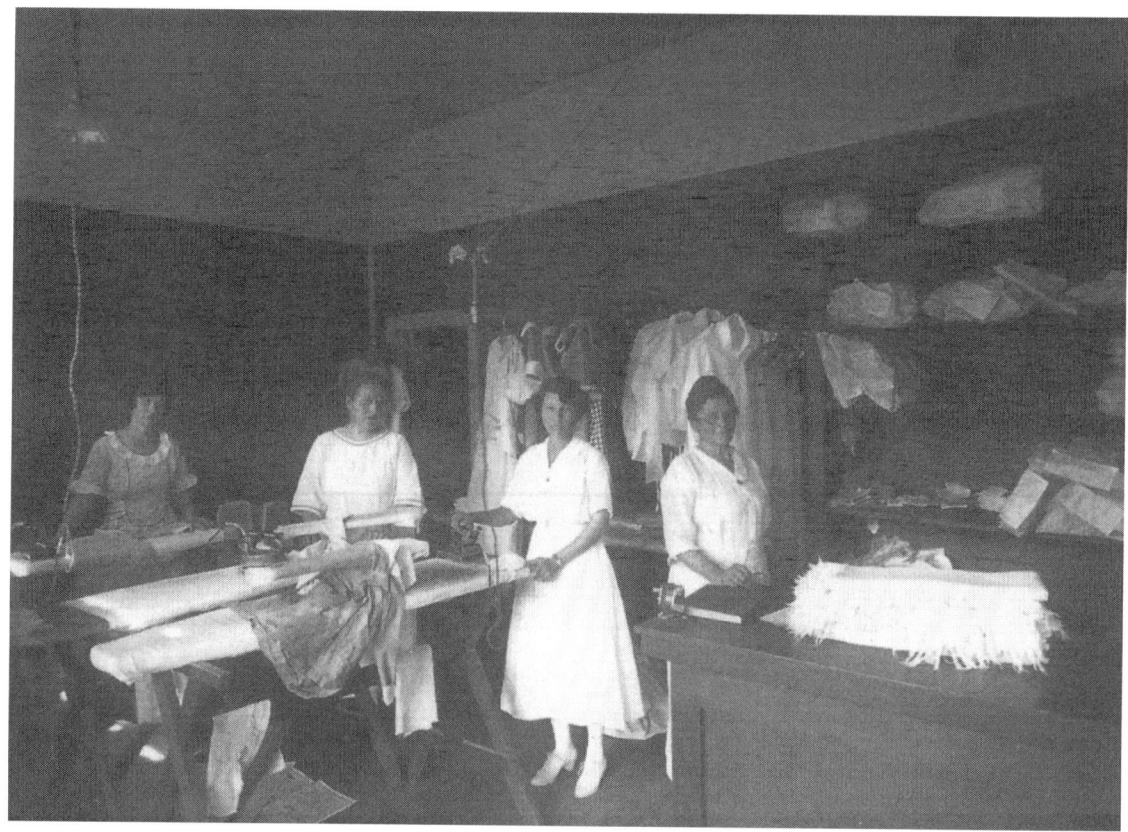

*Interior photo of the Fall River Hand Laundry, established by Elizabeth Hix (far right).*
Photo courtesy of The Taffy Shop, Elkhorn Avenue, Estes Park, Colorado

## The Hix Family of Estes Park

Few families have contributed more to the growth and development of Estes Park than the Hix family. The matriarch was Elizabeth Esther Clauser Hix (1864–1952), who homesteaded 160 acres in Estes Park in 1903, after the death of her husband, Franklin S. Hix (1854–1902). Originally from a German-speaking community in Pennsylvania, Elizabeth came west after Franklin's death to join her brother Milton Clauser (1867–1948), who was living in Denver. Elizabeth's children, ten-year-old Beulah (b. 1893) and seven-year-old Charles Franklin Hix (Sr.) (1896–1984), spoke no English at the time of their arrival in Colorado. It was Milton and his second wife, Winnie, who first introduced Elizabeth, Charles, and Beulah to the village of Estes Park.

Charged with the responsibility of supporting two young children, Elizabeth energetically set about establishing herself and her family in their new community. Beulah recalled her mother's homesteading experiences in this way:

> *She was required to build a habitable house; to cultivate a small area, which she used for a vegetable garden; to pay three dollars an acre; and to live on the tract part of each year for three years. In a short time she made Estes Park her permanent residence and bought a business building in the village, as well as a home nearby.*[44]

Elizabeth's business was the Fall River Hand Laundry, which was located on Elkhorn Avenue. An active participant in the Estes community, Elizabeth was a charter member of the Estes Park Woman's Club, founded in 1912.

Elizabeth's brother Milton was a Haverford (Pa.) College–educated teacher who began homesteading in Estes Park in 1896. Over time he had worked at a number of different jobs, including as a manual training educator in Denver and in Utah, and as the manager of a transportation company and a real estate business in Estes Park. A car enthusiast all his life, Milton owned one of the first Stanley Steamers shipped to Colorado in 1903. Milton also had a number of wives: the first was Ann Hettinger Clauser (1867–1899). Soon after Ann's death, he met Winnie Alvilda Todd Wells, a widow living in Denver, whom he married in 1900. The couple divorced about ten years later. Milton then married Florence Yochum Clauser (1884–1963) in 1911.

Elizabeth Hix's son Charles Franklin (Sr.), who married Elsie Claire Johnson (1902–1982) in Estes Park in 1923, was teller, cashier, and finally president of the Estes Park Bank. A longtime Estes Park booster, Charles was involved with the Estes Park Water Company, and served for twenty-two years on the Town board and eighteen years on the school board. An active member of Rotary and the Community Church of the Rockies, Charles also helped to found the Estes Park post of the American Legion. Charles Sr. and Elsie had two children, Charles Franklin Hix Jr. (1926–) and George Franklin Johnson Hix (1928–2010).

Elizabeth Hix, her sister-in-law Florence Clauser, and her daughter-in-law Elsie Hix, were all members of Chapter AV of the PEO sisterhood, and contributors to the *Tried and True Recipe Book*, first published in 1920.

## Lemon Pie
*(Elizabeth E. Clauser Hix)*

3 eggs
3 tbs. flour
Butter size of egg

2 cups sugar
2 cups milk
1 Lemon

Boil yolks of eggs, sugar, flour and milk in double boiler; then beat whites of eggs with 2 tbs. of pulverized sugar. Put in a baked crust and spread whites of eggs on and brown in oven.

## Brown Bread
*(Elizabeth E. Clauser Hix)*

1 egg
1/2 or 3/4 cup molasses
2 teaspoonfuls soda
1 teaspoonful salt
1/2 cup raisins

1 scant cup sugar
2 cups sour milk
2 1/2 cups graham flour
1/2 cup nut meats

Mix well. If not stiff enough, add little white flour. Bake in two pans.

## Drop Dumplings
*(Elizabeth E. Clauser Hix)*

2 cups flour
4 teaspoonfuls baking powder
Milk

1/2 teaspoonful salt
2 eggs

Sift dry ingredients into bowl, add the well beaten eggs and milk to make a batter as stiff as can be stirred. Drop by spoonfuls into the kettle with meat and vegetables for beef stew. Cover tightly and cook without opening kettle for twenty minutes.

## Ham and Beet Salad
*(Elizabeth E. Clauser Hix)*

2 cups diced ham (cooked)
1 cup diced stuffed olives
1 head lettuce
3/4 cup diced celery
2 cups diced beets (cooked)

Mix first four ingredients, moisten with French dressing or mayonnaise and serve on lettuce.

## Pumpkin Pie
*(Elizabeth E. Clauser Hix)*

1 egg
1 tbs. flour
1 cup milk
1 tsp. cinnamon
1/2 tsp. salt
3 tbs. sugar
1 cup pumpkin
1 tbs. molasses
1/4 tsp. ginger
Butter size of egg.

## Iced Chocolate
*(Elsie Johnson Hix)*

1 1/2 squares chocolate
1/2 cup sugar
4 cups milk (hot)
2 cups water
1/2 teaspoonful salt

Melt chocolate over hot water, add 2 cups water, sugar and salt. Cook until a smooth syrup is formed. Add milk, beat with egg beater. Set in refrigerator and chill thoroughly before serving.

## Almond Caramel Ice Cream
*(Elsie Johnson Hix)*

1/2 cup flour
2 cups cream
1 1/2 cups caramel flavoring
1/8 tsp. salt
1 cup sugar
1 cup ground almonds
2 eggs
2 cups milk

Mix flour, sugar, salt. Heat milk and add; also caramel flavoring and cook in double boiler twenty minutes, stirring frequent. Add well-beaten eggs and return to double boiler. Cook three minutes, stirring constantly. Cool and add cream, nuts, and freeze.

### *Caramel Flavoring*

Prepared by melting 1 1/2 cups sugar in frying pan, when it is brown add 1 1/2 cups boiling water. Boil fifteen minutes.

## Christmas Star Salad
*(Florence Yochum Clauser)*

Simple salad of pickled beets cut in star shape and serve on lettuce leaves or endive. In the center of each star place a tiny white ball made of cream cheese. Serve with French dressing or mayonnaise.

## Date Cookies

*(Florence Yochum Clauser)*

1 cup sugar (brown)
1 tbs. soda
1 cup sour milk
1 cup butter
2 cups flour
2 cups oatmeal

Roll very thin, cut rather large and make turnovers, using the filling.

## *Filling*

1/2 lb dates
1/2 cup water
1/2 cup sugar

Cook until it is soft. Bake.

## Raisin Graham Bread

*(Florence Yochum Clauser)*

1 cup sour milk
1/4 cup molasses
1/4 cup sugar
1 1/2 cups Graham flour
1 teaspoonful each salt and soda
1 cup chopped seeded raisins
2 tablespoonfuls melted shortening

Stir well and pour in greased pan, let stand for ten minutes, then put in moderate oven. Bake three-quarters of an hour.

## Alma and Cornelius Bond

Cornelius Howard Bond (1854–1931), a schoolteacher, visited Estes Park on a camping trip in 1879, and in 1883 he returned from his native Ohio to settle in Loveland. At first engaged in ranching and storekeeping, he soon turned his attention to politics, eventually serving as Larimer County Sheriff (1896–1901) and two terms in the state legislature. As a committeeman investigating the Bald Mountain stage route linking Loveland and Estes Park, he was instrumental in the creation of a new road along the Big Thompson River.

Alma E. Sanborn (1861–1958) married Cornelius in 1896. She was his second wife, his first wife, Friona Sullivan Bond, having died in 1895, leaving Cornelius the single parent of a three-year-old daughter, Doris (b. 1892). Together Alma and Cornelius had four children: the twins Frank[45] and Florence, in 1898; a son Fred E., in 1899; and a daughter, May S., in 1902. In 1905 Cornelius, Alma and the children moved to Estes Park, where Cornelius sold real estate and insurance.

Both Bonds were community leaders from an early date. Cornelius helped plat the town and sell the original lots along Main Street (now Elkhorn Avenue) and Moraine Avenue. He later served on the Estes Park school board and was a board trustee of The Stanley Hotel. Bond Park, located on Elkhorn Avenue in the heart of the Village, was named for Cornelius in 1944 and commemorates his efforts in founding Estes Park. For her part, Alma made significant contributions to community life, not only as a founding member, in 1912, of the Estes Park Woman's Club, but also as the town's librarian, a job she held for eighteen years. As a member of Chapter AV of PEO, Alma provided many recipes to the sisterhood's cookbook published in 1920.

### Punch—Six Quarts
*(Alma Sanborn Bond)*

1 can of pineapple

4 cups of sugar

Boil twenty minutes

Juice of 5 lemons

Juice of 6 oranges

1 pint of grape juice

6 quarts of water

If in season, sliced cucumber, left in a while to season it.

## Salad Dressing
*(Alma Sanborn Bond)*

1 tablespoonful of mustard
3 tablespoonfuls of flour
Yolk of 2 eggs
1 1/2 cups of milk
2 tablespoonfuls of sugar
1 teaspoonful of salt
1 tablespoonful of butter
1/2 cup vinegar

## Brown Sugar Candy
*(Alma Sanborn Bond)*

2 cups of brown sugar
1/2 cup of Karo Syrup
1 cup of nut meats
1 cup of white sugar
1/2 cup of milk or cream

Cook till hard ball, beat until creamy, add nuts and vanilla.

## Mother's Crullers[46]
*(Alma Sanborn Bond)*

2 eggs
3 tablespoonfuls of melted butter
Pinch of salt and soda
6 tablespoonfuls of sugar
3 tablespoonfuls of milk

Mould very hard.

## Chopped Pickles
*(Alma Sanborn Bond)*

Eight pounds of green tomatoes, chopped; 3/4 cup of salt. Let stand over night, then pour off juice and add 4 green peppers, 4 onions, medium; 2 teaspoonfuls of pepper, 3 teaspoonfuls of mustard, 3 teaspoonfuls of cinnamon, 3 teaspoonfuls of cloves, 2 quarts of vinegar. Cook one hour.

*Estes Park in 1908, about the time the Wiests moved to the Village.*
Photo courtesy of the Estes Park Museum

## Wiest Family

Roy Francis Wiest (1877–1961), first mayor of the Town of Estes Park as well as the town's first doctor, moved from Michigan to Longmont soon after the turn of the last century to study medicine with his uncle, Dr. Sard Wiest. In Longmont, Roy met and married Sara Armstrong (1878–1954) in 1906, and the couple then moved to Estes Park, where Roy set up his medical practice in an office on Elkhorn Avenue.

Both Roy and Sara were active personally and professionally in the Estes community. In addition to managing his medical office and running the Estes Park Drug Company, Dr. Wiest was an active member of the Fish and Game Commission, the Rocky Mountain National Park Radio Club, the Estes Park Group of the Colorado Mountain Club; he was also a founding member of The Rotary Club of Estes Park. He served as president of the school board, and was active in the Masons and the Chamber of Commerce. Dr. Wiest is also remembered as an amateur lepidopterist, who, with the couple's son, Donald (b. 1909), amassed a fascinating collection of butterflies, now housed in the Estes Park Museum.

For her part, Sara was active in Chapter AV of the PEO sisterhood, contributing a number of recipes to the group's cookbook in 1920. She also served as PEO president in 1922 and 1924. Her other activities included membership in the Ladies Aid Society, the Missionary Society of the Community Church, and the Estes Park Woman's Club, serving as its second president (1919–1920).

## Butterscotch Pie
*(Sara Armstrong Wiest)*

2-3 cup dark brown sugar  
2 tablespoonfuls milk  
1 tablespoonful butter

Cook these together as thick as possible without burning.

2 egg yolks  
1 1/2 cups milk  
1 heaping tablespoonful flour

Add these last articles to the other mixture and cook until quite thick. Fill crust which has already been baked, beat the whites of the eggs until stiff, add 2 tablespoonfuls sugar, spread on top of custard and brown in oven.

## Eggless, Butterless, Milkless Cake

*(Sara Armstrong Wiest)*

2 cups brown sugar
2 cups water
2 teaspoonfuls cinnamon
1/2 teaspoonful nutmeg
1 teaspoonful soda
1 cup raisins
3/4 cup Lard
4 cups flour
1 teaspoonful cloves
1/2 teaspoonful mace
1 teaspoonful baking powder
1 cup nut meats.

Boil sugar, lard, raisins and spices in 1/2 cup cold water. Cool and add the 2 cups of water and the other ingredients and stir well. Bake in a loaf about an hour.

## Potato Cake

*(Sara Armstrong Wiest)*

One and one-half cups sugar, 3/4 cup butter; cream together 4 eggs beaten (whites added last); 1/2 cup melted chocolate, 1 cup mashed potatoes, 3/4 cup sweet milk, 2 cups flour, sifted with 2 teaspoonfuls baking powder, 1 cup chopped raisins, 1/2 cup English walnuts. Add vanilla and spice to taste.

## Peanut Brittle
*(Sara Armstrong Wiest)*

1 cup sugar                1 cup peanuts

Put sugar on stove and melt, stirring all the time; do not brown. When melted, add cup of nut meats which have been rolled on board. Pour at once on same board, roll out and mark in squares. When cold, break.

## Beef Loaf
*(Sara Armstrong Wiest)*

2 pounds ground beef
1 pound ground fresh pork
3 well-beaten eggs
1/2 cup sweet milk
6 crackers, rolled fine
1 tablespoonful salt
1 teaspoonful sage
1 teaspoonful pepper

Mix well, make into a loaf, put into bake-dish, cover with strips of bacon and bake two hours.

*Albert and Julian Hayden showing off their morning's catch to Mr. and Mrs. Thompson and Mr. and Mrs. Warren Hilton, August, 1899.*

Photo courtesy of the Estes Park Museum.

## The Hayden Family

Emma Cornelia Howe (1856–1935) of Chicago married Ohio-born Albert Hayden (1847–1911) in 1877. Albert was employed in the family's saddlery business, the income from which allowed the young couple to live comfortably in a household run with the assistance of a cook and two servants. Cornelia and Albert's sons, Albert Jr. (1882–1932) and Julian, called "Jude" (1886–1964), were educated as civil engineers at the Illinois Institute of Technology.

Albert Jr. and Julian moved to Estes Park sometime before 1910,[47] where they became "avid mountaineers."[48] In the newly platted village, the pair established an engineering firm, and even-

*The Hayden and Reed families, c. 1915. (Standing): Cornelia Hayden (Mrs. Albert Sr.), Julian Hayden, Belle Brandt Reed, Sallie Ferguson Reed, Charles Reed Sr., and Mildred Frances Ferguson Seaton (Mrs. Walter). (Seated): Mrs. Hayden's housekeeper, Ed Andrews, Anna Louise Reed Hayden (Mrs. Albert Jr.), and Albert Hayden Jr.*
Photo courtesy of the Estes Park Museum.

tually became partners in a real estate business as well. Following the death of her husband, Albert Sr., in 1911, Cornelia Hayden decided to move from Chicago to Estes Park, where she made her home with her younger son, Julian.

In 1912, Albert Jr. married Anna Louise "Louise" Reed (1887–1965), whose parents, Charles and Sallie Ferguson Reed, owned the Brinwood Hotel in Moraine Park. The wedding, which attracted seventy-five guests, was, according to the *Estes Park Trail*, "One of the prettiest . . . that ever occurred in Estes Park."[49] The young couple became the center of much of the social life in the Village during the 1910s and 1920s, and their activities and guests were the focus of considerable interest in the local newspapers.

Albert Hayden Jr. played an important role in the incorporation of the town, serving as mayor in 1921 and 1922 and for ten years as a town trustee. He was also an officer of the Estes Park

*Charles and Sallie Reed's daughter, Anna Louise, in high boots, leather riding gloves, and knickers (n.d.).*

**Photo courtesy of the National Park Service**

Bank. A member of the Estes Park Protective and Improvement Association (EPPIA) and the Estes Park Motor Club, Albert also helped to organize the Estes Park Golf and Country Club. By the same token, Louise was an active member of the community and an officer of the Colorado Ski Club, which was organized in Estes Park in 1924. She was also a member of the Missionary Society of the Community Church and the Estes Park Woman's Club.

Albert Jr. died in 1932, leaving his widow, Louise, to care for the couple's two adopted children, Julian Reed Hayden (1924–1984) and Sally Cornelia Hayden (1925–1985). Eventually, Louise married her brother-in-law, Julian, who became a father to his niece and nephew. Both Cornelia Howe Hayden and her daughter-in-law Louise were members of the PEO sisterhood and contributed recipes to the *Tried and True Recipe Book*.

## Oyster Soup
*(Cornelia Howe Hayden)*

Bring 1 quart of milk to a boil (in double boiler). Drain 1 quart of oysters and put on the stove. Let this come to a boil, then skim. Chop a stalk of celery very fine, add a little water and simmer until tender. Just before this is ready to take off, drop in a clove of garlic, let it remain only a minute, then skim off. Add oysters, oyster juice, celery and a small piece of butter to the milk and bring to a boil.

## Coffee Cake
*(Anna Louise Reed Hayden)*

1 cup flour
1 cup sugar
1/2 cup butter
1 teaspoonful cinnamon

Cream this together. To half of it add 1 egg, 1 cup of flour, 1 teaspoonful baking powder and 1 scant cup milk. Put in baking pan and sprinkle the other half of the first ingredients over the top. Bake twenty minutes.

*Josephine Cheney Hall (left), wife of Charles Byron Hall, and her sister, Hazel E. Cheney (right); the Cheney sisters were originally from Lyons.*
Photo courtesy of Byron Hall

## The Hall Family

Charles Byron Hall (1879–1944) is best remembered in Estes Park as the manager of Freelan O. Stanley's Fall River Power Plant and as manager of the Estes Park Transportation Company. His father was John Bigland Hall (1847–1934), a Scot who immigrated to the United States in 1871. In his younger years, John had been a sailor on the Great Lakes. In 1878, he married Wisconsin-born Hannah Roberts (1860–1939), and their son, Charles Byron, was born the following year. After almost a decade in Illinois the family moved to Lyons, Colorado, where, in 1855, John Hall took up ranching.

At some point shortly thereafter, John met F. O. Stanley, and at Stanley's request, John and Charles built a new road from Lyons to Estes Park along the North St. Vrain River, below the current roadbed of U.S. Highway 36. Stanley also hired Charles to serve as superintendent of construction for the new hotel he was building in Estes Park. Once the hotel was completed, Charles started a transportation company in Lyons, for which he served as manager. At some point during this period, Charles and F. O. became good friends; F. O. trusted Charles so much that he made him the personal financial administrator for the Stanleys' Estes Park holdings. So close did Charles and F. O. become that their relationship extended from Estes Park to the Stanley's home in Newton, Massachusetts. In fact, Charles "was present at Mr. Stanley's bedside when he died."[50]

In 1904, Charles married Josephine Cheney (1878–1956). The couple moved to Estes Park in 1913, where Josephine was active in the Ladies Aid Society of the Community Church. The couple had two children, George B. Hall (1911–1979) and Madge L. Hall (b. 1916), whose descendents continue to live in Estes Park and are still active with projects at The Stanley Hotel. In 2012, the Hall family donated historical artifacts to the hotel's new archive museum.

## Lemon Pudding
*(Josephine Cheney Hall)*

1 lemon–juice and rind
3 egg yolks
1 cup sugar
2 tablespoons corn starch
1 1/2 cups boiling water
Beaten whites 3 eggs

Cook in double boiler and add the stiffly beaten whites of eggs just before taking from the fire and beat well. Serve with whipped cream.

## Scalloped Cheese
*(Josephine Cheney Hall)*

1 1/4 cup grated cheese
1 cup cracker crumbs
2 cups milk
3 eggs
1/4 teaspoon salt
1/2 tsp. mustard
A few grains paprika
1/4 tsp soda
1 1/2 tablespoon melted butter.

Soak crumbs in milk 15 minutes. Add the eggs well beaten, the seasoning, butter and cheese and soda dissolved in a little hot water. Bake one hour in moderate oven and serve in the dish in which it is cooked.

## Sponge Cake for Jelly Roll
*(Josephine Cheney Hall)*

Beat 3 eggs 3 minutes. Add 1 cup sugar, beat 5 minutes. Add 1/2 cup of cold water, beat 3 minutes more. One teaspoon vanilla, 1 3/4 cups of flour into which has been sifted 2 teaspoons baking powder. Bake very thin in a moderate oven and turn out on a cloth. Spread with jelly and roll.

## Preserved Strawberries
*(Hazel E. Cheney)*

Measure 2 quarts strawberries, scald 2 minutes in hot water. Pour off water. Add 4 cups sugar and boil 2 minutes after it bubbles. Remove from fire. When bubbling stops, add 2 cups sugar and boil 5 minutes. Count time as specified. Pour in shallow pan 1 1/2 to 2 inches deep. Let stand all night and can cold the next morning.

# Notes

1. Those families entered the resort business by default rather than by design; for that reason, their stories (and recipes) are featured in this chapter along with other founding families, rather than in chapter 3, "Early Estes Resorts and Inns."

2. James H. Pickering. *America's Switzerland: Estes Park and Rocky Mountain National Park, The Growth Years.* (Boulder: University Press of Colorado, 2005), p. 17.

3. Milton Estes. "Memoirs of Estes Park." *Colorado Magazine* (July, 1939). (Fort Collins: Friends of the Colorado State College Library), p. 124.

4. Martha Ann "Patsey" Stollings, the daugher of Jacob Stollings, a Methodist minister, married Joel Estes in Missouri in 1826 and was the mother of his 13 children. Colleen E. Cassell. *The Golden Pioneer. Biography of Joel Estes, The Man Who Discovered Estes Park.* (Colorado: Peanut Butter Publishing, 1999.)

5. M. Estes, *Memoirs,* p. 9.

6. C. E. Cassell, *Golden Pioneer*, p. 64.

7. I. L. Bird, *A Lady's Life (*1888), p. 95.

8. *Ibid.*, p. 128.

9. James H. Pickering. *"This Blue Hollow": Estes Park, the Early Years, 1859–1915.* (Boulder: University Press of Colorado, 1999), p. 21. At the time of Bird's visit, the Evans children were: Jennie, Llewellyn, Katherine Ellen, George, and Evan. With the addition of Florence Isabella in 1874 and John in 1876, the Evans' children eventually numbered seven.

10. Isabella Lucy Bird. Letter to Henrietta Bird, October 23, 1873. In Kay Chubbuck, ed. *Letters to Henrietta.* (Boston: Northeastern University Press, 2002), p. 175.

11. *Ibid.*, p. 176.

12. *Ibid.*, p. 184.

13. *Ibid.*, p. 188.

14. *Ibid.*, p. 190.

15. Anyone wishing to try the dishes Bird described in her letters to her sister will find recipes for these items in Appendix A. Although these are authentic, nineteenth-century British recipes, they may not be an exact match for those dishes Isabella created in Estes Park in 1873.

16. In 1926, William H. McCreery died tragically in a train fire while aboard a sleeping car en route from Riverside, California, to his home in Loveland.

17. The couple's missionary work was carried on by their daughter Ruth, who was educated at Wheaton College in Illinois. She enjoyed an academic career at Westmont College in California as dean of women and as head of the Department of Christian Education (1938–1950) before leaving to pursue active missionary tasks in Ethiopia in 1951. Later, Ruth served as a teacher in Kenya (1978–1980). In a testimonial written at the time of her death in 2009, she was described as "solid and fearless," whether "killing a king cobra in the girls dormitory in Kenya, [or] scaring bears out of her garage in Estes Park with a broom. . . . Her faith in God instilled in her strength to parallel the mountains she loved." "This Orthodox Woman Was No Shrinking Violet" by Sylvia Dooling. Available online at http://www.vow.org/Documents/Doc0384.aspx (February 20, 2012).

18. Homer E. James (1866–1985), Charles James (b. 1872), Howard Perry James (1874–1928).

19. It was Eleanor who would eventually write of her life at the Elkhorn Lodge. Her *Memoirs,* first published in 1964, was republished in 2010 as *Memoirs of Eleanor E. Hondius of Elkhorn Lodge* (Estes Park, Colorado, Estes Park Museum Friends & Foundation, Inc. Press.)

20. As H. F. Pedersen explains in his book, *Those Castles of Wood* (Estes Park, 1993), "tent cabins came with canvas ceilings that extended down the walls to meet wood at the level of the window sills." P. 65.

21. E. E. Hondius. *Memoirs* (2010), p. 68.

22. In 1923, Howard married Edna B. Cobb Gray, the widowed daughter of Estes Park contractor Al Cobb.

23. *The Hotel Monthly* (July 1910), p. 40.

24. H. F. Pedersen, *Castles*, p. 71.

25. *Estes Park Trail* (August 3, 1912).

26. E. E. Hondius, *Memoirs* (2010), p. 58.

27. E. E. Hondius, *ibid.*, p. 59.

28. Soy sauce was produced by the Oriental Show-You Company of Indiana in 1920.

29. Abner and his sister Areanna were members of the first public school class taught in Larimer County, in 1868.

30. Abner E. Sprague. *My Pioneer Life: The Memoirs of Abner E. Sprague.* (Estes Park: Rocky Mountain Nature Association, 1999), p. xi.

31. H. F. Pedersen recalls that the very first dinner served to tourists at Spragues' was "a culinary triumph," consisting of "chicken, biscuits and gravy, and raspberry jam." *Castles*, p. 255.

32. Carrie Adell Strahorn, 1877, quoted in J. H. Pickering, "This Blue Hollow," p. 97.

33. H. F. Pedersen, *Castles*, p. 255

34. A .E. Sprague, *My Pioneer Life*, p. 256.

35. H. F. Pedersen, *Castles*, p. 271.

36. While Thomas Sprague was the proprietor, Sprague's was known formally as Sprague House.

37. A. E. Sprague, *My Pioneer Life*, p. 183.

38. Nancy Mabel Morrison (1877–1959).

39. *Estes Park Trail* (May 27, 1921).

40. Alberta Sprague's recipes comprised major contributions to the *Tried and True Recipe Book*, published in 1920, as well as to the *High Altitude Cook Book*, published in 1936.

41. *Estes Park Trail* (October, 1969).

42. "The Trail editor was favored last Friday with three of the finest heads of lettuce we have ever seen anywhere, the gift of Dan Griffith. The lettuce was raised by A. Griffith and the heads are remarkably large and sound, and crisp and sweet as one could wish. The season has been very dry, but when such lettuce can be raised in the Park in such an unfavorable year, there can be little question as to the success of the crop in the Estes Park vicinity." *Estes Park Trail* (April 24, 1924).

43. From 1918 to 1963, Dan and Louise ran Rockmount Cottages, which they owned with Dan's sister Lois. The cabins occupied the site of Albin Griffith's original homestead, which was located on Moraine Park Road (now Spur 66), the original road to the National Park.

44. Beulah Clauser Hix. *Some Early Lineages of Berks County, PA.* (Boulder, Colorado: 1959), pp. v–vii.

45. Frank later served a term as Mayor of Estes Park.

46. Although flour is not listed as an ingredient in this recipe, the directive to "mould very hard" assumes the addition of flour to make dough that is stiff enough to hold its shape when twisted into individual crullers.

47. The pair had apparently visited Estes Park with their parents during the summer of 1899, and perhaps even before that.

48. In fact, it was the Hayden brothers who named three lakes "above Forest Canyon: Arrowhead, Doughnut, and Hourglass." J. H. Pickering. "This Blue Hollow," p. 164.

49. *Estes Park Trail* (June 22, 1912).

50. *Estes Park News* (April 13, 2012).

# Three: Early Estes Park Resorts and Inns

*"All the hotels in the park serve an abundance of pure milk from their own dairy cows. None of the hotels have trout on their bills of fare, the hotel-keepers having agreed among themselves, in the interests of their guests, to let their guests do all the fishing, and cook the fish for them."*
— *Hotel Monthly*, "A Week in Estes Park, Colorado, July 1910"

The history of hotels and resorts in Estes Park is a particularly rich one, as after the area was first "discovered" by Joel Estes and publicized in the writings of Isabella Bird, thousands of visitors began to make "this blue hollow" their summer destination. While in the early years many were anxious to engage with the natural setting firsthand and thus preferred simplicity and rusticity in meeting their needs for room and board, others were eager to experience the mountains at a distance, without giving up the luxuries and conveniences available in grand hotels in Chicago, Denver, and San Francisco. Fortunately for all, Estes Park from its beginnings offered something for everyone. In fact, visitors had a range of accommodations from which to choose, from primitive tents and tiny log cabins to elegantly appointed guestrooms, linen-draped dining tables, and indoor plumbing.

Early-day visitors looking for an upscale mountain experience could have their needs amply met at the Estes Park Hotel, built by the Irish aristocrat Windham Thomas Wyndham-Quin, fourth Earl of Dunraven (1841–1926). Known locally as the "English

*Summer visitors enjoying the view from Dunraven's Estes Park Hotel, which set local standards for elegant fare from its beginnings in 1877 until it was destroyed by fire in 1911.*

**Photo courtesy of the Estes Park Museum**

Hotel," Lord Dunraven's hostelry catered to a wealthy and sophisticated clientele. Removed, as they were, some little distance from the Village, those who summered at the Estes Park Hotel appeared to dress in a manner quite different from those willing to "rough it" at the more rustic local resorts.

The only other high-end hotel in Estes Park before 1910 was The Stanley Hotel, built by inventor, musical prodigy, and entrepreneur Freelan Oscar Stanley (1849–1940) of Newton, Massachusetts. Stanley had come to Colorado in 1901 in fear for his life. A consumptive[1] whose doctors had prescribed the palliative effects of mountain air as a sort of last resort for a dying man, Stanley had traveled to Denver from New England with his wife, Flora Jane Record Tileston Stanley (1847–1939). By the time the couple arrived in Colorado, Stanley had already gained fame and fortune as the inventor, with his twin brother Francis Edgar Stanley, of a photographic dry-plate process and a steam car.

During the summer of 1904, and for several summers thereafter, F. O. and Flora traveled to Estes Park, renting Rockside, a cabin

Chapter Three: Early Estes Park Resorts and Inns

*Diners at the "English Hotel" on Fish Creek were treated to lace curtains and white linen in a formal and elegant setting.*
Postcard courtesy of the Old Estes Collection: David and Carol Tanton

*Men, women, and children pose for a photographer, with the English Hotel as a backdrop. That a number of them were able and willing to climb the old pine tree at the center of the group marks a willingness to engage nature on a level not reflected in their fashionable attire.*
Photo courtesy of the Estes Park Museum

belonging to the Elkhorn Lodge. Although the cabin had a small kitchen, the Stanleys, who had brought their own housekeeper from Denver with them, preferred to dine at the Lodge. Indeed, precious few early travelers were as anxious or as willing to involve themselves in high-country cooking as Isabella Bird, expecting,

*The Stanley Hotel opened in 1909 for the summer season.*
**Postcard courtesy of the Bobbie Heistercamp Collection**

rather, to take their meals, of whatever degree of complexity, in hotel or resort dining rooms. The Halletts of Massachusetts actually built a kitchen-less home, "Edgemont," adjacent to Fergusons' guest ranch in 1888[2] and joined the Ferguson's paying guests at meal times for many years thereafter.

In 1908, Stanley decided to build a hotel in the same neo-Georgian style he had chosen for his and Flora's homes in Newton and in Estes Park. More reminiscent of hotels in New England than any west of the Mississippi, the hotel, designed by Stanley himself, was completed in 1909. The appointments that Stanley planned to include in his grand hotel necessitated the creation of a hydroelectric plant that was completed just in time for the hotel's grand opening; the result was the first all-electric hotel west of St. Louis. While never a financial success,[3] The Stanley Hotel was so impressive that it lured guests from far and wide to enjoy its gracious lobby, its expansive porches, and its Longs Peak view.

In addition to Dunraven's English Hotel and The Stanley, the other early example of the "grand hotel" idea in Estes Park was the Lewiston, which opened in 1914.[4] "[S]plendidly situated with

*A* porte cochere *attached to the front porch originally protected arriving and departing Stanley Hotel guests from the vagaries of mountain weather. It was later removed.*

**Photo courtesy of the Estes Park Museum**

a magnificent view of the snowy Front Range and Longs Peak," the Lewiston was for years "considered *the* place to stay" in Estes Park.[5]

While it has not been possible to locate menus and recipes from the English Hotel, nor recipes for The Stanley,[6] evidence of their owners' regard for the importance of a good "table" to the success of their hotels survives in the fastidious attention paid to the designs of their dining rooms and in newspaper accounts of the quality of the cuisine and spirits that were served to hotel guests.

Food preparation at many of Estes Park's earliest hotels and resorts, including the Lewiston, was in the hands of the innkeeper's wife, his daughter, or his mother. Fortunately, most of these women were talented cooks who relied on family favorites as well as published recipes in planning meals for hungry guests. In his memoirs, Abner Sprague talks about his own mother's cookbooks, and her reliance on clippings from the local newspaper's "domestic

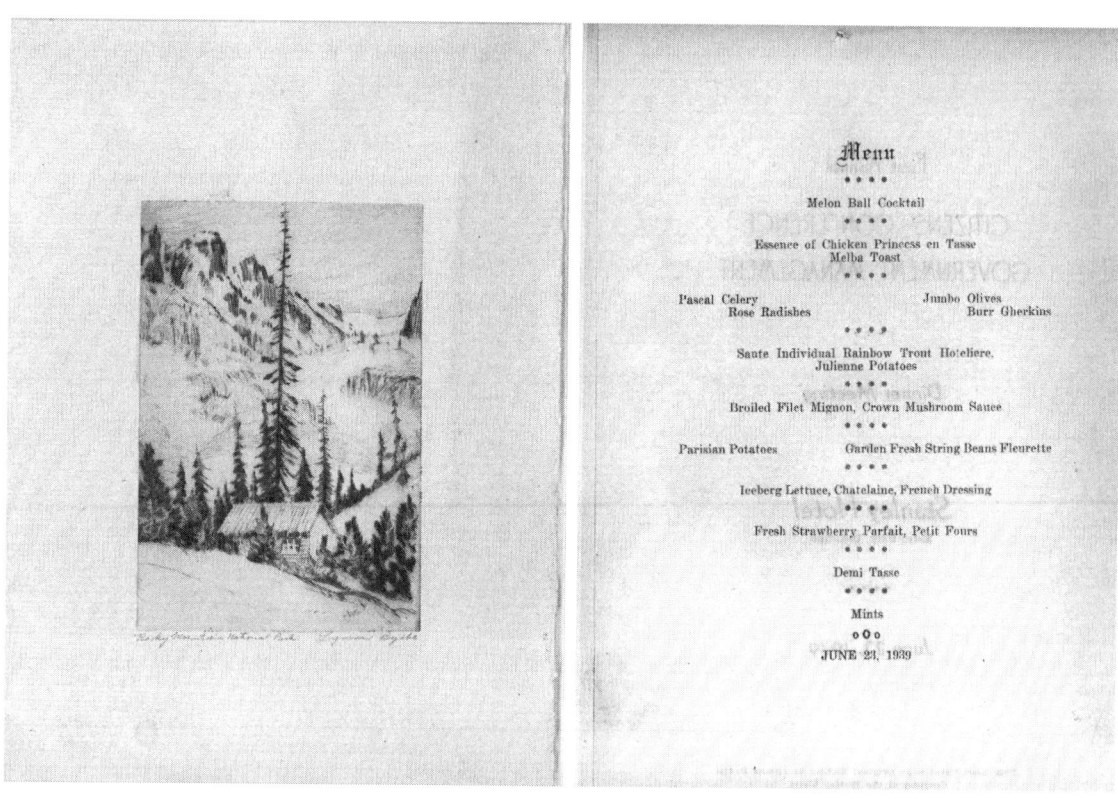

*Sporting an etching by Lyman Byxbe on its cover, this menu from June 1939 offered diners a delightful selection of entrees as well as appetizers, relishes, side dishes, and desserts.*

**Artifact courtesy of the Estes Park Museum**

column for some kind of change of food."7 Of course, professional cooks were hired later, especially in hotels that counted on serving hundreds of people on a daily basis.

The dedication of Rocky Mountain National Park in 1915 focused national and international attention on the beautiful mountains of the Front Range, and from that time on increasing numbers of summer visitors flocked to Estes Park. While some were hikers and climbers destined to stay but a week or two, others required accommodations for the entire summer. To meet the demand, many new hotels, lodges, and cabin camps were built in the Village and in the surrounding mountain valleys. In 1915, guests could book rooms not only at The Stanley Hotel (1909), the Elkhorn Lodge, and the Lewiston Hotel, but at Stead's Ranch (1904), the Hupp Hotel (1906), the Manford Hotel (1908), the Horseshoe Inn

*The Stanley Hotel Lobby, c. 1910. In the early years, guests at The Stanley often came for the entire summer season.*

Clatworthy photo, courtesy of Cheryl Pennington

(1908), Fern Lake Lodge (1910), the Moraine Lodge (1910), the Brinwood Hotel (1911), Hewes-Kirkwood Ranch and Hotel (1911), the Rockdale Hotel (1913),[8] Sprague's Lodge (1914), and the Crags (1914) as well.

The next decade saw the creation of a spate of new businesses both inside and outside the confines of the new National Park. Among those built in the late 1910s and 1920s were the Fall River Lodge, the Baldpate Inn, Copeland Lodge/Wild Basin Lodge, Holzwarth Trout Lodge, Meeker Park Lodge, and Wind River Ranch. While some offered their guests privacy by renting them

*View of Moraine Lodge, looking toward Moraine Park, c. 1925.*
Photo courtesy of the Estes Park Museum

little "housekeeping" cabins in the woods, other larger operations created extensive resorts, which featured communal dining rooms, liveries, and social programs that promised visiting "dudes" an authentic "cowboy experience" along with room and board.

In addition to housing and feeding the ever-increasing numbers of summer visitors, the hotels served the residents of the growing Estes Park community in a variety of important ways. Hotels helped local clubs with fundraising dances, such as those the Estes Park Woman's Club organized in support of the town library. In addition, card parties, club meetings, teas, and luncheons, sponsored by individuals and local clubs, were also held in hotel dining or party rooms. Over time, "milestone" celebrations of weddings, birthdays, and engagements were increasingly held at hotels and inns as well.

*The resort hotel that became known as The Highlands in the 1890s was built by Horace and Sallie Ferguson in 1875. At its height, Fergusons' little resort included the main living quarters, a barn, cabins, and tent houses, all of which are visible in this photograph. Today all that remains of these structures are the foundation stones of the resort's kitchen chimney.*
Photo courtesy of the Estes Park Museum

## The Highlands and the Ferguson Family

*"It was a friendly door that was always open to those who arrived by foot, horse, buggy, or stage from the valley towns for friendship, refreshment and a story told in front of a blazing fireplace about bears.... The Highlands used to welcome you with the smells of food that wafted out of Sallie Ferguson's kitchen."*

—Henry F. Pedersen Jr.

The Highlands resort was the dream of Horace Willis Ferguson (1826–1912) and his wife, Sarah (Sallie) Louise Thomson (1828–1887). A Kentucky native who operated a gristmill in Lebanon, Missouri before the Civil War, Ferguson chose to take his family west at war's end; in 1870 the couple joined a migration colony that was headed for the town of Evans, Colorado, south of Greeley.

*Horace and Sallie Ferguson and their family at The Highlands near Marys Lake (n.d.).*

**Photo courtesy of Estes Park Museum**

Then in 1875, seeking to alleviate Sallie's continuing problems with bronchial asthma, the couple moved their six surviving children[9] again, this time to Estes Park. While their sod-roofed, two-room homestead cabin northwest of Marys Lake offered few amenities, the property featured a freshwater spring and "indescribably beautiful"[10] views of the Mummy Range, Lily Mountain, and the Twin Sisters Peaks. Winters were another matter; the family decided to spend the cold months in Longmont, where Horace had purchased eighty acres.

During the next several summers, the couple began to provide room and board for summer visitors, with Sallie responsible for the cooking. Business was so good that eventually Horace was persuaded to add a new kitchen and dining room and to enlarge the main building, so that by 1878, the Highlands could host sixty guests in the lodge, cabins, and tent houses. For Sallie, who continued to suffer from respiratory problems and had such a large and complex family to care for, the challenges and burdens of running a cabin camp and cooking for literally dozens of strangers on a daily basis must have been monumental.

In 1877, Mrs. M. A. Hallett and her son, William L. Hallett (1851–1941), came west to Fergusons' for the summer and stayed on through the winter, for reasons of William's health. In spite of the distances involved, for the Halletts' home was in Massachusetts, the pair returned in 1879 to purchase land adjacent to the Fergusons' resort and began to build their own frame house. In 1881, William and his New York–born bride, Elvena A. "Vena" Sessions, christened this mountain home "Edgemont" at a party that received considerable attention in the Longmont newspaper. Apparently, William and Vena so enjoyed the cuisine available at the Fergusons' that they saw no need to provide a kitchen in their cottage, preferring to dine at the Fergusons' along with Horace and Sallie's summer guests.[11]

Although the resort thrived during the 1880s, no doubt aided by stories in the *Rocky Mountain News* and elsewhere that extolled an "old-fashioned homestead" and hospitality that crept "out of every door and window,"[12] Sallie's health began to fail. She died in 1887, soon after the marriage of her third daughter and namesake, Sallie (1858–1954), to Charles L. Reed (1859–1944).

With two of the Fergusons' daughters now married[13] and eldest son William Hunter Ferguson (1851–1938) homesteading his own parcel of land in Moraine Park beginning in 1879, it fell to Mildred Frances (Fanny) Ferguson (b. 1855) and James (b. 1869) to run the resort for the family; not only had Horace turned his attention from innkeeping to farming and ranching operations, but he had also taken a new wife, a woman considerably younger than himself. Eventually, Horace and his bride Jennie moved to New Mexico, where he died in 1912.

During the 1890s, the resort was closed for a time. However, when Sallie and Charles Reed decided to reopen the hotel for the summer season in 1898, they moved their four children[14] back to Estes Park from Longmont, where Charles had been working as postmaster. To economize, Sallie herself planted a vegetable garden and kept chickens and cows, selling milk to her neighbors. Even so, they had to augment locally available groceries with "fresh meats, bacon and hams" from Denver. Other than the wild raspberries they were able to pick on Deer Mountain, and make into "delicious jam that was greatly enjoyed by [their] guests,"[15] fresh fruit also had to be brought in from Longmont. In 1903, the Reeds moved back to Longmont so that their children could attend high school.

## Scottish Scones
*(Sallie E. Ferguson Reed)*

2 cups sifted flour
4 level tablespoonfuls butter
2 eggs, beaten very light
4 level teaspoonfuls baking powder
2 teaspoonfuls sugar
1/2 cup sweet cream
salt

## Date Pudding
*(Sallie E. Ferguson Reed)*

6 eggs
1 cup sugar
1 cup fine breadcrumbs
2 teaspoonfuls vanilla
2 level teaspoonfuls baking powder
1 lb. ground dates
1 cup English walnuts

Beat eggs separately. Add the sugar to the yolks and beat. Add breadcrumbs, baking powder, vanilla, dates and nuts. Add whites of eggs, beaten stiff. Bake one-half to three-quarters of an hour in a slow oven. Serve with whipped cream.

*Enos Mills and Scotch; for years Mills' dog was the unofficial "greeter" at Longs Peak Inn.*

Clatworthy photo courtesy of Cheryl Pennington

## Enos Mills and the Longs Peak Inn

*I peeled 150 pounds of potatoes regularly, prepared chickens for cooking and made the coffee. Mr. Mills wanted the coffee very strong, and guests were seen quite often diluting it with hot water.*[16]

— Robert Gookins

Located nine miles south of the Village of Estes Park, Longs Peak Inn was for almost a half century a rustic mountain lodge with a national reputation. Opened in 1902 by the peripatetic author/

lecturer/naturalist and innkeeper extraordinare, Enos Abijah Mills (1870–1922), over time the Inn came to include in its guest registry the names of many of America's rich and famous, from the author Edna Ferber, to U.S. Supreme Court Justice and one-time Presidential candidate Charles Evans Hughes. An avid spokesman for conservation of the natural world,[17] Mills wrote essays and articles for national magazines and spoke publicly and widely on the subject even as he lectured his guests at the Inn on local flora and fauna.

Longs Peak Inn was actually the successor to Longs Peak House, a homestead cabin built by Mills's uncle and aunt, Elkanah and Jane Lamb, in 1875. Mills himself came west from Kansas in 1884, seeking relief from his recurrent indigestion problems. A boy of fourteen, Mills built a tiny homestead cabin across the Valley from the Longs Peak House, and worked for the Lambs as a hiking guide. Mills eventually purchased the property from his uncle and his cousin, Carlyle for $2,000 in 1901.

In 1906, a fire destroyed the main lodge building of the Inn. Seemingly undaunted, Mills rebuilt it within a month, making use of fire- and wind-killed trees, sinuous tree stumps, and gnarled roots, which lent to the Inn a distinctive and singular aspect not duplicated in any other local resort before or since. At an elevation of 9,000 feet, visitors enjoyed a rustic mountain experience amid lush meadows, wildflowers, cool pines, bubbling streams, and unsurpassed views of Longs Peak and Mount Meeker. Yet even in this setting, Mills was able to provide a range of creature comforts that were no doubt as welcome as they were unexpected, including "modern amentities such as steam heat, electricity, plumbing, comfortable beds, flannel sheets and thick towels."[18]

In keeping with the rest of the decor, the furnishings in the dining room were "quaint" and "homemade." However, the meals were well planned and served, and at one time were said to have rivaled the restaurants at Denver's Brown Palace and the Broadmoor in Colorado Springs. Thankfully, one long-ago visitor has provided us with a menu for a Sunday dinner she particularly enjoyed: "Tomato soup, fried chicken, mashed potatoes, gravy, green peas, apple fritters, green tea, lemon pie and chocolate ice cream." She also reported that meals were served at predetermined hours. On Sundays, dinner was at 1:00 p.m., while suppers were always served at 6:00 p.m.[19]

*The dining room furniture at Longs Peak Inn was as rustic as the other appointments at the hotel.*

Postcard, author's private collection

In point of fact, Longs Peak Inn had two dining rooms, one for "regular guests with reserved seating" where meals were available for seventy-five cents (Chicken [any time ordered], twenty-five cents extra),[20] and the other for "transients," who could purchase a chicken dinner for $1.75, or enjoy "light refreshments . . . from early morning till late at night."

According to Mills biographer Alex Drummond, Mills himself provided each table in the dining room with a single flower in a tall slender vase. A detail-driven innkeeper, Mills oversaw the dishes served and paid particular attention to serving healthful foods.

> *Chickens were butchered, plucked, and cleaned by the kitchen staff; meat hung in quarters in a walk-in icebox and was cut into roasts or individual servings. Cooking was done on three wood-fired ranges and in separate baking ovens. Renown[ed] house specialties were fried chicken and raspberry jam. Raspberry jam sandwiches were . . . part of the box lunches prepared for hikers . . . [which] also contained roast beef sandwiches, raisins, an orange, and a piece of chocolate [furnishing] "all the nourishment needed on the trip [up Longs Peak] without loading you down."*[21]

Chapter Three: Early Estes Park Resorts and Inns

*Timberline Hotel (Timberline Cabin) soon after its completion in 1908.*
Clatworthy photo courtesy of Cheryl Pennington

Pedersen (1993) reports that the Inn did not use printed menus but required waiters to recite a litany of available dishes to as many as 100 guests, all of whom could be accommodated in the main lodge and adjacent cabins. Each waiter was responsible for remembering at least "24 separate orders" for each meal. For such hard work, the pay was decidedly meager ... and opportunities for picking up extra money were also limited. Mr. Robert Gookins, who served as undercook during the summers of 1913 and 1914, recalled that "Mr. Mills was strict with employees, dismissing summarily those who broke the rules, and would not allow any tips to be received, for he said 'this was a no tip house.'"[22] Although his travels frequently took him away from the Inn, Mills remained a hands-on manager until his death in 1922.

In addition to the Inn's dining rooms, guests had an opportunity to dine informally at the Timberline Cabin, a tiny and primitive way station that also served as an overnight stop for those attempting an ascent of Longs Peak. Built by Mills in 1908, the little log building, which was "connected to the Inn by telephone," offered meals at the seventy-five-cent rate. Picnicking there was also possible, where location or distance did not pose a problem and where the uniqueness of the setting was a part of the fun. Social notes in the *Estes Park Trail* confirmed one such occasion during the summer of 1912:

> *Frank S. Harrison and wife who are spending their honeymoon at Long's Peak Inn entertained a number of friends on Monday at luncheon at Timber Line Cabin. To reach the cabin it is necessary to cross several hundred feet of snow field. At an altitude of 11,000 feet, Mrs. Harrison cooked and served a delicious repast.*[23]

While the Inn's architecture was considered "Extremely Rustic," Mills established a tone for behavior and entertainment that was "distinctly high brow,"[24] and, according to one guest, visiting "professors [were] as thick as peas in a pod."[25] An evening's entertainment frequently featured a lecture by Mills himself on the natural environment and the importance of stewardship. Everyone was usually in bed by 9:30 p.m.

However, as with other resorts and inns in and around Estes Park, guests at Longs Peak Inn also enjoyed dinners cooked and consumed out-of-doors. Indeed, in spite of the somewhat reserved demeanor that Mills hoped to maintain at his hostelry, guests were invited to participate in campfire marshmallow roasts in addition to his fireside talks recounting "the marvelous ways of birds and beasts, and sometimes a dab of poetry."[26]

In 1916, Mills married his protégé and secretary, Esther Burnell (1889–1946), who had learned nature guiding from Enos during previous summers and had herself proved up a homestead claim on the Fall River. In 1919, the couple became the parents of a daughter, Enda.[27] Named for the famous author Edna Ferber,[28] who had been a frequent guest at the Inn, the baby was born just three years before her father's death in 1922.

It was left to Esther Mills to run the hotel after Enos' death, which she did until her own death in 1946. During that time, the Inn was run very much as it had been when Mills was alive and

*Clatworthy photo of the cabins at Longs Peak Inn*
Photo courtesy of Cheryl Pennington

was as popular a destination in the late 1920s and early 1930s as it had been when Mills and his dog, the faithful Scotch, had been there to welcome earlier visitors at the turn of the century.

Like the Lewiston before it, the Inn burned to the ground in 1949, a victim of a fire that started in a wood stove. Its successor on the site was the Swiss Village Resort, a hotel that served guests for decades before it was sold to the Salvation Army, and renamed Longs Peak Inn.

Until her death in 2009, the Millses' daughter Enda guided visitors on a nature walk that led to her father's little square-log homestead cabin on the lower reaches of the Twin Sisters Peaks. In her later years, she was a well-known figure in Estes Park, where she frequently and charmingly promoted the themes of natural preservation and conservation that her parents had championed when the National Park existed only within the mind's eye of her famous father.

Sadly, no recipes from the Mills family nor the kitchens of Longs Peak Inn are available at this time. However, thanks to

Emerson Lynn, who documented the list of ingredients and their amounts in his family's joint memoir, *The Scottage*, we do have the recipe for Enos Mills's famous trail mix. According to Mr. Lynn,

> *Mills was credited with conceiving the raisin – chocolate diet which was popular among mountain hikers in the early twenties . . . and may still be. He believed that [the trail mix] was sufficient to sustain a hiker for three or four days without harm.*[29]

Given the digestive issues that plagued Mills earlier in his life, it is little wonder that he invented a hiking staple that would serve him well on his many ascents of Longs Peak and the other mountains of the Front Range.

## Trail Mix
*(Enos Abijah Mills)*

12 ounces of raisins
4 ounces of chocolate

*The view of Longs Peak and Mount Meeker from the hillside above the Rustic Hotel in Devils Gulch drew day-trippers and hotel guests to the lodge that Shep and Clara Husted built at the turn of the last century.*
Photo courtesy of the National Park Service

## The Rustic Hotel: The Husted and Lester Families

The cabins that originally constituted the Rustic Hotel were built by Shepherd Newcombe Husted (1867–1942) and his wife Clara Gertrude Crawford (1871–1963), who had arrived in Estes Park in 1893, just a year after their marriage. The Homestead Cabin, built in 1896, was soon followed by a second dwelling, called Shep, in 1897. By the time the Rustic was opened for business in 1901, four additional cabins and a main lodge had been completed. One of the most important selling points for the Rustic was its location. "F. O. Stanley—who was photographed driving his steam car to the Husteds' during his first summer (1903) in Estes Park—thought the view of the Front Range from the Rustic the finest in the park."[30] Husted also raised hay and potatoes as well as vegetables for his table and maintained a dairy herd. Between 1893 and 1909, Shep and Clara had eight children, of whom only four survived.

For a time, the Husteds appeared to enjoy the summer season. But while Shep was a gracious host when he was present, his guiding activities often kept him from home and Clara was left to manage the hotel and handle cooking and cleaning tasks as well. Indeed, it was Shep's reputation as a guide rather than his skills as an innkeeper that locals recalled about him: during his life in Estes Park, he climbed Longs Peak no fewer than 350 times. His skills were acknowledged by no less an expert than Enos Mills himself, who called Husted "a prince on the trail."[31]

In 1907, Shep sold the little hotel that he and Clara had launched to W. G. Edwards, with whom he had formed the Rustic Hotel Company six years earlier. Edwards' tenure was also relatively brief. After only six years, he himself sold the Rustic to Charles E. Lester (1863–1935), who had managed the Earl of Dunraven's Estes Park Hotel until its loss in a devastating fire in 1911.

Charles found ample support for his new endeavor in his wife, Edna May Brush Lester (1869–1949), the daughter of Jared Lemar Brush (1837–1913), a Colorado miner turned Weld County rancher, turned politician, who served two terms as Lieutenant Governor of Colorado and for whom the town of Brush was named. Charles and Edna May had been married since 1894. Thanks to Charles' managerial skills and Edna's considerable culinary talents, the Lesters got off to a good start. Almost immediately, the couple both enlarged the Rustic and gave it a new name: The Lester Hotel. The following year, the *Estes Park Trail* described the hotel under its new ownership:

> *Located at the north end of Estes Park, it faces a magnificent view of the range and an unsurpassed vista of Estes Park itself. It nestles close to the foot of Eagles Rock, and his grounds extend to Devils Gulch just beyond. The main lodge is built of logs and the main floor is ceiled with redwood on the interior. This contains in addition to offices, parlors, dining room, and kitchen, 15 commodious lodging rooms. Nine cottages, providing for from one to five guests each, and a number of tent houses increase the capacity of this hotel to care for 75 people in all.*[32]

In addition to a two-story lodge building designed by Henry C. Rogers, a British architect who had immigrated in 1893, the Lesters offered guests opportunities to play golf, tennis, and croquet in addition to "rambles through the mountains," horseback riding, and trout fishing on their 203-acre ranch at the north end of town.

The Lester Hotel and Cottages, which was known as "a select little family hotel," offered meals on the American Plan, with butter, cream, milk, and eggs for their dining room available from the Lesters' own dairy. Edna took an active role in managing the hotel and superintending the kitchen. The hotel's ads promised "substantial home cooked meals" offered in a "large spacious dining room," and reports in the local press amply documented her culinary skills. For example, an article in the *Estes Park Trail* reported that Edna presided over the tearoom at the Ladies Aid Society's annual bazaar in 1913, where "food fit for the gods"[33] was served.

Although the Lesters were offering the hotel for sale as early as 1922, it was not purchased until 1933, when Julian M. Livingston of Denver assumed ownership. Two years later, Livingston reopened the hotel as the H-Bar-G Ranch,[34] and operated it as a dude ranch until 1958.

## Punch
*(Edna May Brush Lester)*

1 lb. sugar
Rind 1 lemon
1 pt. water
1 tsp. lemon extract
1/2 tsp. bitter almonds

1 qt water
2 cups strong tea
3 lemons (juice)
1 tsp. vanilla extract

Cook sugar, quart of water and rind five minutes and strain; add other ingredients.

## Raisin Pie
*(Edna May Brush Lester)*

1 teaspoonful butter
1 cup sugar (scant)

1 cup raisins

Cover raisins with water and boil until soft. Mix with sugar and butter, flavor. Bake in two crust pie.

*Sprague's Hotel and Ranch, later Stead's Ranch and Hotel, in Moraine Park.*
Clatworthy photo courtesy of Cheryl Pennington

## Stead's Ranch and Hotel: The Stead Family

*"We can truthfully say that no guest ever left Stead's hungry."*
—Stead's Ranch and Hotel brochure, 1937

In 1904 Eudora and James Stead took over the Sprague's Hotel from Abner and Mary Alberta Sprague who, with Abner's parents the Thomas Spragues, had homesteaded the site and built a cabin in 1874. Soon after the sale, the new owners renamed the resort Stead's Ranch and Hotel.

New York-born James D. "J. D." Stead (1859–1931) had been a dairyman in Chicago before traveling west to visit his wife's cousin, Abner Sprague, in 1902. Stead was so taken with Moraine Park and its landscapes that he persuaded the Spragues to take him on as a partner. In fact, Sprague's had become such a large operation that Abner saw a distinct advantage in getting some help. However, when Stead's wife, Eudora Mary "Dora" Wolaver (1859–1931), and Sprague's wife, Alberta, had a falling out, the

*Formally set tables and fern bouquets greeted guests in the dining room at Stead's in 1910.*

Photo courtesy of the Estes Park Museum

situation resulted in the sale of the hotel and most of the property to the newcomers. The Spragues moved, temporarily as it turned out, to Loveland to pursue other interests.

Thanks to an infusion of both time and money, the resort's operation was greatly expanded by the Steads over the period of the next three decades, resulting in the development of one of the premier resorts in Estes Park. Indeed, many summer residents reported receiving their first mountain experiences at the ranch. Stead's also became the hub of Moraine Park cottager picnics, fish fries, dances, and parties, attended by young and old. In his autobiographical account of the summer of 1920, William Allen White wrote nostalgically of his family's Moraine Park days. Mary was an accomplished horsewoman from an early age, preferring to ride over most other pastimes, and she and other young people who summered in Moraine Park were drawn to the activities that Stead's provided for locals and guests.

*Dora Stead on the patio of the stone house J. D. built for her, with Stead's Hotel and Ranch in the background.*

Photo courtesy of the Estes Park Museum

James and Dora Stead were well-respected and contributing members of the Estes Park community. In fact, James was active in the Estes Park Protective and Improvement Association (EPPIA) and helped F. O. Stanley and other businessmen create the Estes Park Bank, serving on the board of trustees when the bank was organized in 1908. Dora belonged to the Ladies Aid Society, which often met at her home. Although James Stead died in 1931, Dora, with the help of her sister Myra Wolaver Lewis and Myra's husband Will, successfully managed the Stead Ranch and Hotel into the 1950s. By then, the resort included both lodge rooms and cabins, dining facilities for 250 guests, a nine-hole golf course, an in-ground swimming pool, and tennis courts.

In *Those Castles of Wood*, H. F. Pedersen described the fanciful Cowboy Dinner menus at Stead's which no doubt delighted several generations of children. With selections such as "Slopgolly, Fodder Salad, Tenderfoot Dream, Smothered Toothbuster Pie and Whoopie Cup, and Slum Gum Soup," guest families' dinners in

Chapter Three: Early Estes Park Resorts and Inns    107

*Will and Myra Lewis, who helped Dora run Stead's Ranch and Hotel after the death of J. D. Stead in 1931.*

**Photo courtesy of the Estes Park Museum**

Stead's dining room must have been delightful and lighthearted affairs.

About 1951, Ed Stopher (1909–2003), beloved nephew of "Auntie Bert" and "Uncle Abner" Sprague, and Ed's wife, Dorothy Hansen Stopher (1917–1958), purchased the Steads' property, and with it the homestead that Thomas and Mary Sprague had claimed nearly eighty years before. By that time, Ed was an experienced manager,

*An extensive buffet was launched by Ed and Dorothy Stopher at Stead's Ranch and Hotel in the 1950s.*

Photo courtesy of the Estes Park Museum

having run Sprague's Lodge during the summers beginning in the 1940s. In fact, he operated both Sprague's and Stead's for a period of about fifteen years.

In the early 1950s, a new chef instituted a buffet at Stead's, which consisted of a sumptuous array of main and side dishes set out on white linen–draped and flower-strewn tables. Although these buffets were popular with guests, time was on the side of the National Park Service, which was anxious to take over the property and return the site to its natural state. The summer of 1962 was the last season for Stead's Ranch and Hotel. As with so many other hotels and resorts within the Park boundaries, the NPS lost no time in razing the buildings and removing all evidence that this expansive and popular resort had ever existed.[35]

*Cooking out was a tradition at Stead's Ranch and Hotel, c. 1950s.*
**Photo courtesy of the Estes Park Museum**

An early newspaper description of summers in Moraine Park captured the essence of what the ranch meant to so many of its guests over the years:

> *Stead's is not a hotel in the ordinary sense of the word. It is more of a stopping place, where tired people from the city can come and forget that there ever was such a thing as business or worry. Where one may be alone with nature, or, if inclined that way, join with the other guests in the hotel for company. Where everyone does just as he pleases, and life is full of joy.*[36]

## Ice Box Doughnuts

*(Eudora Wolaver Stead)*

3 eggs
1 cup sugar
3 tbs. melted butter
1 tbs. vanilla
Nutmeg to taste
1 cup sweet milk
4 cups flour
2 tsp. baking powder

Beat eggs until lemon color, add sugar and beat until grain disappears; add butter, vanilla and nutmeg, milk, added alternately with flour and baking powder (flour and baking powder must be sifted four times). Place in ice box for three or four hours. Roll out, cut and drop into hot fat immediately, without adding more flour.

## Stead's Ranch Ice Cream French Toast

*(Edgar and Libby Stopher)*[37]

2 eggs, beaten
1/2 c. cream
1/2 tsp. vanilla
dash of salt

Mix well together, dip bread in batter and fry in butter til brown. Cut into 3 corner squares, sprinkle lightly with powdered sugar. Serve with 1/4 inch slice of orange.

Delicious served with a small dip of French vanilla ice cream for a luncheon.

*Charles and Sallie Ferguson Reed's Brinwood Hotel in Moraine Park, c. 1915.*
Photo courtesy of the Estes Park Museum

## The Brinwood Hotel: The Reed Family

*"A ranch where the hospitality and friendly atmosphere of the 'Old West' gets you and makes you a part of it, and formality is forgotten."*
— Brinwood Hotel Advertisement

After taking a break from running The Highlands, the resort founded by her parents Horace and Sallie Ferguson in 1875, Sallie Ferguson Reed and her husband Charles Lowry Reed decided once again to turn their hands to innkeeping in Estes Park. Married in 1886, the couple had been dividing their time between Estes Park and Loveland for some years. This new venture promised to be a challenge, but the potential rewards were an incentive as more and more visitors were able to travel to the Estes Valley every year, thanks to improved roads.

To launch their new enterprise, the couple purchased the land in Moraine Park homesteaded before the turn of the century by Sallie's older brother, Hunter Ferguson, and in 1910 Sallie, Charles,

*Charles and Sallie Ferguson Reed, who, with Sallie's brother Hunter, started the Brinwood in Moraine Park.* Photo courtesy of the Estes Park Museum

and Hunter built the Brinwood Hotel on 290 acres. Located near the present-day Cub Lake Trailhead, the new two-story hotel opened for the summer season the following year as a "first class summer resort hotel."[38] Sallie and Hunter's youngest sibling, James Ferguson, joined them in its operation.

The Brinwood offered tents, cabins and lodge rooms, which boasted hot and cold running water and a few en-suite rooms. Somewhat fortuitously, the Brinwood's grand opening coincided with the demise of the Earl of Dunraven's Estes Park Hotel, which was destroyed by a disastrous fire in 1911; many of Dunraven's displaced guests sought accommodations at the Reeds' lovely new resort. Over the course of the next few years, the Reeds added a number of other buildings on the site to accommodate additional guests as well as their own relatives and the hotel staff. By 1925, the resort was going by the name of the Brinwood Ranch and Hotel.

*The Brinwood dining room as it looked in the 1920s. Sallie Reed personally ran the kitchen and was noted as a first-rate cook.*
Postcard courtesy of the Bobbie Heistercamp Collection

Pedersen reported that "Grandma Sally [sic] Reed commanded a considerable drawing power for Brinwood as her culinary abilities extended over most of the years of the Reeds' ownership."[39] And even after she allowed the hiring of a number of additional cooks, she herself planned the menus and ordered the supplies. Cooking at the Brinwood was managed on kitchen ranges that burned aspen logs. Although most meals were served in the resort's spacious dining room, the Reeds also provided breakfast rides and all-day rides that offered lunch halfway through.

Their brochure from c. 1930 assured prospective guests that

*the Brinwood has a wide reputation for its delicious and appetizing meals prepared by first class women chefs. Only the best foods the market offers are served. Fine wholesome milk and cream from our dairy of tested cows, and fresh vegetables in large varieties (partly from our own garden) are served in abundance. We employ only high class college girls and teachers in our dining room.*

As noted, the Reeds maintained their own garden, raising potatoes, peas, and beans, and also kept dairy cows and pigs. Any surpluses were sold in the Village as an additional source of revenue.

In 1932, Charlie and Sallie sold their hotel to the National Park Service with the understanding that they could continue to run it for another twenty years. In 1947, after Charlie's death, Sallie sold their lease to two local couples, who operated the resort until 1958. Today the Brinwood is only a memory, its buildings having been torn down and removed in 1959 as part of the NPS Mission 66 effort to restore the Park to its natural state.

## Spanish Soup
*(Sallie E. Ferguson Reed)*

4 cups brown stock
2 cups tomato pulp
1 large green pepper, chopped fine
1 medium onion, chopped fine
5 tablespoonfuls flour
4 tablespoonfuls butter
2 tablespoonfuls grated horseradish
1/2 tablespoonful Worcester sauce
1/2 cup hot cooked rice
Salt, cayenne or a few drops of tabasco

Cook the pepper and onion in butter for five minutes, add flour, stir until well blended and delicately browned, then add gradually the stock and tomato pulp. Simmer twenty minutes. Rub through a sieve and season with salt and add other seasonings.

## Lemon Cream Filling
*(Sallie E. Ferguson Reed)*

Warm a piece of butter the size of a hen's egg, add beaten yolk of an egg and 1/2 cup of powdered sugar, then the grated rind of 1 lemon and the juice from half of it. Add powdered sugar to spread nicely, beat hard. Use as frosting or filling.

*In its heyday, Columbine Lodge was a center for social activities in the Tahosa Valley.*

Clatworthy photo, courtesy of Cheryl Pennington

## Columbine Lodge

*The Columbine Lodge is 10 miles west of Estes Park, Colorado. Nearest resort to Longs Peak, cottages in the pines, hiking trails, horseback riding, good home-cooked food, good beds, superb view, reasonable rates.*

— *Estes Park Directory*, 1930

The Columbine Lodge, or "The Columbines" as it was familiarly known, was located in the Tahosa Valley nine miles south of Estes Park on Highway 7. It was originally built in 1908 by Harry W. Bitner (1860–1925), a patent attorney and entrepreneur who had moved to Colorado from Michigan. Bitner was also something of an inventor, having patented a "hanging doll-house," which could be folded up for easy storage and transport. From the outset,

*In addition to the fine food served and the friendly and casual atmosphere offered at the Columbine Lodge, reasons for the resort's popularity over the years included the privacy enjoyed by guests housed in the many tiny cabins tucked away in among the lodgepole and ponderosa pines.*

Photo courtesy of the Estes Park Museum

Bitner's wife, Edna Evangeline Sperry Bitner (1873–1947), took an active role in running the little inn. Harry and Edna had been married in 1892 and were the parents of three children: Albert, Catherine, and Melville.

Life for guests at the Columbine Lodge was much more casual and less restrained than the one visitors experienced at nearby Longs Peak Inn. Instead of lectures on the flora and fauna, which so often characterized evening activities planned and conducted by Enos Mills, Bitners' guests enjoyed amateur theatricals, bonfires, and music played outdoors on a Victrola as part of an evening's entertainment. Anticipating the needs of families with small children, the Lodge also provided a swing and merry-go-round on the grounds. In addition, the Bitners operated cars that ferried guests to and from the Valley. The Columbines operated on the American Plan, serving up hearty meals to their guests three times a day. The Lodge was also the site of dinner parties given by summer residents from nearby cabins, who entertained one another in the Columbine's rustic dining room.

In 1912, the Bitners hired Dr. Ira D. Scott, a Boulder dentist, to manage their resort for the summer.[40] Scott brought his wife

*Dinners in the Columbine Lodge's spacious dining room were served to "locals" as well as hotel guests.*
Postcard courtesy of the Bobbie Heistercamp Collection

Callie and the couple's two small children with him for the season, an event that was noted in the local paper. At some point the following year, Harry Bitner ran off with Callie Scott. This episode created a scandal that not only rocked the Tahosa Valley community but also played for weeks in the Boulder newspapers. While Ira and Callie seem to have managed a reconciliation at some point after this event, the Bitners did not.[41]

Left alone to run the lodge and its cabins the following summer, Edna Bitner had little choice but to sell out, which she did, to her Tahosa Valley neighbor and friend, the Chicago architect Edwin Gillette. For several years, Edna stayed on and continued to run the hotel for Gillette, with assistance from her son Albert. That she did so with some considerable success was evident in the gracious account of life at Columbine Lodge that appeared in the *Estes Park Trail* in 1914:

*A visit to the Columbines is a treat that was enjoyed by the writer one day last week. Every hotel in Estes Park has its own individuality, and something that especially appeals to the visitor. One no sooner enters this little nook than he feels the restfulness of the situation. The Columbines is not a hotel with many rooms as one would expect, but a number of beautiful little cottages settled in the pines, each entirely remote from the other, making it possible for a company or family to be as retired as in their own home. The dining room is built entirely to itself, and is indeed a "thing of beauty." The reception room and office, just across a most beautiful stream from the dining room, is most restful and quaint.*

*The large fireplace, with its pillars of the pines from timberline that have been twisted by the winds for centuries, is remarkably beautiful. . . . Mrs. Bitner, the manager of this place, is most genial, and always makes one feel at home. She does everything in her power to make one comfortable and happy.*[42]

Ultimately, however, Edna chose to leave the Tahosa Valley for Boulder. Then, in 1922, she returned to the Village to run her own small resort, eponymously named Bitner's Cabins.

Meanwhile, in 1916, Edwin Gillette sold the Columbine Lodge to Indiana-born Charles H. Alexander (1865–1962) and his wife Anna (b. 1874). Married in 1907, the couple had considerable experience in hotel management, having previously worked in a hotel for consumptives in Denver and at the Hot Springs Hotel in Idaho Springs. As the new owners of The Columbines, Alexander and Anna expanded the resort to include, in addition to the main lodge, a new dining room, and a number of additional guest cabins, many outfitted with bathrooms. From all accounts, the Alexanders ran The Columbines efficiently and well until 1945, when they sold the resort.

During the next decade, the resort had a number of owners. In 1959, a Texan, Ruth Eugenia Harms Bliss (1911–1993), widow of Jack E. Bliss (1910–1955) of Midland, Texas, took over active management of The Columbines. A former journalist and sports editor for the Paris (Texas) *News*, Harms ran the hotel with the assistance of her second husband, Denver attorney Horace B. "Van" Van Valkenburgh.

In the 1990s the Salvation Army acquired the property and converted it into a summer camp and conference center; nearby, the organization built a retreat on the site of Enos Mills's fabled Inn.

## Columbine Chicken in Sherry Barbecue
*(Genie Harms Bliss)*

Prepare in the usual manner enough breasts of chicken for the number to be served. Lightly brown on all sides in deep golden corn oil or vegetable oil. Then cover chicken with a sauce made from combining prepared tomato sauce plus 1/2 tsp. Beau Monde seasoning plus 2 tbsp. Worcestershire sauce and 1/2 to 3/4 c. cooking sherry.

Cook over low heat under cover until tender. Approx. preparation time 30 min.

Serve with a fresh fruit salad topped with Columbine Poppyseed Dressing.

## Columbine Poppyseed Dressing
*(Genie Harms Bliss)*

1 1/2 c. granulated sugar
2 tsp. dry mustard
2 tsp. salt
2/3 c. vinegar
3 tbsp. onion juice
2 c. salad oil (we use Wesson oil or Mazola)
3 tbsp. poppy seeds

Mix salt, sugar, vinegar and mustard. Add onion juice and stir well.

Add oil slowly beating constantly and continue until thick. Store in cool spot or in refrigerator but not where it will be close to a freezing unit. We get onion juice by putting a large onion in a Waring Blender and then straining. It can be obtained by grating the onion, however. The Secret of This Dressing Is In The Long, Long, Long Beating With The Electric Mixer.

*Clatworthy photo of the ranch in Horseshoe Park, as Willard and Grace Ashton might have seen it their first summer in Estes Park.*
Photo courtesy of the National Park Service

## The Ashton Family's Horseshoe Inn

Horseshoe Inn was the short-lived dream of Willard Herbert Ashton (1869–1947). Born in Illinois, Ashton and his wife, Grace E. Jones Ashton (1867–1943), were living in Massachusetts with their three children when, at the suggestion of a land speculator, they came to Estes Park to spend the summer of 1905. Willard was immediately taken with the beauty of the mountains, and purchased the 160-acre Horseshoe Ranch, which lay about seven miles west of the village of Estes Park, on the Fall River. He decided to expand the farmhouse and take up innkeeping in his adopted home. Unfortunately for the family, Willard and Grace divorced shortly after their summer in Estes Park; Grace departed taking the couple's three children with her.[43]

Although in 1907–1908 Ashton had the noted architect Frank Lloyd Wright draw up plans for a remodeled ranch house and

*Flowers and linen napkins greeted guests at Willard Ashton's Horseshoe Inn dining room.*

**Photo courtesy of the Estes Park Museum**

lodge building for the inn, in the end Willard chose the familiar log style more in keeping with the mountain setting.[44] Willard's brother handled the construction, with the help of local artisans and contractors. In order to ensure the installation of the latest in bathroom amenities, the Ashton brothers hired the local firm of E. D. Lindley & Son to install the plumbing.

An avid and talented gardener, Willard Ashton maintained a lush kitchen garden, which provided fresh vegetables for guests. Although the location of the hotel, which opened in 1909, was certainly appealing to some summer visitors, many may well have been drawn by the promise of rooms "just like home," complete with "hot and cold water in every room," and "home-cooked food."[45] Ashton also promoted the Inn, set among open fields of wildflowers, by promising guided nature hikes. In addition, Ashton maintained a small-scale fishing camp at Lawn Lake, for the convenience of hotel guests and other summer visitors.

Willard's tenancy of the Inn was relatively short-lived; he sold it to a consortium of businessmen from Fort Collins in 1915. However, Willard and his second wife Cora maintained a residence in Little Horseshoe Park until Willard's death in 1947. Cora later wrote: "This place was his heart's delight and he loved the rains, the hail, and the snow—the solitude, where he found much peace."[46]

Today there is little left to remind contemporary visitors of Horseshoe Inn or of Ashton's property on Deer Mountain. If the Ashton family has left a legacy, it is without doubt the *Handbook of Rocky Mountain Plants* written by Willard and Grace's daughter Ruth Elizabeth Ashton Nelson (1896–1987); the book is still in print—a classic botanical guide born of Ruth's love for the wildflowers that surrounded the Ashton's Inn in Horseshoe Park.

*Joe and Ethel Mills with their children, Mark Muir and Eleanor Ann, at the Crags, c. 1920.*

Photo courtesy of Patricia Yeager Washburn

## The Crags: Joe and Ethel Mills

*"Through their stomachs you can reach them."*

— Joe Mills

Few family names are as familiar to residents and visitors to Estes Park as is the name of Mills. Even at a distance of ninety years and more, Enos Abijah and Esther Burnell Mills are still recognized and honored for their lasting contributions to Estes Park history and local lore. However, there was another Mills family—the family of Enoch Josiah "Joe" (1880–1935) and Ethel M. Steere Mills (1884–1969)—which left its mark on the town and established a wonderful hotel, the Crags Lodge, as a lasting legacy for visitors to this beautiful valley. In addition, we have, in the recipes so carefully typed out in Ethel's loose-leaf notebook, ample evidence of the careful management style and the cuisine that made staying at the Crags such a memorable experience.

*The notebook in which Ethel Mills kept typed and detailed recipes she prepared at the Crags for the couple's guests.*

**Artifact courtesy of Patricia Yeager Washburn**

Joe and Ethel were arguably the most popular couple in Estes Park from the 1910s into the 1930s. Joe Mills himself was revered for his unabashed boosterism of Estes Park and its activities, as well as his prowess on the gridiron (at the University of Denver). The charming, if idealized, story of Joe's life, *A Mountain Boyhood*, which he published in 1926, remains a "must read" for those hoping to capture the essence of life in the Rockies at the turn of the twentieth century.[47]

Joe and Ethel, who met and married while Joe was the coach at Baylor University in Waco, Texas, in 1908, began their innkeeping lives in 1911 by managing The Forks Hotel in Drake, Colorado. In spite of becoming parents to a new baby, Eleanor Ann, who arrived in September that same year, the couple threw themselves into

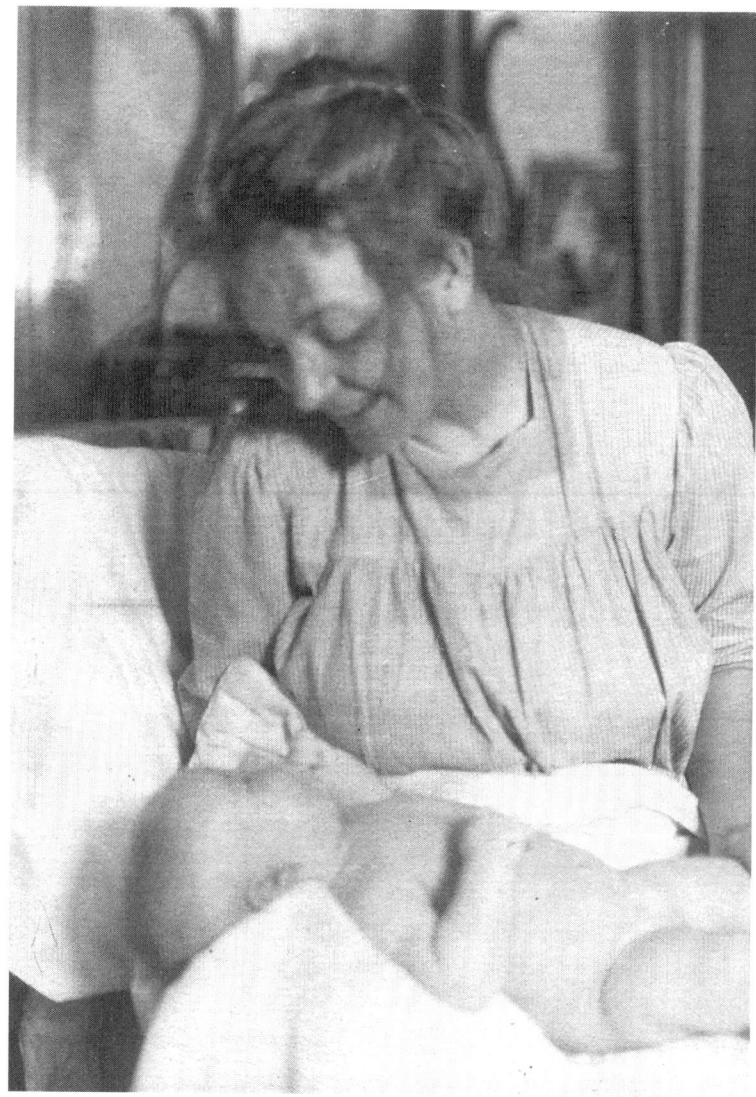

*Ethel Mills with Eleanor Ann, who was born in 1911.*
Photo courtesy of Patricia Yeager Washburn

making The Forks a profitable enterprise. In addition, Joe ran a climbing school and wrote articles in the evenings. Advertisements for the hotel assured the traveling public that though

> *our furnishings are plain and simple, our rooms are clean and comfortable. Our meals are prepared by a woman who preserves the natural homey flavor, and are served to you on clean, rustic tables, family style, no menu and no excuse for tipping.*[48]

Their three-year partnership in Drake served the young couple well, for they were to spend the next twenty-one summers hosting visitors at a hotel of their own in Estes Park. Often referred to as the "House on the Hill," the Crags Lodge opened its doors to the public for the summer season in 1914. It was perhaps prophetic that the Millses would erect their inn on the north side of Prospect Mountain, which, from the multi-paned windows in the dining room, commanded a view of the Village and of Lumpy Ridge and the peaks of the Never Summer Range beyond.

The original inn was a two-story building with twenty-one rooms. The kitchen, in which Ethel produced meals for family and hotel guests, was located on the first or basement level; the dining room and public areas were on the main level. A third story was added in the 1920s, as was a second dining room. Conveying the food from kitchen to dining room was managed by means of dumbwaiters, located at the east end of the main dining room. Ethel's wood-burning range,[49] which was "retired from service" in the late 1990s, can be seen today in Enoch's Dining Room.

Guests at The Crags took their meals on the American Plan, and it was left to Ethel to plan menus and manage the cooking, including the famous "campfire suppers" that she and Joe hosted every summer. An excellent cook fond of gourmet recipes, "she was renowned for her birthday and wedding cakes," her granddaughter Patricia Washburn recalls, and she "ran the kitchen and dining room with an iron hand."

Menus were not printed for guests, although Ethel posted each day's meal plans in the kitchen. On any given day, guests might partake of

> "Fresh frog legs, Hashed lamb, Lobster wiggle, Mutton ragout, Planked lamp chops à la Tarbeaux, Salt codfish, Boiled calves tongues, Boned ham baked with sherry and frosted, Cottage meat pie, Crab flake timbales, Dunkirk meat pie, Spaghetti rarebit . . . and Burr Oak farm potatoes."[50]

As at The Forks Hotel, Joe and Ethel promised good food served hot and family style in cheerful surroundings. The Crags' brochure prepared for the 1929 season set the tone: "The Crags is not a dressy place. Most folks come for relaxation and a good time outdoors. Old clothes are fashionable here. . . . Tipping is not

*Ethel Mills was often called on to bake special desserts for the Woman's Club, local parties, and weddings. In 1929 she created this airplane cake in honor of her son Mark's eleventh birthday.*

Photo courtesy of the Estes Park Museum

necessary." Snobs, grouches, and dogs were, however, invited to stay away.[51]

Joe was not unaware of what would keep the Crags' 200 guests happy. The secret of successful innkeeping, he was sure, lay in the quality of the kitchen. "A resort hotel," he wrote,

*offers many opportunities, though no more than the average business, for reaching its patrons in pleasurable and profitable ways. One of the chief amusements of a resort hotel is the indoor sport of eating three times a day. Through their stomachs you can reach them.*[52]

In addition to their responsibilities at the Lodge and their roles as parents of two young children (their son, Mark Muir "Bud" Mills, was born to the couple in August 1918), Joe and Ethel were both involved in the social and civic life of the Village, where they were good friends with both year-round and summer residents. Ethel was active with the Estes Park Woman's Club, functioning in 1920 as resident expert on the League of Nations, and serving as its president the same year. Joe was busy with the Rocky Mountain Hotel Association, the school board, the Chamber of Commerce, and the Estes Park Golf and Country Club, for which he served as president in 1920. As a couple, Joe and Ethel made contributions in support of the new library planned for Bond Park and hosted many fundraising events for a variety of local charities and causes. One such event was a public fish fry for the Woman's Club in 1921. Billed as a "campfire wizard," Joe served as "head chef" for the event, where 200 people were served "[f]ried trout, camp-cooked bacon, deviled eggs, baked potatoes, corn, homemade hot rolls, homemade jelly, pickles, camp coffee, watermelon, and homemade cookies."[53]

According to the Millses' granddaughter Patricia Washburn, "Joe was very much on site at the Crags during the season and did his travelling after the hotel closed for the winter. When his family moved to Boulder, he was still at the Crags in the summer." It is a testimonial to the esteem with which Joe was held in Estes Park that, in 1949, the National Park Service named a peak Joe Mills Mountain. Rocky Mountain National Park Superintendent Canfield summed up the contributions that Mills had made to the local community, but cast them in terms of larger goals:

> [H]e gave his full energies to the preservation of the scenic splendor of the area. He climbed peaks within the National Park, explored and photographed the area for years. . . . A naturalist, author, and lecturer, he made known the beauty of the country and contributed to its fame.[54]

After Joe's tragic death in an automobile accident in Denver in 1935, Ethel assumed total responsibility for managing the resort she and Joe had founded, and continued to engage actively in community life. Although fiercely competitive at the bridge table, she frowned on the use of alcohol in any form. Indeed, as a founding member of the Colorado Chapter of the Women's Christian Temperance Union (WCTU), Ethel would have "been appalled that her bridge room would later be used to house the hotel bar."[55]

## York County Pot Pie
*(Ethel Steere Mills)*

4 to 5 lbs. stewing chicken
1 teasp. saffron (optional)
1/4 teasp. pepper
2 medium potatoes, quartered
2 medium sweet potatoes or yams, quartered
2 eggs, slightly beaten
1/4 teasp. salt
2 quarts water
2 teasp. salt
1/2 cup chopped celery
2 onions, cut in half
1/2 cup chopped parsley
3 Tables. milk
2 1/2 cups sifted all-purpose flour

Cook chicken in water to cover, about 2 quarts, with saffron, salt, pepper and celery. Add more water as necessary.

When chicken is tender, (2 to 3 hrs), removed meat from bones. Add meat, potatoes, sweet potatoes and onions to broth. Cook 10 minutes, or until vegetables are nearly tender.

Combine egg, milk, salt and flour. Dough should be dry, not sticky.

May have to knead dough with hands. Divide in half. Roll dough on lightly floured board 'til very thin. Cut into 3" squares. Broth in pan should cover meat and vegs. Add hot water if necessary. Add parsley. Place squares of dough, on one by one over chicken and vegetables spooning small amount of broth over each square. Cover. Cook for 20 minutes. It (sic) desired, thicken broth slightly with flour diluted with cold water.

Serves 4 to 6. 590 calories per serving. Vitamins A-B-C

## Baked Tomatoes
*(Ethel Steere Mills)*

2 medium tomatoes  
1 small onion, minced  
Salt  
1/2 teasp. prepared mustard  
1 teasp. Worcester sauce  
2 tbsps. buttered fresh bread crumbs  

Wash tomatoes, cut out stem ends, half crosswise.  
Place in baking dish, cut sides up  
Spread with prepared mustard, top with onion, Worcestershire sauce, sprinkle well with salt, then with crumbs.  
Bake uncovered in 375 oven for 30 minutes.

## Meatloaf with Mustard Sauce
*(Ethel Steere Mills)*

1 1/2 cup bread crumbs  
4 egg yolks  
1 1/2 tbsps. horseradish  
3 tbsps. chopped onion  
1 1/2 lbs. ground lean beef  
1 1/2 teasp. salt  
3 tbsps. green pepper, chopped  
1/3 cup catsup  

Mix above ingredients, put in 9" casserole. Bake 30 minutes in 375 degree oven.  
Beat egg whites 'til foamy.  
Add 1/4 teasp. cream of tartare  
Beat till stiff.  
Fold in 4 tbsps. mustard, gently.  
Swirl on hot meat loaf. Return to oven, bake 20 to 25 minutes longer.

## Spiced Peach Salad
*(Ethel Steere Mills)*

1 large can peach halves
1/4 teasp. salt
3/4 teasps. whole cloves
2 pkgs. orange gelatine
1/4 cup chopped pecans
1/4 cup vinegar
4 2" long cinnamon sticks
Boiling water as directed
1 3 ounce pkg. cream cheese

Drain syrup from peaches - add enough water to syrup to make 1 1/2 cups.
Simmer 10 minutes, after adding vinegar to spices, etc. Add enough water to make 3 cups liquid.

## Apple Roll
*(Ethel Steere Mills)*

4 apples
2 cups water
Sugar and cinnamon
1 1/2 cups sugar
1 tablespoon butter

Put sugar and water in pan 6 x 12 x 2
Cook about 5 minutes over slow fire
Roll biscuit dough into oblong, about 1/2 inch thick
Spread finely chopped apples over it - and roll up like jelly roll.
Cut this roll into 1 ½" pieces
Place pieces cut side down in syrup.
Dot with butter and sprinkle with cinnamon and sugar
Bake in hot oven (450) till crust is golden brown, about 25 minutes
10 to 12 servings.

## Blueberry Tea Cake With Crumb Topping
*(Ethel Steere Mills)*

2 cups sifted flour
1/2 teasp. salt
3/4 cup sugar
1/2 cup milk
2 teasps. baking powder
1/4 cup butter or margarine
1 egg, unbeaten
2 cups blueberries, fresh or frozen

### *Crumb topping*

1/2 cup sugar
1/2 teasp. cinnamon
1/4 cup flour
1/4 cup butter or margarine.

Sift together flour, baking powder and salt. Cream butter, gradually beat in sugar. Add egg and milk, beat until smooth. Add dry ingredients. Fold in blueberries. Spread batter in a greased and floured 8 or 9 inch square pan. Sprinkle with crumb mixture. Bake in hot oven - 375 40-45 minutes. Cut into squares.

Crumb mixture - Mix together sugar, flour and cinnamon. Cut in butter to form coarse crumbs.

## Pastete
*(Ethel Steere Mills)*

A delicious concoction of ground veal beef and pork, spread with sautéed mushrooms, and chicken livers, and then rolled and cooked in buttered parchment paper.

## Annie's (Turner) Lemon Chiffon Pie
*(Ethel Steere Mills)*

Place on stove and bring to boil
| | |
|---|---|
| 1 quart water | (1 cup) |
| 1 1/2 cups sugar | (3/8 cup) |
| 1 teasp. salt | (1/4 tsp) |
| 2 Tablsp. grated lemon rind | (1/2 Tablsp.) |

Drops of lemon coloring [if] desired

Stir in
| | |
|---|---|
| 1 cup cornstarch | (1/4 cup) |
| 1 cup fresh lemon juice | (1/4 cup) |

Dissolve cornstarch in lemon juice, beat rapidly to prevent lumping, after adding to first mixture. Leave in double boiler over fire while preparing the following.

Beat
| | |
|---|---|
| 1 pint egg whites | (1/2 cup) |
| 1 cup sugar | (1/4 cup) |

until very dry and ragged

Fold in 1 cup sugar    (1/4)
till well blended.

By this time the first mixture should be ready. Pour it slowly over meringue, folding with a large wire whip, until well blended. Pour into baked pie shells and place in refrigerator to chill. Decorate on top with whipped cream.

This amount makes 4 nine-inch pies. [Alterations for one pie are in parentheses.]

*Perched on a cliff overlooking the Village, the luxurious Lewiston Hotel commanded a spectacular Front Range view in both winter or summer.*
Photo courtesy of the Estes Park Museum

### The Lewiston Hotel: Gus and Aneta Lewis

The Lewiston had its beginnings rather unpretentiously, as the home of Augustus Denby "Gus" Lewis (1873–1957) and his wife Aneta, who arrived in Estes Park in 1912 from Nebraska with their two little girls, Leora (b. 1899) and Maurine (b. 1905). The Lewises' third daughter, Dorothy, was born in 1918. Entering the business community as cashier of the Estes Park Bank, Gus turned innkeeper when the tents and tent-houses that the couple set up on their property for the summer season proved to be immensely profitable.

It was Aneta Fannie Jackson Lewis (1879–1959), the daughter of a postmaster in Fairmont, Nebraska, who provided the energy and culinary skills to launch the couple into the resort business. That the Lewises were immediately successful in their endeavor was duly noted in the local paper, which also suggested the reason. "The host," the paper reported, "is ably assisted in the management . . . by his estimable wife, who has personal charge of the cuisine and serving of the meals, as well as leading in the entertainment of guests."[56]

*The stately dining room at The Lewiston Hotel, where Aneta Lewis' home-cooked gourmet dishes were served.*
**Postcard courtesy of the Bobbie Heistercamp Collection**

So popular was the fledgling resort that the couple soon enlarged their house to include additional guest accommodations, and by 1920 the Lewises had erected a new three-story hotel. When completed, the Lewiston included seventy guest rooms, each outfitted to deliver hot and cold running water; there were also multiple dining rooms, three kitchens, a third-floor ballroom with organ, and a roof garden.

At its zenith, The Lewiston served its guests in surroundings of considerable sophistication, offering a Japanese Tea Room on the third floor. The spacious and cheery dining room was fully carpeted and graciously appointed with an abundance of porcelain chandeliers and white linen. A brochure from the 1930s describes the experience that awaited hotel diners:

> *Mealtime is an event looked forward to with eager anticipation, induced by appetites set on edge by the pine-scent mountain air and ideal altitude (7,800 feet). The dining service is unexcelled. Good food, carefully selected and tastily prepared.*

*Estes Park lost one of the Village's few luxury hotels to fire in September 1941.*
Photo courtesy of the Estes Park Museum

In addition to its elegance, The Lewiston's remoteness from the downtown area and its panoramic views of the Front Range from the two verandas installed on the hotel's south side made the hotel a rival to The Stanley as a summer destination for the wealthy.

Once their hotel was built, the Lewises remodeled their own house to accommodate families with children. In addition to their expansive resort, Aneta and Gus also owned a number of related businesses in the Village and in the Estes Valley, including the Lewiston Chalets (now Marys Lake Lodge) and the Lewiston Café on Elkhorn Avenue.

Ironically, the demise of the Lewiston—"the grand lady of the hotel industry"—was precipitated by "excessive culinary zeal in staging a gala dinner" for a group of Rotarians who had driven up from Denver in September 1941. According to Pedersen, "All of the fireplaces were blazing and every oven was in use baking the one hundred hens and thirty-seven turkeys required. The flues up in the attic were glowing bright red, obviously overloaded" so that in the end, the rafters caught fire,[57] and the hotel burned to the ground. The entire town turned out to fight the fire, including the Estes Park High School football team.[58]

### Rochester Soup
*(Aneta Fannie Jackson Lewis)*

2/3 cup almonds, chopped fine
little salt
1 sliced onion
4 tablespoonfuls cold water
3 cups chicken broth
3 stalks of celery, cut fine

Let this simmer one hour. Melt 3 tablespoonfuls butter, add 1 tablespoonful flour and stir until well blended, then pour on the first cooked ingredients gradually. Add 2 cups milk and 1 cup thin cream, salt and pepper to taste, bring to a boiling point and serve at once.

### French Cauliflower
*(Aneta Fannie Jackson Lewis)*

Separate a fine head of cauliflower in uniform portions and boil in salted water until tender. Dip each piece in well-beaten egg, to which add 3 tablespoons cold water, 1/2 teaspoonful of salt and a few grains of cayenne.

Roll in cracker crumbs mixed with grated cheese and place in a buttered dish. Brown richly and quickly. Place each piece on a round of buttered toast and surround with a little well-seasoned hot cream sauce.

## Cheese Cream
*(Aneta Fannie Jackson Lewis)*

Sift a saltspoon each of dry mustard and salt over 3 unbeaten eggs and beat to a foam. Pour over them a cupful of rich milk brought to the boiling point. Turn into a double boiler and cook until mixture coats spoon. Add 4 heaping tablespoonfuls grated cheese, 1 level tablespoonful gelatin softened in cold water, turn into a chilled bowl, set into a pan of ice water and beat until thick. Then fold in a cup of whipped cream. Serve with the coffee as an after-dinner savory.

## Wellesley Fudge Cake
*(Aneta Fannie Jackson Lewis)*

3 sq. chocolate  
2/3 cup sugar (brown)  
1/2 cup milk

Cook ten minutes and add 1 teaspoonful of vanilla

### Cream

1 cup sugar (brown)  
1/2 cup sour milk  
2 cups sifted pastry flour  
1/4 teaspoonful salt  
1/2 cup butter  
2 eggs (well beaten)  
1 teaspoonful soda

Add above mixture. Bake in layers.

## German Coffee Cake
*(Aneta Fannie Jackson Lewis)*

Beat whites of two eggs stiff, then add yolks with 2 tablespoonfuls sugar. Mix 1 yeast cake in a little warm water, fill cup with milk. Make soft dough in the morning, add 1/4 cup butter, 1/2 cup sugar and mix stiff. Mix down once more, roll out and cover with butter, cinnamon and sugar.

## Cheese Soufflé
*(Aneta Fannie Jackson Lewis)*

Three rounding tablespoonfuls flour moistened with 1/2 cup of milk; heat 1 cup of milk in a double boiler, add flour and cook until thick; add 1 cup of cheese and cook until cheese is melted. Stir into this the yolks of 4 eggs, well beaten, salt and dash of red pepper. Add the whites of the 4 eggs, beaten very stiff, last. Bake in a moderate oven in a pan of boiling water thirty-five or forty minutes.

## Salmon Mousse
*(Aneta Fannie Jackson Lewis)*

To 1 cup salmon, picked fine, add yolks of 3 eggs, well beaten. Add a sauce made from 1 tablespoonful butter, 1 tablespoonful flour, 1/2 cup milk and salmon stock, cooked until thick like cream. Add whites of the 3 eggs, beaten. Set in pan of water and bake for one-half hour, or until it springs back at touch.

## Smothered Sausage
*(Aneta Fannie Jackson Lewis)*

Cook little link sausages until brown and rather crisp. Arrange them in a casserole, pour a little water over them and cover thickly with tart apples (sliced to correspond to sausage). Sprinkle apples with dark brown sugar. Cover and bake slowly 3/4 to 1 hour. Serve steaming in casserole, placing on large plate garnished with parsley.

*The historic Baldpate Inn, located off Highway 7 south of Estes Park (c. 1920), continues to serve lunch and dinner to summer visitors in a delightful mountain setting.*

Photo courtesy of the Estes Park Museum

## The Baldpate Inn: The Mace Family

*"Where hospitality is king."*
—Baldpate Inn advertisement, 1953

The Baldpate Inn opened for the first time in 1917 on land homesteaded three years earlier by the family of William and Mina Aitken Mace. In fact, William and Mina and their little boys[59] had immigrated to Denver from England in 1890 at the urging of Windham Thomas Wyndham-Quin, fourth Earl of Dunraven, the Irish aristocrat whose initial intention had been to buy up large portions of the Estes Valley to support his growing cattle operation. In 1889, Lord Dunraven had built a fine, three-story hotel near the Village along Fish Creek. Perhaps hoping to establish a community of the likeminded nearby, the Earl had persuaded the Maces to leave their homeland and risk their fortunes and their futures in the American West.

*The Baldpate Inn dining room has undergone very few changes during its 100-year history.*

Postcard courtesy of the Bobbie Heistercamp Collection

During the summer of 1910, William's son Gordon McLeod Mace and his bride, Mary Ethel Prickett Mace (1889–1983), spent their honeymoon near Estes Park. They were so charmed by the mountain setting that they homesteaded three years later, and, assisted by Gordon's two brothers, Charles and Stuart, they built a cabin on the northern slope of Twin Sisters Peaks.

Soon thereafter, the Maces decided to add a number of small tourist cabins, which they rented out to enhance the family income. This venture proved so successful that the couple enlarged their business by constructing a beautiful and rustic three-story inn. Located directly on the old road linking the Village to the Tahosa Valley, the Maces' hotel offered tourists breathtaking views of the Estes Valley from its dining-room windows.

Unlike the Earl of Dunraven, the Mace family had limited financial resources and thus relied on their own carpentry skills, which were considerable,[60] and hand-hewn logs from their own property in constructing the building. Gordon himself created much of the furniture, including the writing desks. The Western Stick-style structure, featuring a front gable, "overhanging eaves, and projecting porch,"[61] was completed in 1917. Stone fireplaces provided heat and hot water; the hotel also offered electric lights and indoor plumbing. In 1918, a dining-room wing was added to the original structure, where, for over thirty years, meals served to guests garnered the prestigious Duncan Hines Award, which promised "good eating."[62] Another wing was built in 1921, and enlarged in 1935. The open porch, a major feature of the original Inn, was enclosed in 1930.

By the middle of the 1930s, the Maces could offer their guests twenty-one lodge rooms and twelve bathrooms, a dance hall, four guest cabins, and a livery stable. In addition to drawing visitors from around the world, the Inn was a favorite with local residents, as well as Greek-letter fraternities from Front Range colleges, which frequently held dances there.

The Maces named their inn The Baldpate at the suggestion of Earl Derr Biggers, a visiting author whose mystery novel, *The Seven Keys to Baldpate,* had been adapted for the Broadway stage (1913) by George M. Cohan. In line with this theme, the Maces began to present guests with small sets of keys as souvenirs, a practice that was abandoned during World War I because of the rising cost of metal. Guests, dismayed at the loss of these mementoes, began a new tradition of their own— leaving keys to mark their visits. To house their growing collection, which ranged from the mundane to the exotic, the Maces created a Key Room and for a time even offered tours for "a nominal admission charge."[63] Over the last ninety-five years, the Inn has collected over 20,000 keys.

In the 1970s ownership of the Inn passed to Gordon and Ethel Mace's daughter Leanne Vick, who put her own stamp on the place, particularly the cuisine, reopening the dining room, which had been closed for many years, and updating the menu to include entrees named for characters from Biggers' novel that "its ingredients and style of preparation" seemed to most reflect. In addition, she drew on family recipes, assuring guests that "Everything is made from Scratch."[64]

The Smith family purchased the Inn in 1986. Since that time, Lois Smith has made a concerted effort to preserve Baldpate history and the building, which has been on the National Register of Historic Places since 1996.

*The main building at the Fall River Lodge as it looked in the 1940s.*
Photo courtesy of the Estes Park Museum

### Fall River Lodge: Dan and Minnie March

*"Spend your vacation at Fall River Lodge, where there are modern conveniences and reasonable rates."*

—Fall River Lodge brochure, 1915

Fall River Lodge was the inspiration of Daniel J. March (1863–1923), a Canadian-born blacksmith, who, with his wife Minnie E. Brown March,[65] first came to the Estes Valley from Greeley in search of a more salubrious climate for Dan's respiratory problems. In 1907, the couple purchased property on the Fall River west of the Village, and four years later added 125 acres more to their

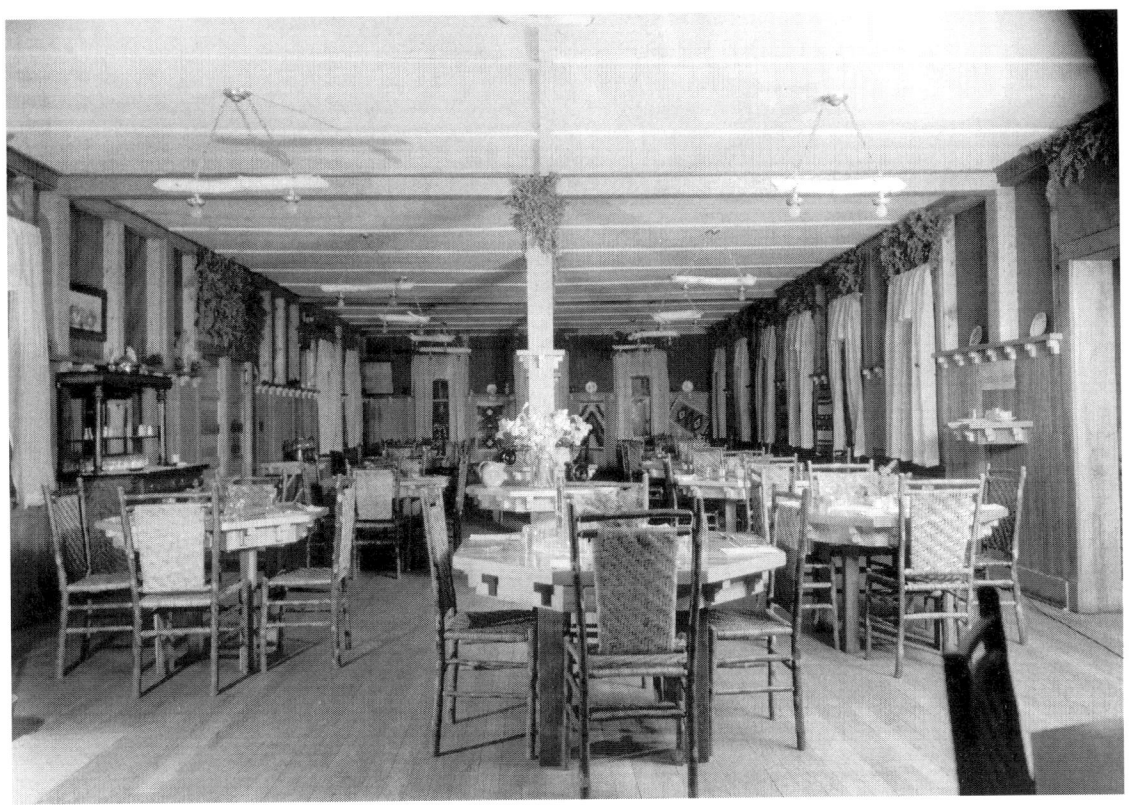

*The dining room at the Marches' Fall River Lodge.*
Photo courtesy of The Estes Park Museum

homestead holdings. Their intention at the start was to take up farming. However, when they realized that their land was situated in a place that encouraged tourism, they decided to build a lodge and enter the hotel business. Minnie later wrote,

> *Since our first summer in the park we had visions of a hotel in that quiet valley. Those visions never left us, and as the summer wore on, and the winter's wood piled up, we talked and thought of hardly anything else.*[66]

In making their "vision" a reality, the couple overcame enormous challenges as their land was not only remote from the Village but very swampy. However, Dan was able to use his own timber to build a home, barn, and corral, and over time the lodge he had designed that first winter in the mountains began to take shape.

The lodge's grand opening on July 4, 1915, coincided with the dedication of Rocky Mountain National Park, the ceremony for which took place nearby just eight weeks later. Over the course of the next six years, the Marches added one- and two-room cabins, and in the spring of 1923 the lot was expanded through a purchase from the Marchs' neighbor, Pieter Hondius. Unfortunately, Dan's enjoyment of the Inn and its lovely surroundings was tragically short; he died the following fall. Minnie, who by that time was, herself, past 50, continued to run the lodge Dan had built for her, eventually adding a barn, a recreation hall, and staff housing to the Fall River Lodge complex.

Then, in 1935, Minnie married an old friend, Samuel M. Service,[67] an Irish immigrant and owner of a general store, which was itself a longtime Village landmark. At the time, Service was a widower with eight grown children. The Village greeted the news of Minnie and Sam's marriage with enthusiasm, for as individuals and as a couple they were as loved in the community as they were at the Lodge. For the next two summers Minnie served up three delicious meals a day in the Lodge kitchen, and Sam[68] entertained guests in the living room with stories of early Estes Park and its unique characters.

Sam died in 1937, but Minnie continued on at the Lodge until its purchase by John Russell "Russ" McKelvey (1900–1970) and his vivacious wife Florence Mason McKelvey (1899–1972) in 1941. No stranger to the hotel business, Russ had served as an assistant manager at the Lodge in the 1920s; just before buying Fall River Lodge, he managed The Lewiston Hotel until fire ended its history. Although the McKelveys made few changes in the Lodge, they did add a 600-square-foot extension to the dining room.

Fall River Lodge continued to flourish as a family-friendly resort under its new owners and was long remembered as the site of square dances, picnics, canoeing, marshmallow roasts, lawn games and first-rate fishing. In 1959, it was taken over by the National Park Service and the buildings were razed. Its demise was viewed with sadness by residents and former guests, who would later recall "the gracious manners of the hosts and hostesses of Fall River Lodge through the years, together with the tasteful and rustic elegance of the Lodge's appointments, [and] its lovely location."[69]

## Tomato Salad

*(Minnie E. Brown March Service)*

2 cans tomatoes
2 bay leaves
6 cloves
1 1/2 teaspoonfuls paprika

Boil until thoroughly done, strain, add 2 1/2 teaspoonfuls gelatin and put in moulds.
Serve with lettuce, dressing and whipped cream.

## Fruit Salad

*(Minnie E. Brown March Service)*

1/2 lb. almonds
4 oranges
1 can pineapple
3 bananas
1/2 cup cherries
1 cup powdered sugar

Blanch almonds and chop, slice the oranges, cut the pineapple in dice, slice bananas and add sugar. Add the following dressing and chill: One-half cup lemon juice, 2 tablespoonfuls sherry or wine, 2 tablespoonfuls Maraschino liquor, 1/4 cup pineapple juice, and 1 cup sugar. Cook down to a syrup. Grated cocoanut can be used instead of almonds, peaches and pears instead of bananas.

*Lobby of Clem Yore's Big Thompson Hotel, completed in 1917.*
Photo courtesy of the Estes Park Museum

## Clem Yore's Big Thompson Hotel

Clement Yore (1875–1936) was one of Estes Park's most colorful innkeepers. A prolific author who wrote novels (mostly westerns),[70] short stories, poems, and erotica, the St. Louis–born Yore had worked as the city editor for the Chicago *American* newspaper before coming to Estes Park. Yore had big plans for his hotel, which he commissioned local contractor Fred Anderson to build near Beaver Point, just west of the Village. The Big Thompson Hotel was a seasonal business, which permitted Yore to winter in Long Beach, California, beginning in the 1920s.

Yore's life story is an extraordinary one. As a boy of twelve, he left his home in St. Louis to travel around the Midwest before going to El Paso to join the Texas Rangers, which he apparently did at the age of fifteen. He then "punched cows" and drove a stagecoach for a time before trying his hand at prospecting in Creede, Colorado, in the 1890s. Eventually, he returned to school, first at a military academy in Virginia and then at Washington University Law School in St. Louis. In 1896, he turned to journalism, and his first assignment was to cover the gold rush in the Yukon. This career turn was short-lived, however, as the excitement posed by the Spanish-American War drew him to join the army. Once the

*Alberta McAuley Plonke Yore was talented composer and an active participant in the cultural life of the Estes community.*
Photo courtesy of the Estes Park Museum

war was over, Yore went back to journalism, this time in California, and finally in Chicago. In 1897 he married Olive, and their daughter Juanita (1898–2000) was born the following year.

Given Yore's peripatetic life style, it is perhaps not surprising that his first marriage ended in divorce. Then in 1915, Yore married his protégé, Alberta Evelyn McAuley Plonke (1879–1959), and the couple honeymooned in Estes Park. Both Clem and Alberta fell in love with the area's mountains, and they decided to stay. A gifted pianist and published composer in her own right, Alberta frequently wrote musical scores for her husband's poems. As early as 1921, she served as president of the Estes Park Music and Study Club and often provided programs for the group that featured her own compositions.

After relocating to Estes Park, Yore was able to turn his full attention to writing, and at least one critic believed that his new surroundings had a profound effect on the depth and development of his poetry.

> *Since his sojourn in Colorado, mountains have found a place in his soul, his verse teems with the bigness and freshness of the West, and has earned for him the laurels of Colorado's State Poet. In his poem "Colorado" is evidenced the versatility of his pen and the lessons the vasts have taught him.*[71]

His poetic themes were also transformed, from "slime to sublime," as one critic put it. Once preoccupied in the gritty urban landscapes he had observed at close hand as a police reporter, Yore came increasingly to reflect in his work his love for the majestic peaks of his adopted state. In a verse from "Colorado," for example, he wrote:

> *Here are the valleys that are yet nameless*
> *And mountains that spike the sky,*
> *And the true blue spruce, to e'er produce*
> *A charm to seduce the eye.*
> *There are canyons that yawn as they grip you,*
> *There are sentinel rocks austere—*
> *There are operas unsung, there are pictures unhung*
> *And silences made to hear.*

As both writer and resident, Yore was not alone in seeking inspiration from the natural beauty that surrounded him. There was, in fact, a local literary community that included Emporia (KS) *Gazette* editor and Estes Park summer resident William Allen White, fellow Kansan and poet/philosopher Walt Mason (b. 1862), and of course, Enos Mills. Robert W. Service and Jack London were also sometime guests at the Big Thompson Hotel.[72]

Yore was very proud of his hotel, which could accommodate 200 guests, and of its kitchen. Cuisine at Yore's hotel was standard American fare, on a typical day offering diners sirloin steak, roast pork, roast prime rib of beef, corn on the cob and apple pie.

*Clem and Alberta Yore, Estes Park c. 1930s. Thanks to the beauty of the natural world that the couple experienced on a daily basis, Clem turned his poetic attention from "tenderloin to timberline" and became the "laureate of the Rocky Mountains."[73]*

Photo courtesy of the Estes Park Museum

## Clem Yore's Own Pudding

*(Clement Yore)*

1 cup grated cocoanut
12 marshmallows, cut in halves
1 cup milk
1/2 cup sugar
2 eggs
1/2 teaspoon almond extract

Put 1/2 cocoanut into greased baking dish, 1/2 marshmallows on top of this. Pour mixture of milk, sugar, eggs and flavoring over cocoanut and marshmallows. Carefully add the rest of the cocoanut and marshmallows and bake twenty-five or thirty minutes. Serve either hot or cold with whipped cream.

*Johann and Sophia Holzwarth and their children, gathered at the family dinner table in 1920.*

Photo courtesy of the National Park Service

## Holzwarth's Trout Lodge[74]

In the summer of 1917, Johann and Sophia Holzwarth packed up their four children[75] and moved to a homestead claim in the Kawuneeche Valley on the Grand (Colorado) River north of the town of Grand Lake. Born in Germany, Johann "Johnnie" Gottlob Holzwarth (1865–1932) had come to Denver in 1880 or 1881, and there he met and married (1894) Sophia "Sophie" Lebfromm (1870–1953), a fellow German immigrant. Although a butcher by trade, Johnnie eventually purchased a saloon and boarding house, which provided a good living for himself and his family. Unfortunately for the Holzwarths, the state legislature moved to ban the sale and consumption of alcohol beginning on January 1, 1916.[76] Since the law effectively put an end to Johnnie's business, he had little choice but to find a new occupation in a new place.

At the start, Johnnie and Sophie planned to establish a ranch on their 160-acre homestead tract, and to that end they put up a sod-roofed log cabin. Containing only a single room, the cabin, which they called "Mama Cabin," was soon followed by a number of other cabins and structures as the couple worked to get their new enterprise up and running. Their first move in expanding their holdings came in 1918, when they purchased the adjacent homestead proper-

*The dining room at Holzwarth's Trout Lodge. Sophie stopped serving meals at the Lodge after Johnnie's death.*
Postcard courtesy of the Bobbie Heistercamp Collection

ties of one Joseph Fleshuts. The acquisition of Fleshuts's property increased the Holzwarths' land to more than 900 acres. The couple's dream of owning a cattle ranch seemed within their grasp.

Not long thereafter, however, Johnnie suffered an injury that made the launching of a full-fledged cattle operation untenable. At this point, the Holzwarths decided to increase the number of their rental cabins and go into the resort business. Running an inn was right up Sophie's alley—she was good-humored and loquacious, and ready and willing to handle the cooking responsibilities. The first guests arrived in 1919. By all accounts, Holzwarth's Trout Lodge was a favorite with the traveling public right from the start.

With the opening of Fall River Road over the Continental Divide in 1920 and the increase in the number of visitors that desired accommodation near Grand Lake, the Holzwarths expanded their resort to include Fleshuts's original homestead cabin, which lay on the other side of the Colorado River. During the 1920s additional cabins were built there, and a new lodge building was completed in 1929. The site was called the Never Summer Ranch.

Holzwarth's Trout Lodge provided a reasonably priced vacation in a rustic setting. For a charge of $11.00, a guest could procure: a week's lodging, which included breakfast, lunch, and dinner; the use of a saddle horse; and all the trout he or she could eat. The resort's popularity no doubt depended on both the geniality of the host and the "scrumptious home-cooked meals, including trout, deer, grouse, chicken and fresh eggs and milk," that Mama Holzwarth prepared on a wood-burning range ordered from the Montgomery Ward catalog. In addition to traditional western fare, the menu at the Trout Lodge featured many ethnic German dishes, some recipes for which came from German newspapers. Perhaps believing cleanliness to be next to godliness, Sophie held herself and her family to high housekeeping standards, refusing to allow anyone into her home unless all public areas were spotless.

When Johnnie died in 1932, Sophie decided to make the cabins self-catering, and she ended her career as the Trout Lodge cook. She continued to own and run the ranch, however, and when she herself could no longer manage, the Holzwarth children continued its operation. In 1973, the Holzwarth Trout Lodge and the Never Summer Ranch were sold to The Nature Conservancy, which sold it to the National Park Service the following year, with the understanding that the land would be preserved as open space. The NPS now maintains the Trout Lodge and the Never Summer Ranch as historic sites.

### Sauerkraut
*(Sophia Lebfromm Holzwarth)*

Use one tablespoon pickling salt with each large head of cabbage.

Slice cabbage as fine as possible and place in large tub. Sprinkle salt over the cabbage and mix well with hands.

Juice will start forming. Continue mixing until very juicy.

Place the mixture in a crock and pound with a potato masher until all cabbage is under its own juice.

Place a plate over the mix, weighted down with a rock, to hold the cabbage down under the juice.

Let stand at room temperature until as sour as desired, usually two or three weeks.

Place in a saucepan and bring to a boil, then simmer for half an hour.

## Gewurzkuchen (Spice Cake)

*(Sophia Lebfromm Holzwarth)*

Ingredients:

| | |
|---|---|
| 2 cups flour | 1 teaspoon baking powder |
| 1/2 teaspoon baking soda | 2 teaspoons cinnamon |
| 1/2 teaspoon cloves | 2/3 cup butter |
| 2 cups sugar | 4 egg yolks (beaten) |
| 1 cup buttermilk | 4 egg whites |

Sift flour and measure two cups. Sift again two times with baking powder, baking soda, cinnamon and cloves. Stir butter until soft.

Add sugar a little at time and stir constantly. Then stir beaten egg yolks for five minutes with the other ingredients.

Alternately add buttermilk with the rest of the dry ingredients.

Beat egg whites stiff and fold in.

Bake in two layer tins at 375 degrees for 35 minutes. An orange or lemon filling is best.

### *Icing*

Mix 2 cups of sifted powder sugar with whipping cream and vanilla or add three tablespoons orange juice and one tablespoon lemon juice. If necessary, add a little cold water. Pineapple juice can be substituted for orange juice.

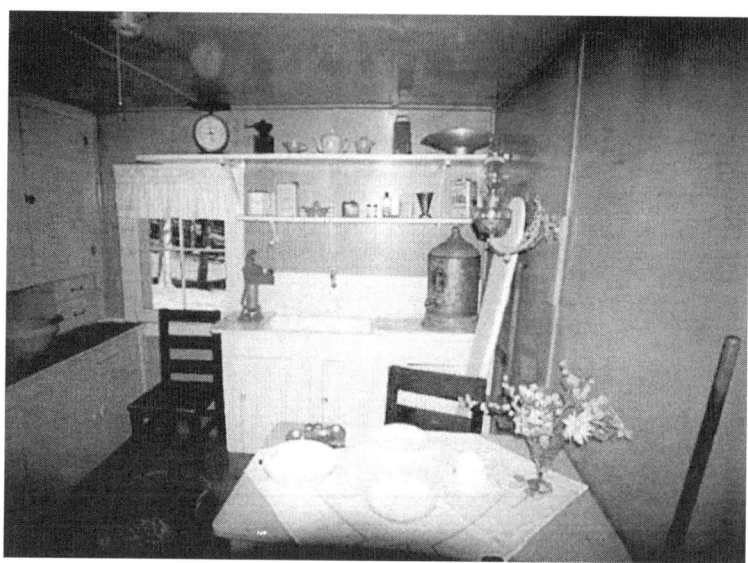

*Kitchen of Mama Cabin at Holzwarth's Trout Lodge. Sophie Holzwarth was a fastidious housekeeper as well as a first-rate cook.*

Photo courtesy of National Park Service

## Schokoladenkuchen (Chocolate Cake)

*(Sophia Lebfromm Holzwarth)*

Ingredients:
- 4 oz bitter chocolate
- 1 1/2 cups sugar plus 3 tablespoons (separate)
- 3 teaspoons tartrate or 2 teaspoons double-acting baking powder
- 1/4 cup boiling water
- 2 cups sifted cake flour
- 1/2 teaspoon salt
- 1/2 cup butter
- 3 egg whites.

Put chocolate in a double boiler along with three tablespoons of sugar and one quarter cup boiling water.

Stir until the chocolate is melted and cool. Meanwhile, take sifted cake flour and sift again two times with the baking powder and salt.

Stir butter until creamy and add one-and–one half cups sugar a little at a time. Then add the chocolate mixture. Beat egg whites and fold in.

Bake in two or three layer tins at 350 degrees for 25 to 35 minutes.

*The Tahosa Valley homestead cabin of Elkanah and Jane Lamb, which the couple built at the foot of Longs Peak in 1875.*
Photo courtesy of the National Park Service

## Wind River Ranch: The Hutchinson Family

Wind River Ranch, which continues to operate today as a Western-style family resort, had its origins in the 1920s. However, the property itself was homesteaded several generations earlier by Elkanah J. Lamb (1832–1915) who had traveled west from Kansas in 1875 to establish his family on property at the foot of Longs Peak.

Lamb had first come to Colorado in 1860, in the company of his Kansas relatives,[77] on what turned out to be a fruitless prospecting junket. Then in 1871, he undertook a second trip, this time as an itinerant preacher for the Church of the United Brethren, with a mission to organize churches "along the South Platte and the valleys of the Poudre and Big and Little Thompson" Rivers.[78] Four years later, with his second wife Jane,[79] the couple's only child, a

Chapter Three: Early Estes Park Resorts and Inns    157

three-year-old daughter Jennie, and Elkanah's son Carlyle, Lamb moved his family into a log house and began supplementing his preacher's salary by launching a modest ranching and farming operation.

Within a year or two, Lamb's Ranch, now called "Longs Peak House," became an overnight stop and launching site for climbers heading for Longs Peak; Elkanah and Carlyle were often hired as hiking guides. In addition, father and son built a road from the Tahosa Valley to Estes Park in order to enable summer visitors to travel more easily from the Village to Longs Peak House. Eventually, Enos Abijah Mills, Lamb's nephew, whose homestead cabin was located on the lower slopes of the Twin Sisters Peaks across the valley from the Lambs,' purchased Longs Peak House and in 1902 opened Longs Peak Inn on the site. At that time, the Lambs built a second homestead cabin, "Mountain Home," at Lamb's Notch, on property they owned at the northern end of the Tahosa Valley.

In 1911 Mountain Home was purchased as a summer retreat by Chicago journalist John Dickinson Sherman (1859–1926) and his wife Mary Bell King Sherman (1862–1935). Married in 1887, Mary Bell was a political activist and ardent supporter of the National Park movement. She was also leading member in the General Federation of Women's Clubs, serving as its national president from 1924 to 1928. The couple summered in their Tahosa Valley home for thirteen years before selling the property to another Chicago couple, Dr. and Mrs. Robert James Gay.[80]

The Gays expanded the property over time until it included some 520 acres, and built a number of log cabins as summer homes for their relatives. The Gays' daughter and her husband later turned what had been her family's vacation compound into a commercial enterprise by renting the cabins to paying customers. Then in 1944, the resort was sold on a lease option to Robert B. and Helen Cornish Hutchinson,[81] who added new cabins and a recreation hall built around Mountain Home's original fireplace.

Wind River Ranch really came into being as a result of the Hutchinsons' skills as innkeepers, which inspired such loyalty in their guest families that they began to make summering at Wind River an annual tradition. Generations of guests were called to meals by the tolling of a large dinner bell, with the expectation that all would arrive on time. Before entering the dining room for the evening meal, guests were encouraged to socialize with one another in the den, immediately adjacent to the dining room, which offered a fire in the fireplace, a piano, and, sometimes, musical entertainment. The Wind River guest book was also kept in the den on a low table, so that each person in the family could sign his or her name as part of the registration ritual.

At mealtime, family members were seated together and served by waitstaff usually clad in white aprons. Because on the American Plan meals were included with the cost of lodging, the menu changed daily and included gourmet items as well as more standard fare, served family style. It was also during meals that the Wind River's wranglers would sign up individuals and families for various rides being offered, including the breakfast ride, which was always a favorite.

The Hutchinsons retired in 1973. Subsequent owners Robert and Nan Irvin and, later, the Blakeways, took particular pride in preserving the historic barn (built in 1889), the rustic atmosphere, the traditions, and the artifacts that made staying at Wind River Ranch a premier summer experience for over fifty years.

## Avocado Ring with Lobster or Crabmeat Salad
*(Bob and Helen Cornish Hutchinson)*

1 tbsp. gelatin - soften in 1/4 c. water
1 c. avocado pulp
1/2 c. mayonnaise
3 tbsp. lemon juice
2 tbsp. lime juice
1 tsp. salt

Combine all ingredients above stirring in the gelatin thoroughly.
   Add: 1 c. heavy cream, whipped, folding into avocado mixture.
Pour into a ring mold and chill at least 3 hrs. or til stiff and firm.
   Unmold the ring and fill the center with a salad of lobster or crabmeat.
Arrange overlapping slices of tomato around the edge of the ring on the platter.

*Meeker Park Lodge as it looked in the 1930s.*
Postcard courtesy of the Bobbie Heistercamp Collection

## Meeker Park Lodge: The Dever Family

Meeker Park Lodge, which is located along the North St. Vrain Creek ten miles south of Estes Park, was the vision of Owen Leroy "Roy" Dever (1885–1973) and Harry Gaylord "Gay" Nowels (1875–1961), who purchased the 160-acre property together in 1922. Both Dever and Nowels were teaching school in Longmont at the time and hoped to augment their incomes by catering to tourists who flocked to Estes Park every summer.

The Lodge was built on land that had originally been homesteaded as "Good View Ranch" in 1888 by Franklin L. Hornbaker (1866–1918). Hornbaker first erected a sod house on the property, but over time he improved his holdings with a five-room log house and a number of outbuildings. As was so often the case with homesteaders in Estes and beyond, Hornbaker soon began to provide rooms and meals at his home for summer visitors. Eventually he sold his fledgling Meeker Park resort to Fred Earl Robinson (1872–1920), who had homesteaded an adjacent property. It was

*The dining room at the Lodge featured rough-hewn logs and a twisted log staircase. The simple mountain furniture was made by Gay Nowels, a gifted carpenter.*

Postcard courtesy of the Bobbie Heistercamp Collection

from Robinson's widow, Harriet Lucinda "Hattie" Robinson (1876–1964), that the Devers and Nowels acquired the property in 1922.

Dever was a newlywed, having married Crete Mildred Childers (1892–1993) that same year, while Nowels and his wife, Hattie Leota Alter Nowels (1878–1930), had been married almost thirty years at the time the land was purchased. While their husbands turned their hands and attention to building the first of the cabins that they planned to rent out or to sell outright should buyers appear, Crete and Leota transformed Hornbaker's log house into an inn, eventually renting guest rooms upstairs and providing meals to travelers in the tearoom on the main level. A little grocery store was also added soon thereafter.

At the outset, the cabins were primitive affairs that lacked both indoor plumbing and electricity. The first upgrade made to the cabins was the addition of small "refrigerated" boxes for butter, milk, and bacon, cooled by water carried from a nearby creek via a ditch; later, the same stream and ditch provided running water to the Lodge and the cabins. A 1920 Ford engine and generator provided the electricity.

After Leota's death in 1930, Gay Nowels sold his interest in the resort, although he continued to assist the Devers when they decided to erect a large log lodge in 1930, designing the twisted log stairway in the Lodge and making pine beds, dressing tables, wash stands, dining tables, chairs, and bookcases. When completed in 1935, the lodge complex included the store, a gas station, and a livery. In the 1950s, a recreation hall was built for square dances.

Roy and Crete Dever's descendants continue to own and run Meeker Park Lodge, which today, as in times past, rents lodge rooms and housekeeping cabins to summer visitors.

## Ice Water Cake
*(Crete Mildred Childers Dever)*

Cream: 1/2 c. shortening and 1-1/2 c. sugar.
Add alternately: 3 c. flour and 1-1/2 c. ice water.
Fold in: 4 beaten egg whites to which has been added 3 tsp.
   baking powder, 1 tsp. vanilla, and 1/2 tsp. lemon extract.
Bake in sheet or layers.

Maraschino Cherry variation of ice water cake—Use half water and half juice of maraschino cherries. Add 1/2 c. nuts, chopped and 1/2 c. chopped maraschino cherries. Frost with boiled frosting using some juice instead of water.

## Boiled Frosting
*(Crete Mildred Childers Dever)*

Boil to a thread stage:
1-1/2 c. sugar
1/2 c. water
1-1/2 tsp. vinegar.

Beat 3 egg whites to which a pinch of salt and 1 tbsp. water has been added.

   When syrup spins a thread, start adding to beaten egg whites 1/3 at a time. Put syrup back on stove and boil while eggs are whipping, a few seconds. Then add 1/2 of the remaining syrup and repeat the third time. Whip until the frosting stands in peaks. Add 1/2 tsp. vanilla.

*The Lodge and cabins at the McGraw Guest Ranch hosted generations of vacationing families, including Alf Landon, former governor of Kansas who ran for President against Franklin Roosevelt in 1936.*
Photo courtesy of the Estes Park Museum

## Roughing It with Ease: The McGraw Guest Ranch

When newlyweds John and Irene McGraw first visited Denver and the mountains of the Front Range to the northwest, few would have imagined that this Pennsylvania-born couple would found one of the most enduring and endearing resorts in the history of the Estes Valley.

John J. (1882–1918) and Irene McGlathery McGraw (1888–1972), who were married in Philadelphia in 1907, had been staying at the Brown Palace in Denver when they decided to extend their stay in Colorado to include some time in the high country. In Estes Park they rented a little log cabin, and during their stay they met Hugo

*Ruth and Frank raised their five daughters at the McGraw Ranch in the 1960s.*
**Photo courtesy of Fran and Jay Grooters**

and Mary Miller, owners of a ranch on Cow Creek. The couples became instant friends, and within two years, the McGraws had purchased the Millers' ranch, the Double Bar=Y. John, who had been employed with his father in the construction business, initially planned to use the Ranch as a summer home, and in the years until his death in 1918 the family traveled back and forth across the country so that the couple's four children could spend the summers out of the city and in the mountains.

The property itself had been homesteaded in 1884 by Peter J. Pauley, who sold out to the Millers in 1897. When John McGraw died, Irene at first considered selling the land but instead decided to run the Ranch herself with the help of a foreman. In 1936 she changed the ranch's name to the Double Bar=X, and opened the ranch to summer visitors as the McGraw Guest Ranch.

For almost fifty summers thereafter, the Ranch provided guest families a "cowboy experience" in a beautiful setting. Among Irene's most famous summer guests was Alf Landon and his family, who sought solitude and a retreat from the public eye the summer before his unsuccessful run for the Presidency in 1936. In deference to their famous guest and his entourage, and to ensure their privacy, the McGraws moved into town for the duration of the Landons' stay.

In 1946, Irene's son Frank (1913–1983) married Ruth Hodson (1916–2010). Ruth had initially come west to Estes Park to live near her parents at a time when her father was employed at Rocky Mountain National Park.[82] At first, the young couple ran the livery at the Ranch, where they maintained a string of seventy saddle horses for use by guest ranch visitors. In addition, they owned and maintained 200 head of cattle. Then, in 1955 Ruth and Frank took over the entire Ranch and its resort operations, where they assured summer guests that they would "Rough It with Ease."[83]

The McGraws emphasized the cowboy lifestyle; for example, upon check-in each guest was assigned a horse to ride. However,

*Frank and Ruth McGraw made the McGraw Guest Ranch a popular destination for Estes Park visitors for decades.*
Photo courtesy of Fran and Jay Grooters

the accommodations were hardly rustic, and the dining room offered good meals nicely served. Although the McGraws hired a cook to run the kitchen on a daily basis, Ruth managed the Ranch's three dining rooms and took over cooking duties herself one day a week. Frank pitched in too, often serving up the beef and beans at the Ranch's Thursday-night steak fries. In addition to Frank's beans, Ruth's "cowboy" cookies and "ranch" cinnamon rolls were signature menu items.

The McGraws were early risers, and personally greeted their guests each morning to discuss with them their plans for the day. By this time, of course, the wranglers had already eaten, for their days began at 4:30 a.m., and their breakfasts were served before any of the guests appeared. In his book Pedersen outlined a typical day's menu:

> *Breakfast was between 7 and 8 A.M., that consisted of pancakes, eggs any style, bacon or sausage or ham—or whatever the guest wanted*

*in the breakfast line. Lunch was at 12:30 P.M. and large helpings of homemade soup, freshly made pastry . . . was the fare. Dinner, served at 6:30 P.M., had chicken, turkey, great steaks, potatoes, vegetables, salad, juice appetizer, and those looked-forward-to ice cream sundaes.*[84]

The McGraws sold the ranch in 1973 but continued to run it for another seven years for the new owners.

The parents of five daughters, Ruth and Frank were well known and popular in the Estes Park community. Frank gave his moral and financial support to the Rooftop Rodeo and served a term as the president of the Estes Park Hotel Association, several terms as president of the Colorado Dude & Guest Ranch Association, and many years on the Larimer County Planning Commission. Ruth herself was active on library and hospital foundation boards and with the Elizabeth Guild and the PTA. She also enjoyed memberships in PEO, the Quota Club, and the Estes Park Woman's Club. Used to an active lifestyle, Ruth continued to ride, hike, snowshoe, and cross-country ski well into her eighties.

Today the McGraw Ranch is owned by Rocky Mountain National Park, which has kept the main portion of the ranch intact and completed extensive and authentic restoration projects. Since 1988, the fourteen buildings erected at the site from 1880 through 1948 have been listed on the National Register of Historic Places.

### McGraw Ranch English Toffee Squares
*(Ruth Hodson McGraw)*

1 c. butter
2 c. flour
1 c. brown sugar
1/2 tsp. salt
1 tsp. vanilla
1 egg

Mix thoroughly with electric mixer. Spread thin on 2 cookie sheets, each 12 x 18. Bake 15 min. 350° oven. As soon as out of oven, ice with frosting made of powdered sugar, cocoa and milk. Sprinkle with finely chopped nuts. Cut while hot.

## McGraw's Guest Ranch Cowboy Cookies
### *"An Old Dude Ranch Recipe"*
*(Ruth Hodson McGraw)*

Butter 1 cup, room temp
Brown sugar 3/4 cup, packed
Vanilla 1 1/2 tsp.
Baking soda 1 tsp.
Salt 1 tsp.
Oats 3/4 cup
Sugar 3/4 cup
Eggs 2
Flour 2 cups
Baking powder 1/2 tsp.
Chocolate chips 1 cup
Nuts 3/4 cup, chopped

Cream together butter and sugars. Add eggs and vanilla; beat well. In separate bowl, sift together flour, baking soda, baking powder and salt. Add a little bit at a time to the butter mixture, stirring well. When thoroughly combined and smooth, stir in chocolate chips, oats and nuts. Drop big spoonfuls (cowboys like their cookies very large in size) onto a lightly greased cookie sheet. Bake in a preheated oven at 350 degrees for about 15 minutes, until lightly browned. These may be frozen and thawed within minutes. Hide some away. They go fast!

## McGraw Flank Steak
*(Ruth Hodson McGraw)*

Honey 3 tablespoons
Ginger 1 1/2 teaspoons
Oil 3/4 cup
Vinegar 2 tablespoons
Soy sauce 1/4 cup
Flank steak 1 1/2 pounds scored diagonally

Mix honey, vinegar, ginger, soy sauce, and oil.
Pour over steak and let marinade [sic] 4 or 5 hours.
Cook on a hot grill for just a few minutes for rare meat. Longer if desired.
Cut into strips. Serves 4.

## McGraw Guest Ranch Cinnamon Rolls
*(Ruth Hodson McGraw)*

Yeast 3 cakes
Water 1 cup, lukewarm
Salt 2 teaspoons
Water 4 cups, boiling
Walnuts 1 cup, finely chopped
Brown sugar 2 pounds
Cinnamon 12 tablespoons
Vanilla 1 tablespoon
Powdered sugar 3 cups

Eggs 2
Sugar 1/2 cup
Shortening 1/2 cup
Raisins 1 cup golden
Flour about 5 lbs
Oleo 3/4 pound, melted
Frosting: Canned milk 1/2 cup
Oleo 1 cup, browned

Beat yeast, eggs, and lukewarm water until foamy. In a separate bowl, mix together 1/2 cup sugar, salt and 1/2 cup shortening. Pour four cups of boiling water over this mixture and set aside to cool. Add raisins and walnuts to the yeast mixture. Add enough flour to make a soft dough. Kneed [sic] and let dough rise once. Form it into a round ball. Combine brown sugar, 3/4 pound melted oleo and cinnamon. Roll dough to 1/2 inch thickness. Spread brown sugar mixture evenly over dough. Roll and cut into slices – 1 1/2 inches thick. Place slices on greased baking sheet about 3 inches apart. Let rise for 20 minutes. Bake in a preheated oven at 300 degrees for 30 minutes.

For frosting: combine canned milk, vanilla, one cup of browned and cooled oleo and powdered sugar. Beat or stir until smooth. Drizzle the frosting over rolls once they are removed from the oven. Note: This recipe makes enough to feed the whole ranch.

*Marge Machin in front of the Machin's Cabins office.*
Photo courtesy of the Estes Park Woman's Club

## Machin's Cabins in the Pines

In 1946, Marge and Ralph E. Machin moved to Estes Park from Manhattan, Kansas, with the idea of renting out cottages to the traveling public. Previously, the Machins had vacationed in the high country to escape the heat of Kansas summers. On these trips, Marge and Ralph often stayed at the Deer Ridge Chalet.

Machin's Cabins in the Pines, which continues to host tourists each summer, is unusual in that the property lies entirely within the confines of Rocky Mountain National Park. The Machins' small business began with a cozy 8' × 10' cabin, which the couple built soon after their arrival. Although it still stands in its original location, it has been enlarged three times over the years to five times the size of the original building.

Having decided to offer rental accommodations, the Machins soon added additional cabins to their little resort, either by building them themselves or purchasing adjacent properties. Today the resort offers seventeen cabins and cottages to visitors from all over the country. But the Machins' very first guests were Marge's parents, Chester E. and Bertha G. Pierce of Manhattan, Kansas, with whom the couple had lived for a time during the Great Depression.

Marge and Ralph were active in their adopted community, involved with a number of charitable and philanthropic organizations. A member of Eta Omega chapter of Epsilon Sigma Alpha, Marge also served a term as president of the Estes Park Woman's Club from 1961 to 1962.

## Marge's Rolls
*(Marge Pierce Machin)*

Crumble a cake of yeast into a bowl with 1/3 c. of warm water and a tbsp. of sugar.

Scald 1 c. milk and add 4 eggs, 1 tsp. salt and 1/2 c. sugar, beat and then add to the yeast mixture. Beat in 4 c. flour and add 1/2 c. real butter (melted). Add enough more flour to make a soft stiff dough. Do not knead. Let rise until double in bulk and then make into your favorite shape roll and let rise again, then bake in oven 450 degrees for 12-15 min.

### Grandma Carlson's Sugar Cookies
*(Marge Pierce Machin)*

2 c. sugar
1 c. sour cream
2 tsp. soda, or 1 1/2 tsp baking powder
1/4 tsp salt
1 tsp. nutmeg
3 eggs
1 scant c. lard or shortening
4 c. flour

Mix and roll thin. Cut cookies and bake 350 degrees until brown. Approx. 12 min.

### Fudge Brownies
*(Marge Pierce Machin)*

Beat 2 eggs, add 1 c. sugar, stirring in gradually. Add 1/2 c. melted butter or oleo, 2 sq. melted chocolate, 1/2 c. pastry flour–sifted and 1/4 tsp. salt. Beat well and add 1/2 c. oatmeal, 1 tsp. vanilla and 1/2 c. nut meats. Stir well.

Bake 1/4 inch thick in pan. Bake 20 min. at 350 degrees F. Cut while warm. Sprinkle with powdered sugar. Makes 24 cakes 1 1/2 inch square.

### Ice Cream
*(Marge Pierce Machin)*

Cook:  2 egg yolks, 2 c. sugar
       2 rounding tbsp. flour
       1/2 tsp. salt, with a qt. of milk

Cook until the mixture coats a spoon. Cool. 2 egg whites, stiffly beaten and add 1 pt thick cream, 1 tbsp. vanilla. Then add enough milk to fill a gallon freezer to within 3 inches of top. Mix well and freeze.

*The Fischer brothers of St. Louis built a new resort, called the Swiss Village, on the site of Enos Mills's Longs Peak Inn.*

Photo courtesy of the Estes Park Museum

## The Swiss Village

The Swiss Village was the successor to Enos Mills's fabled Longs Peak Inn. After Mills's death in 1922, his widow, Esther Burnell Mills, ran the Inn, trying to keep alive her husband's message of conservation and environmental stewardship. In 1946, she sold the Inn to Robert Loren Fagan and his wife, Irmel, who moved to Estes Park to run it. The Inn suffered a terrible fire in 1949 that destroyed the main lodge building. The couple was ultimately able to reopen the Inn, making use of some of the original structures. But in 1953, the Fagans sold the property to the Fischer brothers

*Swiss Village cabins featured scalloped trim along the roofline; the two-story structure on the right in the photo was a "leftover" from Mills's Longs Peak Inn.*

**Photo courtesy of the Estes Park Museum**

from St. Louis, who recreated the resort as a new hotel, which they called the Swiss Village.

During the next few years, a number of small cabins were built. Trimmed with scalloped edging along the eaves, the intent was to make the resort take on an "alpine," aspect; the main lodge, which featured a split-timbered and stucco façade and a clock tower, provided a lobby, guest rooms, a café, and a dining room. In spite of the resort's location at the base of Longs Peak, with its panoramic views of Meeker, Longs, and the Twin Sisters, the hotel failed to thrive.

*The dining room at the Swiss Village, c. 1955, was furnished with pine tables and chairs, typical of many Estes Park restaurants at mid-century.*
Photo courtesy of the Estes Park Museum

In 1972, Robert and Virginia Akins purchased the resort, and in 1975 they changed the name back to Longs Peak Inn. Ultimately the property was sold to the Salvation Army, and is now a family camp and retreat center for its members.

The Swiss Village survives today on picture postcards, in ads from back issues of the *Estes Park Trail*, and now, happily, in a wonderful recipe for wilted lettuce salad that was a contribution to *A Treasury of Famous Recipes from Estes Park* in 1965, by the recipe's creator, Paul Fischer.

## Swiss Village Kopfsalat Mit Speck (Wilted Lettuce with Bacon)
*(Paul Fischer)*

Rinse with cold water and drain well greens such as Romaine, Endive, and Iceberg lettuce (enough to make a <u>small head</u>). Pat dry and tear into pieces. Cover and chill in refrigerator. Hard cook and peel <u>1 egg</u>. Slice crosswise and set aside. Dice <u>6 slices bacon</u>, fry til crisp. Pour off fat and reserve.

Combine in a small skillet:

1/4 c. cider vinegar
1/4 c. bacon drippings
2 tbsp. sugar
1/2 tsp. salt
1/8 tsp. pepper

Heat mixture to boiling, stirring well. Add crumbled bacon. Immediately pour vinegar mixture over lettuce and toss lightly to coat greens thoroughly. Garnish with hard-cooked egg slices and pimento strips. Eat while hot!

*The entrance to the Work's resort off Fall River Road, in the 1960s; the resort has accommodated the traveling public at the same site for over half a century.*

Postcard courtesy of the Bobbie Heistercamp collection

## Workshire Lodge: The Work Family

In 1945, Virginia Hays "Pep" Work and her husband Jim[85] bought a rustic resort in Estes Park and launched their dream. The "resort" they purchased was the Blue Spruce Cabins, which had been owned for some years by Ron Smith, an old friend of Jim's from Fort Morgan, Colorado. Pep and Jim, who were married in 1934, had three children, Albert (Al), James (Jim), and Carol Ann. During the war years, the couple had been looking for an established business to buy, but their search had been stymied by gasoline rationing, which limited their ability to travel back and forth between their home in Denver and the mountains. With its location along the Fall River west of Estes Park, the cabin camp's setting suited the couple, even though the cottages themselves were very primitive.

In all there were six small cabins, three outhouses, and a shower house that also included a laundry. The two-bedroom "office" cottage that the previous owners had used as their home was just as rustic as the rest of the little buildings—its kitchen had a coal range and no hot water. Still, the Works were determined to upgrade the amenities. A pipe fitter with a job in Denver, Jim settled his family into their new home and then went back to the city, where he decided to keep his job in case the business did not prosper. During their first season as innkeepers in the mountains, Pep operated the cabins by herself with the assistance of her mother, Ethel Hays.

Neither Jim nor Pep liked the idea of a divided family, and after that first summer they sold their Denver home and Jim moved to Estes Park. During the next few years Jim took a number of local jobs during the winter and the couple ran the resort together during the summers. He later was co-owner and operator of the Mountain Home Plumbing and Heating Company.

Soon after the Works took over the little resort, they had a number of odd visitors—men who came by at night, asking for "Dad." Even though Jim and Pep explained that the property was under new management, the strange "visits" persisted for some time. Much later, a horse that had gotten loose and was running in back of the cabins literally fell into a deep hole. Upon close examination, it became clear that the "hole" actually held an underground still. The mystery of the nighttime requests for "Dad" had been solved!

In 1947, the Works changed the name of the resort to "Workshire," a reference to their Scottish lineage; the word "Lodge" was added sometime later. Jim and Pep continued to own and run the Lodge into the 1980s.

## Scalloped Corn
*(Donna Work)*

Saute 1/4 onion, chopped in
   2 tbsp flour
1/2 tsp. paprika
dash of pepper

Blend in 2 tbsp. flour
1 tsp. salt
1/4 tsp. dry mustard

Add one #303 can cream style corn. Sir in one egg slightly beaten. Pour in 1 qt baking dish, bake in oven 350 degrees 20 min.

## "Good Ol' Mrs. Work's Potato Salad"

*(Virginia R. Hays Work)*

4 medium size potatoes (preferably new potatoes) cooked in their jackets.
2 hard cooked eggs
1/2 teaspoon dried onion crisped in a tablespoon or so of cold water. (Add the water, too, when mixing the salad.)
1 teaspoon salt
2 tablespoons cider vinegar
1/2 teaspoon celery seeds
dash black pepper

Equal parts of mayonnaise and Miracle Whip Dressing to moisten (about two heaping tablespoons each).
Mix all together and let stand an hour before serving, if possible.
A few tips: Make the salad while the potatoes are still warm. The flavors seem to blend more. Always use real Miracle Whip—no other dressing has quite the same flavor. If the salad seems bland, add a little salt and a little more vinegar, sparingly, tasting until it seems right.

## Barbecue Beef

*(Virginia R. Hays Work)*

Cook a small pot roast.
Drain off all fat except about 2 T.
To drippings add 1 cup water, 1 cup ketchup, about 2 T vinegar, 2 T sugar, dash of cinnamon or four cloves, salt and pepper to taste, ½ tsp chili powder, 1 tsp prepared mustard. Simmer about ½ hour.
Add sliced meat. Heat. Leave meat in sauce as long as possible.

# Notes

1. A person suffering from tuberculosis.

2. Early in the 1890s Fergusons renamed their hotel The Highlands.

3. As long as he owned The Stanley Hotel, F. O. brought cash along with him from Newton to pay for any financial shortfall the hotel might sustain during the summer.

4. It should be remembered that by the time The Lewiston opened, the Estes Park Hotel was only a memory; it burned to the ground in 1911 at the hand of a disgruntled employee.

5. H. F. Pedersen, *Castles*, pp. 230–231.

6. Mr. Stanley himself was very food conscious; possibly his own health concerns made him sensitive to nutritional issues. As a recovering consumptive, Stanley relied on a high-protein diet consisting mainly of beef, eggs, and dairy products typical of the times. "According to some accounts, he typically dined on roast beef every night, followed by a tall glass of milk (as a teetotaler he was actually quite fond of milk)." James Merrick, Stanley Museum Archivist, Kingfield, Maine (personal communication, February 2012).

7. A. E. Sprague, *My Pioneer Life*, p. 138.

8. It is interesting to note that the original Rockdale Hotel was later expanded and acquired by A.D. Lewis, who renamed it the Lewiston Chalets. Today, a small portion of the original Rockdale Hotel survives as a part of Marys Lake Lodge.

9. The Ferguson children were: William Hunter (1851–1938), Anna R. (b. 1853), Mildred Frances (b. 1855), Sallie E. (1858–1954), Mary L. (b. 1864), and James M. (b. 1869). Horace V. (1861–1873) died of pneumonia before the family came to Estes Park.

10. Frederick Chapin, quoted in James H. Pickering, Carey Stevanus, and Mic Clinger, *Estes Park and Rocky Mountain National Park (Then & Now)*, (Westcliff Publishers, 2006), p. 150.

11. William L. Hallett eventually joined Ferguson in a ranching business, and also developed his own cattle operation. However, today he is best remembered for the prominent mountain that dominates Bear Lake, which Frederick Chapin (1852–1900), a noted author and early photographer, mountaineer, and amateur archaeologist, named Hallett's Peak in his honor.

12. *Rocky Mountain News* (August 27, 1882). Quoted in J. H. Pickering, *"This Blue Hollow,"* p. 121.

13. His oldest daughter, Anna, married Richard Hubbell in 1876.

14. Anna Louise (b. 1887), Mabel (b. 1889), Charles L., Jr. (b. 1891), Roland F. (b. 1895).

15. Sally Ferguson Reed. "Family Reminiscences of a Real Pioneer of Estes Park." In *A Pictorial History of Estes Park, Colorado.* (Estes Park, CO, 1968), pp. 33–34.

16. Robert Gookins, third cook at Longs Peak Inn in 1913. H. F. Pedersen, *Castles*, p. 81.

17. His energy and ideas soon brought him to the attention of President Theodore Roosevelt, who, sharing Mills's enthusiasms, asked him to become a "Government Lecturer on Forestry." Mills used this opportunity to promote his idea for a national park all over the country, a dream that came true in 1915, when Rocky Mountain National Park became a reality.

18. "A Brief History of Enos A. Mills." Available online at http://www.enosmills.com/historypg2.html (accessed September 26, 2013).

19. Mary Belle Totten, quoted in Pedersen, *Castles*, p. 83.

20. *The Hotel Monthly* (July 1910).

21. Alexander Drummond. *Enos Mills: Citizen of Nature.* (Niwot, CO: University Press of Colorado, 1995), pp. 130–131.

22. H. F. Pedersen, *Castles*, p. 81.

23. *Estes Park Trail* (July 6, 1912).

24. H. F. Pedersen, *Castles*, p. 82.

25. *Ibid.*, p. 83. As noted, Longs Peak Inn was remarkable for the clutch of cultural, political, and financial icons it hosted over the years, including Cornelia Otis Skinner, Douglas Fairbanks, Helen Keller, Frank Lloyd Wright, Eugene V. Debs, Lowell Thomas, and John D. Rockefeller, to name just a few.

26. A. Drummond, *Citizen*, pp. 131–132.

27. Raised in Estes Park by her mother and a beloved aunt, Enda attended Colorado College, the University of Colorado, and Pamona (CA), as well as the University of Denver. Before her marriage to Robert Kiley in 1946, Enda served in the Navy. Afterwards she worked for American Airlines and also helped her husband in businesses in Denver. The couple had four children.

28. Enda's name was misspelled on her birth certificate and her parents did not correct it.

29. A cabin, the Scottage, built by Charles Scott of Iola, Kansas in Moraine Park in 1898 still stands; it is situated between the Moraine Park Visitor Center and the William Allen White Cabin. The Estes Park Museum, the Estes Valley Public Library, and Rocky Mountain National Park have copies of *The Scottage, A Medley*, (an unpublished series of reminiscences written by Emerson Lynn, Carruth Scott, Angelo Scott, Dorothy Carnine Scott, and William Lindsey White).

30. J. H. Pickering, et al., *Then and Now*, p. 140.

31. J. H. Pickering, "*This Blue Hollow*," p. 158.

32. *Estes Park Trail* (September 5, 1914).

33. *Estes Park Trail* (August 6, 1913).

34. "H" for Husted, "G" for Livingston's sister, Helen Gates.

35. Ed Stopher went on to manage The Stanley Hotel for a time, before moving on to run hotels in Indiana and in Steamboat Springs. He was instrumental in persuading the Rocky Mountain Nature Association to publish his uncle Abner's memoirs.

36. *Mountaineer* (July 23, 1908).

37. Ed Stopher married Dorothy Eleanor Hansen Stopher (1917–1958) in 1941; the couple had two children. After Dorothy's death and Stead's was closed, Ed married Elizabeth W. Stopher (1924–2002), with whom he had four children.

38. S. F. Reed, *A Pictorial History*, p. 34.

39. H. F. Pedersen, *Castles*, p. 144.

40. The Scotts were neighbors of the Bitners in Boulder, where the Bitner family spent the winters.

41. In 1925, Harry Bitner took his own life.

42. *Estes Park Trail* (September 12, 1914).

43. Grace embarked on a somewhat nomadic odyssey that took her and the Ashton children east to Illinois and then to Massachusetts. She chose to homeschool the children, whom she thought would learn more from experiencing nature firsthand than from more formal in-school instruction. Grace brought the children back to summer in Colorado from time to time.

44. It is ironic to note that the only structure in Colorado that Frank Lloyd Wright personally designed was never built.

45. H. F. Pedersen, *Castles*, p. 91.

46. *Idem.*

47. *Joe Mills of Estes Park: A Colorado Life*, a new biography by James H. Pickering, was published in 2013 by the Estes Park Museum Friends & Foundation, Inc. Press.

48. H. F. Pedersen, *Castles*, p. 242.

49. The stove was eventually converted to gas, perhaps when the Crags reopened after War War II.

50. H. F. Pedersen, *Castles*, p. 243.

51. *Ibid.*, p. 247.

52. *Ibid.*, p. 248.

53. *Estes Park Trail* (July 21, 1921).

54. Quoted in James H. Pickering, "Introduction." *Joe Mills: A Mountain Boyhood*. (Lincoln: University of Nebraska Press, 1988), p. xli.

55. Patricia Yeager Washburn (personal communication, 2012).

56. *Estes Park Trail* (August 29, 1914).

57. H. F. Pedersen, *Castles*, p. 237.

58. *Idem.*

59. The Mace family consisted of William (1849–1933) and Mina Aitken (1854–1928) Mace and their sons: Stuart Garfield (b. 1882), Gordon McLeod (1884–1959), and Charles Eric (1889–1973).

60. William Mace had been trained in England under the tutelage of his own father, who had been a master carpenter.

61. J. H Pickering et al., *Then and Now*, p. 152.

62. Duncan Hines (1880–1959) was a traveling salesman from Chicago who used his decades of experiences of dining on the road to pioneer the practice of restaurant rating. In 1935 he turned the notes he had made over his career into a self-published book of recommendations, titled *Adventures in Good Eating: A Directory of Good Eating Places Along the Highways of America.* Restaurants that Hines considered "highly recommended" were entitled to hang a "Duncan Hines" sign to that effect, and the traveling public soon began to look for these when seeking restaurants in unfamiliar surroundings. Many also purchased copies of the book before leaving home and based their own travel plans, as well as lodging and dining decisions, on Hines' testimonials. In the 1950s he launched, with Roy Park, Hines-Park Foods, marketing a line of 250 boxed, bottled, and canned products under the Duncan Hines label. The company was later purchased by Procter & Gamble. Duncan Hines cake mixes can still be found on supermarket shelves.

63. *Estes Park Trail* (July 12, 1974).

64. *Estes Park Trail Gazette* (June 22, 1984).

65. Dan and Minnie March were married in Canada in 1890 and immigrated to the United States in 1896. The couple had no children of their own, although census records for 1900 indicate that they had adopted a little girl, Hannah Headley. By the time the Marches moved to Estes Park, she was no longer listed as a member of their household.

66. H. F. Pedersen, *Castles*, p. 147.

67. Service had come to the United States in 1882. Eight years later he married Sadie (1869–1931), with whom he had nine children (eight surviving). The family lived in a large frame house next to Sam's store on Elkhorn Avenue. When Service married Minnie March in 1935, she was sixty-six and he was seventy-four. For all the years thereafter until her own death in 1963 at the age of ninety-four, Minnie chose to use her full name, Minnie March Service, to honor both of her husbands.

68. Sam was a longtime resident and was related to a number of other pioneer families through marriage. A niece, Elizabeth Buchanan (1890–1980), eventually married Charles A. Chapman (1879–1951), Abner Sprague's nephew, and ran the Moraine Park Post Office. Sam's daughter, Rhoda Service (b. 1895), married Leland Tallant (b. 1893), son of local artist R. H. Tallant.

69. H. F. Pedersen, *Castles*, p. 156.

70. Some of his more colorful titles include: *The Six-Gun Code* (1932), *Hard Riding Slim Magee* (1929), *Hard Country and Gold* (1935), *Dusty Dan Delaney* (1930), and *The Two-Gun Kid* (1932). In addition, Yore wrote two brochures on Rocky Mountain National Park for the Burlington Railroad.

71. *National Magazine* (May 1918).

72. *American Magazine* (May 1918). New York: Crowley Publishing Co.

73. *Idem.*

74. Over time, Holzwarth's has been known variously as the Holzwarth Trout Ranch, the Holzwarth Trout Lodge, and Holzwarth's Trout Lodge.

75. The Holzwarths were the parents of three daughters and a son: Julia (1896–1967), Maria (1898–1919), Sophia (1900–1972), and John (1902–1983).

76. In fact, Colorado was one of the first states to go "dry," anticipating by three years the passage

of the Volstead Act in 1919, which banned alcohol nationally.

77. These included Ann and Enos Mills, Sr., the parents of Enos Abijah Mills.

78. J. H. Pickering, *"This Blue Hollow,"* p. 99.

79. Elkanah J. Lamb married Jemima Jane Spencer (1829–1917) in 1868, a month after the death of his first wife, Welta Jane "Hattie" Lamb. In addition to Carlyle (1862–1958), Hattie and Elkanah were the parents of nine children, five of whom lived to adulthood.

80. Robert James Gay (1877–1950); Bessie A. Henderson Gay (1872–1956).

81. Robert B. (1901–1975) and Helen Cornish Hutchinson (1904–1989) had two children, Robert B. III, born in 1930, and Mary in 1931.

82. Ruth was the daughter of George G. Hodson, a ranger in the National Park Service who served in both Glacier and Rocky Mountain National Parks.

83. H. F. Pedersen Jr. *"Rough It with Ease:" The Story of The McGraw Ranch*. (Estes Park, CO, 1990).

84. *Ibid*, p. 108.

85. Virginia R. Hays Work (1914–2002); James G. Work (1911–2001).

# Four: Estes Park Villagers

In the 1880s and 1890s, the little clutch of buildings and tents that began to appear at the intersection of two dirt roads near the confluence of the Fall and Big Thompson Rivers in the Estes Valley included only the home of John and Margaret Cleave, a post office, and a community building that served as church, meeting hall, and school. Further development of the village proceeded slowly, so that in and around the "Corners," as the area was locally known, early travelers had either to bring camping gear and foodstuffs with them or depend on the kindness of the area's pioneer families to provide a bed and a seat at the family table.

The site for a village was chosen by Cornelius Bond and his associates, who, in 1905, platted and sold lots along the two main roads. By that time, merchants had begun to establish small businesses to meet the needs not only of Estes's residents but also those of the growing number of flatlanders who arrived each summer. A hotel-building boom of sorts was launched by Josephine Hupp in 1906 with the opening of her first hotel; this was followed by the Manford in 1908 (which Hupp eventually purchased), the Sherwood Hotel and Prospect Inn in 1915, and the Josephine Hotel in 1916. Visitors could now enjoy complete meals and overnight accommodations downtown as well as less substantial fare in a growing number of tearooms, cafés, and confectionaries.

*Open-sided stagecoaches like this one, photographed on Elkhorn Avenue just after the turn of the last century, transported visitors to the mountains from the valley communities of the Front Range. The bumpy and dusty trip took most of the day.*

**Photo courtesy of the Estes Park Museum**

Although, as the heart of a resort community Estes Park's Elkhorn Avenue featured a spate of hotels, tearooms, cafes, and stables that catered to the needs of summer visitors, in other respects the dusty road resembled the "Main Streets" of other small towns with their storefront businesses, offices, and shops. Of course, in Estes many stores also stocked items for the tourist trade: Western clothing, hats, and gear; Indian pottery, rugs, and curios; and souvenir postcards.

Despite the rapid increase in businesses along Elkhorn Avenue after the platting of the Village, not all the structures on the main street were commercial entities. In addition to the Cleaveses' home, a large, two-story frame dwelling housed Sam Service and his family next to his store at the corner of Elkhorn and Virginia Drive.

*Chez Jay's art deco furnishings were intended to invoke the fictional Himalayan lamasery, Shangri-La, from James Hilton's classic novel,* Lost Horizon. *Its East Asian motifs and modern appointments provided residents and visitors an experience that was markedly different from the western cowboy style that dominated Estes Park in the 1930s and 1940s.*
Photo courtesy of the Old Estes Collection: David and Carol Tanton

Other families, such as the Macdonalds, Gooches, and Godfreys, lived in back of or above their respective shops.

With the coming of Riverside Amusement Park in 1923 with its Dark Horse Tavern, and the addition of the Chez Jay Café and Lounge a decade and a half later, nightlife also became a regular part of the Estes Park experience. Perhaps because most downtown pubs and restaurants, then as now, were comfortable and unpretentious, tourists and townies came to frequent their favorites many times during any given summer and year after year. As the years passed, many of these, like the Plantation Café

*Most downtown businessmen belonged to the Estes Park Rotary Club in the 1920s.*

**Photo courtesy of the Estes Park Museum**

(later the Old Plantation Restaurant), Roth's, Crowley's Café, and Coolidge's Café, developed local specialties and signature dishes, which made them memorable and enduring destinations for hungry visitors.

Because a number of the early shops were shoestring operations destined to fail when the mountain town's summer seasons were shorter than expected or the national economy flagged, the look of the town tended to change a little from year to year. However, many stores and restaurants survived to become local landmarks, with ownerships passed down in families for many decades. Thanks to the mountainous terrain and rock outcroppings, which effectively limited downtown development beyond the main thoroughfares, "many of the original buildings remain, altered by face lifts and remodeling to be sure, but recognizable all the same."[1]

*The congregation gathers for a group photo in front of the Presbyterian Church of Estes Park on Elkhorn Avenue about 1910.*
Photo courtesy of the Estes Park Museum

Perhaps for this reason, Estes's visitors and residents continue to feel nostalgic about the Village and its historic structures in ways that are unusual in a day when the new is so often embraced at the expense of the old.

This chapter brings together recipes from the families of early business owners, as well as those of popular eateries that flourished during the early and middle decades of the twentieth century. The first one included here is the time-honored scalloped chicken recipe created by the ladies of the Presbyterian Community Church of the Rockies in the 1930s. Still going strong more than one hundred years after its formal organization, the Community Church actually had its beginnings in the 1870s, when early residents met

*The Sunday school class poses on the steps of the Estes Park High School in the summer of 1933.*

**Courtesy of the Presbyterian Community Church of the Rockies**

in private homes on Sundays to sing hymns together and hear a sermon. In the years before the turn of the century, itinerant ministers, such as Elkanah Lamb and Albin Griffith, handled preaching duties. In 1907, the church was officially organized as the Presbyterian Church of Estes Park; the following year, the congregation purchased a lot on Elkhorn Avenue, and, using locally milled lumber and donated labor, completed the church building.

For many years the Presbyterian Church was the only Protestant congregation in town and, perhaps to reflect this reality, the church officially changed its name to the Community Church of the Rockies in 1952. The church was always well supported by the local residents and expanded as the need arose. Still, when in the summers the congregation swelled by many hundreds of people, services were moved to the high school auditorium. A new church, located on Brodie Avenue, was completed in 1982. As a remembrance of times past, the congregation carefully removed the stained glass windows that had been donated to honor the early church's parishioners and installed them in the new sanctuary. Likewise, the bell from the original church tower was placed in a bell tower made especially to receive it.

## Community Church of the Rockies Scalloped Chicken

*(Serves 10 to 12)*

Combine:

1 cooked chicken cut into small pieces
2 c. moist breadcrumbs
1 c. cooked rice
1 teasp. salt
1 small can pimento
2 egg yolks
1/4 c. broth plus milk to make 1 pt.

Fold in: 2 beaten egg whites.
Bake 1/2 to 3/4 hr. at 350° in a 9 x 13 inch greased pan.

### *Sauce:*

Melt 1 tbsp. butter in double boiler and stir in 1/4 c. flour until well blended. Gradually add 1 pt. of broth, stirring constantly.

Add:   1/4 tsp. salt
       1/2 c. mushrooms
       2 slightly beaten egg yolks
       1/2 tbsp. lemon juice

Continue cooking a few min. until thickened. Serve hot over warm squares of Scalloped Chicken.

*Julius Edward Macdonald's general store, located at the intersection of Elkhorn and Moraine avenues, originally belonged to Homer James.*
Photo courtesy of Estes Park Museum

## Macdonald's Store

Jessica Chapin Macdonald (1874–1957), the wife of J. Edward Macdonald, was born in Denver, the only child of Howard C. and Louisa Chapin, who had come west in 1877 from Massachusetts to manage Denver's Grand Central Hotel. In the 1880s, the family moved to Leadville, where Mr. Chapin (b. 1841) served as the manager of the Clarendon House Hotel. Built in 1879, the same year Leadville's Silver King, Horace A. W. Tabor, erected his Opera House, the hotel was a three-story structure with elaborate furnishings and appointments. The largest and arguably the most elegant hostelry and barroom in town, the Clarendon soon became a meeting place for Tabor and other mineral barons who had made their fortunes in Leadville's fabled silver mines.[2] Even though Leadville was booming—by 1884 the town would number 60,000

*About 1913, the Macdonalds moved their store further east on Elkhorn, into a building erected by Al Cobb. The Macdonalds' log home, which later became Jessica's bookstore, can be seen on the left.*
Photo courtesy of the Estes Park Museum

people—it still ranked as a wide-open Western town, where claim jumpers were publicly hanged, desperados patrolled the streets, and beer halls and dance parlors entertained customers into the wee hours of the morning.

After the death of her mother, Jessica Chapin and her father returned to Denver in 1900, where Howard's occupation was listed for a time as a gold miner, although he eventually resumed his career in hotel management. For her part, Jessica was a kindergarten teacher and then in 1903 the principal of a local school. During her first visit to Estes Park, she met Julius Edward "Ed" Macdonald (1861–1932), a widower who was thirteen years her senior. The couple was married in 1905, and three years later moved back to Estes Park and purchased a little log cabin that had been built by the Forest Service in 1907. Ed Macdonald then opened a hardware store at the corner of Moraine and Elkhorn Avenues. A

*Jessica Chapin Macdonald.*
Photo courtesy of Paula Steige

unique feature of the enterprise was a corner devoted to the sale of books.

Several years later, Ed built a new general store, which he operated with Ralph, his son from his previous marriage. Ralph and his wife Betty had moved to Estes Park from Denver with Ed and Jessica.[3] Jessica and Ed's daughters, Louise and Maria, were born in 1906 and 1908 respectively.

When Ed retired in 1928, Jessica opened a little book and gift shop in their home, further down the block on Elkhorn. So successful was she that soon the shop took over the entire first floor. Selling candles, cigars, candy, school supplies, office supplies, magazines, stationery, and books, Jessica's shop thrived, and she soon became known as "the little lady at the book store." In addition to operating her business, Jessica was a founding member of the Estes Park Woman's Club in 1912 and a member of the PEO sisterhood. She was especially proud of her membership in the Territorial Daughters of Colorado. One of her most prized possessions was a little locket given to her by Horace Tabor's wife, Augusta, when Jessica was a little girl in Leadville.

After Ed's death in 1932, Jessica continued to run the little store, living above the shop until her own death in 1957. The Macdonald Bookshop, an Estes Park icon and Elkhorn Avenue landmark, remains in the Macdonald family, now owned and operated by Jessica's granddaughter, Paula Laing Steige.

## Raspberry Shrub
*(Jessica Chapin Macdonald)*

Four quarts red raspberries, 1 quart vinegar. Put vinegar over berries and let stand for four days, strain through jelly bag. For each cup juice, add cup of sugar. Boil twenty minutes, bottle and keep in dry place.

---

## Hungarian Goulash (For Seven Persons)
*(Jessica Chapin Macdonald)*

| | |
|---|---|
| 1 pound lean veal | 1/2 pound lean beef |
| 3 tablespoons lard | 1 large onion |
| 12 potato balls | 6 small white onions |
| 6 carrot balls | 6 turnip balls |
| 1 teaspoon salt | 1 bay leaf |
| 1 whole clove | 1 chopped chili pepper |
| 1 teaspoon paprika | 3 cups boiling water |
| 2 heaping tablespoons flour | |

Slice the large onion and brown it in the lard. Remove onion and put in the meat cut in small pieces. When brown put meat in a baking dish, add paprika and boiling water and cook one and one-half hours in oven. Fry vegetables in hot fat and add salt, bay leaf, clove, and flour mixed with cold water, pepper and another cup of boiling water, and bake another hour and a half.

---

## Curry
*(Jessica Chapin Macdonald)*

Put 3 slices of bacon cut in tiny pieces into very hot frying pan. Add small amount of onions cut very thin. Mix heaping tablespoon flour and one teaspoon curry powder, add to bacon and onion. Add enough milk (if chicken is to be used) or meat stock (if veal or pork) to make a thick gravy. Put in a cup full of cooked meat diced. Add one cup of tomatoes and cook about half an hour. Serve with rice.

## Yorkshire Pudding
*(Jessica Chapin Macdonald)*

2 eggs
2 cups milk
2 cups flour
1 teaspoon baking powder

Beat the eggs until very light, add milk, flour and baking powder. Put three large tablespoons of the gravy into bread pan, and when boiling pour in the batter. Bake thirty minutes, cut into squares and serve around the roast.

## Scalloped Potatoes
*(Betty Marguerite Abildgaard Macdonald)*

Slice as many potatoes as needed. Put in covered baking dish, season with salt and pepper, cover with milk (Columbine milk diluted with water) and sprinkle with grated cheese. Remove cover when potatoes are soft and brown well.

*Fred Clatworthy's first permanent studio on Elkhorn Avenue in Estes Park. He moved the studio to another location in 1922.*
Photo courtesy of the Estes Park Museum

## Ye Lyttel Shop: The Clatworthy Family

As is true for so many residents both past and present, the Ohio-born, Colgate-educated Fred Payne Clatworthy (1875–1953) chose to settle in Estes Park after only a brief visit. In Clatworthy's case, his introduction had come on one of several bicycle trips he made as a travel reporter for a Chicago newspaper. Although he graduated from the University of Chicago with a business law degree in 1899, he decided to take up photography, the skills for which he acquired on his own. He was especially interested in photographing the mountain landscapes of the West, and soon began to experiment with Autochrome Lumière, a color process that had been developed in France. By the time he moved to Estes Park in 1905, Clatworthy was already an accomplished landscape photographer whose works had been widely published in East Coast magazines and in railroad advertisements.[4]

Clatworthy set up his first photographic studio in a tent on Elkhorn Avenue, but he soon built a proper darkroom where he could safely develop his photos. Eventually, he also opened the

Chapter Four: Estes Park Villagers   195

*Fred and Mabel Clatworthy on the steps of their home on East Riverside Drive in the Estes Village (n.d.).*
Photo courtesy of the Estes Park Museum

curio and souvenir store called Ye Lyttel Shop. Stocked with all kinds of items from stationery to Navajo rugs, the store was one of the first retail operations in town. Of course, he also offered a line of his own black-and-white, autochrome, and hand-colored photographs and postcards, and provided developing services to the growing number of amateur photographers who visited the mountains each summer.

In 1910, Fred met Sarah Mabel Leonard (1885–1971) in the Denver home of mutual friends. They were married the following year. The daughter of Dr. Harsey King and Ada C. Starkweather Leonard, Mabel had been born in upstate New York. Educated at Cook Academy, a private boarding school and college founded in the town of Montour, Schuyler County, New York, in 1872. Mabel's considerable interest in literature and music, and her love for the outdoors, might well have been due to the influence of her mother's family, which included Dr. J. C. Burroughs, the first president of the Old University of Chicago,[5] and John Burroughs (1837–1921), the famous naturalist. Although her prior experiences of mountains had been in the green and leafy Adirondacks, she soon fell under the spell of the Rockies, as had her husband not long before.

The Clatworthys' first home in Estes Park was a tent cabin which they occupied while their permanent residence was under construction. In addition to their own home, the couple built a number of guest cabins along the Big Thompson River. Fred and Mabel, with the assistance of Fred's mother, Emma Payne Clatworthy,[6] rented these cabins (Known as the Wigwam Cottages) to summer visitors. In the winters, the couple frequently traveled to California with their children: Fred Jr. (b. 1912), Helen Margaret (b. 1915), and Barbara Louise "Bobbie" (1921–2011).

Both Fred and Mabel were civic and social leaders of Estes Park during the opening decades of the twentieth century. Ever generous in their support of local clubs and groups, the Clatworthys

*Mabel Clatworthy posed for her husband's camera, fishing the Big Thompson River.*

**Clatworthy photo courtesy of Cheryl Pennington**

were noted for donating his photographs as prizes or premiums for charitable causes. Fred served as the town's second mayor. In addition, he invited the newly formed (1910/1911) Estes Park Business Men's Association to hold its meetings at his shop. In order to promote the town as a tourist destination, Fred singlehandedly convinced the Beta Theta Pi Fraternity to hold its national convention at The Stanley Hotel in 1921. His photographs also helped to promote the establishment of Rocky Mountain National Park.

Mabel was a charter member and officer of the Estes Park Woman's Club in 1912.[7] She also belonged to the Ladies Aid Society and the Estes Park Music and Study Club, activities that kept her equally busy with civic, charitable, and cultural endeavors. A contralto, Mabel's vocal talents were often on display at club programs and performances, as were her dramatic readings and recitations.

## Rhubarb Pie

*(Sarah Mabel Leonard Clatworthy, submitted by Bobbie Clatworthy Gish)*

2 3/4 C. Rhubarb (cut up)
1 Egg
1 Tbsp Lemon Juice
1 1/2 Tbsp Lemon Rind, grated
2/3 C Flour
1 1/2 C Sugar
1/4 tsp Nutmeg
1/4 tsp salt

Combine rhubarb, egg, lemon juice add rind (use almost one lemon complete). Blend together flour salt nutmeg and sugar, add to rhubarb mixture.
400 degrees for 10 min - reduce to 300 degrees
bake 40–45 minutes in favorite pie crust mix.

## Boiling Water Pie Crust

*(Sarah Mabel Leonard Clatworthy)*

1/2 cup shortening
1/4 cup boiling water
1 1/2 cups flour
Salt
Pinch of baking powder

Let cool.

```
- Clatworthy Studios -
ESTABLISHED 1905
PHOTOGRAPHS — DEVELOPING — PRINTING
COLORADO ALABASTER
```

*The ruins of Al Birch's stone house sit atop the Knolls above Elkhorn Avenue in Estes Park. The structure burned in 1907.*

Photo courtesy of Estes Park Museum

## Jacob's Ladder: The Home of Al Birch

Albert George Birch (1883–1972), whose stone and frame dwelling on the Knolls above the Village of Estes Park burned to the ground in December 1907, was a Washington D.C.–born newsman who joined the *Denver Post* in 1903. The following year, Birch purchased property in the little village he had visited the previous year and hired the local blacksmith turned stonemason, Carl Piltz (1867–1926), to build a house for him in the "rustic bungalow" style. The dwelling was unique in design and construction, and offered wonderful views of the mountains of the Front Range through the large windows that Piltz had installed in the structure's massive stone walls.

*Al Birch, in black hat, was a well-known summer resident of the Estes community as well as a publicist for the* Denver Post. *His original stone bungalow is now a ruin, but the summer cabin he built later survives to this day.*

**Photo courtesy of the Estes Park Museum**

Unfortunately, Birch had little time to enjoy his wonderful house, for Jacob's Ladder[8] caught fire shortly after it was built and burned to the ground. The cause may have been overheated wooden joists under the hearth catching fire on a particularly cold December night when a fire had been kept burning in the fireplace for many hours.

The following year, Birch built another cabin just north of the charred ruins of his home, which served as the family's summer retreat for more than seventy years.[9] The *Mountaineer* noted its construction:

*The new house will be less pretentious than the old one, and will be what Mr. Birch is pleased to call a workshop, where he will do his lit-*

*erary work this winter. The house is hidden among the rocks and trees, and requires a search to find it.*[10]

In addition to his remarkable ruin that still overlooks the Village, Al Birch is remembered for publicizing an elaborate hoax that involved passing off a young woman, in the guise of a "Modern Eve," as living in the wild within the confines of Rocky Mountain National Park. Park Superintendent Lewis Claude Way (1877–1920) ultimately confessed that he had devised the scheme as a publicity stunt, arranging to have "Eve" hidden away for the week at Fern Lake Lodge and enlisting Birch's help in sensationalizing the event in print.

In 1940 Birch married Phoebe Katherine Phillips, a woman thirty-two years his junior; six years later their daughter Briana was born. The couple moved to California for a time but eventually returned to Denver. Briana Birch contributed the following:

> *Here's a recipe for Succotash, a dish my mother used to frequently make for dinner at the cabin. I believe it was originally my father, Al Birch's, recipe. It was a hike to the ruins, up the steep steps carved into the rocks, and food needed to be minimal and nutritious. Succotash fitted the bill perfectly.*

## Succotash

*(Albert George Birch)*

1 cup corn
1 cup lima beans
butter
1/2 cup cream
salt and pepper

## Osborn's Garage

One of the "pioneer businesses of the Village"[11] was Osborn's Garage, which originally housed a fleet of Stanley Steamers that conveyed visitors from Loveland to Estes Park. The firm was founded by Daniel Obediah Osborn (1841–1926), an Illinois-born entrepreneur who had traveled west with his parents to Denver in 1860. Soon thereafter, Daniel enlisted in the 3rd Colorado Cavalry of the Union Army. His unit, which was retained in Colorado to guard against problems with the Clear Creek Indians during the Civil War period, eventually took part in the Sand Creek Massacre in November 1864. Osborn's role in the massacre remains unclear.

Mustered out of the army at war's end in 1865, Daniel moved back to Denver, where he remained until 1870, when he moved to Valmont. In Valmont, Osborn eventually met and, in 1879, married Sarah (Sadie) Murchland (1845–1885). The couple moved to Berthoud two years later. At that time he was engaged in farming, pioneering the use a steam plow, which was something of a novelty at the time.[12]

Daniel and Sarah were the parents of six children: five sons,[13] Will, Otto, Estes, Ralph, and Dellie, and a daughter, Dora Estela. Unfortunately, Sarah Osborn and her two youngest children died within sixteen months of each other in 1884 and 1885. The following year, Daniel, now a widower with four little boys aged one to nine, met and married Sarah C. Haley, and in 1895 he moved the family from Berthoud to Loveland. Interestingly, the couple had been active as parishioners in the Church of the United Brethren, whose pastor, Albin Griffith, summered in Estes Park.

In 1904, Daniel and sons Will, Otto, and Estes purchased the Estes Park Stage Line, which carried visitors up the Big Thompson canyon from Loveland to Estes Park in horse-drawn coaches. Within the next three years, the trio had transformed the stage line into a transportation company, the Loveland-Estes Park Auto Company, which operated five-passenger Stanley Steamers able to make the three-hour trip to Estes Park twice a day. The following year, the Osborns added three 9-passenger Stanley buses, making it possible to transport 100 passengers a day into the mountains. Then in 1909, twelve-passenger Stanley Mountain Wagons were added to the run.

While the addition of the mountain wagons marked a major improvement in transportation since the days when visitors were driven into the mountains aboard horse-drawn stagecoaches, the trip was not without its discomforts. In fact, passengers were at the mercy of the weather, as the Osborns' vehicles were open to the elements, without tops, side curtains, or windscreens. Still, the use of these vehicles made it possible to carry an estimated 3,000 passengers up the Big Thompson Canyon to Estes Park during the summer of 1909.[14]

> OPEN THE YEAR ROUND
> 
> **Osborn Garage**
> 
> PHONE 17-R2
> 
> Goodyear and Miller Tires
> 
> Exide Batteries and Charging Station
> 
> Chevrolet Parts Depot          Ford Parts

The Osborns continued to operate the business until they were bought out in 1916 by Roe Emery's Rocky Mountain Parks Transportation Company. They continued to manage the operation, however, and later took over F. O. Stanley's stage lines from Lyons to Estes Park as well. During this period, the series of tents that provided overnight housing for the Osborns' steam cars gave way to a huge, multi-lot concrete garage that was built on the upper end of Elkhorn Avenue.

While he was still living in Loveland, Daniel's third son, Lawrence Estes Osborn, married Bessie Alberta Charter (1883–1947), an Iowa native who had moved to Loveland with her family in 1900. The couple moved to Estes Park some few years later, where they became the parents of two children.

Estes Osborn operated Osborn's Garage in Estes Park for many years thereafter, but in 1923, he and Bessie decided to try their hands at fox farming, which they hoped would be the start of a new industry for the town. The farm itself consisted of a forty-acre tract west of the Village and south of Old Man Mountain,[15] and the initial stock consisted of four pairs of black silver foxes. Later, they added chinchillas. The business prospered, and within a year Estes had sold the garage in order to devote his full attention to the farm. Apparently a man of infinite interests, Estes later gave up fox farming and opened an art store on Elkhorn Avenue as a venue for his own paintings, mostly landscapes of scenes in Rocky Mountain National Park.

Although the fox farm idea seems not to have caught on as a commercial enterprise, Estes and Bessie were well known and liked in the Village, and helped the developing community through a variety of activities and projects. Estes was an avid golfer as well as an active member of the Chamber of Commerce. In 1923, he also joined Sam Service and Byron Hall on a committee that the Chamber charged with mapping the town and naming the streets.

As was true of many Estes Park matrons in the 1920s and 1930s, Bessie attended bridge parties and other social occasions on a regular basis. In addition, she was a charter member of the Estes Park Woman's Club, a member of the Ladies Aid Society, and a member of the local chapter of the PEO sisterhood. She and Estes were generous in their charitable support of the library building fund, and lent the garage as the setting for at least one of the Woman's Club's fundraising bazaars.

## Whole Wheat Muffins
*(Bessie Alberta Charter Osborn)*

3/4 cup white flour  
3/4 cup whole wheat flour  
1 heaping teaspoon baking powder  
1 tablespoon shortening (rounded)  

1 teaspoon salt  
1 egg  
1 1/4 cups sweet milk  

Sift dry ingredients together, add milk and beaten egg and lastly the melted shortening. Bake in muffin tins in quick oven about 15 minutes.

## Baking Powder Biscuits
*(Bessie Alberta Charter Osborn)*

2 cups flour  
1 cup milk  

1 heaping tablespoon Snowdrift  
1 teaspoonful rounding of baking powder  

Work the shortening, salt and baking powder into the flour, add the milk. Bake in hot oven.

## Sweet Potatoes Southern Style
*(Bessie Alberta Charter Osborn)*

Cut cold boiled or baked sweet potatoes cross way in half inch slices; cover bottom of dripping pan and spread thickly with butter, sprinkle with sugar and salt; place on each piece of potato 2 or 3 small pieces red pimento and dried currants. Bake 15 minutes.

*"This served on platter garnished with parsley makes a most attractive dish."*

## Preston's Garage

Although the Osborn's large garage came to dominate West Elkhorn Avenue, the Preston family was also involved in the automobile industry in early Estes Park. Harry Cornelius Preston (1872–1962), a Loveland blacksmith who moved to the Village at the turn of the century to establish an auto repair shop, became the local agent for Buick, Nash, Ford, and Dodge cars and sold used cars as well.

In 1895, Harry married Ada Mary Ream (1879–1908), and the couple had two children, John (b. 1897) and Glenard Harry (b. 1900). Two years after Ada's death, Harry married for a second time. His new bride was Mary M. Redman Brinkley (1870–1960), a young widow with two sons, George Earl Brinkley (1895–1920) and Bert Brinkley (1897–1933).

Preston's Garage was a Village landmark for thirty years, before it was replaced by Brodie's Market. In its day Preston's was a very up-to-date service station, handling auto repairs and selling gasoline. Preston's even provided a ladies restroom. As a public service, Harry maintained a lost and found for car parts retrieved in the Big Thompson Canyon, advertising a list of these items in the local paper. Harry served on the Larimer County Commission in 1913 when that body was planning the construction of Fall River Road.

Harry and Mary were very active in social and commercial activities in the Estes Park community during the 1920s and 1930s. In addition to raising four boys, Mary was a member of the Ladies Auxiliary of the American Legion, taught a Sunday school class at the Presbyterian Church, and supported the Woman's Club's library project with both monetary and book donations. The activities of the Woman's Missionary Society, for which Mary served as president in 1922, were many and varied. In addition to missionary outreach, the group also supported young matrons in the community. A headline featured in the *Estes Park Trail* in 1923 included an invitation to a unique party:

> *Babie's* [sic] *reception. Will all the babies please take notice.*
> 
> *On Friday afternoon at three o'clock at the home of Mrs. Harry Preston, the Missionary Society will tender a reception to all the babies of the community. Each baby is requested to bring its mother and as many friends as possible, for while the reception is the babies' own everyone else will be very welcome. Now let every baby keep this date*

*in mind, take the afternoon nap early and be present on the dot at this meeting.*[16]

Two weeks later, the *Estes Park Trail* provided a follow-up:

*Reception for mothers. The Missionary Society gave a reception to Estes Park babies October 19 and nineteen babies took advantage of the attentions heaped upon them that afternoon at the home of Mrs. Harry Preston. Now it is the wish of the society to honor the mothers of the community and Friday, November 2, a Mother's reception will be held at the Manse at 3 o'clock that afternoon. Every mother of the community should consider this notice an invitation to attend.*[17]

Harry and Ada Preston's second son, Glenard, grew up in Estes Park and worked at his father's garage until he met and married Leora A. Lewis (1899–1976), the daughter of Gus and Aneta Lewis, owners of the Lewiston Hotels. Shortly thereafter, Glen went to work for Leora's parents in the Lewiston Hotel Company. Active in politics as well as commercial endeavors, Glen[18] served a term as mayor, where he promoted a limited role of government and a business approach to town governance; his other activities included service on the Board of Directors of the Estes Park branch of the Colorado Mountain Club, which promoted skiing as a winter sport in Estes Park; he also helped install a skating pond in Bond Park. Finally, Glen supported the effort to purchase a warplane in 1943, the Estes Park Avenger, for which $113,000. was raised in just six weeks.

Leora, an active member of Chapter AV of the PEO sisterhood and the Women's Missionary Society, was also an avid bridge player. Leora and Glen were the parents of one son, Alvin "Jack" Preston (b. 1926). Both Leora and her mother, Aneta Lewis, contributed recipes to the *Tried and True Recipe Book*.

## Harvard Beets

*(Leora A. Lewis Preston)*

Wash 12 small beets, cook in boiling water until soft. Remove skins, cut beets in thin slices, small cubes or fancy shapes, using French vegetable cutter. Mix 1/2 cup sugar and 1/2 tbs. cornstarch; add 1/2 cup vinegar and let boil five minutes; add beets and let stand on back of stove one-half hour. Just before serving add 2 tbs. butter.

## Rich Cookies

*(Leora A. Lewis Preston)*

1/2 cup butter
1/3 cup sugar
3/4 cup flour
1/2 teaspoonful vanilla
1 egg well beaten
Raisins, nuts, or citron

Cream butter, add sugar gradually, egg, flour and vanilla. Drop from tip of spoon in small portions on buttered sheet two inches apart. Spread thinly with knife first dipped in cold water; put four Sultana raisins on each cookie. Almonds blanched and cut in strips or citron cut in small pieces.

*The Gooch family in 1910. From left, Edward, Ernest (seated), Carl, Julia and Harry.*

Photo courtesy of Michael Morris

## Gooch's Ready-to-Wear Shop

*"Outfitter for Mountain Vacations"*
— Advertisement, *Estes Park Trail*

Harry Augustus Gooch (1860–1918), a native of Braintree, Essex, England, immigrated to the United States in 1883,[19] settling with his wife, Julia Fincham Gooch (1855–1938), first in Illinois and then in Saratoga, Kansas. The first of the couple's three sons, Edward Augustus Gooch (1884–1966),[20] was born soon after their arrival in Saratoga. Edward was joined two and a half years later by a brother, Ernest Clifford Gooch (1887–1949). Shortly after Ernest's birth the family moved to Colorado, where in 1890 Julia gave birth to a third child, Carl Frederick Gooch.[21]

As a young man in England, Harry, who was the son of a "merchant traveler," had been trained as a draper's assistant. During his years in Denver he held a variety of jobs, at first as a bookkeeper and later as a clerk at Daniels, Fisher & Company Dry Goods store.²² After more than ten years in Denver the family moved to Loveland, where Harry purchased the Golden Rule Store in 1910. The Golden Rule was a retail operation, one of a chain of stores owned by James Cash Penney, who would later found the J.C. Penney Company. For a time, Julia was herself employed as a salesperson at the Golden Rule.

At the time of the Gooch family's move to Loveland, the town was undergoing a boom time as the regional hub for the manufacture and distribution of farm equipment in Larimer County. Edward and Carl went into business together there, owning a garage and car dealership. In 1907, Ernest went off to Colorado Agricultural College (later Colorado State University) to study chemical engineering. On June 13, 1913, Ernest married Alma K. Mulvaney (1890–1948), the daughter of Daniel and Maria McCarthy Mulvaney of Loveland.

At that time, Harry Gooch's health was beginning to deteriorate, and he and Julia decided to sell their Loveland store and move to a cabin near the little mountain community of Estes Park. After hearing that a small ice cream shop was for sale in town, they chose to invest in the property. Julia borrowed $3,000 from an Estes Park friend, the banker Charles F. Hix, and set up a shop on Elkhorn Avenue. The venture, which sold dry goods and clothing, was a success from the beginning. In fact, "Gooch's Ready-to-Wear Store" expanded quickly and within two years Harry and Julia purchased a more permanent building on the same block. During this time, the couple lived in an apartment behind the store.

When Harry died in 1918, Julia ran the store by herself until her son, Ernest, returned to Estes Park to take over operations.

*Alma Mulvaney Gooch, wife of Ernest Gooch, with the couple's daughter, June (c. 1919).*

**Photo courtesy of Michael Morris**

*Alma and "Ern" Gooch and Alma's sisters in front of Gooch's Sports Wear, 1940s.*

Photo courtesy of Michael Morris

At the time, "Ern" was working as a field engineer for General Electric in Schenectady. Months after Ern and Alma's daughter, June Elizabeth Gooch,[23] was born in 1919, the young couple left New York for Colorado.

Ern and Alma lost little time in expanding the Gooch store. In 1923, they completely remodeled the interior, buying out the other occupant of the building and using the additional space to store their increasing inventory. The building soon became known as "the Gooch building." The couple changed the name of the store several times, eventually settling on "Gooch's Sports Wear."

At the same time, the couple began contributing to the town as active members of the business and social communities. Ernest served as president of the Estes Park Chamber of Commerce and also captained his local bowling team. Alma was active in the Estes Park Ladies Aid Society. Ern and Alma were also enthusiastic Estes Park boosters, often donating prizes for local contests and consistently supporting the local library, which was built in 1922.

Alma Gooch passed away at her Estes Park home in 1948. Later that year, Ernest Gooch married a fellow Estes Park resident named Edna Morgan (1892–1969). Ernest and Edna remained in Estes Park until 1964 when Ern's health necessitated a move to Arizona, where he died in 1976.

## Nut Bread
*(Alma Mulvaney Gooch)*

1 egg
3/4 cup sugar
1 cup milk
2 1/4 cups of flour
2 tsp. Calumet baking powder
1 cup nuts chopped fine
1 tsp. salt

Beat eggs, add sugar and other ingredients. Let stand 20 minutes before putting in oven. Bake 1 hour in oven 325 degrees.

## Apricot and Cheese Molded Salad
*(Alma Mulvaney Gooch)*

Drain juice from two no. 2 1/2 size cans of best apricots. Run pulp through sieve. To half of the juice add enough water to make 1 quart, bring to boil and add 2 packages of lemon jello. Add pulp and let set until partly congealed.

Cheese Mixture: Whip 1/2 pint of cream and add 2 packages of Colorado cream cheese. To this add 1/2 envelope gelatin which has been soaked in 1/4 cup cold water for 5 minutes and dissolve in 1/2 pint of hot apricot juice and allowed to cool.

Molding: Before mixture gets too hard to mold, pour 1/2 pint apricot mixture into mold, let harden. Pour cheese mixture on this and when congealed add balance of apricot mixture. When completed you have a very colorful and tasty salad with a yellow layer on top and bottom with white cheese mixture in center. May be sliced or cut in squares and served with any good whipped cream salad dressing.

*Fern Lake Lodge was built amid a stand of lodgepole pines at the edge of the lake.*

Photo courtesy of the Estes Park Museum

## National Outing Company: The Higby Family

*"Cliff Higby, the all Year Guide. Anywhere, Anytime, Anyway."*
—Advertisement, *Estes Park Trail*

The Higby family made many contributions to early Estes Park, but their name may not be as familiar to contemporary residents as those of the Spragues, MacGregors, Macdonalds, or Millses.

Harry and Nina W. Higby[24] left their school teaching jobs in Schenectady, New York, in the 1880s to homestead in Manville, Wyoming. They were drawn to Estes Park by their sons[25] Clifford and Reed, who managed Fern Lake Lodge in 1914 for a Dr. Workman and who purchased the Lodge the following year. The pair were also involved in a variety of other activities over the next decade, including a stint as managers of the Hupp Hotel. Another venture was the National Outing Company, located on Elkhorn Avenue, which not only included a taxidermy museum, with stuffed animal heads offered for sale, but also sold camping and hiking equipment and a line of ladies' clothing that included

*A feature unique to the Fern Lake Lodge dining room was a large round table, the center portion of which revolved. Meals were served family style, with shared dishes, condiments, and utensils placed on the central "lazy susan." Rotating the "susan" eventually put all dinner items within easy reach of each diner.*

Postcard courtesy of the Bobbie Heistercamp Collection

furs and sweaters. While Nina was in charge of running the store, Clifford conducted tours through the National Park, northern Colorado, and southern Wyoming. His byline, which appeared in the store's ads, read: "Cliff Higby, the all Year Guide. Anywhere, Anytime, Anyway."

Harry was not often in Estes Park during those years, having elected to remain in Wyoming to run a ranch.[26] However, Nina took an active role in Estes Park activities, which included the Music and Study Club, the Ladies Aid and Missionary Societies, and the Community Church of the Rockies' prayer group and youth programs.[27] That Nina was a profound influence in the lives of both Cliff and Reed is evidenced in their participation, along with their mother, in the Community Church, for which Cliff served as a trustee and Reed as clerk.

*Clifford Higby was a man of many talents and interests. An avid outdoorsman as well as a resort owner and writer, he later became an ordained minister.*
**Photo courtesy of the Estes Park Museum).**

In 1916, Cliff Higby married a young widow, Frances DeVol Wood (b. 1883), whose son, Edward DeVol (b. 1905), Cliff adopted and came to consider his own. About 1918, Cliff became affiliated with the YMCA, and, with his family, traveled to Europe as the organization's representative. The family lived in Milan from 1919 to 1921, during which time Edward attended school and Frances took voice lessons. Upon their return, both Cliff and Frances shared their considerable talents with the Estes Park community.

Cliff served as scoutmaster for the local Boy Scout troop, in addition to writing pieces for a brochure describing hiking paths in Rocky Mountain National Park for the National Park Service and articles for the local newspaper. He also assisted with backcountry search and rescue operations. "A student of nature and human nature,"[28] Cliff purchased half interest in the Rocky Mountain Boys Club on Cow Creek in 1923, a program founded by John Timothy Stone.[29] Frances, whose voice was described as "exquisite,"[30] sang in church and performed operatic pieces by Puccini and Donizetti for programs of the Estes Park Woman's Club and the Estes Park Study and Music Club, of which she was a member. She also served a term as president of the local Parent Teacher's Association. Trained as a bookkeeper, and employed for a time by the National Park as an information clerk, Frances was an early proponent of founding a local museum for Estes Park.[31]

All three Higby brothers were active in promoting winter sports in Estes Park. One activity was the installation of a skating pond in Bond Park. However, this initiative was emblematic of a much broader vision that involved creating a winter industry that would bring visitors to Estes Park in the "off-season" every year. To this end, Cliff Higby and the Estes Park Outdoor Club made overtures to the directors of the Colorado Mountain Club to visit

*Eunice and Reed A. Higby on the steps of Moraine Lodge.*
Photo courtesy of the Estes Park Museum

Fern Lake Lodge, with the idea of promoting the site as the center for skiing, snowshoeing, and other outdoor activities. And so a tradition was born. Until 1934, an outing to the Fern Lake Lodge cabin was a Colorado Mountain Club annual event. Cliff was also a founding member of the Colorado Ski Club.

## Molasses Cookies
*(Nina Wright Higby)*

1 cup molasses
2/3 cup sugar
1 cup hot water
1/2 cup shortening
1 egg
2 level teaspoons soda
1/2 teaspoon each of ginger and cinnamon
Flour to stiffen enough to handle.

*In the 1930s, the Deer Ridge Chalet was located on Fall River Road just east of the entrance to Rocky Mountain National Park.*

Photo courtesy of the Estes Park Museum

## Deer Ridge Chalet

The history of Deer Ridge Chalet began in 1915 when Orville W. Bechtel (1892–1964) built a store catering to summer tourists. Bechtel sold his own photographs, along with film and processing services for amateur photographers. Eventually he added a small guest lodge, cabins, and a snack bar. The site he chose for his store was scenic Deer Ridge, within the confines of Rocky Mountain National Park.

In 1925 a widow, Emma Schubert of Roggen, Colorado, purchased the 224-acre property and Bechtel's business. Emma, called Bomma, had seven hard-working children who helped her run the little resort. Bomma's timing was fortuitous, as the tourist traffic that passed Deer Ridge on its way into the Park greatly increased with the completion of Trail Ridge Road in 1932. To take full advantage of this turn of events, the Schuberts added a liv-

*Toots and Bert Schubert at the front entrance of their family's business in 1934.[32] Toots handled the cooking, while Bert managed the store.*
                    Photo courtesy of the National Park Service

ery, a kitchen, and dining hall, offering "good home cooking" produced on a coal stove by Bomma's daughter Adele, called "Toots." The observation tower, with its magnificent Front Range views, soon became a local landmark. The Schuberts worked closely with

*The dining room at the Deer Ridge Chalet featured knotty-pine furniture and a collection of beautifully detailed models of covered wagons.*
Postcard courtesy of the Bobbie Heistercamp Collection

Charles Eagle Plume to identify and stock authentic Indian artifacts in the gift shop, and he often brought rugs down from his own shop on Highway 7 to sell from the Schuberts' porch. Four of the children—Emil, Bertha "Bert," Anna, and "Toots"—took over ownership of Deer Ridge in 1927.

Initially, the guest cabins at Deer Ridge were very primitive. Although each one had a wood-burning stove for heat, there was no indoor plumbing, and guests were obliged to use a common outhouse and a common shower housed in a separate building. (It was widely "rumored that Berta and Toots had a portable bathtub secreted away for their personal use."[33]) In 1945, when Emil, Bert and Toots sold the business to their youngest sibling, Edward, his wife Eleanor took over the kitchen duties.

In its prime, the Deer Ridge Chalet "campus" included—in addition to the viewing tower, livery, and high-quality gift shop—a rock shop, a miniature train, a white-tailed deer herd, a hairdressing salon, and the Covered Wagon Dining Room, famous for its oversized cinnamon rolls, popovers, and chicken pot pie.

By the late 1950s, Ed's sister Pat Schubert Webermeier and her husband John joined the family business, and in 1960, after Deer Ridge Chalet and most other private commercial in-holders in the Park had been evicted by the National Park Service, the family relocated their business to the Fall River Entrance of the Park, and named it the National Park Village.[34]

Four generations of the Schubert family have served the community, and many of Estes Park's young people had their first jobs bussing tables or working as waitstaff in the Chalet's dining room.

## Lemon Freeze

*(Eleanor Schubert)*

3/4 cup KELLOGG'S Corn Flake Crumbs
2 tbsp sugar
1/4 cup butter or margarine, melted
2 eggs separated

1 can (1 1/3 cups) BORDEN'S EAGLE BRAND SWEETENED CONDENSED MILK
3 tbs sugar
1/3 cup fresh or bottled lemon juice
1/2 tsp grated lemon peel

Combine Corn Flakes Crumbs, 2 tbs sugar, and melted butter in 8 in pie pan or ice cube tray, mix well. Remove 2 to 4 tbs crumbs mixture and reserve for topping.

Press remaining crumbs mixture in firmly around sides and bottom of 8 in pie pan or in bottom of ice tray.

Beat egg yolks until thick and lemon colored; combine with Eagle Brand Condensed Milk. (It's a special blend of whole milk and sugar.) Add lemon juice and lemon peel; stir until thickened.

Beat egg whites until stiff but not dry. Gradually beat in the 3 tbs sugar. Fold gently into lemon mixture.

Pour into Crumb-lined pan; sprinkle with reserved Crumbs.

Freeze until firm. Cut pie into wedges or bars to serve. Yields: 8 servings.

# Sweet Bread Dough (Cinnamon Rolls)
*(Eleanor Schubert)*

1 cup cream
2 tsp. salt
2 cups milk (luke warm)
7 egg yolks + 1 whole egg
2 pkgs. dry yeast dissolved in 1/2 cup water with 1 tsp. sugar
3/4 c sugar
1/2 cup butter or oleo
1 tsp. vanilla

Beat egg yolks + 1 egg with sugar, add cream, milk, butter, vanilla, and yeast mixture. Add 8 or 9 cups of sifted flour to make a soft dough. Cover, let rise in warm place until double in size. Work down and let rise again til double. Then shape into various rolls + coffee cakes.

Makes 3 to 4 dozen cinnamon rolls, depending on size.

For cinnamon rolls (filling): Roll out dough + spread with melted butter. Sprinkle generously with cinnamon-sugar mixture. (1 cup sugar to 3 tsp. cinnamon.)

Roll up tightly and cut into 1 to 1 1/2 inch pieces. (Raisins can be added before rolling.)

Place side by side in pan. Let rise about 20 min. Bake at 350 degrees for about 20 min. till golden brown.

*Lora and Dugald "D. F." Godfrey and their dog pose in front of their original home in Estes Park in 1927.*

Photo courtesy of the Estes Park Museum

## Godfrey's DeLuxe Store

*"We've been in Estes Park for a long time, have tried to make it a better town to live in, and we believe Estes Park folks know they can trust us, and depend on us for square service."*

—Advertisement, *Estes Park Trail*

The store the Godfrey family founded in Estes Park served residents and visitors to the Village for more than twenty years. Dugald Floyd "D.F." Godfrey (1882–1941) was born in Ohio. Orphaned at an early age, D.F. was raised by his aunt and uncle and attended Dennison University before becoming a school teacher. He moved to Colorado in 1911, where he met and married Lora Lee Byrant (1891–1977) of Denver in 1918. The couple moved to Estes Park and opened a store the following year.

*Godfrey's store on Elkhorn Avenue in 1925. The store carried men's and women's clothing as well as western wear.*

Photo courtesy of the Estes Park Museum

Godfrey's store occupied the first floor of the Josephine Hotel on Elkhorn Avenue,[35] and shared the space for a time with the *Estes Park Trail*. During this period, the newspaper used the store's front windows to post "time-sensitive" news items, in particular, the scores of baseball and college football games. In addition, D. F. sometimes worked as an editor.

Godfrey's was primarily a clothing store, and as such it carried a wide variety of apparel. From the many and various advertisements that appeared in early editions of the *Estes Park Trail*, it is evident that the store featured men's and women's "ready-to-wear;" fishing, hunting, and western wear; sporting equipment; dress shirts; shoes; hats; and Vanity Fair lingerie. In 1923, the Godfreys added phonographs and records to their inventory, and the following year they initiated a pre-season sales promotion that promised "post season prices." Both Lora and D. F. worked in the store, running a laundry and cleaning business alongside their retail operation. When the Godfreys decided to expand their store in 1925, it was front-page news.

In addition to their efforts at the store, both D.F. and Lora Godfrey were active participants in the social and civic activities in town during their Estes Park years. Both played bridge, and their names were often listed among attendees at bridge gatherings large and small. Lora was a member of the Estes Park Woman's Club, serving as its president in 1925–1926. She was also a member of the Ladies Aid Society, headed up Red Cross drives for the Presbyterian Church, and served as an officer in Chapter AV of the PEO sisterhood. In addition, she took on the position of town librarian for a time in 1923. A partial list of D.F.'s local commitments included the Chamber of Commerce and the Presbyterian Church, for which he served as Church clerk, elder, trustee, and superintendent of the Sunday School.

Both Lora and D.F. were acknowledged Village boosters. Their store served as a "lost and found" for the town and as a collection site for used clothing during various civic fundraising activities. The Godfreys used ads in the local paper to state publicly their belief in the town and in their perceived role in its economic development: "we believe in the future of Estes Park, its people, its institutions, and all its enterprises," one ad ran. In another, Lora and D.F. described their civic responsibility in this way:

> *Godfrey's of Estes Park. Not just "Estes Park" but "of Estes Park"—There's a difference. When you boost your town, back up its enterprises, and its charities, and plug for its progress, you become a part of it.*[36]

## Mint Sauce

*(Lora Lee Bryant Godfrey)*

1/4 cup vinegar (not too strong)
2 teaspoonfuls powdered sugar
1/4 cup chopped mint leaves.

Combine and allow to stand until well blended. Strain and serve with roast lamb.

## Sour Milk Waffles

*(Lora Lee Bryant Godfrey)*

2 eggs (well beaten)
2 cups sour milk
2 cups flour
1 teaspoonful soda
2 teaspoons baking powder
1/4 teaspoonful salt
2 tablespoonfuls butter (melted)

First beat eggs, stir in milk and flour in which the soda and baking powder and salt has been sifted. Add melted butter and beat thoroughly.

## Asparagus with Cheese Sauce

*(Lora Lee Bryant Godfrey)*

2 cups milk
4 tablespoonfuls flour
Salt and pepper to taste
1 cup grated cheese
1 can asparagus
Chopped pimentos

Rub milk and flour together, add a little water, cook until smooth and add salt and pepper; slowly stir cheese and beat until smooth. Heat asparagus, arrange on slices of toast, garnish with pimentos and pour cheese sauce around toast, with just a tablespoonful on each slice. (Good substitute for meat.)

*The Estes Park Music and Study Club meeting at the National Park Hotel.*
Photo courtesy of the Estes Park Museum

## Lindley & Son, Estes Park Plumbers

Elmer D. Lindley (b. 1862) arrived in Estes Park from Illinois before 1910, a widower with several children, including Robert Henry Lindley (1896–1960). Although Elmer seems to have been a janitor back in Rockford, in Estes Park he founded a plumbing firm that handled the installation of water systems and bathrooms for commercial and residential enterprises. Given the building boom in Estes Park between his arrival and the 1920s, Elmer ended up running a very successful business. By 1921, his son Robert had joined Elmer in Lindley & Son, Estes Park Plumbers.

In 1921 Robert married Mary R. Piel (1893–1978), a woman four years Robert's senior. Their union, though childless, seems to have been a happy and productive one. Robert, who served in the Marines from 1918–1919, was a charter member of the local chapter of American Legion and had a hand in numerous building projects in and around Estes Park. Mary was active in many social and civic groups, including the library building committee of the Estes Park Woman's Club, the Missionary Society of the Presbyterian Community Church of the Rockies, the PEO sisterhood, and the American Legion Auxiliary. Mary was also an officer and frequent hostess for the Estes Park Music and Study Club. A knowledgeable woman with both literary and musical interests, Mary was also a brilliant storyteller, a talent marked by the newspaper's account of a program she presented to the Club in 1921: "Mrs. Lindley held the audience spellbound," the paper opined, "with [stories of] the weird traditions of castles on the Rhine River."37

### Ham en Casserole
*(Mary R. Piel Lindley)*

Peel and slice 3 or 4 medium-sized potatoes. Place in sauce pan, salt to taste and let simmer for 15 minutes.

Cut one fairly thick slice of smoked ham into squares about one inch. Chop fine half an onion. Butter casserole; place layer of hot potatoes on bottom, then add layer of ham and sprinkle over with chopped onion; then another layer of potato and one of ham. Add butter size of teaspoon, cover with milk. Bake in moderate oven 45 minutes.

### Golden Corn Bread
*(Mary R. Piel Lindley)*

1 cup yellow corn meal
1 cup flour
4 level teaspoonfuls baking powder
3 tablespoonfuls sugar
1 teaspoonful salt
1 1/2 cups milk
1 egg
2 tablespoonfuls shortening.

Mix and sift the dry ingredients; add milk, beaten egg, and melted shortening; beat well and pour into greased shallow pan. Bake in hot oven about twenty-five minutes.

## Apple Custard

*(Mary R. Piel Lindley)*

Six medium-size apples
2 cups boiling water
1 pint scalded milk
1 tablespoonful cornstarch
1/2 teaspoon extract lemon
1 cup sugar
3 cloves
2 eggs
1/4 cup sugar

Mix 1 cup sugar and water and heat to boiling point. Add cloves. Peel and core apples and drop them into boiling syrup; cook slowly until the apples are tender, but not broken. Lift to a serving dish and cool. Boil down the syrup one-half and pour over apples. Mix cornstarch and 1/4 cup of sugar with beaten eggs. Add scalded milk slowly and cook until thickened and smooth. Remove from fire, cool, add flavoring and pour around the apples. Garnish with a little bright colored jelly.

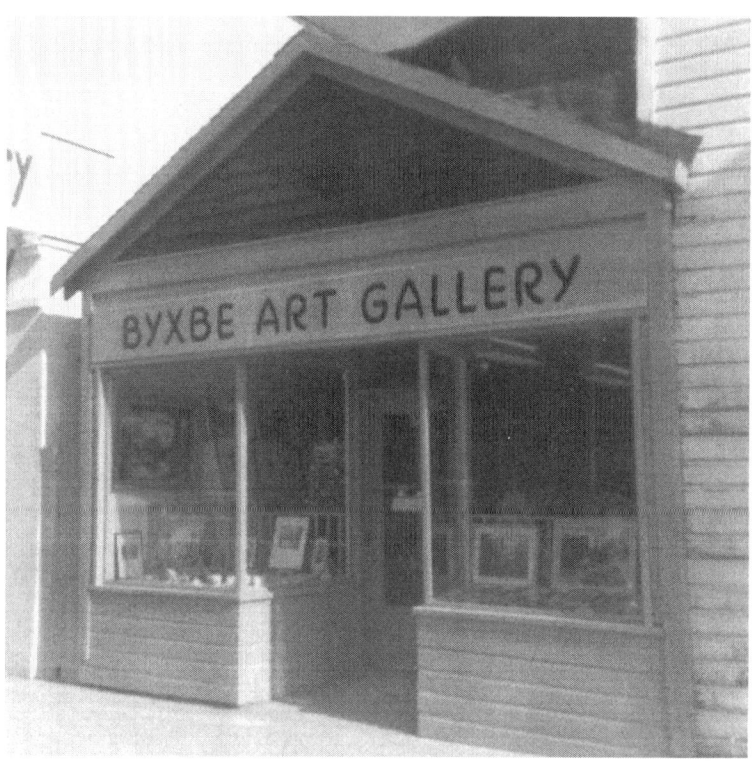

*Byxbe's Art Gallery on Elkhorn Avenue.*
Photo courtesy of the Estes Park Museum

## Byxbe Art Gallery

Henry Lyman "Byx" Byxbe (1886–1980) was a prolific watercolorist, oil painter, and sketch artist, whose talents for etching and printmaking were as widely known and appreciated in his lifetime as they are today. The Byxbe family, which consisted of Lyman's wife Geneva and their daughter Alice, began summering in Estes Park in the 1920s, making the long and dusty drive from Omaha to the mountains each year. During the early years, Byxbe considered these trips working vacations, during which he continued to create etchings and woodcarvings that he sold through local gift shops. On at least one occasion, he hung and sold prints from a clothesline near the shops on Elkhorn. By 1935, however, Byxbe had set up a summer studio in Estes, which his wife ran when he was away. His dream was to make a living in the mountains he loved by marketing his prints, paintings, and sketches directly to the traveling public. At this the Byxbes were ultimately successful. In fact, by

1951, the couple owned two large retail operations on Estes Park's main thoroughfare.

Born in Illinois, Byxbe had first worked for a newspaper in Bloomington until 1909, when he enlisted in the army. One of his first assignments took him to Omaha, where he met Geneva Mildred Blackwell (1893–1971). The couple was married in Council Bluffs, Iowa, in 1911 and chose to make Omaha their home. Lyman worked as a clerk and as a bookmaker before he was able to find a job as a commercial artist. Later, he taught commercial art and etching at a local technical school. During those years, Byxbe drew inspiration for his etchings from the city, from his rural surroundings, and from sites visited on vacations—especially the Rocky Mountains.

From an early date, Byxbe was recognized for the excellence of his prints. During the Depression he participated in projects for the Public Works Administration (WPA), and in 1937, the Smithsonian Institution honored Lyman with a one-man show.

*Lyman Byxbe sketching near Estes Park in 1920.*
Photo courtesy of the Estes Park Museum[38]

Geneva Byxbe was a woman of varied talents and interests. While at the University of Nebraska, Geneva had learned how to raise White Leghorn chickens, an avocation that she pursued while the young couple was living in Omaha. Eventually, Byx needed the chicken coop for a studio, so Geneva moved the chickens into the basement. In Estes Park, she assisted her husband and his business in a variety of ways, for example, as timekeeper and quality control for the business. In addition, while Lyman continued to produce exquisite etchings of the mountains that surrounded the town, Geneva, known familiarly as "Ma," participated in the printmaking by hand tinting Lyman's prints with oil paints. Indeed, printmaking at the Gallery was a family affair. The Byxbes worked together in the artist's workshop, while their daughter Alice (1912–2006)[39] and her husband Rudolph F. "Rudy" Anspauch (1923–1996) ran the shop on Elkhorn Avenue. Alice, who had married Rudy in Greeley in 1947, also often helped her father in his studio. In addition to handling Gallery sales, Rudy took over

Chapter Four: Estes Park Villagers     229

the task of making prints from Byxbe's small (3.5 × 5 inch) plates so that Lyman could concentrate on oil painting.

Because Byx never did learn to drive safely, Geneva and daughter Alice took over driving duties on their trips to and from Nebraska, and around the Village as well. Apparently, Geneva also drove her husband to sketching sites inside and outside Rocky Mountain National Park. In his *Catalog Raisonné*, Byxbe biographer Robert Crump provides an anecdote of one such outing: "The single-lane dirt roads had only an occasional passing spot," Crump recalls

Ma Byxbe worked with her husband in his studio hand-coloring his etchings.
Photo courtesy of the Estes Park Museum Friends & Foundation, Inc. Press

*Ma would stop the car and let Byx out to sketch, and then, since rock slides were common . . . she would go back up the road with a flag to hold up traffic, telling the other motorists that 'there's a little problem up ahead. I'll come and tell you when it's OK,' so that Byx could finish his sketch without being run over. The other motorists thought that it was just another rock slide and Byx or someone was clearing it.*[40]

Geneva Byxbe was a delightful woman with a keen sense of humor, who was not above dressing up as a cave woman when circumstances dictated. In addition, she was widely considered a talented cook. At times when the couple was particularly busy, Lyman hired local people to help with the hand-coloring process and with printmaking. Coyt Hackett was one such employee, who, writing in 1990, extolled Ma's culinary skills as well as the atmosphere that permeated the workplace they all shared:

*When we worked at the house I was the only employee and I would bring my lunch, but it was often scrumptiously supplemented. Byx had diabetes and was supposedly limited on what he could eat. On the other hand Mom loved to bake so there was many a morning that our labors over the presses were enriched by heavenly odors from Mom's kitchen. Of course I knew I would be the beneficiary and Pop knew he wouldn't! Her pecan pie was beyond belief. She would also share secrets with me—always put an egg yolk in the pie dough and the crust would be extra flaky.*[41]

## Byxbe Canapé
*(Geneva Mildred Blackwell Byxbe)*

2 cans sardines [drained]
vinegar to taste
4 tablespoons of Wesson Oil
salt and pepper to flavor

6 tablespoons water
7 crackers finely crushed
3 shakes paprika

spread on buttered crackers or toast

## Walnut Brittle
*(Geneva Mildred Blackwell Byxbe)*

6 cups walnuts
12 tablespoons sweet milk

2 cups sugar
1 teaspoon vanilla

Cook sugar and milk to a thread add vanilla and stir in nuts.

## High Altitude Devil's Food Cake
*(Alice Byxbe Anspauch)*

1/2 cup shortening-minus 2 tbsp.
1 1/2 cup sugar minus-5 1/2 tbsp.
2 eggs (cream this till like whipped cream).

2 cups flour
1/2 cup cocoa
1/2 tsp salt

Dissolve 1 tsp. soda in 1/2 cup plus 2 tbsp. sour milk
(Just barely mix with creamed mixture).
Add 1/2 cup boiling water all at once and mix quickly.
Vanilla
Bake in layers 30 min. at 350 degrees. If electric mixer is used, add flour by hand.

## Never Fail Pie Crust
*(Geneva Mildred Blackwell Byxbe)*

1 1/2 cups flour
1/8 teaspoon salt

1/2 cup shortening
1 egg yolk beaten in 1/4 cup of milk

Makes 2 crust pie.

## Fluffy White Frosting
*(Alice Byxbe Anspauch)*

1 cup sugar   1/2 cup water   1/4 tsp. cream of tartar

Boil til threads and pour over 3 egg whites beaten very stiff. Add vanilla.
*"This frosting will never get hard"*

## Delicate Fluffy Pancakes
*(Geneva Mildred Blackwell Byxbe)*

3 eggs   1 2/3 cups buttermilk
1 tsp soda   1 1/2 cup sifted flour
1 tsp. baking powder   1 tbsp. sugar
1 tbsp. melted shortening.

## Byxbe Noodles
*(Geneva Mildred Blackwell Byxbe)*

2 egg yolks   4 tbsp. cream
Flour to make a stiff dough.

Roll out on floured board, flour lightly and let stand 1/2 hour.
Roll up and cut in strips. Cook in boiling salted water, blanch in boiling water.

## Strawberry Jam
*(Alice Byxbe Anspauch)*

*"The berries stay whole."*

1 qt berries   4 cups sugar   2 tsp. lemon juice

Put the berries with 2 cups sugar in sauce pan and boil five minutes. Add lemon juice to other 2 cups sugar and add to berries and let boil 10 or 15 minutes longer.
Remove from fire and let stand 24 hours. Stir up and can cold.

Estes Park Trail *photo of the Town's new library in Bond Park, c. 1922.*
Photo courtesy of the Estes Park Woman's Club

## The Estes Park Public Library

*"Then the women took over."*
—Eleanor Estes James Hondius

Building a public library in the Village was a project and dream of the Estes Park Woman's Club, which had been founded in 1912 by a group of ladies who had initially banded together as an auxiliary and fundraising arm of the Estes Park Protective and Improvement Association. When it became clear that the all-male EPPIA had no intention of accepting the women as equal decision-makers, the auxiliary, which included the wives of many of the EPPIA members, literally "walked out" and founded their own organization. Now over one hundred years old, the Woman's Club continues to make significant contributions to the town of Estes Park.[42]

*Ora Carr in front of the Library she ran for more than a quarter of a century.*

**Photo courtesy of the Estes Park Woman's Club**

Founding a town library was one of the Woman's Club's first goals. Initially, the books donated for the library were set up in various locations in town as the Club proceeded to raise money for a permanent building. Finally, in 1921, the clubwomen were able to purchase property for a library on Davis Hill, located on Moraine Avenue. However, in order to forestall the removal of the National Park Service headquarters from Estes Park to another location, the Woman's Club decided to donate their property to the NPS for a new building in exchange for the Park's assurance that their headquarters would remain in the Town. The Club then selected a new location for the library. They chose the public park situated in the very heart of the Village.

The Library was completed in 1922. The first librarian was Alma Bond, who served the needs of library patrons as a volunteer for well over eighteen years. In 1940, Woman's Club member Ora L. Mabie Carr took on the responsibilities of town librarian.

A Kansas native who married Lawrence H. Carr (1892–1972) in 1916, Ora Carr (1893–1977) taught in a rural school in Wyoming before moving to Estes Park, where Lawrence was hired by the Forest Service. Before taking charge of the Library, Carr worked for the Mountain States Telephone and Telegraph Company. The couple had one child, daughter Virginia, born in 1917.

Carr joined the Estes Park Woman's Club in 1928, serving as its president during the 1935–1936 club year. Her long run as librarian extended from 1940 to 1970, during which time the library building underwent a number of additions, and expanded its programs for adults and children. Carr's recipes appeared in the *High Altitude Cook Book*, published by the Estes Park Ladies Aid Society.

## Cooked Oil Mayonnaise
*(Ora L. Mabie Carr)*

1 egg or 2 yolks
2 tbsp. sugar
1/2 tsp. salt
1 tsp. mustard
1/2 tsp. paprika
1/4 cup vinegar
3/4 cup olive oil

Place in bowl, but do not stir. To 1 cup water add 4 tbsp. cornstarch. Place on stove and boil until thick and clear, then add this immediately to other ingredients and beat five minutes.

## Mexican Orange Candy
*(Ora L. Mabie Carr)*

1 cup sugar caramelized
1 1/2 cups hot milk
2 cups sugar

Add hot milk to caramelized sugar. Then add rest of sugar and stir until dissolved. Cook until almost hard ball stage. Add grated rind of 2 oranges, pinch of salt, 1/2 cup butter, one cup nut meats. Cool and beat until creamy.

## Pinwheel Icebox Cookies
*(Ora L. Mabie Carr)*

1 cup butter  
3 eggs, beaten  
1 tsp. baking powder  
1 tsp. cinnamon  

2 cups brown sugar  
4 1/2 cups flour  
1 tsp. soda  
1/4 tsp. salt  

### *Filling*

1 1/2 cups dates  
1/2 cup of sugar  

1 cup nut meats, ground  
1 cup water  

Cook filling 5 minutes. Roll dough out thin and spread with date mixture. Set in a cool place over night. Separate dough in three parts.

## Pineapple Upside Down Cake
*(Ora L. Mabie Carr)*

1 cup brown sugar  
1 small can of pineapple  

1/2 cup butter

Put sugar and butter in an iron frying pan and place on top of oven. Allow to warm just enough to make them melt and blend nicely. Drain pineapple and spread it evenly over the melted sugar and butter. Chop nuts and spread on top.

### *Cake Part*

1 cup sugar  
1 tbsp. corn starch  
1/4 tsp salt  

1/3 cup pineapple juice  
3 eggs  
1 cup flour  

First mix the cornstarch and pineapple juice, then beat egg whites till stiff and gradually beat in sugar, well beaten yolks and juice. Beat well. Add flour and salt. Cut and fold. Pour over mixture in frying pan. Bake in moderate oven.

*The Old Plantation in the 1930s.*

Photo courtesy of the Burgess family

## The Old Plantation Restaurant: The Burgess Family

*"The trout today you think a treat, slept last night in Thompson Creek."*[43]

Few landmarks on Elkhorn Avenue were as familiar to generations of Estes Park visitors as the Old Plantation Restaurant, founded by the Burgess family and operated by them for more than sixty-one years. The original restaurant was located in an old building that had been the home, studio, and café of local artist Reginald H. Tallant[44] and his wife Louise. Tallant's mother, Helen Tallant (b. 1828), had also operated a confectionary shop on the main floor at one time, but by 1930, the shop had become a sandwich and souvenir store called the Pinecone Inn. In 1931, the Tallants sold the building to Thelma Porter Burgess (1898–1976), a young widow from Texas.

Thelma was a newcomer to Estes Park, having moved with her two little boys shortly after her husband died to be closer to her parents, Curran Rutilious (1855–1939) and Sarah Elizabeth (Lizzie) Tadlock Porter (1865–1946), in a place that her husband had loved. Now that the Porters could look after her children, William Endsley "Bill" Burgess (1923–2005) and Robert E. "Bob"

*Thelma Burgess moved her family to Estes Park in 1931 and established the Old Plantation, a landmark restaurant on Elkhorn Avenue.*
Photo courtesy of the Burgess family

Burgess (1926–2004), Thelma was able to go to college in Greeley. Her plan was to earn a teaching certificate that would enable her to teach in Colorado schools.

Through a friend, Thelma heard that the Pinecone Inn on Elkhorn Avenue was for sale. Thinking it a good investment, she used her husband's life insurance money to make the purchase and launch a new business, which she called the "Old Plantation." She was initially assisted in running the restaurant by her youngest brother, Carl Porter (b. 1901), and her mother. Many years later, when asked why Thelma chose to name her restaurant the Old Plantation, her son Bob recalled: "Mother wanted a Southern name; she picked 'the Plantation.' We stuck with it forever," he said. "[We] wouldn't think of changing it now." The opening of the new restaurant was front-page news in December 1931.[45]

Soon thereafter, Thelma met and married Clay Warren "Chappie" Chapman (1889–1956). Although he had no restaurant experience, Chappie was an astute businessman, and after he took over management tasks, the Old Plantation began to thrive. In those early years, cooking duties at the restaurant were the responsibility of a series of part-time chefs. Bob began working at the restaurant at an early age, pitting cherries for the restaurant's hallmark pies. As the years passed, he worked his way up, at first to busboy and, later, to host.

Both of Thelma's sons enlisted in the service during World War II. Bob recalled later that wartime rationing necessitated some changes in food services—one little packet of sugar, one pat of butter, and meatless days were examples. After the war, the Old Plantation underwent considerable redecorating, and the kitchen was enlarged. Bob returned to run the Old Plantation almost immediately.

In 1950, Bill married Harriet Rose Bittner (1925–2012) at the Community Church of the Rockies. Harriet's family had spent many summers in Estes Park during her childhood, and her father, Dr. Silas P. Bittner, was a Presbyterian minister who often preached at the local church. Dr. Bittner officiated at Bill and Harriet's wedding; among attendants were Pieter Hondius Jr., Harriet's sister Ruth Bittner Shaw, Howard (Bud) James, and Bob Burgess; the photographer was none other than Fred P. Clatworthy Jr.

After Chappie died suddenly in 1956, Bill and Harriet decided to return to Estes Park and the Old Plantation Restaurant, which

*The Plantation Café's first menu (1931) featured a steamboat and a black cover, in line with Thelma's carefully designed color scheme and overall theme.*

**Courtesy of the Burgess family**

*Bob and Janet Burgess' daughters took a turn at waitressing at the Old Plantation in the 1970s.*

Photo courtesy of the Burgess family

the couple owned with Bill's newly (1956) married brother Bob and Bob's wife, Janet Rae Bovee Burgess. For the next twenty-two years, Bill took on managerial responsibilities, Harriet served as bookkeeper, and Bob—who had been mentored by Chappie—was the chef. Bob and Janet took over sole ownership when Bill and Harriet retired in 1979, and together ran the Old Plantation until it closed in 1992. Bob continued to share his recipes thereafter in the local newspaper. In a 1981 interview, Bob summed up what the restaurant had meant to him: "I've spent my life at the Plantation."[46]

The Old Plantation, which was open year-round, was known for its American cuisine: Yankee pot roast, liver and bacon, fried chicken, trout and duck dishes, and, of course, the restaurant's signatures: homemade pies and mint juleps.[47]

## Mint Julep
*(Thelma Porter Burgess Chapman)*

Muddle mint in the bottom of a Kentucky Derby official glass with simple syrup

Fill glass with ice
Add 1 oz of Kentucky bourbon
Fill with club soda to top
Finish with mint garnish

## Thelma's Lemon Sauce (For Plum Pudding)
*(Thelma Porter Burgess Chapman)*

Beat 2 egg yolks and add 1 c. powdered sugar, 1 c. coffee cream or half and half cream, 4 tbsp. butter and 1 tbsp. lemon flavoring (extract).
Stir constantly and cook over slow fire until thick. Serve hot over plum pudding. Top with maraschino cherry. Serves 6.

## Plantation Gooseberry Pie Filling
*(Robert E. Burgess)*

2 #10 cans Gooseberries
Drain juice from fruit and bring to boil.
12 OZ. W-13 [Thickener]
2 cups Water
Few Drops Yellow Food Color

Add to boiling juice and stir until thick and clear then remove from fire.
6 LBS. white sugar
Add to thickened juice and mix and pour over fruit, mix, refrigerate.

## Chappie's Meat Loaf
*(Harriet Rose Bittner Burgess)*

1 lb. ground round
1 egg
1 small pimento, chopped fine
1/4 green pepper, chopped fine
1/4 small onion, chopped fine
Celery leaves to taste
Salt and pepper
1–1/2 slices dry bread rolled fine into crumbs
1 small can tomatoes

Mix whole tomatoes into meat mixture, reserve liquid
After thoroughly mixing all ingredients, shape in loaf.
Pour tomato juice over and place 1 or 2 slices of bacon on top.
Bake 1 1/4 hours at 350.
[For mild meat loaf, use regular canned tomatoes. For nippy or hot loaf, try canned tomatoes with green chilies.]

## Plantation Sauce Robert[48]
*(Robert E. Burgess)*

4 lbs Minced onions
8 oz. Margarine
2 Quarts dry sherry
6 quarts brown sauce
1 cup Dijon mustard

Sweat onions in margarine until onions are transparent
Add sherry to onions, reduce by 1/3
Add brown sauce to onion-sherry mixture and bring to a boil
Add mustard, but do not boil

## Liver and Bacon/Onions[49]

*(Robert E. Burgess)*

Dip calves liver in salt and peppered flour. Shake off excess.
Fry desired number of bacon slices and set aside
Fry desired amount of sliced onions
Fry liver for only 2 1/2 minutes each side and serve immediately

## Scotch Eggs

*(Robert E. Burgess)*

1 pound pork sausage
1/4 cup cracker crumbs
2 egg whites
1 teaspoon Worcestershire sauce
2 egg yolks, beaten
1 or 2 cups cracker crumbs
6 peeled hard-boiled eggs

Place sausage, cracker crumbs, egg whites and Worcestershire in mixing bowl with dough hook and combine. Or mix with your hands. Make six equal-size balls.

Made a cup in a sausage ball with your thumb. Dip egg in egg yolks and place in sausage cup. Completely surround egg with sausage. Make sure egg is completely covered with sausage meat.

Roll egg in cracker crumbs. Drop one or two at a time in a 350-degree fryer.

Cook for six minutes. Check first egg to be sure the sausage is cooked through.

Serve hot or cold with salt, pepper and mustard. They are terrific!

[Recipes for the Old Plantation's Soup Luncheon of Cock-A-Leekie Soup and Cucumber, Watercress and Cream Cheese Sandwich, can be found in Appendix B.]

*Interior of the Dark Horse Tavern showing the bar with its trademark barstools. This unique and popular Estes Park bar was built in 1933 by Ted Jelsema, who operated it until 1946.*

**Courtesy of the Estes Park Museum**

## The Dark Horse Tavern

The Riverside Amusement Park, an Estes Park "hot spot" for decades, was built by Estes pioneer Frank C. Bond (1898–1980) and Michigan-born Theodore Charles "Ted" Jelsema (1891–1970) in 1922–1923. Originally a complex of buildings featuring a ballroom, lunch counter, and ice cream parlor, over time the Riverside complex grew to include a dance floor, a heated swimming pool with sand beach, a bowling alley, a shooting gallery, and a roller rink. From 1945 to 1969, theatrical performances were offered on a

*A Dark Horse brochure provided stories about all of the famous horses after which their carousel counterparts in the bar had been named.*
**Courtesy of the Estes Park Museum**

stage that had been built over the swimming pool. Although it was a particular favorite with college students, visitors of all ages came from near and far for the entertainment and for the Wednesday-night "theme" dances that were held every summer.

With the end of prohibition in 1933, Jelsema opened the Dark Horse Tavern, which took its name from the merry-go-round horses that Jelsema converted into bar stools and wall decorations inside the bar and outside over the entrance.[50] Each horse carried the name of a famous rodeo mount, and Jelsema distributed a four-page brochure that provided information on each one. In the tavern's heyday, Jelsema published a newspaper touting the week's coming attractions; sadly, the Dark Horse was demolished in 1970, but only after a community gala was held to mark its passing.

## Dark Horse Special
*(Dark Horse Tavern)*

1 jigger light rum
2 jiggers lemon juice
1 tsp. sugar
1/4 lime
1/2 jigger cherry brandy
1 orange slice
1 maraschino cherry

Fill tall frosted glass with crushed ice. Add rum, lemon juice, lime juice, and lime rind. Fill glass with Canada Dry soda, add sugar and stir to dissolve. Top off with cherry brandy and garnish with orange slice and cherry.
Sip slowly!

*The Holland Inn as it looked in the 1930s.*
Photo courtesy of the Estes Park Museum

## The Holland Inn/Dunraven Inn

The historic structure that would one day carry the name of the Irish aristocrat Windham Thomas Wyndham-Quin, the fourth Earl of Dunraven, was built at "the Y-Junction" in 1907. When the National Park Service chose a nearby location for its Big Thompson entrance into Rocky Mountain National Park, the road past the house was transformed into a major thoroughfare, the Moraine Park Road. It is likely the house was turned into a restaurant about this same time.

In 1935, Albert Benjamin Servey (1889–1936) and his wife Kathryn moved to Estes Park and purchased the building, opening their new business as the Holland Tavern. Unfortunately, the following year Albert suffered a heart attack and died while on a

*The Dunraven Inn dining room, c. 1970, featured plaid carpeting and bright red table linens.*

**Postcard courtesy of the Bobbie Heistercamp Collection**

fishing expedition in Horseshoe Park. Kathryn was left to carry on by herself, and she eventually converted the business from bar to a restaurant, complete with soda fountain. The new restaurant was named the Holland Inn.[51]

By the 1940s, the Inn had been sold to Mr. and Mrs. C. H. Mohr, who advertised steaks, chicken, and trout as house specialties. Then in 1970, Neil Quirk purchased the building and, after finishing an extensive renovation, re-launched the restaurant as a steak house, the Dunraven Inn, complete with plaid carpeting and split timber décor in honor of the Earl's Irish roots.

Over the next decade, the ethnic themes at the Inn changed from English steak house to Mexican restaurant. Then, when Julius "Jules" Schneidkraut (1931–1998) and his wife Marcia (1932–1988) purchased the Dunraven in 1979, they introduced an Italian menu. It was "Jules" who added the sobriquet "Rome of the Rockies" to the restaurant's sign, and the multiple prints of Da Vinci's famous painting, *La Giaconda* (Mona Lisa) to the interior décor. Even so, many of the interior appointments in wall design and carpeting of the earlier restaurants were retained. Jules was both a convivial host and a "hands-on" manager. In his signature black leather vest, he personally welcomed every guest, whether local or tourist, with the same enthusiasm and charm.

After Jules' death in 1998, the Dunraven was purchased and operated by a Florida couple, Dale and Laurel Hatcher. Adopting Jules' décor, including a bar full of dollar bills affixed to walls and ceilings, and his personable management style, the Hatchers maintained the Dunraven as a community favorite until 2012. Andy Morgan (b. 1974) and wife Cindy Saurino Morgan (b. 1973), current owners, returned to their Estes Park roots when the Hatchers retired and are continuing the Dunraven's tradition of Italian dishes served in a casual, family atmosphere.

The historic building that houses the Dunraven Inn survives today in substantially the same form as in its early days, and the interior layout, in terms of bar area, dining room, and kitchen, belie that of the original building. Today, however, the restaurant's front door, which faces on Spur 66, is located on what was originally the structure's back side, next to the kitchen, and the building has been repainted. Even so, it is still recognizable as the Holland Inn to those who take the time to look closely.

*The main dining room at Gartner Haus as it appeared in the 1960s.*
Postcard courtesy of the Bobbie Heistercamp Collection

## Gartner Haus

*"Dine with your friends."*

—Gartner Haus slogan

The Gartner Haus was located on Highway 34 just east of the Village of Estes Park. It was established by Hans (1911–1993) and Catherine Schaffer Gartner (1913–2002), who were married in 1933 in Chicago and moved to Colorado in 1935. Hans, a butcher by trade, was the son of German immigrants. For this reason, it is not too surprising that the restaurant he and Catherine founded specialized in European cuisine, with signature dishes of sauerbraten, wiener schnitzel, and potato pancakes. Their kitchen also served up classic American menu items, as well as the obligatory trout dinner.

Newspaper ads for the restaurant assured potential customers that "imported beer and wine" would be served to them in a "friendly atmosphere." Over time, the restaurant, which was popular with Estes Park residents as well as the traveling public, was enlarged to comprise a cocktail lounge, dining room, and rooms for banquets and receptions.

## Hungarian Goulash[52]

*(Hans and Catherine Gartner)*

1 lb. beef
1 lb. veal or pork
1/4 c. flour
1/2 tsp. salt
1/4 tsp. pepper
3 T. fat
3 T. diced onion
2 T. minced parsley
1 T. paprika
Cooked noodles

Cube meat, roll in flour, salt, pepper, and brown in fat. Add water, cover tightly, simmer 1 1/2 hours or when meat is done. Add remaining ingredients and heat to boiling point, and simmer 10 minutes. Serve with cooked noodles.

## Sholty Food Market

The Sholty Food Market on Elkhorn Avenue was founded in 1933 by Clarence Earl "C.E." Sholty (1885–1974), who had moved to Loveland from Ohio soon after the turn of the century. In 1910, Sholty married Chloe S. Beery Wurfel (1885–1972), a young widow with one little girl, Grace Mildred, born in 1904. Together the Sholtys had three children, twin sons Chalmer and LeRoy and a daughter Helen. Sadly, the little boys did not survive infancy, but Helen grew up to marry Bert J. McConnell (b. 1899), an Estes Park pharmacist, in 1930.[53] In Loveland, C.E. owned and managed Kelly & Sholty Grocery and Meat Market with the help of a partner.

Sholty was a capable horseman, and a licensed mountain guide. He continued these activities even after he opened a little grocery store in Estes Park. In fact, during the 1930s and early 1940s, Sholty essentially ran two businesses, the market on Elkhorn and the Arrow Livery[54] on Devil's Gulch Road. The livery was owned by Charles and Sadie Mae Evett. With the Evetts, Sholty constructed a complex of buildings at the Arrow, which came to include a barn, a bunkhouse, and a corral. When the Arrow was sold to Eva Jane Reece Price and her daughter Margaret in 1939, Sholty stayed on to help them manage the operation.

Clarence Sholty may be best remembered as a founding member of the Estes Park Lions Club, while Chloe's activities with the Estes Park Ladies Aid are reflected in the recipes that she contributed to the group's *The High Altitude Cook Book*.

## Soft Ginger Bread

*(Chloe S. Beery Wurfel Sholty)*

1/2 cup sugar  
1/2 cup shortening  
2 1/2 cups flour  
Last, add 2 well beaten eggs  
1 cup sorghum or molasses  
1 tsp. each ginger, cinnamon, cloves, and salt  
2 tsp soda dissolved in 1 cup boiling water  

Bake in moderate oven 30 minutes.

## Steamed Pudding and Hard Sauce

*(Chloe S. Beery Wurfel Sholty)*

3 cups flour  
1 cup raisins  
1 cup sweet milk  
1 tsp. nutmeg  
1/2 tsp. salt  
1/2 cup nut meats  
1 cup suet (chopped)  
1 cup sorghum or molasses  
1 tsp. soda dissolved in a little hot water  
2 eggs beaten  

Mix in order given. Steam 2 hours and serve with hard sauce.

### *Hard Sauce*

Cream together: 1 cube butter  
2 cups powdered sugar  

Add one small egg  
Chill and use.

## Lemon Apple Pie

*(Chloe S. Beery Wurfel Sholty)*

Grated rind 1 lemon
2/3 cup sugar
1 egg yolk
2 tbsp. flour
2 apples pared and grated
2 tbsp. lemon juice
1/3 cup corn syrup
1 tbsp. melted butter
1/4 cup hot water
1 egg white

Mix grated rind of lemon, lemon juice, sugar, syrup, egg yolk (slightly beaten), melted butter, flour and hot water. Then add apples. When well beaten, fold in stiffly beaten egg white, bake between 2 crusts.

# Village Gift Shops: The Seybold and Herzog Families

Two families who followed in the footsteps of the first generation of Main Street merchants (e.g., the Clatworthys, the Godfreys, and the Gooches) were the Seybolds and the Herzogs, whose shops were Estes Park icons beginning in the 1940s. Even though these business were not among the first ones to occupy prime spots on Elkhorn Avenue, their owners' family roots tie them to Estes Park's earliest days.

The first member of the Seybolds' extended family to arrive on the local scene was Alfred Lewis Cobb, who had come west from Missouri with his family before the turn of the last century. A. L. "Al" Cobb (1863–1938), as he is most often referred to in local histories, was a skilled carpenter, builder, and architect. Among his early achievements in the Village was the stucco and river-rock structure, at the edge of the public park, that he designed to house the Estes Park Public School. While the school exists now only in memory, three other Cobb buildings still stand today as reminders of the man and his talents. From 1907 to 1909 Cobb served as contractor for Mr. Stanley's neo-Georgian hotel, and in 1908 he built for the Macdonalds not only their house on Elkhorn but also the little lodgepole cabin in its backyard, which has since been moved and preserved at the Estes Park Museum. Cobb also designed[55] and built Estes Park's original Presbyterian Church, which has since been transformed into a "mini-mall," called The Old Church Shops.

Al Cobb was a popular figure about town, whose activities and travels were amply documented in the local press of the time. He was also one of Estes Park's civic leaders, serving a term as the town's third mayor. The Cobb and Seybold families were linked through Al's daughter Edna B. Cobb,[56] whose own daughter, Jeanne Gray, married Jack Seybold.

John Ross "Jack" Seybold's parents, John Ross "Ross" Seybold Sr. (1889–1946) and wife Loua N. Steinmetz Seybold (1889–1970), came to Estes Park in 1920 from Fort Morgan, Colorado. A Kansas native, Ross Seybold operated a gas station in town for a number of years before managing a tourist park. Ross and Loua's son Jack Seybold (1917–2004) was a child of only three when his parents brought him to Estes Park. After attending the local schools, he helped his father run the family's businesses. Jack enlisted in the

*Herzog's Gift Corral was frequently the site for fundraising activities along Estes Park's Elkhorn Avenue.*

Photo courtesy of the Estes Park Woman's Club

navy during World War II, and, upon his return, he worked with the highway department to improve the canyon roads and local roadways in the Town. For twenty years, Jack owned and ran a Texaco station on Elkhorn Avenue. He also worked for a time at Rocky Mountain National Park where he was maintenance director at the Hidden Valley Ski Area. His local civic activities included the American Legion, Lions Club, the Masons, and the volunteer fire department. Jack and Jeanne's son, James S. "Jim" Seybold, was born in 1940, delivered by Estes Park's first doctor, Roy Wiest.

In the 1940s, Charlie Herzog[57] and his wife Doris moved from Denver to Estes Park with their two children, where, over a period of fifty years, they established and operated businesses at various locations downtown. The two-story, wood-frame building that they purchased to house Herzog's Gift Corral was, in itself, an historic building—it had been built as a home for Sam Service and his family. Like the Seybolds, the Herzogs were full participants in the life of the town as well as community boosters. Indeed, in the early days they, along with many other downtown merchants, would close up shop to attend football games at the high school. Charlie served two terms on the Estes Park Board of Trustees, was president of the Rotary Club of Estes Park (Noon Rotary), and was instrumental in the formation of the Estes Valley Recreation District. Doris developed a keen interest and knowledge of Indian jewelry and was generous in sharing her expertise in programs she presented to local civic clubs. She was also a charter member of Estes Park's Quota Club, an international organization that raises funds to help disadvantaged women and children. Finally, the Herzogs provided both moral and financial support to local non-profits by donating the coins that were dropped into the Gift Corral's in-store wishing well.

When Jim Seybold (1940–2000) married Charlie and Doris's daughter, Dianne, the newlyweds decided to open their own downtown business: Seybold's Gifts. For over fifty years the shop provided a range of western, Native American, and mountain-related gift items and collectables, linens, apparel, and home décor. Their Elkhorn Avenue store became a town landmark. During these years, Dianne and Jim continued their families' dedication to service projects in addition to their support for the economic development of the town. Jim's activities included the Estes Park Fire Department, the Chamber of Commerce Board, and the Lions Club.

## Edna James' Texas Pecan Pie

*(Dianne Herzog Seybold)*

4 eggs (yolks separated from whites)
1 1/2 c. sugar
1 c. raisins
2 T. butter (melted)
1 T. vinegar
1 c. pecan meats

Beat 4 egg yolks together with the 1 1/2 c. sugar. Place 1 c. raisins in boiling water for 15 minutes. Drain. Add the raisins, melted butter and vinegar to first mixture. Add 1 c. pecan meats. Mix well. Add 4 well-beaten egg whites. Pour into a (9 inch) unbaked crust. Bake 40–45 minute at 325°.

## Batter Bread/Coffee Can Bread

*(Jeanne M. Gray Seybold)*

1 pkg. dry yeast
1/2 c. warm water
1 can evaporated milk (undiluted)
3 T. sugar
1 tsp. salt
2 T. salad oil
4 c. flour (unsifted)
Crisco

In a large bowl, dissolve yeast in the warm water. Set in warm place about 15 minutes. Add sugar, milk, salt, salad oil. Beat with a mixer at low speed. Add the flour, one cup at a time. As it becomes heavy, mix by hand. Divide dough into 2 well-greased (1 lb.) coffee cans. Cover with greased plastic lids. Let stand in a warm place until the lids pop off or rise an inch or two above tops of cans. Bake standing up in a preheated 350 degree oven about 50 minutes.

## Cream Cheese Ball

*(Dianne Herzog Seybold)*

*"This recipe is a favorite with everyone who tries it."*

2 pkg. (8 oz) Philadelphia cream cheese
1 small can crushed pineapple (drained)
1/2 c. pecans (chopped)
1/8 c. green pepper (chopped)
1 T. onion (finely chopped)
1/2 tsp. salt.

Beat cheese with a fork adding all ingredients except the pecans. Place 1/8 c. pecans in the mixture. Shape into a ball and chill. Roll chilled ball in remaining chopped pecans. Serve with assorted crackers; fairly bland ones work best.

## Ginger Cream Cookies
*(Doris Romig Herzog)*

1 c. shortening
1 c. dark molasses
3 tsp. baking soda
1 tsp. cinnamon
1/4 tsp. salt
Flour (sifted) (as much as can be worked into dough)

1 c. sugar
1 1/2 c. sour milk
1 tsp. ginger
1 tsp. nutmeg
2 eggs

Cream shortening and sugar together. Add molasses and mix well. Add sour milk and stir. Sift next 5 ingredients together with first cup of flour and add. Stir in the 2 eggs and continue adding the flour until dough is very stiff and must be worked by hand. Roll dough on floured board and keep it fairly thick. Cut with cookie cutters.
Bake at 325 degrees oven until golden.
Frost with powdered sugar-milk icing and decorate.

## Beef Bourguignon
*(Dianne Herzog Seybold)*

3 lb. chuck or round steak (cubed)
1 1/2 tsp. salt
1 c. canned consommé
1/2 lb fresh mushrooms or 1 small can

3 T. flour
1/2 tsp. pepper
1 c. dry red wine
1/2 c. onion (chopped)

Brown meat cubes in hot oil. Stir in flour, salt, and pepper, scraping bottom of skillet well. Pour into 2 1/2 qt. casserole. Pour consommé and wine over meat; cover. Bake at 325 degrees for 2 hours. Add mushrooms and onions and continue baking for 1 hour and 30 minutes or until very tender. Add more consommé and wine as necessary during cooking. Skim fat and thicken gravy. Serve over rice. Or leave meat in serving portions, add all ingredients, and cook 15 minutes in pressure cooker at 15 lb. pressure.

## Angel Cookies
*(Dianne Herzog Seybold)*

### *Dough:*

1/2 c. butter  
1 egg  
1/8 tsp. salt  
1/4 c. sugar  
1/4 c. flour (sifted)  
1/2 tsp. vanilla  

### *Toppings:*

2 eggs beaten  
1/2 c. flaked coconut  
2 T. flour  
1/2 tsp. salt  
1 1/2 c. brown sugar  
1 c. pecan meats (chopped)  
1/2 tsp. baking powder  
1 tsp. vanilla  

Make dough first by creaming the butter and sugar together until well blended. Add the egg and beat in well. Combine the flour and salt and add them in about 3 parts to the butter mixture, blending well. Work in the vanilla and using your hands, pat the dough evenly in a (9 x 12) pan. Bake about 15 minutes in preheated 350° oven. Spread with the topping mixture and bake about 30 minutes. When cool, ice with: 1 1/2 c. confectioners sugar thinned with milk. If desired, omit the coconut in topping mixture and use 1 1/2 c. nutmeats instead. Cut the cake into oblongs.

*Sundeck Restaurant at Beaver Point, c. 1950s, with signs presenting restaurant specials and directing visitors to Anderson's Wonder View resort. Both establishments continue to host summer vacationers to Estes Park.*
Photo courtesy of the Estes Park Museum

## Sundeck Restaurant

*"The Sundeck has been run by a single family for over 65 years. We've found that the only way to keep serving up great food for that long is to care about what we do."*

—Online webpage, www.sundeckrestaurant.com

The Sundeck Restaurant is an Estes Park favorite that has been owned and operated by the Hoerner family for over sixty-five years. Before the coming of the Sundeck, its site, at the intersection of Moraine Avenue and Marys Lake Road at Beaver Point, had been the location of a variety of early eateries over the years, including several tea rooms, a market, Hap's Glorified Hamburger Haven, and the Wheeler Inn.

The Sundeck was the creation of Fred Hoerner (b. 1917) and his wife Marian, who moved to Estes Park from Chicago, purchasing the Wheeler Inn in 1948. However, as the couple's son Vick explained, it was left to Marian to get the restaurant up and running while Fred "settled things in Chicago." At first, the restaurant "was simply the kitchen area of our current restaurant. . . . Shortly after his arrival," Fred purchased the motel next door, which he ran while "mom ran the restaurant."[58]

The Hoerners wasted little time in expanding their operation by adding an open-air deck. However, the deck area was almost immediately enclosed due to the vagaries of the mountain weather. Fortunately, the views of the Twin Sisters, Taylor, Otis, Hallett and Flattop peaks as well as Prospect, Rams Horn, Eagle Cliff, and Deer mountains were still visible from the dining room's expansive picture windows.

From the beginning, the Sundeck was operated on a seasonal basis, in June, July, and August. During the off-season, the Hoerners lived first in Arizona and then in Boulder, where Fred and Marian purchased and ran the 4-H Motel.

The Sundeck's diverse menu, which includes Rocky Mountain trout, Forelle Blau, Viennese goulash, prime rib, and chile rellenos, is a combination of Hoerner family favorites and recipes they have discovered on their travels.

## Forelle Blau (Blue Trout)
## (also known as Truite au Bleu or Poached Trout)

2 quarts of water
2–3 three cups of red wine (we use a burgundy)
1/4 cup cider vinegar
1/2 to 1 cup Pickling Spice (loose or in a cheese cloth)
1 lemon quartered and squeezed (both juice and quarters)
Bring to a boil and let it simmer for a minimum of 20 minutes

When the above broth is ready, put your trout (gutted and cleaned) to steep for 6–12 minutes. This depends on size and quantity of trout you are cooking. Once the eyes are white and or the meat pulls away from the bones, then it is ready to serve. If the trout is freshly caught it will bow and that is good.
Serve with melted butter and lemon, salt and pepper to taste.
Side dishes that go well are parsley potatoes and a good wine.

*Bon Appetit*

---

# Sun Deck Cafe

### FINE FOODS

**NEW LARGE MOTEL**
Under construction and will be opened about May 1.

— At Beaver Point —
on Hwy. 262 West of Estes Village

*Early photo of the Wheel Bar, c. 1940s.*
Photo courtesy of the Estes Park Museum

## The Wheel Bar

The Wheel Bar on Elkhorn Avenue has been a family affair from its beginnings over sixty-five years ago. The business was the idea of Orlando Michael Nagl (1914–1998), who was born in Carroll, Iowa. In 1937 Nagl married a fellow Iowan Margaret Ann Brannan (1913–1943). The couple moved to Eugene, Oregon, soon after they were married and then relocated to Seattle, Washington, two years later where Orlando Mike worked as an instructor for the Boeing Aircraft Company. Tragically, Margaret Ann died after a brief illness in 1943. At the close of World War II, Orlando Mike married his widowed sister-in-law, Leola Byrnes Nagl (1920–2008),[59] and the couple moved from Las Vegas to Estes Park. The Nagls purchased Ben Vance's Estes Park Beer Parlor, which they renamed Mike's Tavern. The bar was located in the old Josephine Hotel, built on Elkhorn Avenue in 1916.

In an effort to make the business an Estes Park landmark with its own distinctive style and traditions, the Nagls sponsored a contest to rename the bar. The name "The Wheel" was chosen from among countless entries because, as they said, it was a "hub" of community activity and the meeting place for all the influential people in town. Adopting motifs reminiscent of the gambling

*Estes Park Woman's Club members and friends counted coins collected for the March of Dimes on the bar at Nagl's.*
Photo courtesy of the Estes Park Woman's Club

casinos in Las Vegas, the couple ran not only the bar downstairs but also a restaurant, Orlando's Steakhouse, upstairs. In December 1955, the bar barely escaped its demise when the Riverside Hotel, located above the bar, was destroyed in a fire.[60] In 1977, ownership of The Wheel passed to the Nagls' son Steve and his wife, Gay.

Mike and Lee Nagl were Estes boosters and community supporters whose activities helped raise substantial amounts of money for various philanthropic organizations. Among these were: the Wheel Open Golf Tournament; City League basketball teams; the March of Dimes; the Wheel Streak, a benefit for the EP visitor center; and the Estes Park Duck Race.[61]

## Wheel Cocktail
*(Orlando Mike Nagl)*

1 oz. dry gin  
1/2 oz. Benedictine  
1/3 oz dry vermouth

Stir gently—strain into a footed cocktail glass.

*Sign board for the Harmony Guest Ranch located on Fall River.*
Photo courtesy of the Estes Park Museum

## Harmony Guest Ranch

*"Amani Mgeni Uwanda"*

"Amani Mgeni Uwanda," Swahili for Harmony Guest Ranch, was built by Matilda E. "Tillie" and Scott Wilbur Hayes in 1953–54. An Illinois-born chicken farmer turned big-game hunter, Scott Hayes (1898–1960) made trips to Europe, Africa, and India in search of the trophies he used to decorate the couple's Estes Park motel. Located on Fish Hatchery Road, near Rocky Mountain National Park's Fall River Entrance, the Hayes' resort occupied a forty-two-acre site that featured a swimming pool, a three-hole golf course, and a small lake. A two-story dining hall served motel guests,

*Guests in the Harmony's lounge were served by a uniformed bartender, while the bar's contemporary décor and appointments were augmented by stuffed animals: a polar bear and a seal.*

while the bar, named the Polar Bear Lounge for the animal Hayes killed in Norway, was a popular local watering hole for Estes Park tourists and residents.

In the late 1960s, a group of local businessmen purchased the Hayes's resort to use as an alcoholic rehabilitation center, which it remains to this day.

## Harmony Ranch Special Cider Cocktail
*(Matilda E. Hayes)*

Heat to boiling:   2 c. apple Cider
6 whole cloves
1 tbsp. red candy cinnamon

Add: 1/2 c. sugar and Simmer 10 min. Remove clove, pour into ice tray. Freeze to mushy state. (It won't freeze beyond that.)

Wash, core, and dice red apples, leaving skins on. Section oranges (pineapple) drain and dice (canned). Arrange in sherbet glasses and pour cider over the fruit.

## Harmony's Special Glog
*(A famous cold weather drink from Sweden)*

*(Scott Hayes)*

3/4 c. granulated sugar
2 oz. Angostura bitters
1 pt. Claret
1 pt. Sherry
1/2 pt. Brandy

Combine ingredients and heat in saucepan until piping hot, but do not boil. Preheat Old-Fashioned glass with boiling water and place in bottom of it 1 large raisin and 1 unsalted almond; place spoon in glass to prevent breaking and fill 2/3 full with hot wine mixture.

*Crowley's Restaurant on East Elkhorn, c. 1955.*
Postcard courtesy of the Bobbie Heistercamp Collection

## Crowley's High Country Restaurant

Crowley's was one of a number of popular restaurant businesses in Estes Park owned and run by members of the Crowley family[62] in the middle years of the twentieth century. J. Harold Crowley (1920–2013) and his brother Joseph W. "Joe" Crowley (1908–1993) moved to Estes Park from Wyoming in the mid-1950s and, over the years, operated a number of local eateries: The Dinner Bell Restaurant, the Round-Up Grocery and Delicatessen, and Crowley's Restaurant.[63] Harold and his wife Peggy[64] also ran Peg's Drive-In, which was located across the street from Crowley's, as well as the Dairy Bar Delicatessen. After twenty-five years on Elkhorn Avenue, the brothers moved Crowley's to a site on Highway 34, and renamed it Crowley's High Country Restaurant.

## Crowley's Famous Cheese Soup

*(Mrs. Joe W. Crowley)*

*Makes 2 qt.*

4 tbsp. butter
1/2 c. diced green pepper
1/2 c. diced celery
2 tbsp. flour
6 oz. young cheddar cheese, grated
salt to taste
white pepper
few drops of yellow food coloring
1/2 c. diced carrots
1/2 c. minced onion
1 qt. well seasoned chicken stock (or chicken bouillon cubes and water)
6 oz. well-cured, cheddar cheese, grated
milk

Melt butter in upper part of double boiler. Add the vegetables and braise til tender. Do not let them brown.

Blend in flour and cook 1 min., stirring constantly.

Pour in stock and stir til thickened.

Put the pan into the lower part of double boiler, in which the water is boiling. Add the 2 cheeses, stir till melted.

Thin to cream consistency with milk, season with salt and pepper, strain.

To reheat use double boiler. Serve very hot.

*Highway sign directing people to Crowley's.*
Photo courtesy of the Estes Park Museum

## Crowley's Restaurant Danish Rolls

*(Mrs. Joe W. Crowley)*

1 c. warm water
1/4 c. sugar
1/4 c. dry milk
4 eggs
1 pkg. (4oz) dry yeast
1/2 c. shortening
1/2 tsp. salt
3 to 4 c. flour

Combine yeast, warm water, and sugar, stirring until yeast dissolves.

Stir in 2 1/2 c. flour and the salt. Beat for a couple of minutes; add eggs, and stir to make soft dough.

Turn onto lightly floured surface, using remaining flour gradually knead for a couple minutes.

Cover and let rest in warm place until doubled. Roll out on floured surface and with a brush spread with melted butter, roll out again and repeat with butter three more times.

Roll out and put on cinnamon and sugar. Roll up dough and cut in 1/2 in. pieces. Place on greased pan and bake at 350 degrees for about 35 min. After you take out of oven you can put prepared pie filling in center of roll. May need more flour than recipe calls for.

## Brownfield's Trading Post

An Estes Park landmark for well over fifty years is Brownfield's Trading Post. The original store, which dates from the mid-1950s, was the inspiration of Lincoln, Nebraska-born Gerald Francis "Jerry" Brownfield and his wife Vera Mae Hill Brownfield.[65] Married in 1931, the couple moved to Estes Park in 1956 to open a summer business. In coming to the mountains, Jerry left his corporate career behind him in order to follow his dreams. Although today the store offers outdoor gear and souvenirs to town visitors, the Brownfields' first shop specialized in western and leather goods: tack, western clothing, and boots. Jerry enjoyed repairing and restoring old saddles in his spare time, a hobby that reflected his lifelong passion for horses, horseback riding, and rodeos.

The couple's first shop was located in Gaslight Square on Moraine Avenue. The family, which included their son Gerald F. Brownfield Jr.—the current owner and manager of Brownfield's Trading Post—lived in the basement of the store during their initial summers in the high country, and returned to their home in Lincoln for the winter. Within just a few years, the Brownfields decided to move the store to Elkhorn Avenue, and in 1961 they located a wood-frame house, built between 1909 and 1915 as a home for Glen H. Preston and his family. While Brownfields' continues to occupy this same site, the building has been remodeled a great many times (the most recent being the addition of Barlow Plaza, in 1991), in keeping with a business that has consistently updated its marketing focus in line with changing tastes and trends.

When Jerry and Vera ran the store, Vera assumed most of the managerial responsibilities. In addition, she belonged to a number of social clubs in town. Jerry continued his interest in horses through activities such as chairing the Rooftop Rodeo committee. In fact, for many years Jerry was the "voice" of the rodeo parade and the annual Estes Park Horse Show, providing "local color" as the announcer for both events. The Brownfields were community boosters in their adopted town. Vera was a member of Eta Omega chapter of Sigma Epsilon Alpha, and contributed a number of recipes to the organization's 1965 cookbook.

Jerry and Vera's son Jerry continues to serve the varied needs of Estes Park's summer visitors. Brownfield's website, which he created and maintains, promotes not only the store and its goods but town news and events as well.

## Pheasant Dinner

*(Vera Mae Hill Brownfield)*

Disjoint pheasant, roll in flour to which has been added salt and pepper. Brown in iron skillet. After pieces are all brown, turn flame low and cover pheasant with sour cream. Let it cook slowly for 1 or 1 1/2 hrs.
Serve with casserole of wild rice and grapefruit salad.

## Wild Rice Casserole

*(Vera Mae Hill Brownfield)*

1 c. wild rice, well washed and soaked for several hrs.
1 c. grated American cheese
1 c. chopped or sliced mushrooms
1 c. chopped ripe olives
1/2 c. chopped onion
1 c. hot water
1/4 c. salad oil
1 c. canned tomatoes
salt and pepper

Drain rice well. Add all other ingredients and place in casserole. Cover and bake at 350 degrees for 1 hr.

## Roth Family Restaurant

*"We were known for chicken and roast beef and just good old-fashioned food. So that's how we grew."*[66]

—Rex Roth

When Shirlee Ann and Rex Roth[67] arrived from Rockford, Illinois, in 1967 with their three young sons, they probably never suspected that they were embarking on a journey that would take them from Allenspark to Estes Park and extend over a period of almost thirty years. In fact, their initial goals in coming to the mountains were decidedly more spiritual than culinary, for Rex, an ordained minister, had been hired to direct the Covenant Heights Bible Camp. Shortly after their arrival, a group of Allenspark residents decided to create a nondenominational congregation, and take over the little log Episcopal Church that had been built in the village in the early 1960s. Rex and others in the area were invited to serve as guest ministers for Sunday services, and in 1972 the Community Church of Allenspark was formally established. In 1974, the congregation called Rex to the pulpit on a permanent basis.

During this same period, the couple decided to try their hands at running a vintage mountain resort, and to that end they bought Wild Basin Lodge in 1971. The property surrounding the almost seventy-year-old rustic building comprised twenty-two acres and offered visitors ten cabins in addition to the thirty-five guest rooms available in the main lodge building. After cleaning and sprucing up the Lodge, the Roths opened their doors to summer visitors in 1972.

When Shirlee and Rex took over the kitchen and the menu at the Lodge, they made many changes, including adding "family recipes for fried chicken and other home-style foods that were extremely popular."[68] The smorgasbord provided by the Roths was one innovation the couple added to the dining room, almost by accident. The idea came about one night when the cook failed to show up for work; having the guests serve themselves was the Roths' spur-of-the-moment solution to an innkeeping crisis. In its heyday, the Lodge could and did accommodate between 200 and 300 diners a night.

Unfortunately, like so many aging wood structures in and around the mountain communities of the Front Range, the Lodge was extremely vulnerable to fire; in 1980, it burned to the ground.

*The Roth Family Restaurant on U.S. Highway 34 was the last of the Roths' businesses in Estes Park.*
Postcard courtesy of the Bobbie Heistercamp Collection

Although the Roths rebuilt it in short order, they decided to sell it anyway and try their hands at running a restaurant in Estes Park.

There, on Highway 34, the couple opened the Roth Family Restaurant, which the Roths operated from 1984 to 1994. In addition, the Roth family owned the Dairy Dream on Highway 7. In its day, Roths' was very popular with visitors and residents alike. In an interview in 2005, Rex explained their success in this way: "We were known for chicken and roast beef and just good old-fashioned food. So that's how we grew."

## Rex's Baked Chicken
*(Rex Roth)*

Chicken pieces
Skin side up.
Brush with butter, pepper, and paprika

Little water in Pan (1/3 cup for 25 pieces)

Don't Cover
325 degrees     1 hour & 1/2 (?)

Then cover
Turn off Oven
Let stand on top rack of oven 1/2 hr.

*The dining room of the Cottage Inn.*
Photo courtesy of the Old Estes Collection: David and Carol Tanton

## Hart's Cottage Inn Restaurant/Buffeteria

Hart's Cottage Inn Restaurant was another popular Elkhorn Avenue eatery in the middle decades of the twentieth century. Owned and operated by Dave Hart, it featured an all-you-can-eat buffet, which made it a favorite destination for high school boys of the time.[69]

*Postcard of Estes Park at mid-century. The Hart's Cottage Inn sign in the right foreground locates the restaurant, which offered both table service and a buffet.*

**Courtesy of the Old Estes Collection: David and Carol Tanton**

## German Kaese Kuchen (Cheese Cake)

Ingredients for one 8 inch cake:

1 lb. 3 oz. of cream cheese
5 1/2 oz. granulated sugar
pinch salt
1 tsp. vanilla
1 oz. fresh lemon juice
6 oz. fresh eggs

For Crust: Mix together 6 1/2 oz. crushed graham crackers, 2 oz. melted butter and 1 1/2 oz. granulated sugar.

Preparation:
1. Place cheese in mixer and mix at high speed til cheese is light.
2. While mixer is in motion add sugar, salt and flavoring slowly to cheese mixture. Then add eggs slowly and continue mixing at high speed until the mixture is light and fluffy. (The mixture or batter should be about double its original volume.)
3. Line 8 inch cake tin with graham cracker crust mixture and fill pan with cheese batter.
4. Place filled cake tin in a baking sheet or on cookie sheet which has the bottom covered with water and bake in oven at 350 degrees for 30–35 min. (longer at higher altitude) When cake is done remove from oven and cool thoroughly overnight, if possible.
5. When thoroughly cooled, ice the top of the cake with a topping mixture of equal parts sweet cream, sour cream, salad dressing, with sugar added to taste and cover the top of the cake about 1/4 inch thick.

To serve cut with thin wire or hot, very thin knife to avoid crumbling.

# Glen Haven

*"We want Glen Haven to be the most restful, enjoyable mountain home site in the country. We hope to avoid overcrowding and public commercialism, and to retain as much as possible Glen Haven's mountain wildness, and the simple neighborhood atmosphere, yet have as many conveniences as possible."*

—1925 Report: Glen Haven Resort

The little community of Glen Haven, nestled in the Canyon of the North Fork of the Big Thompson River, has its own unique history and stories to tell. It was founded by the Knapp family of Illinois,[70] who came west in the 1890s, settling first in Estes Park, where they started a sawmill. Orrin Smith Knapp (1835–1914) and his wife Eizabeth Catherine Althouse Knapp (1839–1917) had been in the lumber business before moving to the mountains. The couple was accompanied by their two sons and their families: Ira Owen (1859–1944) and Delia Dunkelberg Knapp, and Mason and Florence Knapp. Ira is credited with "discovering" the heavily wooded gulch while hiking in 1893. The Knapps subsequently opened a sawmill in Glen Haven in 1896, and for a time the tiny settlement was called Knappville.

During the earlier years, the village existed only as a summer retreat, not only for the Knapps (who wintered in Loveland) but also for a number of other families who escaped to the cool temperatures of Glen Haven from the foothill and flatland communities east of the Front Range. It remained so for more than sixty years—people did not stay in Glen Haven year-round until the 1950s.

In 1890, Rev. William H. Schureman (1853–1941), a Presbyterian lay missionary who traveled the villages and towns of the Front Range establishing Sunday schools, visited Mason Knapp, an old friend of his from Illinois. Schureman was thrilled with the quiet and secluded nature of the area and thought it an ideal retreat site for Presbyterians from the Boulder area. To that end, he founded the Presbyterian Assembly Association in 1903, which purchased land from the Knapps and began to sell lots in the Canyon for $50 each. Because Rev. Schureman considered "Devil's Gulch," as the area was by then being called, highly unsuitable for a community of Christians, he changed the name to Glen Haven. In the early years at least, the village was a sort of Presbyterian colony, and, as might be imagined of a community founded on religious principles, liquor was banned.

In order to provide goods and services to those first summer residents, the Association built a grocery store about 1921, run initially by a Reverend Benjamin and his wife from Greeley. Shortly thereafter, Mae (Ira's second wife, b. 1891) Knapp added a dining room to the store and began serving "chicken dinners and pies."[71]

The general store and grocery, the town hall, and a number of other historic buildings and businesses in the Glen Haven community were either severely damaged or destroyed in a catastrophic flood that hit the little communities of Larimer county, including Estes Park and Glen Haven, in September 2013. Many summer and year-round homes in Glen Haven were also swept away. Residents and business owners are in the process of rebuilding, with help from volunteers, including college students who have traveled to the mountains from around the country to provide necessary manpower to remove the debris left in the flood's wake. Many are optimistic that some semblance of normalcy will be restored to Glen Haven by summer 2014, when it is hoped that the legendary homemade cinnamon rolls, long a tradition at the general store, will be available to locals and visitors once again.

*The Knapp homestead in Glen Haven, as it looked shortly after it was built.*
Photo courtesy of the Estes Park Museum

## The Inn of Glen Haven

*"One of the most romantic places ever."*

In 1931, Ira Knapp built the Homestead Ranch in Glen Haven. Initially, it consisted of a dining room and rental cottages. Five years later, Knapp added a second story to the ranch house, moved the dining room upstairs, and renamed the resort Knapp's Homestead Ranch. Menus at the Homestead offered chicken dinners for sixty cents and steak and chop dinners for seventy-five cents. By 1938, Knapp's resort was known as Homestead Lodge, and offered to summer visitors saddle horses from its own livery in addition to room and board.

During the 1950s and 1960s, the Glen Haven Lodge, as it was then known, changed hands a number of times. One owner-couple was Mr. and Mrs. J. B. Sparks, of Houston, Texas. Finally, in 1967, the lodge was purchased by an Iowa couple that renamed it the Glen Haven Inn. The young couple, Bill and Doris Wells, were commercial artists from Des Moines who worked for Meredith Publishing's bestselling magazine, *Better Homes and Gardens*. The Wellses ran the Inn as a seasonal business, but because they lived in Estes Park year-round, they could open the lodge for short periods in the winter as well. One of their innovations included a twelve-night celebration at Christmas, a tradition that was picked up and promoted by the Inn's subsequent owners.

Wilbur Lavern Wells (1926–2008) and Doris Evans Wells (1928–2003) were Iowa natives who joined the art department of *Better Home and Gardens* (Des Moines, Iowa) soon after graduating from art school. After purchasing the Lodge, the couple launched a major interior renovation, moving the dining room to the main level and redecorating the upstairs rooms. Bill not only cooked for the restaurant but also designed and installed stained-glass windows, which gave the Inn a unique and distinctive countenance. In 1972, the Wells' Inn was featured in Betty Crocker's *Sphere Magazine*. Because the Inn offered a gourmet menu designed for the sophisticated palates of adults, it did not provide a children's menu. Instead, the Wellses offered youngsters the option of vegetable soup, which Bill created from his own recipe.

When the couple sold the Inn in 1978, they retired in Estes Park, where they were active in the community until Doris's death in 2003. The couple was also instrumental in founding, in 1979, the Saint Francis of Assisi Anglican Church in the Little Valley area of Estes Park, which Bill designed himself in the style of the Saint Francis Chapel in Assisi, Italy. He created most of the artwork that was installed in the tiny church, and also wrote sacred music, played the organ, and directed the choir. In 1992, he himself was ordained a priest in the Traditional Anglican Communion.

Ted and Karen Haynes purchased the Inn from the Wellses and ran it in the 1980s, adding the wine cellar. Then, in 1989, the Inn was sold to Tom and Sheila Sellers. A B&B as well as a restaurant, the Inn garnered consistently high ratings from Inn guests as well as permanent residents from across the Estes Valley. A disastrous flood in September 2013 devastated the Glen Haven community. The Inn was heavily damaged, but plans are underway to make repairs and reopen this historic business, including its popular dining room, in the near future.

*Wilbur Lavern "Bill" Wells was both owner and cook at the Inn of Glen Haven in the 1970s. Under the Sellers, the Inn continued to serve a gourmet menu to diners.*

Photo courtesy of Sphere Magazine

### Inn of Glen Haven Vegetable Soup
*(Wilbur Lavern Wells)*

1 lb lean beef stew meat, cut up
1 mild onion, chopped
2 stalks celery, chopped
3–1/2 c water
1/2 tsp celery salt
1/4 tsp thyme
2 or 3 whole cloves
1 tsp instant beef bouillon
snipped parsley
3 c tomato juice
2 carrots, sliced
3 potatoes cut into cubes (3/4 inch)
1/2 tsp garlic salt
1 tsp Worcestershire sauce
1 bay leaf
1 tsp instant chicken bouillon

Brown meat. Place in large pot and add tomato juice. Simmer 15 minutes. Add vegetables and water and bring to a boil. Cover and reduce heat, simmer 1 hour, stirring occasionally. Stir in rest of ingredients, except parsley. Cover and refrigerate 24 hours. To serve, reheat soup to boiling reduce heat, and simmer 5 minutes. Garnish with parsley.

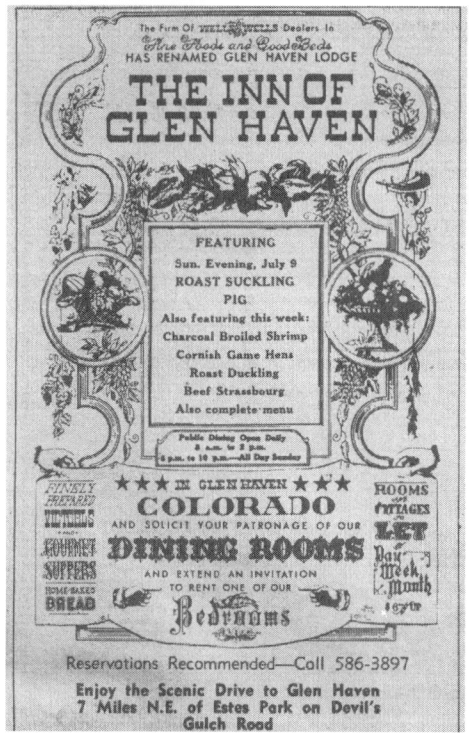

*Calico Kate's Gift Shop was a hub of local social activity as well as a favorite tourist destination in Glen Haven in the 1950s and 1960s.*
Photo courtesy of the Estes Park Museum

### Calico Kate's Gift Shop: The Fergusons

While the Inn clearly dominated the little community of Glen Haven for many years, no discussion of food in the village would be complete without recipes from a lady who was arguably the town's most famous former inhabitant, Dorothy Elizabeth Walters "Dottie" Ferguson—a.k.a. Calico Kate. In 1956, Dottie opened Calico Kate's Gift Shop, which quickly became the informal social center of the little community.[72]

Dottie Ferguson (1914–1993) was born in Greeley, the daughter of Herman Walters (1876–1944), a German-born baker of considerable talent, who had immigrated to the United States in 1886. Lured to Ouray, Colorado, by the prospect of silver mining, Walters soon abandoned his dream and settled instead in Denver. There, in 1907, he married Henrietta Erdbruegger (b. 1887). In Greeley, Herman launched a business in partnership with Claude H. Hackett (1884–1963): Hackett & Walters Bakery.

Beginning in the summer of 1914, the Walterses began summering in the mountains. Later, Dottie would recall:

> *Family meals, freshly baked bread, coffee cakes, and pies were produced on little Lulu, a shiny black coal range that "was the joy of my mother!"*

*Mother was never happier than when baking and she generously shared the results of her labors. Dad was an old-time German Baker and his strong hands could knead a loaf of bread into silken tenderness—his rye bread was an old world taste treat.*

No doubt inspired by her parents' examples as well as their recipes, Dottie soon developed her own culinary talents, first by creating frozen cookie dough, which she successfully marketed as "slice and bake,"[73] and later by publishing a line of popular original cookbooks. When they opened the shop, Dottie and her husband David Frank Ferguson (1908–1976) moved to Glen Haven. Eventually, Dottie would open "Calico Kate's" shops in Scottsdale, Arizona and Disneyland.

Dottie lived in Glen Haven until her death in 1993. The little building that once housed her shop was swept away in the flood of September 2013.

### Calico Kate's Applesauce Pancakes (*Aebleskiver*)
*(Dorothy Elizabeth Walters Ferguson)*

*"Just the thing to serve after a mountain hike in the early morning."*
2 cups milk
2 cups flour
1/2 teas. salt
2 tbls. sugar
3 eggs
applesauce

Beat egg yolks, add sugar.
Sift dry ingredients & add alternately with milk.
Fold in stiffly beaten egg whites.
Place bit of fat in each aebleskiver pan & fill 2/3 full with batter. Then place a small teaspoonful of applesauce on top of the batter, carefully add a bit more batter to each one.
Cook until bubbly. Then turn carefully & cook on other side.

*Serve with syrup or "Calico Kate's" preserves. Sometimes just dust with powdered sugar. These call for a pot of hot coffee and good big appetites. Just the thing to serve after a mountain hike in the early mornings.*

# Mother's Wonderful White Bread

*(Henrietta Erdbreugger Walters)*

*"There is no perfume that can compare with the fragrant smell of bread baking in the oven."*

2 cups scalded milk
2 tbls. sugar
2 teas. salt
2 tbls. shortening
1 cake of pkg. yeast
5 1/4 cups sifted flour

Measure out scalded milk. Set aside a small amount to cool for dissolving yeast. Pour the rest over shortening, sugar & salt. Stir 'til sugar and salt are dissolved & shortening is melted.

Add half the flour & beat well. When lukewarm add dissolved yeast & remaining flour. Mix well & knead 300 times (about 6 min) on floured bread board. Put dough in greased bowl, cover & let rise until doubled in bulk (about 50 min). Keep in warm place.

Punch down dough & let rise again until doubled (about 30 min.). Punch down & divide dough in half. Roll each half into a ball & let rest on board 10 min. Shape into loaves, put into greased pans 7 1/4 x 3 1/4 x 2 1/2. Cover & let rise until again double in bulk (about 45 min). Bake in 400 oven 45 to 50 min. Makes 2 loaves.

*The Devil's Gulch Tea Room in Glen Haven in the 1950s would become The Red Stallion Inn, a restaurant and bar, a decade later.*
Photo courtesy of the Estes Park Museum

## The Red Stallion Inn: The Van Horn Family

*"Where the West is Still for Real"*

Paul H. Van Horn (1912–2000), the founder of the Red Stallion Inn in Glen Haven, was born in Loveland, Colorado, the son of George N. and Mariah Belle C. Van Horn. George (b. 1871) had come west from Pennsylvania in the 1880s, and was a successful attorney. In Greeley in 1898 and Loveland in 1900, he served as lawyer for both F. O. Stanley and Enos Mills.

Paul graduated with a degree in civil engineering from Colorado A&M (later Colorado State University) in 1935. While working for the Bureau of Reclamation, he took a leadership role in the creation of the Alva B. Adams Tunnel, which brought water to Estes Park from the western slope of the Rocky Mountains. His responsibility as an engineer was to make sure that the two tunnels, one from each side, were successfully aligned. After the tunnel project was completed in 1948, Paul, who had married Mary

*Poster announcing the opening of the Red Stallion Inn in Glen Haven in 1960.*

Poster courtesy of Bill Van Horn

Jo Janosec, founded his own engineering firm and purchased the Hobby Horse Dude Ranch on Highway 34. The family ran the ranch until 1959.

In 1960 Van Horn opened the Red Stallion Inn in Glen Haven. The building, which had previously housed the Devil's Gulch Tea

*The western mural in the Red Stallion, created by Arizona artist Monte Flagg, made the bar a unique venue for residents and visitors to Glen Haven.*

Photo courtesy of Bill Van Horn

Room, was the work of Ronnie Eastwood. Fir logs harvested on the site were used in the building's construction. During the 1960s, the Red Stallion was frequently the site of benefit dances for local charities and drew crowds from many of the Front Range communities. The most dramatic features at the Inn were large murals in the bar and dancehall, created by Arizona artist Monte Flagg (1929–1985).[74] Flagg was well known for his paintings of cowboys and cowboy themes, and the popularity of his work earned him the sobriquet "cowboy Rembrandt." Today Flagg is chiefly remembered for his portraits of Indian children.

When the Van Horns sold the Red Stallion in 1998, the log building was converted into an art gallery of the same name. Today the building is a private home.

## Italian Bread

*(Paul and Mary Jo Van Horn)*

1/4 c. olive oil
1 cake yeast
6 1/4 c. flour
2 c. lukewarm water (little more if needed)

Fill bowl with flour. Make hole in center and add water, salt and crumble in yeast. Mix thoroughly. Add olive oil. Knead, cover and let rise—punch down when double in size and knead again. Form into 2 loaves in oiled bread pan. Let rise. Bake at 350 degrees 35–50 min.

## Red Stallion Minestrone Soup

*(Paul and Mary Jo Van Horn)*

Soak several hours 1/2 c. dried kidney beans and 1/2 c. small lima beans. Cook until tender.

| | |
|---|---|
| 1/2 c. salt pork, diced (dried out) | 1/2 c. onions, diced |
| 1/2 c. carrots, diced | 1/2 c. celery, diced |
| 1/2 c. short spaghetti | 1 c. tomatoes |
| 2 potatoes, diced | 1 c. zucchini squash, diced |
| 1 c. turnips, diced | 2 c. cabbage, shredded |
| 1/4 c. parsley, chopped | 1/2 tbsp. basil |
| 1 tbsp. Parmesan cheese | 1 clove garlic, crushed |
| salt and pepper to taste | 2 1/2 qt. meat stock |

Fry salt pork with onions, garlic, carrots, and potatoes (until onion is yellow). Add other ingredients to meat stock and cook 30 minutes. <u>Don't overcook</u>. Serve with Parmesan cheese for topping, with Italian Bread. (Also freezes well).

*Fawn Brook Inn Dining Room as it looked in the early days.*
Postcard courtesy of the Bobbie Heistercamp Collection

## Allenspark's Fawn Brook Inn

The Fawn Brook Inn opened to paying guests in the 1930s, having been built in 1927 and first used as a general store. In its almost ninety years of service as an Inn, the Fawn Brook has had only seven owners. Certainly the first one, Augusta Mengedoht (1892–1977), was one of the most colorful. An heiress from Nebraska who purchased the Inn in 1935, Mengedoht initially ran the Inn as a hunting lodge. Standing well over six feet tall, Augusta was imposing figure. A woman of strong convictions, constitution, and skills, she was able to handle blacksmithing, horseshoeing, plumbing, electrical work, roofing, and embalming with equal aplomb. She was also a fine cook. Specialties of the house during her tenure at the Inn included buffalo steak and bison stew.

Born in Omaha, Augusta ("Gussie") was the sixth and youngest child of German immigrants (1869) Frederick "Fritz" Mengedoht (1844–1924) and his wife Augusta Wilhelmine Mengedoht (1853–

*In this photo dating from the 1930s, Gussie Mengedoht shares a shooting "outing" with Cleo Tallman (b. 1908) in Allenspark.*
Photo courtesy of the Carnegie Library for Local History, Boulder, Colorado

1892). Sadly, Augusta died within a month of her daughter Gussie's birth, and soon thereafter, Frederick, a successful businessman and realtor who worked for the Union Pacific, married Bertha Heidt (1879–1962),[75] a woman thirty-four years his junior.

Gussie experienced a privileged childhood. Trained as a violinist and as a concert pianist, she married an artist, Augustus William Dunbier (1888–1977) in 1918. The union was an unhappy one; the couple lost a baby in 1918 and ultimately divorced in 1927. Shortly thereafter, Gussie moved to Colorado. Her first job after arriving in Allenspark was as manager of the Point-of-Pines Lodge and an adjacent resort called the Highlands Cabins, which eventually became part of Highlands Presbyterian Camp.

In an extraordinary turnaround from what appears to have been an early focus on the arts, Gussie embraced an outdoor life and became an avid and able hiker and fisherman. After purchasing the Inn in 1935, she often served as a mountain guide for her guests and organized hunting parties that she herself led. She was also active in promoting the development of Allenspark as a skiing destination. Her practice of carrying two guns led to the sobriquet "gun woman."[76]

Gussie Mengedoht was followed by a number of capable successors at the Inn, beginning with Ann and Charles Wetig, who purchased the Inn in 1946. From the 1950s through the 1970s, the Inn was owned first by Rose and John Reinhold, next by Mary Beth and Dick Alford, and finally by Kathy and John Richards. The Richardses sold the Inn to its present owners, Hermann and Mieke Groicher, in 1978. The Inn is open year round and remains a popular dining destination for local residents across the Estes Valley. The Groichers published a cookbook of Fawn Brook Inn recipes in 2008.

# Notes

1. J. H. Pickering, et al, *Then and Now*, p. 80.
2. Interestingly, the hotel was connected by a passageway to the Tabor Opera House next door. After Horace Tabor (1830–1899) met Elizabeth McCourt "Baby" Doe (1854–1935), he installed her in an apartment in the hotel so that he could meet her discreetly without his having to pass through the hotel lobby.
3. Ralph Russell (1884–1958) and Betty Marguerite Abildgaard (1880–1929) were married in Chicago in 1908. Ralph later owned and managed the Estes Park Laundry.
4. Over the course of his career, more than one hundred of his photographs, taken all over the American West, Hawaii, Mexico, and New Zealand, appeared in *National Geographic*. The beauty of his work and his expertise with autochrome plates earned him a national reputation, and he was much sought after as a lecturer on the process. His tours often took him away from Estes Park and his family for weeks at a time.
5. The Old University of Chicago, the precursor of the University of Chicago, was a Baptist institution that offered both undergraduate and graduate degrees. Situated on beautiful lakefront property donated for the purpose by Senator Stephen A. Douglas, it was closed for financial reasons in 1886.
6. Emma (1853–1936) played the organ for the Presbyterian Church.
7. On the occasion of the fiftieth anniversary of the Club's founding, Mabel provided this description of the first meetings and early days:

> "One bright afternoon in 1912 Mrs. Hondius met Mabel Clatworthy in front of the Hupp Hotel and askt [sic] her to be Secretary of the Estes Park Woman's Club. Meetings were held at private homes and as I remember about a dozen members organized the club. Once in particular we met at the home of Mrs. Ed Macdonald. In order to get a quorum two of us went up & down the streets in quest of the proper numbers to be present."

Harriet Rose Burgess. *Then The Women Took Over: A Hundred Years of the Estes Park Woman's Club*. (Estes Park Museum Friends & Foundation, Inc. Press: 2012), p. 4.

8. The name either recalled the steep stone steps that provided access to the house from the town below or the stained-glass panel in the front door the colors of which recalled "Joseph's biblical coat of many colors." J. H. Pickering et al., *Then and Now*, p. 84.
9. In 2001 the Town of Estes Park purchased the 20-acre site, which included Birch's second cabin, as well as the ruins of Jacob's Ladder. Added to the Colorado State Register of Historic Properties in 2001, Jacob's Ladder is now managed by the Estes Park Museum.
10. *Mountaineer* (July 30, 1908).
11. *Estes Park Trail* (April 30, 1926), p. 9.
12. *Rocky Mountain News*, Denver (Feb 28, 1882).
13. William Alexander (1876–1941), Otto Leslie (1877–1930), Lawrence Estes (1882–1939), and Ralph Marion (b. 1885).
14. J. H. Pickering, *America's Switzerland*, p. 64.
15. *Estes Park Trail* (January 5, 1923).
16. *Estes Park Trail* (October 12, 1923).
17. *Estes Park Trail* (October 26, 1923).
18. Glen and Leora moved to San Diego, California, where Leora died in 1976. The following year, and just two months before his own death, Glen married Leora's younger sister Maurine A. Lewis (b. 1905).
19. Harry and Julia Gooch sailed from Liverpool to Londonderry (Ireland) to Montreal on their honeymoon in September 1883.
20. Edward "Ed" Gooch married three times—to Elinor Crumrine (1887–1909) in 1908, Ethel Milheim

(1876–1928) in 1913, and Katherine Weber (1897–1993) in 1929. His daughters were Marianna Gooch (b. 1916) and Charmayne Gooch (1930–2013). Marianna continues to live in the Loveland/Estes Park area.

21. Carl Gooch (1890–1966) and his oldest brother, Ed Gooch (1884–1966), remained close for much of their adult lives. They lived and worked in Loveland, and together owned and operated the Lincoln Avenue Garage in Loveland through much of the Great Depression. Carl was married twice—to Ethel Briggs (1890–1938) in 1911 and to Mary Chamney Wild (1892–1969) in 1939. He and Ethel had one child, Lorene Gooch (1912–1976).

22. The Daniels, Fisher & Company store later became the May D&F Company. Its clock tower, which remains a Denver landmark, was salvaged when the original D&F building was torn down.

23. June Gooch (1919–1976) married Joseph Morris (1918–1979) in 1943 after both graduated from the University of Colorado in Boulder. They had four sons—James Morris (1944–2002), John Morris (b. 1946), Larry Morris (b. 1950), and Michael Morris (b. 1952).

24. The Higby family included: Harry LeRoy Higby (b. 1854); Nina Wright Higby (1865–1965); and three children: Clifford Starr Higby (1885–1977), Reed Andrews Higby (1888–1976), and Lester Wright Higby (1894–1983).

25. The Higbys' youngest son, Lester, served in the navy during World War I, and upon his return seems to have split his time between Estes Park and Wyoming, where he was for a time a Ranger for the Forestry Service. He and his wife Nina Harris Higby were the parents of two sons.

26. Harry and Nina eventually divorced in 1926.

27. While she was living in Wyoming, Nina was a charter member of the Women's Christian Temperance Union and also promoted the establishment of Carnegie libraries in both Cheyenne and Laramie.

28. *Estes Park Trail* (September 1923).

29. Clifford eventually became an ordained minister.

30. *Estes Park Trail* (May, 1923).

31. "Another Appeal for a Museum by Frances DeVol Higby." *Estes Park Trail* (January 25, 1924).

32. H. F. Pedersen, *Castles*, p.168.

33. *Ibid.*, p. 167.

34. A number of the Chalet's wonderful log buildings were moved to Highway 7 near downtown Estes Park, where they were incorporated into what is now the Masonic Lodge.

35. The Wheel Bar now occupies the site of Godfrey's original store.

36. *Estes Park Trail* (March 28, 1924).

37. *Estes Park Trail* (December 16, 1921).

38. The photos of the Byxbes and the Art Gallery are reprinted here from: R. L. Crump. *The Prints of Lyman Byxbe, Omaha to Estes Park: An Artist's Legacy and Catalog Raisonné*, David Tanton, ed. (Estes Park: Estes Park Museum Friends & Foundation Inc. Press, 2011.)

39. Alice's recipes often appeared in the "High Altitude Recipes" column in the *Estes Park Trail* in the 1940s and 1950s.

40. Robert L. Crump. *The Prints of Lyman Byxbe (1886–1980), A Catalog Raisonné: In Competition with Souvenirs, Photos, Postcards and the Like.* (Wayzata, Minn: Studio K, 2002.)

41. R. L. Crump. *The Prints of Lyman Byxbe, (1886–1980), A Catalog Raisonné*, p. 149.

42. For a complete history of the Estes Park Woman's Club and details of its founding, see H. R. Burgess. *Then The Women Took Over: A Hundred Years of the Estes Park Woman's Club.* (Estes Park: Estes Park Friends & Foundation, Inc. Press, 2012).

43. A saying printed on Old Plantation menus in the 1930s.

44. R. H. Tallant (1853–1934) preferred to use the name Richard or Dick rather than Reginald.

45. "The owners, Mrs. W. E. Burgess and her brother, Carl Porter, plan to make the café a symphony in black and white they say. The most startling color combination in the world has been chosen for the walls, trim, tables and other furniture. An extensive search was made for the drapes by Mrs. Burgess before finding the ones selected which picture the passage of an old Mississippi river steamboat in an appropriate setting. The antique lamps would delight the heart of a collector of wrought iron. Considerable search was necessary before the right ones were found to carry out the old plantation motif, something new for Estes Park. During the summer season a colored mammy will help attend to the wants of the tourists." *Estes Park Trail* (December 18, 1931).

46. "Plantation Restaurant history and the art of Richard Tallant." Presented by Bob Burgess and Rhoda Service Tallant, April 23, 1981. Estes Valley Library Archives.

47. The Burgess brothers added the Coat of Arms Tavern to the restaurant in 1968 and began to serve alcoholic beverages. The recipe for the restaurant's signature mint juleps, however, had come from their mother, Thelma Porter Burgess Chapman.

48. Sauce Robert was created as an accompaniment for the Old Plantation's Old Sizzling Steak. The steak itself was a 10-ounce sirloin, which was served with sauteed mushrooms and sauce Robert on a sizzling platter.

49. "The secret to delicious liver according to my Dad was not to cook it too long. Waitresses had to come and 'fire' their liver five minutes before they were ready to pick it up and serve to their table. Liver came standard with bacon, but you could also have onions or both." Elizabeth Burgess Eggert (personal communication, 2013).

50. As the story goes, Jelsema purchased a merry-go-round for the Riverside, but when it arrived he discovered that the carousel's motor was missing. Not one to let this obstacle stand in his way, Jelsema salvaged all the carousel horses, and then used them as bar décor.

51. It seems likely that the Holland Inn was operated as a summer business during the years of Kathryn Servey's ownership, as she managed the Greeley Country Club during the winter months as late as 1944. *Greeley Tribune* (December 18, 1944).

52. *Estes Park Trail Vacation Edition*, 1964.

53. McConnell was first employed by Brinkley Drug Co., but he eventually opened his own store, McConnell's Pharmacy, which was located on the corner across from the City Hall. It not only carried drugs but also featured a soda fountain. The store's advertisement in 1944 read, "The Friendly Drug Store. We make our own ice cream fresh daily."

54. It had formerly been the Blue Ribbon Livery.

55. A Seybold family story credits a drawing by Alfred Cobb's little daughter Edna with suggesting to her father the original design for the building.

56. Edna B. Cobb (1890–1979) was married in 1905 at the age of fifteen to a man named Arnold. The couple had one daughter, Clara Lois, born in 1908. By 1920, Edna Cobb Arnold had married Walter A. Gray, by whom she had a daughter, Jeanne. Within four years, Edna had married for a third time; her new husband was William and Ella James's son Howard (1872–1928). Howard and Edna had two children together, Howard James (b. 1924) and Eleanor James (b. 1926). After Howard's death, Edna in 1932 married John Russell Myers (b. 1898), a partner in Boyd's Market in Estes Park.

57. Charles Lewis Herzog (1909–1985) and Doris Hope Romig Herzog (1911–1992).

58. Vick Hoerner, (personal communication, 2013).

59. Leola was the widow of Orlando's older brother, Linus, an Air Force sergeant, who was killed in Italy in 1945.

60. *Estes Park Trail-Gazette* (August 27, 1971).

61. The brainchild of Lee and Mike's son Steve Nagl, the Duck Race was "adopted" by the Estes Park Rotarians in 1988. Proceeds from the sale of tickets directly benefit dozens of Estes Park's non-profit agencies.

62. Erma Nell Crowley (1913–2004) also lived in Estes Park, where she owned the For Beauty's Sake beauty parlor.

63. Today, Ed's Cantina occupies Crowley's original Elkhorn Avenue site.

64. Peggy J. Hackleman Crowley.

65. Gerald F. Brownfield (1908–1983) married Vera Mae Hill (1905–1982) in 1931 in Lincoln, Nebraska.

66. Rex Roth, interview 2005. Estes Valley Public Library.

67. Shirlee Ann Kendle Roth (1930–2011) and Rex Roth (1932–).

68. Sybil Barnes. *Estes Park* (Images of America). (Charleston, SC: Arcadia Publishing, 2010).

69. Dave Tanton (personal communication, 2012).

70. Transcript of Lennie Bemis interview with Duke Sumonia, August 16, 1990. Estes Valley Public Library.

71. Knapp, Joseph G. *The Glen Haven Story.* (Boulder: Johnson Publishing Co., 1967).

72. Knapp, *ibid.*, p. 61

73. *Idem.*

74. Monte Flagg was born into a family of talented artists. His parents, James and Irene Flagg, and his three sisters, Claudine, Rita, and Irene, were all artists; his brother Dee was well known for his wood carvings. Today the Flagg Family Art Collection, which features paintings, wood carvings, photographs, and family memorabilia, is on display at the Bison Museum in Scottsdale, Arizona.

75. Bertha was an artist and philanthropist, whose estate provided money for art students' scholarships that to this day continue to be awarded annually. She was also a major benefactor of the Joslyn Art Museum in Omaha.

76. "Gun Woman a Jack of All Trades in Allenspark." *Boulder Daily Camera* (January 18, 2013).

# Five: Cottager Communities

*Take what trail you will, go where it leads, and return when the day is old, you will know that the spirit of beauty and of rest has been with you all the way, and that tomorrow and always you may find on the trail the strength for days of trial or stress, comfort for the time of sorrow, fellowship for the lonely hour, a heritage of blessing for all the year, and as the years go by, returning summer will find you again and again renewing your spirit in the fellowship of Estes Park.*[1]

While before the turn of the twentieth century the year-round population of Estes Park remained tiny, the number swelled every summer as hundreds and then thousands of "seasonal residents" descended into "this blue valley" to escape the heat and pace of plains and cities or to find relief for asthma and other respiratory problems experienced at lower altitudes. Drawn as they were either by necessity or by a desire to enjoy the mountain air, the solitude and quiet, or the adventures of fishing, hiking, climbing, and horseback riding in a such beautiful place, it is not surprising that so many of these flatlanders would move to formalize their love of the area through personal ownership of sometimes elaborate but more often primitive summer residences.

Before long, the knots of little cabins that began to appear about 1900 soon took on the semblance of neighborhoods; sometimes one person would purchase a large acreage and then sell lots to friends from home, while in other cases clusters of friends might

*Grandma Hallett, her daughter-in-law Elvena Sessions Hallett, and Elvena and William's children on the front steps of Edgemont, which beginning in 1881 served as the family's summer home.*
Photo courtesy of Dr. and Mrs. Eugene Oja

buy land or cabins close to those they knew. In this way, communities of "cottagers" began to appear in Moraine Park (or Willow Park as it was then known), along Fish Creek, in the Tahosa Valley, and on Prospect Mountain. Over time, these cottage collectives came to be known by specific names—the Fort Morgan Colony, University Heights, the Country Club, High Drive, Broadview, Glen Comfort, Dunraven Heights, Woodland Heights, and the Cliffs, to name just a few. The depth of the attachment to these little communities, within the larger frameworks of Estes Park, Colorado, and of the Rocky Mountains themselves, experienced by so many of the first generation of seasonal families was evinced in the passing of cabins from parents to children and then to grandchildren, a tradition that continues to this day.

Beginning in the 1920s, many of these seasonal residents achieved a sense of "belonging" in Estes Park through membership in the Summer Residents Association, which was created to introduce newcomers to one another and to the area. However, it should be noted that during the first decades the distinction between summer residents and Estes "year-rounders" was not necessarily predicated on length of stay in any given year but on the types of activities in which a family engaged; initially, at least, most of the "first" merchants, innkeepers, and professionals wintered at lower altitudes, returning in the summer just in time to welcome tourists and cottagers back to the mountains.

That the cottagers were regarded as important members of the community was marked by the fact that the local newspaper described their comings and goings, their social outings, and their visitors in some detail. In fact, *Trail Talk*, published in 1920, announced that a reporter would make the rounds of cottager communities each week to find out who was doing what and with whom. These accounts, even at the distance of a century, provide intriguing glimpses into the social, cultural, and economic activities of both part-time and full-time residents of Estes Park.

*Mary White riding her horse in Willow Park, c. 1920. She, her brother Bill, and their parents, William Allen and Sallie White summered in their Willow (Moraine) Park cottage beginning in 1912.*

**Photo courtesy of the National Park Service**

## Cottagers in Moraine (Willow) Park

*It was surrounded on three sides by snowcapped mountains that looked down into a valley, a peaceful green valley through which the Big Thompson River wound its way.... And it was to be for all our lives a haven and a refuge.*[2]

Although Willow Park (or Moraine Park as it is now called) was the year-round home of the likes of Abner and Alberta Sprague, the

*View of the back and side of Moraine Lodge, c. 1920. Built by Imogene "Mother" McPherson, the resort eventually included a recreation hall and guest cabins.*

Photo courtesy of the Estes Park Museum

Dutch rancher Pieter Hondius, and Imogene Green McPherson (who built the Moraine Lodge), by the end of the nineteenth century the area was being shared with a group of summer residents from Kansas. Beginning with a clutch of college professors from Lawrence—the Hodders, the Melvins, and the Higginses—the community soon expanded to include the families of two Kansas journalists, Charlie Scott from Iola and William Allen White of Emporia, and a doctor, William J. Workman of Ashland.

In spite of political differences[3] that may have dominated their relationship when in Kansas, Scott and White, together with the other Kansans in Willow Park, eagerly sought out one another's company during their summers together. White described what these vacations meant to him in his autobiography, and what the experience was like for his children.

> *We turned them loose then with the children of the academic people from Kansas University on the hillside and in the valley. We could*

*locate Mary with our field glasses by the little red ribbon topknot on her towhead, a mile away in the meadow by the brook that played through the grass.*[4]

As with so many members of cottager communities across the valley, the Whites were fully engaged in the life of the town. Sallie White was a member of the Estes Park Woman's Club, son Bill led visitors on fishing trips to remote lakes and streams, and daughter Mary rented burros to tourists and participated in youth conferences at the YMCA of the Rockies. Both Young Bill and Mary, along with the many neighborhood children, attended parties and dances at Stead's Ranch. William Allen White himself took part in local groundbreakings and writing contests, and was a frequent and popular speaker for Estes Park clubs and organizations. For the Whites, their summers in Moraine Park, so rich in memories, were the happiest of their lives.[5] And their feelings for the town were reciprocated: when the Whites' sixteen-year-old daughter Mary died in a riding accident in Emporia in the spring of 1921, her death was headline news in the *Estes Park Trail*.[6]

*Charles Frederick Scott of Iola, Kansas, who built the Scottage in Moraine Park as a summer home for his family.*
Photo courtesy of Dorothy Scott Gibbs

### The Scotts of Moraine Park

Charles Frederick "Charlie" Scott (1860–1938) of Iola, Kansas, owner and editor of the *Iola Register* (1882–1938), and five-term U. S. Congressman (1900–1912), had first come to Estes Park with a number of young friends during the summer of 1880 or 1881. The group was probably part of a Kansas University natural science "class," organized and led by the distinguished biologist and scholar Francis Huntington Snow (1840–1908).[7] Like so many high-country visitors before and since, Scott's visits ultimately led him to secure a piece of Moraine Park for himself and his family.

After his marriage to May Brevard Ewing (1869–1929) in 1893, Scott purchased land just south of what is now RMNP's Moraine Park Visitor Center, and built a log house there that he and May named the "Scottage." This cabin, a two-story log dwelling designed and built in 1898 by Abner Sprague's nephew, Charles A.

*May Brevard Ewing Scott, 1895.*

Photo courtesy of Dorothy Scott Gibbs

Chapman (1879–1951), has been the summer home of six generations of the Scott family.[8]

By contemporary standards, the Scottage was, and remains, rustic, although it has been somewhat altered over the years. Because

*The Scottage as it looks today. Built well before the turn of the twentieth century, the cottage still hosts members of the Scott family every summer.*
Photo courtesy of Don Stewart

it lacked its own well, water to meet the family's needs had to be carried up from the Big Thompson River in two pails suspended from a shoulder yoke. Even so, May Scott managed to feed her family of six there in fine style; in fact, Charlie reported that May's "kitchen range produced the most succulent comestibles that ever graced a gullet."[9]

Charlie and May were the parents of four children: Ewing Carruth (1894–1965), Ruth Merriman (1897–1955), Angelo C. (1899–1968), and Charles F. Jr. (1906–1965). Ewing earned degrees in chemistry from Stanford University (1917),[10] the University of California at Berkeley (1918), and the University of Chicago (Ph.D., 1928). In 1926 he married Dorothy Carnine, a fellow Kansan whom he had met in Chicago. The young couple then moved to Virginia, where Ewing held a professorship at Sweet Briar College from

*Charlie and May Scott's grandchildren, the children of Ewing C. Scott and Ruth M. Scott Lynn, photographed on the front steps of the Scottage.*
**Photo courtesy of Dorothy Scott Gibbs**

1927 to 1945. So captivated was Ewing by the Scottage in Estes Park that he had a log home built for his own family near the Sweet Briar campus. His wife, Dorothy, who studied art in Lynchburg, Virginia, under Elizabeth Hunt Barrett, became an accomplished lithographer. The couple had three children: Dorothy, Betty Ruth,

*Ewing Scott's recipe file, cards, and book of cocktail recipes.*
**Artifacts courtesy of Dorothy Scott Gibbs**

and Peter. Dorothy Scott Gibbs continues to live year-round in Estes Park. As a child she spent many summers in Moraine Park at the cabin her grandparents built.

Ewing's wife, Dorothy Carnine Scott, was also a contributor to the family's memoir, *The Scottage*. In it, she recalled details of the Scottage larder:

> We had crates of eggs, sides of bacon, buckets of corned beef in addition to cases of canned goods and great quantities of flour, sugar, cornmeal, etc. Mother used to make our bread. I remember she had a bucket with

*a sort of dasher like in an ice cream freezer which made it possible to sort of knead the bread just by turning a crank. We kept the eggs and such under the house at the back. . . . We got our fresh vegetables from a huckster who used to drive around to the summer cabins in a wagon at least once a week, sometimes twice. It was always a thrill when he came, and oh! What goodies he had.*[11]

According to his daughter Dorothy Gibbs, Ewing was a good cook in his own right, who kept his recipes in a file box left over from his days as a chemist at Sweet Briar. Each card was individually coded and then filed by food category. Dorothy's grandmother, Oma Carnine (1877–1975), was also an accomplished cook, and a copy of her favorite cookbook was kept at the Scottage for its use by subsequent generations of Scott family cooks.

## Boiled Fruitcake

*(Oma Josella Langellier Carnine)*

1 C sugar
1 C currants
1/2 C shortening
1 teas cloves
1 C water
1 C raisins
1 teas cinnamon
1/2 teas salt

Boil all for 3 minutes. Cool to luke warm. Add 2 cups flour, 1 teas soda.
Bake one hour in moderate oven.

## Corn Relish

*(Oma Josella Langellier Carnine)*

1 large cabbage, chopt fine
1/2 dozen onions
2 Cups sugar
1 Tbls. Salt
1 teas tumeric powder
1 dozen ears sweet corn
4 peppers (2 green, 2 red)
1 quart vinegar
1 Tbls. Mustard

Boil 30 minutes.

## Bath Tub Gin

*(Ewing Carruth Scott)*[12]

| | |
|---|---|
| Oil of Juniper berries | 16 oz |
| Oil of Angelica Root | 20 cc |
| Oil of Angelica Seed | 20 cc |
| Oil of Coriander | 40 cc |
| Oil of Lemon | 60 cc |
| Oil of Sweet Orange | 20 cc |
| Oil of Neroli | 5 cc |
| Oil of Geranium Rose | 5 cc |

Alcohol,* as much as you need to make 1 gallon.

[*Note: That Ewing Scott was a chemist is evident in his recipe. Ironically, today commercially distilled Gin must be used to supply the alcoholic content. The use of grain or denatured alcohol produces a poisonous concoction that is, quite literally, "to die for."]

## Bread Pudding[13]

*(May Brevard Scott with modifications by Ewing C. Scott)*

Scald 1 pint milk, pour over 1 cup bread crumbs and soak until the milk has cooled. Beat yolks of 3 eggs and 2/3 cup sugar together until light and mix all with 1 tablespoon melted butter, add 1 teaspoon vanilla and bake 1/2 hour. Beat whites with 4 tablespoons powdered sugar. When the pudding is done spread thin layer of meringue over top, cover with preserves or jelly, spread over this remainder of meringue and bake a delicate brown. Serve either hot or cold with cream or sauce.

    Don't make a meringue – just fold the beaten egg whites [with a little sugar added, or none] and the vanilla right into the cooled milk mixture and bake in a greased casserole like a soufflé at 350° for a half hour. Forget the fancy preserves! I never make this for company because the timing is too difficult – it needs to be eaten right out of the oven. However, it's awfully good cold the next morning for breakfast.

## Company Bean Soup
*(Scott Family Cookbook)*

Soak 2 cups of Great Northern beans overnight. Bring to a boil, add soda, stir, drain, and then add sufficient water to boil them properly together with a bay leaf, ½ onion, a clove of garlic, a piece of heavy bacon, salt, 1/8 tsp. pepper, and 1/16 tsp. cayenne. When beans are very soft remove bacon and puree the rest. Add an almost equal quantity of top milk and heat to boiling. Serve with a thin slice of lemon and a handful of croutons to each bowl.[14]

## Berry Pie
*(Scott Family Cookbook)*

Line pie tin with plain crust. For a pie requiring 2 large cups of either blackberries or raspberries, use one tablespoon of flour mixt dry with 2/3 cup of sugar, put half this in the bottom of pie, put in the berries previously crushing about half of them to form juice, sprinkle remainder of sugar and flour on top of berries, roll out the top crust and make several openings in it to allow steam to escape, wet edges of crust with a little cold water and pinch well together to retain the juice and bake in hot oven till light brown. If berries are very dry add 1 tablespoon water. For gooseberry pie put berries on back of stove with only enough water to steam, add equal measure of sugar and cook slightly then put in pie. Cherries require equal measure of sugar and one teaspoon butter for each pie.

*Dr. William J. Workman of Ashland, Kansas and Moraine Park, 1910.*
Photo courtesy of the Estes Park Museum

## Dr. Workman's Moraine Park Legacy

In addition to building and operating Fern Lake Lodge, Dr. William Jacob Workman (1852–1943) was "one of the pioneers in Moraine Park,"[15] homesteading sites there in 1902 and 1906 on land he purchased from Abner Sprague. His personal journey had been a unique one. Having received his medical education at universities in Missouri and Pennsylvania, Workman first set up a practice in his hometown of Knob Noster, Missouri. He married Katherine "Kate" Jane Elbert (1852–1880) in 1872, just before finishing his degree, and together the couple had a daughter, Jennie (1873–1928), and a son, James Elbert (1875–1954). A year after Kate's death, Workman married Emma Wells Howard (1865–1887), and together the couple had three children, Milo (b. 1882), Dessa (b. 1884), and Alberta Grace (1887–1965). Because the business end of his medical practice had not been a success, he moved his office and his family to Ashland, Kansas, in 1885, where he not only practiced medicine but also ran a ranch and developed an interest in agriculture. In addition, he invented new kinds of stucco and plaster and pioneered the use of poured concrete in the construction of domestic and commercial buildings.[16]

Dr. Workman took a third wife in 1888, Julia Lulu Ripley Oliphant (b. 1854), a widow of thirty-four. By 1900, the family had moved again, this time to Denver, where Dr. Workman again established a medical practice. However, his love of fishing took him to Estes Park, where he homesteaded two sites and completed Fern Lake Lodge by 1911. Workman lost Lulu to pneumonia in 1914, and the following year he took wife number four, Florence Jane Mount (1891–1982), a nurse he had worked with in Denver. Two daughters were born to the couple, Florence Wilma (1916–1990) and Dorothy J. (1918–2010).

*Dr. Workman with his baby daughter Florence Wilma in Moraine Park, summer 1916.*

Photo courtesy of the Estes Park Musuem

Although he continued to pursue his medical career in Denver for a time, Dr. Workman moved the family to Moraine Park in the summers so he could run Fern Lake Lodge. Eventually he began to sell off lots on the moraine to flatlanders who hoped to make the mountains around Estes Park their permanent summer homes. The descendents of two of the families continue to enjoy and maintain cabins as Moraine Park inholders:[17] the Hineses and the Bissells.

*The cabin Fred and Hilda Hines built in Moraine Park.*
Photo courtesy of Roger and Verlene Thorp

## The Hines Family

Dr. Frederick H. Hines (1874–1928) and his wife Hilda O. Nelson Hines (b. 1878) were neighbors of Dr. Workman in Ashland, Kansas. An Illinois-born dentist who had been educated in Chicago and Kansas City, Frederick married Hilda in 1908 in Wichita. The parents of five children, Fred and Hilda were active in the Summer Residents Association in Estes Park during their many years as cottagers in Moraine Park. Their cabin was "next door" to the summer house that Dr. Workman built for Florence. Dr. Hines continued to enjoy the Moraine Park cabin until he suffered fatal injuries when a bus in which he was traveling collided with a truck full of tractors near Mayfield, Kansas.

Frederick and Hilda's son Walter Frederick (1915–2012), who was only thirteen when his father died, married (1939) Rachel Marie Donabauer (1913–2012), a teacher in the Kansas City public schools. Both Walt and Rachel were career teachers in Topeka, and highly respected in their profession; husband and wife died within a few months of one another, both just shy of living one hundred years. Their children, Donald and Deborah, now own the Hines cabin, where they continue to summer with their families and friends.

### Hines Chili
*(Rachel Hines)*

Don wrote:

> *My mother introduced us to the idea of making chili to include the usual bean, tomato mash & meat . . . but also vegetables such as celery, green peppers and tomatoes . . . & in some instances frozen corn. The idea here is to add these extra fresh items after all else is thoroughly cooked, then serve when still somewhat crisp. This alteration, which by now has been improvised and altered to individual taste, has been received often with wide acclaim.*

## Bissell Family

Seeking relief for his hay fever, James Russell Bissell (1908–1994)[18] first brought his wife, Catherine "Ky" Gibson Bissell (1908–1995), to Estes Park in 1921 from their home in St. Louis. The couple stayed at Stead's Ranch and Hotel in Moraine Park that summer and many summers thereafter; and were active in the Summer Residents Association, serving as co-presidents in the 1920s. In 1945, the couple purchased one of Dr. Workman's original cabins, owned at that time by the heirs of a Mrs. Yelm, who had recently died. According to James and Ky's son Russell (d. 2012), the purchase was made on the spur of the moment, with the Bissells buying the little cottage "furniture, clothes, and all."[19]

The cabin originally consisted of three rooms and a screened porch, and was significantly enlarged by the Bissells in 1948. However, until the 1950s, the Bissell family took its meals at Stead's Ranch, which lay below them at some little distance. In 1957, James and Ky moved permanently to Estes Park, where they were both active members of local service organizations, Ky in the Estes Park Woman's Club and Epsilon Sigma Alpha, and Jim in Rotary. In 1962, James was one of the original directors for the Estes Park Area Historical Museum, Inc., the predecessor of the Estes Park Museum Friends & Foundation, Inc.

## Hot Crab Dip

*(Catherine "Ky" Gibson Bissell)*

2 T. cream
1 large pkg. calorie wise cream cheese
Mix until soft. Add:
2 T. horseradish
1/2 tsp. dehydrated onion
1 can crab meat
Slivered almonds.

Bake at 350 degrees—until bubbles. Can be served cold, also.

## Smoked Trout

*(Catherine "Ky" Gibson Bissell)*

Soy sauce
Sherry
Sugar
Pepper
Ginger powder

Amounts vary according to taste and size of trout. Marinate 24 hours, turning flattened trout. Bake slow oven until dry.

## Bread Boat

*(Catherine "Ky" Gibson Bissell)*

1 loaf Vienna or French bread
6 eggs (hard boiled, coarsely chopped)
1 1/2 c. celery, (diced)
1/2 c. stuffed green olives (chopped)
1/4 c. onion (chopped)
Butter or margarine
1 clove garlic (minced)
3/4 tsp salt
1/4 tsp. pepper
1/2 c. mayonnaise
2 T. prepared mustard

Crumble enough bread (taken from center of bread) to make 1 c. crumbs; add eggs, celery, olives, onions, salt and pepper. Combine mayonnaise and mustard, add to egg mixture and toss lightly. Fill loaf, replace top, brush loaf with butter. Wrap in foil. Bake in hot oven 425 degrees for 30 to 35 minutes or until heated through. Slice loaf in 8 servings. ["I add 1 lb. hamburger, browned. Ham, fish, chicken, etc. would be great."]

*Lincolnites of the Dunraven Heights Cottager Community, c. 1920. Far left on lowest step, Dr. Taylor; Ida Robbins, on first landing, fourth from right; Mariel Gere, standing behind Robbins.*

Photo courtesy of Lawrence Day

## Cottagers of Dunraven Heights

The little cottager community of Dunraven Heights, located near Fish Creek in the Estes Valley, was carved out of property that was initially purchased by Burton D. Sanborn[20] and F. O. Stanley from Windham Thomas Wyndham-Quin, fourth Earl of Dunraven. Sanborn (1859–1914), a land developer and entrepreneur who wintered in Greeley, acquired, as his portion, the sites of Dunraven's hotel and ranch properties. Over time, this property came to be dotted with little summer cabins owned by vacationers from Lincoln, Nebraska. Their number included many distinguished

Lincoln families, including the Taylors, the Clapps, the Robbinses, and the Geres.

One of the first, if not *the* first, to acquire land for a cabin from Sanborn was Dana X. Bible (1891–1980), a former coach and athletic director at the University of Nebraska. Bible, in turn, sold off properties to two other Lincoln families: the Raymond G. Clapps, whose cabin was built in 1920 by local contractor Alfred "Fred" Anderson, and the William G. Langworthy Taylors.

Raymond Gustavus Clapp (1875–1967) was a Yale-educated athlete and athletic educator who as a young man distinguished himself in track and field events. In fact, his skill in the pole vault earned him a place on the 1896 U.S. Olympic Team. As a professor at the University of Nebraska, he served as chair of the Department of Physical Education. An energetic spokesperson for college athletics, Clapp enjoyed a national reputation for introducing wrestling as a major collegiate sport in the 1930s and 1940s, and for serving on the U.S. Olympic Wrestling Committee in 1940. Dr. Clapp and his wife, Anne Louise Barr Clapp (1865–1945), were the parents of two daughters, Catherine and Margaret. The original Clapp cabin now serves as the summer home of Edgar M. Morrill Jr., and his family.

William George Langworthy Taylor (1859–1941) and his wife Frances Chamberlain Brown Taylor (1861–1925) were scholars who also taught at the University of Nebraska. A Harvard University graduate, Dr. Taylor's academic specialty was political economics. However, he was also a skilled horseman who taught riding during his winters in Lincoln and in 1925 published *The Saddle Horse: His Care, Training, and Riding*. Taylor's wife Frances ("Fannie") earned A.B. and M.A. degrees from Smith College before completing graduate work at the University of Chicago and Oxford University. A community leader in Lincoln, Frances' interests included civic improvement and women's suffrage. The Taylors had one child, a son, Edward (1899–1974). The Taylors' cabin in Dunraven Heights, which was named Owaissa Lodge (a name based on a phonetic spelling of the Arapaho word for "bluebird"), eventually passed to the Coles family, descendents of W. G. Langworthy Taylor's second wife, Florence Dye Coles (b. 1884); it was later purchased by another Lincoln family.

A third lot was sold to Lincoln-born Edgar Lamprey Morrill (1876–1945), a Fort Collins physician. The Morrills traced their family's American roots back to Abraham Morrill, who emigrated from England to Massachusetts in 1632. Among Abraham's distinguished descendents were Justin Smith Morrill (1810–1898), a founder of the Republican Party,[21] who "fathered" the 1862 Morrill Act that enabled the establishment of land-grant colleges in the American West; and Justin's grandson, Charles Henry Morrill (1842–1928), a New Hampshire–born Civil War veteran who settled his family in Stromsburg, Nebraska, in 1873. Charles' assistance to the Burlington Railroad in identifying routes through the western part of the state and his promotion of geological exploration in Nebraska made substantial contributions to the development of his adopted state. Named a University Regent in 1890 (he served as Board president from 1892–1902), Morrill was a major benefactor to the University's museum, to which he donated his extensive collection of Native American cultural artifacts as well as funding to maintain the museum that still bears his name.

The Morrill family continues to summer in Dunraven Heights, in the Clapp family's original cabin. The two families were united when Edgar Miner Morrill, the grandson of C.H. and Harriet Currier Morrill (1843–1917), married Catherine Barr Clapp (1909–1984). The original Morrill cabin has passed out of the family's hands.

The three cabins that now constitute "Westward O," the summer home of the Olson family, were built by Charles Oscar Bourk (1886–1979) between 1920 and 1933 on land purchased from B.D. Sanborn.

Others who built cabins on the hillside above Fish Creek in the 1930s were Rev. Elliott W. and Isabel Noyes Boone of Longmont, whose rustic mountain cabin[22] was built between 1936 and 1939, the Gere sisters,[23] and the Robbins family. The three Gere sisters—Mariel (1874–1960), Frances (1877–1965), and Ellen (1875–1941)—were the daughters of Charles H. Gere (1838–1904), a Civil War veteran, a regent of the University, and the founder and longtime editor of the *Nebraska State Journal*. The Geres' vacation home included a main cabin plus a number of small "bedroom" cabins that were scattered amongst the rock outcroppings on their property.

The water for the early Dunraven Heights cottagers came from a natural spring that had once served the Estes Park Hotel. The spring is now supplemented by a well drilled in the 1970s; it still provides water to a dozen or so of the cabins "on the hill," whose members belong to the Dunraven Heights Water Association.

*Ida Robbins (1903) built a cabin in Dunraven Heights in 1920–21.*

Photo courtesy of Day Heusner McLaughlin

## Robbins/Day Cabin

Ida Lewis Robbins (1869–1947), an Iowa-born schoolteacher from Lincoln, Nebraska, built her cabin in Dunraven Heights about 1920. When Ida's widowed mother Harriet (b. 1842) died in 1896, Ida was left to care for two younger siblings, Edith Lillian (1884–1957) and Charles Burton "Bert" (1877–1943).[24] As the twenty-eight-year-old head of the Robbins family household, Ida had already experienced a great deal of grief, having previously lost many other family members, including her father, Lewis "Lute" Robbins (b. 1835) in 1893, and two little sisters, May E. Robbins (b. 1873) in 1874 and Julia L. Robbins (b. 1875) in 1885.

Ida graduated with a master's degree in education from the University of Nebraska in 1901. She is remembered today as a leader in the suffragette community, a champion of social causes, and "a woman of fine intellectual ability, active in public and world affairs."[25] Among Ida's activities were the League of Women Voters and the Red Cross, and she was also a founding member of the Lincoln YWCA and Lincoln General Hospital. In the years before World War I, Ida traveled to Europe several times, taking her sister Edith with her in 1900.

Ida never married, and upon her death she left her cabin in Dunraven Heights to her sister Edith, a 1907 graduate of the University of Nebraska who had married a civil engineer, Warren French Day (1883–1976), in 1908.

When Edith Robbins Day died in 1957, the property passed to her four surviving children, Helen, Margaret, George, and Lewis, her son Warren "Heavy" Day having been killed in the Battle of the Bulge on Christmas Day 1944.

The Robbins/Day cabin is still being enjoyed by Ida's descendents, who no doubt love it as much as she did for the thirty summers that she entertained her family and friends in Dunraven Heights. Ida's great niece, Day Heusner McLaughlin, recalls her own summers at the cabin in this way:

> *The sleeping arrangements upstairs in the cabin were dormitory style—a curtain separated the boys from the girls. Whichever adults*

*Edith Robbins Day with her son George, on the running board of the family car, arriving at the cabin after traveling from Lincoln to Estes Park, summer, 1918.*

Photo courtesy of Day Heusner McLaughlin

*George, Warren, and Lewis Day in Estes Park, c. 1922.*

Photo courtesy of Lawrence Day

*were in charge slept downstairs in a bedroom in Aunt Ida's bed. My great Uncle George (my grandfather's brother) was an admiral in the US Navy. His telescope is at the cabin and we would use it to look out at the mountains. My Uncle Lewis taught us a lot about the out-of-*

*Ida Robbins, second from left, and her siblings, Harriet, far right, with Bert and Edith, right, in 1930.*

**Photo courtesy of Day Heusner McLaughlin**

*A picnic for members of the Robbins/Day families and the Gere sisters, hosted by Charles and Agnes Levings (front row, far right) at Graystone, located in the Tahosa Valley on the lower slopes of the Twin Sisters Peaks.*

**Photo courtesy of the Estes Park Museum**

*doors, took us on hikes where we were also able to safely simply stick our heads in the stream waters if we were thirsty!*[26]

One Robbins/Day cabin tradition, now over ninety years old, is the guest book, which constitutes not only a permanent record of cabin visitors over time but also an historical chronicle of family summers spent in Estes Park.

The recipes below belonged to "Grandmother Day," and were retrieved from a cigar-box collection of handwritten sheets. "The pickles were something that Edith made every other day during the 'cuke' harvest."[27]

## Grandmother Day's Favorite Bread and Butter Pickles

*(Edith Robbins Day)*

4 qts sliced cukes
1 green and 1 red pepper, slice thin
6 onions sliced
1/3 C salt

Wash & slice onions, cukes, & peppers. Sprinkle salt over in layers, well mixed through. Cover with crushed ice, stand in refrigerator 3 hours, drain well.

Add to boiling syrup – 2 kettles.
3 C vinegar
1–1/2 Tsp turmeric
2 Tbsp mustard seed
5 C sugar
1–1/2 Tsp celery seed
Heat pickles just to boiling, pack in sterile jars.

## Venison Roast

*(Day family)*

Soak venison in vinegar & water (½ of each) overnight or 8 to 10 hours. Then rinse and wipe off and soak for 2 hours in cold water. Put in baking pan – put a little Crisco in bottom of pan – salt and pepper it. Put in a Bay leaf. Then 2–1/2 hours at 450 degrees – then ½ hour at 400 – then about 1 hour or so at 300 degrees & O boy it's delicious!

## The Sweets of Historic Fish Creek

The acreage along Estes Park's Fish Creek, which offers views of Lumpy Ridge, the Never Summer Range, and peaks of the Front Range, attracted many early summer visitors to invest in summer cabins along its length. One such family, the Sweets, built a large Austrian-style chalet, Tyrolerne, in 1912.

William Ellery Sweet (1869–1942) was a philanthropist and politician who was elected Governor of Colorado in 1922. After graduating from Swarthmore College (Pennsylvania) in 1890, Sweet married a classmate, Joyeuse Lennig Fullerton[28] (1866–1962), two years later. Joyeuse was herself a Phi Beta Kappa scholar, having graduated from Swarthmore College and Cornell University. After their marriage, the couple relocated to Denver, where William became an investment banker. He retired at the age of fifty-three to pursue a political career as a Progressive.

A founding member of the YMCA of the Rockies, William brought his wife and family to summer in Estes Park for the first time in 1900. According to Channing Fullerton Sweet,[29] it was at Joyeuse's insistence that the family began vacationing in the mountains, to provide the children some relief from the heat of Denver summers. At the outset, William Sweet secured lodgings for the family at a number of local resorts, including the Elkhorn Lodge, the Rustic Hotel (later the H-Bar-G Ranch), and the Estes Park Hotel. After the destruction of Dunraven's hotel in 1911, Sweet invested in 160 acres of his own near the site of the Earl's ill-fated resort.[30]

At that time, the Sweet household included—in addition to William and Joyeuse and their four young children—a cook, two maids, and a chauffeur. The chauffeur was responsible for driving Joyeuse to the Village to shop almost every day. When not so occupied, he chopped wood and milked the family's cow, and even slaughtered the chickens served from the Sweets' kitchen on Sundays.

A conservative woman, Joyeuse was known for the frugality with which she maintained her household and the generosity she extended to her family in times of need. During her summers in Estes Park, she continued to ride her horse each day, until well into her eighty-seventh year, in spite of her innate fear of horses. Over time she abandoned a proper riding habit (divided skirt, black boots and "upturned straw hat" for "riding pants . . . with a three-quarter length fitted black coat under which she wore a man's shirt and tie. She never approved of women of any age wearing slacks." For this reason she did not like to be photographed in her riding attire.[31]

While it is unlikely that Joyeuse herself prepared the following recipe for Floating Island, the dish has French origins and has been a Sweet family favorite for generations.

## *Île Flottante* (Floating Island)

*(Submitted by Nancy Sweet)*

4 eggs
1 cup sugar
2 cups milk
1/8 teaspoon vanilla
1/2 cup sugar
1/2 cup water

Put egg whites in a mixing bowl and beat slowly at first. As they thicken, add 1/4 cup sugar and increase speed until they hold very stiff peaks. Scald milk and add 1/4 cup sugar and vanilla. Poach egg whites in milk 4 to 5 minutes, turning once. Remove to serving platter. Beat yolks with remaining 1/2 cup sugar in a bowl and add the hot milk, stirring vigorously. Cool and Strain. Make a caramel by boiling 1/2 cup sugar and 1/2 cup water to a syrup. Serve the cooled milk and egg mixture with the islands and drizzle caramel on top.

*Early photo of the administration building, Wind River Lodge, and guest cabins at the YMCA of the Rockies.*
Photo courtesy of the Estes Park Museum

## The Overlook at the YMCA

After the founding of the YMCA of the Rockies in 1902, a number of families wanted to invest in property nearby. Guy LaCoste (1875–1934), a Denver entrepreneur, had built a small resort anchored by his two-story, fourteen-room Wind River Lodge (opened in 1902) in an area known as the Overlook.[32] LaCoste had also built a more substantial homestead adjacent to his original dugout cabin, and it was this house that became the summer home of the family of Alexander and Ida Hyde of Wichita, Kansas.[33]

Laura Taylor tells her family's history in Estes Park in this way:

*The Taylor cabin, nestled in the pines near the grounds of the YMCA Conference in Estes Park, as it looks today.*

Photo courtesy of Marcia Taylor

*My family has been enjoying summers at the YMCA of the Rockies for six generations, starting with my Great Grandfather Hyde, . . . around the turn of the twentieth century. When his youngest daughter, my grandmother, [Martha Jane] Patti Hyde, married Houston Barclay (in 1919), he gave her one of his cabins as a wedding gift. [Patti and Houston Barclay] would spend every summer at the Barclay Cabin. Their four children continued the tradition, bringing their children to share with my grandparents the beauty and wonder of that cabin on the Y grounds. I have many fond memories of the time spent with them there.*

Cooking was obviously an important feature of these long-remembered summers. According to Laura:

*During these summer visits, my grandmother would preside over the family, orchestrating all the busy comings and goings. I remember the many hymn sings and tea parties she would host. We would hike, ride horseback, and have youth camp adventures. In the evenings, we attended square dances and nature programs. . . . My grandfather would rise each morning and, still in his robe, feed the birds on the porch. . . . On a Saturday, my grandfather, along with all the men folk there at the time, would make loaves and loaves of this aromatic bread. His Dilly Bread recipe sparks so many memories every time I smell it baking.*[34]

*Houston Barclay and his grandchildren.*

Photo courtesy of Laura Taylor

## Grandpa Barclay's Dilly Bread
*(Houston Barclay)*

*(Makes 2 loaves)*
1 pkg. active dried yeast
1/4 C lukewarm water
1 C creamed cottage cheese (lukewarm)
2 Tbsp sugar
1 Tbsp instant minced onion
1 Tbsp butter (soft)
2 tsp dill seed
1 tsp salt
1/4 tsp baking soda
1 unbeaten egg
2 1/2 C flour

Soften yeast in water, set aside. Combine cheese, sugar, onion, butter, dill seed, salt, soda and egg. Stir in yeast, then flour. Let rise in a warm place (85–90 degrees) until doubled in size (50–60 min.). Stir down dough, divide in halves and turn into two well-greased pans. Let rise in a warm place until doubled (30–40 min). Bake @ 350 degrees for 40–60 min., until golden brown. Remove onto cooling rack, brush with soft butter and sprinkle with salt.

## Cottagers of the Cliffs: "Holy Hill"

Across the road from what is now the entrance to the YMCA conference center grounds was another "unique mountain community,"[35] known familiarly as Preacher's Hill or Holy Hill. The creation of this cluster of summer homes was the idea of John Timothy Stone (1868–1954), minister of the Fourth Presbyterian Church on Michigan Avenue in Chicago from 1909 to 1930 and president of McCormick Theological Seminary. An evangelist who spoke at the funeral of Billy Sunday in 1935, Stone oversaw the construction of the Presbyterian Church's magnificent Gothic Revival cathedral, now the oldest building on Chicago's "Miracle Mile." He was also a prolific writer on spiritual and biblical themes.

Captivated by the Rockies on his first trip to the YMCA Camp in 1909/1910, Stone and his wife, Bessie Panning (b. 1874), subsequently built there a beautiful, two and one-half story, Rustic-style, stone-and-log vacation home they called "Mountainside." Stone was a frequent summer preacher during YMCA conferences, and was known for his commonsense rather than philosophical sermons. He also liked to entertain his friends. In 1923, the *Estes Park Trail* reported on a fish fry at Mountainside:

> *Dr. John Timothy Stone and a party of friends spent several days in Wyoming fishing, returning the latter part of the week. On Saturday afternoon Dr. Stone entertained about 165 friends at a fish fry on Mountainside, his summer home above the Y. There was more trout than the party could stow away, and in addition roasted corn, watermelon, etc., were served. A huge bonfire and impromptu speeches completed the occasion. Several noted Doctors of Divinity and Governor William E. Sweet were among the guests.*[36]

Beginning in 1917, Stone purchased additional parcels from the YMCA, the Earl of Dunraven, and Guy LaCoste, eventually acquiring almost 200 acres. It was upon a portion of this property that he built eleven log cabins. As time went by, the charismatic Dr. Stone began to "invite [fellow] Presbyterian[37] ministers to stay" in one of these cabins for a few weeks in the summer. Those individuals and families whom he felt would "fit in to the roughness of mountain living" he encouraged to buy into his little community.[38] Later, the property was managed by the Cliffs Association, which sold lots ranging from 1.75 to 6.9 acres, and costing between $895 and $3,450. Stone often visited his friends living at the Cliffs,

*Dr. Stone enjoyed entertaining friends and colleagues at Mountainside and created a spacious and elegant dining room for the purpose.*
**Postcard courtesy of the Bobbie Heistercamp Collection**

bringing a portable organ that he always carried with him in his car for use when he held alfresco church services.

Because of the religious calling of the first property owners, it is not surprising that Holy Hill had a covenant dictating "acceptable" behavior and activities, especially relating to the use of alcohol:

> *The Christian Sabbath shall be observed with decorum and no nuisance shall be allowed to exist upon said property nor shall intoxicating liquors ever be manufactured in or upon said premises, or sold, given away or otherwise disposed thereon.*[39]

In cabins named variously TreeTops, Cliff Crest, Dalcliffs, Rock Cliff, and the like, the descendents of these early cottager families continue to enjoy Holy Hill and the peace, quiet, and natural beauty that drew Dr. Stone to invest in the property in the first place. At present there are twenty-four cabins on Holy Hill.[40]

Stone's own home, Mountainside, was used briefly as a hotel, and finally purchased by the YMCA of the Rockies. Now listed on the National Register of Historic Places, the house atop Emerald Mountain continues to be a landmark and hiking destination for "Y Camp" visitors.

*The Clark family poses for the camera on the porch of their summer cabin on Holy Hill.*

Photo courtesy of Donna Clark

## The Clark Family

The Cliffs, the summer home of the Clark family of Chicago, was built about 1919 for a New York–born Kansan, William Coffin ("W. C.") Coleman (1870–1957), who summered at the YMCA Camp for years with his wife, Fanny Lucinda Sheldon, and the couple's two sons, Robert and Clarence. Coleman is best remembered today as the inventor of the Coleman Arc Lamp in 1905 and founder, in 1913, of the Coleman Lamp and Stove Company. Coleman also manufactured camping equipment, as well as munitions, all of which were used by the U. S. Army in both World Wars. The Colemans were staunch supporters of the YMCA Conference and camp; in fact W.C. was responsible for bringing electricity to the Y grounds.

Coleman originally intended the cabin on "Preacher's Hill" as a surprise gift for his wife; however, she refused the gesture, saying that it was too large and would require too much work. It was subsequently rented to the Drake family of Chicago, the owners of the Drake Hotel on Michigan Avenue, who would spend twenty-five summers on Holy Hill. Tracy Corey Drake (1864–1939), his wife Annie D. (b. 1868), and their sons Carlos and Francis had first come to Estes Park as guests at Dr. Stone's Mountainside early in the 1920s.

Belonging once again to Dr. Stone by 1943, The Cliffs was offered to Harry Martin Clark (1895–1975), his wife Marie M. Van Malsen Clark (b. 1903), and their two daughters, Helen and Donna, of Chicago. Donna Clark recalls, "This was the beginning of our love for the mountain community that never faded from our vision." Dr. Stone sold The Cliffs furnished, and on one condition: he could come over at any time and play the cabin's square piano. "Almost every week," Donna continues,

*we had hymn sings at our cabin, with Dr. Stone at the keyboard. We lived in a close, loving community and often gathered round to listen to Dr. Stone's many stories. It was quite a privilege to have grown up in such a beautiful setting. Preacher's Casserole was a Holy Hill favorite.*

### Preacher's Casserole
*(Submitted by Donna Clark)*

2 T water
1 C. sour cream
1 t salt
1 t pepper
1 t basil
8 green onions, chopped
3 T butter

2 10 oz packages of frozen spinach
1 c. shredded Cheddar cheese
1/2 c. grated Parmesan cheese
1 c. shredded Monterey Jack cheese
1 t. oregano
12 large mushroom caps
1 1/2 lb ground beef

Thaw spinach in water in saucepan and drain well. Mix in sour cream. Mix half the shredded cheeses together and set aside. Mix remaining cheeses with Parmesan cheese, seasonings, and half the green onions. Combine with the spinach mixture. Spread in 8 x 12 inch baking dish. Sauté mushroom caps in 2 T butter in skillet. Arrange over spinach. Brown ground beef with remaining green onions in 1 T butter in skillet, stirring frequently—drain. Spoon in mushroom caps and top with reserved cheeses. Bake @ 350 for 25 minutes.

## The Dorsey Family

The relationship between the Dorsey family of Dallas, Texas and the YMCA of the Rockies began many years ago. Having made a fortune in the printing business in Dallas, (Thomas) Henry Dorsey (1863–1928) provided funds for the construction of a large classroom building, "the Texas Cottage," on the Y grounds, at least in part to ensure public recognition of the Texas presence at the Estes Park Conference, as it was then known. Then in 1956, Henry Dorsey Jr. (1901–1972) donated an antique school bell, nicknamed "Duke," for the new tower and renovation of the little church that became known as Hyde Chapel.

Lula Ward Dorsey (1898–1980), daughter of Henry Sr., and sister of Henry Jr., and herself a teacher, continued this spirit of benevolence by paying to move salvageable portions of the old Wind River Lodge building (built in 1902) to a new location. Originally erected above what is now the Y Camp Livery, the Lodge was first moved to a site near the Administration Building, and then in 1977, to its present location to make room for the Walter E. Ruesch Auditorium, which was built in 1979.

Thanks to the efforts of Dorsey descendent Lulabeth ("Lulie") Melton and her husband Jack, the Lodge has been preserved as the Lulu W. Dorsey Museum. The Meltons moved to Estes from Dallas in 1979 to bring their conservation and museum experience to the preservation of YMCA Camp documents, photographs, and artifacts. Lulabeth provided the family recipe below.

## Devil's Gulch Potatoes
*(Submitted by Lulabeth Dorsey Melton)*

*When I was a little girl spending my summers in Estes Park in the 1950s and 1960s, one of the things my family did often was to picnic in Devil's Gulch. Any time we had company, rain or shine, we prepared a huge feast and headed to our favorite spot by the river. I remember that we always cooled our pop in the frigid water.*

*We usually cooked hotdogs and hamburgers at the picnic area, but the one food I always looked forward to was the Devil's Gulch Potatoes. The recipe died with my mother and aunt, but my best remembrance of it was it was like scalloped potatoes only better.*

*My mom cut several raw potatoes into cubes. I think this kept them hotter longer. Then she would grease a Pyrex bowl and layer potatoes, grated American cheese and slices of butter until the bowl was full. I think she put in some salt and pepper as well. Then she added about a cup of milk and put the dish in to bake at about 350 degrees. She baked it until the cheese and milk got saucy and brown on top. Then she wrapped the Pyrex in several layers of foil for the long trip down the switchbacks. (This was before the days of insulated casserole warmers.)*

*When we got to Devil's Gulch, the Pyrex would sit on the barbeque grate to keep it warm while the burgers and dogs cooked. Thinking about how good these potatoes taste, makes me want to go home and make up a batch.*

*The Fort Morgan Colony cottage of Emma and Fred W. Carruth and their five children. Their descendents continue to summer in Estes Park.*
Photo courtesy of the Carruth family

## The Fort Morgan Colony

The forty-acre property upon which the Fort Morgan (Colorado) Outing Club established its vacation community was a portion of the 160-acre claim homesteaded in 1901 by Charles Jeremiah Latshaw (1855–1950). Zenas McCoy (b. 1848), a Loveland real estate agent, purchased the acreage in 1903 and then sold it four years later to two prominent Fort Morgan businessmen, the pioneers Burton W. Jackson (1870–1921) and Fred W. Carruth (1869–1934). Then in 1911, Jackson and Carruth, together with another banker, George B. Riker, sold the property to the newly incorporated Fort Morgan Outing Club.

The original plan for the colony, which was located "west of Highway 7, east of Hyde Park, and north of University Heights,"[41] was to identify lots and sell them to Club members. An amendment to the original plat for the Fort Morgan Colony was completed in 1936 "to eliminate 'open space' and adjust some lot lines."[42] Another amendment was completed in 1958, when the area—by then known as the Fort Morgan Colony Addition—was "officially annexed to the Town of Estes Park."[43]

*The Fisher cabin, c. 1905, in the Fort Morgan Colony was built before the Colony's expansion.*

Photo courtesy of Millie Miller

According to the late Jerry Miller,

*Outing Club members were granted the use of a lot in the Colony in exchange for their membership. They could build cabins on them, as many members did, but had to follow rules pertaining to not driving across neighboring lots, using care when picking wild flowers (not by the roots!) and maintaining outhouses, to name a few of the published rules. They also had to abide by the unpublished rules as was common for the time: members were limited to those who were of a specified race, creed and color.*

When people ceased to be Outing Club members, their lots were generally deeded back to the Club, which would then give the deeds to other Club members. In this way, the officers of the

Club were able to retain control over who could, and could not, use and occupy lots in the platted area.

Given the process through which the community was created and the covenants that governed "membership" and ownership, it is not surprising that the members of the Colony should constitute a close-knit group. Ample evidence for this supposition exists in social notes in various editions of *Trail Talk,* which chronicled events and activities of Colony residents on a regular basis. During the summer of 1920, for example, the paper reported that

> *On Monday night, the young people on the Fort Morgan hill had a marshmallow roast on Prospect Mountain. . . . The Fort Morgan people enjoy many outings together. On Tuesday, 30 of them had a picnic at Brinwood. On Tuesday evening, they had a marshmallow roast at Gieses.*[44]

The meadow at the intersection of Morgan Lane and Morgan Street was used as a community center for the Fort Morgan Colony, as it was here that neighbors gathered for picnics and croquet.

## "Thisisit:" The Berryhill and Woodward Families

In the 1930s, Lot 18 in the Fort Morgan Colony was sold to Florence (Mrs. Edward) Hellstern and Mildred Bessie Vermazen Berryhill (1897–1962), wife of Albert Clyde "A.C." Berryhill (1894–1970). The Berryhills lived in Fort Morgan, where Mr. Berryhill was a realtor. He was also the founder of the Fort Morgan Savings and Loan. Eventually, the Hellsterns sold their interest in the property to the Berryhills, who subsequently named their cabin "Thisisit."

A. C. and Mildred were the parents of John R. "Jack" Berryhill, who was born in Estes Park in 1923. In 1944, Jack married Doris F. "Perry" Perrenoud (b. 1921) in Sioux Falls, South Dakota. Perry recalls that as a new bride, she lacked housekeeping experience, and that it was "Mother" Berryhill who taught her how to cook.

When Albert Berryhill died in 1970, the property was sold to Paul Woodward, who enlarged the Thisisit cabin. Upon Mr. Woodward's death in 1990, ownership of Thisisit passed to his daughter and son, Kathleen Woodward Thompson and Merrill H. Woodward (d. 1992). In 1993, Kathleen Thompson became the sole owner.

### Apple Pudding
*(Mildred Bessie "Mother" Berryhill)*

1 egg beaten lightly
3/4 cup sugar
1 1/2 cups diced apples (not peeled)
1/2 cup nuts
1/3 cup flour
1 heaping teaspoon Baking Powder
1 teaspoon vanilla

Bake 30 minutes at 350 degrees. Serve with whipped cream (or plain cream)

## Lickin' Good Cherry Dessert[45]
*(Doris F. Perrenoud "Perry" Berryhill)*

1 cup flour
1 cup sugar
1/2 tbsps. powdered sugar

Blend together thoroughly as for crust. Pat down evenly on bottom of baking dish (8 x 12) and bake in a 350 degree oven until golden brown (about 15 minutes).

2 eggs beaten
1 cup sugar
1/4 cup flour
1/2 tsp baking powder
1 tsp. vanilla
Pinch of salt
3/4 cup chopped English Walnuts
1/2 cup coconut
1 No. 2 can pitted red cherries (about 2 1/2 cups)

Cherries must be well drained. Allow to stand in colander 1 to 2 hours.
Mix all of above ingredients together in order given and pour into crust. Bake 30 minutes in a 350 degree oven. Serve with whipped cream.

## Cabbage Pockets *(Kraut Baroks)*

*(Kathleen Thompson)*

*This recipe seems to be ethnically connected to Morgan County. It is from German-Russian people who immigrated to this area (Fort Morgan) around 1900. I borrowed this recipe from a German friend and it is in the form she gave to me.*

1 package dry yeast
1 cup water
1/4 cup sugar
1/4 cup oil
1 tsp. salt
1 egg
4 cups flour

### *Filling*

1 head cabbage, shredded
1 1/2 lb. hamburger
3–4 onions, chopped
salt & pepper to taste

Dissolve yeast in water; add oil, salt, sugar and egg. Mix well. Add flour and mix. Cover and let rise 45 minutes. Knead and cut dough about 3 inches in diameter and form ball. Roll out to about 1/4 in. thick and cut into 4-inch squares. Put about 3 tablespoons filling in center of rolled-out dough. Bring corners together at top, pinching edges securely. Put in greased pan seam down and bake at 350 degrees for 30 minutes or until brown. Makes about 12. Filling: Fry hamburger and add cabbage, onion, salt & pepper. Fry until cabbage is done.

*The Big Thompson Canyon was dotted with many little businesses that provided goods and services to the cottagers who built summer cabins along the river. Mother's Inn was one of them.*

Postcard courtesy of the author

## Cottagers of Loveland Heights

Located in the Big Thompson Canyon, Loveland Heights constituted a small community of cabins built by residents of Loveland around the turn of the twentieth century. In fact, the oldest cabins in Loveland Heights date from 1898. As in other small cottager communities in and around Estes Park, summer residents of Loveland Heights engaged in any number of family outings and activities planned for residents in their immediate area. An article in *Trail Talk* in 1920 reported on an evening's entertainment that drew people from the Canyon communities of Loveland Heights, Pine Knot, and Glen Comfort:

> *Everyone enjoyed a community sing with Mrs. Russell at the piano. Then the spelling school, in charge of Mrs. Loyd, occasioned much merriment. Miss Grover gave some pleasing vocal selections, and Mrs. Loyd delighted with a couple of readings. Mr. Turner, editor of the Loveland Herald, convulsed the crowd with his funny stories, and then the [honorary] Mayor, Mr. O. D. Shields, was called upon to make an address. His remarks were well received and he was presented with a cabbage head which he expected to have for dinner the next day, but it was stolen before the evening was over.*[46]

Chapter Five: Cottager Communities    343

*Alberta Rutledge waits on a customer at the resort store she and her husband purchased from the Redmonds in 1951.*

Photo courtesy of Jerry Rutledge

## Loveland Heights Court: The Rutledge Family

*"Everything Planned for Your Comfort"*
—Advertisement, *Estes Park Trail*

The Loveland Heights community included a number of cabin camps, including Dick's Harbor (now Loveland Heights Cottages), which was built by Dick Wilson. In 1919, Ernest "Ern" and Mildred Rutledge built a cabin across the road from Dick's Harbor. The cabin was moved in 1937 when the road was widened. Ern and Mildred first came to the mountains because their son Lyle suffered from asthma; the family continued to summer in the Big Thompson Canyon for the rest of their lives. In 1951, when Lyle and his wife, Alberta,[47] were looking for a retirement activity,

*Jerry Rutledge, behind the meat counter, at his family's Loveland Heights store.*

**Photo courtesy of Jerry Rutledge**

the couple bought out Peter and Connie Redmond, the owners of Loveland Heights Court, a small resort that included rustic cabins and a store. Alberta ran the business for the next twenty years.

Lyle and Alberta's son Jerry worked at the family's grocery store and the gas station from 1952 through 1956. The Rutledge family still owns property in the Big Thompson Canyon.

## Aunt Blanche's Lemon Sponge Pudding
*(Myrtle Keever)*

| | |
|---|---|
| 1 cup Sugar | 1 square-inch Butter |
| 2 large tablespoons Flour | 1/2 teaspoon Salt |
| 2 Eggs separated | 1 cup Milk |
| Juice of 1 Lemon(s) | 1 Lemon rind - optional |

Cream butter and sugar. Sift flour and salt 3 times. Add beaten egg yolks and milk. Last, fold in stiffly beaten egg whites. Bake 1 hour in ungreased pan set in a pan of water. Moderate oven.

*This was one of Grandma Keever's favorite recipes for dessert. Very easy to fix, too. As I recall, a 9x13 pan or baking dish.*

—Jerry Rutledge

Chapter Five: Cottager Communities

*Interior of Hewes-Kirkwood Ranch and Inn.*
Postcard courtesy of the Bobbie Heistercamp Collection

## Cottagers of the Tahosa Valley

By the latter years of the nineteenth century, most of the land in the upland valley south of Estes Park and known variously as the Vale of Elkanah and the Tahosa Valley, was owned by Charles Edwin Hewes of Hewes-Kirkwood Ranch and Inn, Enos Mills of Longs Peak Inn, and Charles Levings, a Chicago engineer. These three, in turn, began to sell lots "on the low slopes of the surrounding mountains, unobtrusively tucked amongst the Lodgepole and Ponderosa pines."[48]

Among the buyers were two families from Lincoln, Nebraska—the Ameses and the Sanders. Both had come to Estes Park soon after the turn of the twentieth century, staying in local hotels before claiming acreages for their own. While concern for their son John's health was a motivating factor in bringing Fred and Jessie Sanders to Colorado in the first place, there is little doubt that they, as well as the Ameses, were drawn to the Tahosa Valley

*Hewes-Kirkwood Inn with Estes Cone as a backdrop.*
Photo courtesy of the Estes Park Museum

by the astonishing views of Longs Peak and the solitude afforded by their remoteness from the hustle and bustle of the growing town of Estes Park.

Not far from this little Tahosa Valley community were summer homes clustered in the area of Charlie Hewes' dream, the town of Hewes-Kirkwood. Originally the town was planned to include Perkins Trading Post/WhatNot Inn as well as the Don-Jon Market. Katherine Garetson's Big Owl Tea Place and the Steiner cabins were located nearby on Big Owl Road.[49]

*Grace Ames and her children, Jack and Peg, c. 1913.*
Photo courtesy of John and Diane Roehl

## Broadhearth: The Ames Family

Beginning in 1905, Ernest Capron ("Colonel") Ames (1874–1957),[50] his wife Grace Andrews Ames (1880–1979), and their children Margaret ("Peg") and John H. ("Jack") left their home in Lincoln, Nebraska every year to summer in Estes Park. In 1913, the couple built "Broadhearth," a cabin erected on the lower slopes of the Twin Sisters across the valley from Enos Mills's famous Longs Peak Inn. It was the second home to be built on the "Hill," the first, "Graystone," having been built in 1910 by Charles and Agnes Levings of Chicago. Levings, a prominent civil engineer, designed Graystone himself.[51]

The Ameses eventually purchased Graystone from the Levings family. In the 1940s Ernest and Grace added a third house to their

*Grace and Ernest "Colonel" Ames, with grandchildren Eli and John Roehl, c. 1955.*

Photo courtesy of John and Diane Roehl

compound. Named Stove Hurst, after a small wood stove that provided the cabin's heat, the cabin served as the family's guesthouse for many years. All three homes are owned by Ernest and Grace's grandchildren, some of whom are now year-round residents on the Hill.

Colonel Ames, who was an avid horseman, maintained a four-stall stable and corral adjacent to the cabin to house his horses. Grace, who was known as a gracious hostess and excellent cook, loved hiking and horseback riding as well. The couple joined the Summer Residents Association in Estes Park as charter members in 1941, a relationship that Grace maintained until her death in 1979.

*Colonel Ames in front of his fireplace at Broadhearth.*
Photo courtesy of John and Diane Roehl

## Crunchy Chicken Casserole
*(Grace Andrews Ames/Elizabeth Ames Shoffner)*

*(Serves 4–6)*

1 1/2 cups chicken, cut in small pieces
1 cup chopped celery
3/4 cup mayonnaise
1/2 cup sliced toasted almonds
1 can cream of chicken soup
1 1/2 cups cooked rice
1/2 cup water chestnuts (sliced)
1 tsp. grated onion, seasonings

Mix, put in casserole. Cover with buttered crumbs if desired. Bake 30–45 minutes at 350 degrees. (Cook fresh chicken breasts in salted water or can use pre-cooked chicken.)

## Oatmeal Cookies
*(Grace Andrews Ames)*

1/2 cup butter, or Crisco or bacon drippings
1/2 tsp soda mixed in 2 Cups flour
1 1/2 tsp cinnamon
2 Cups rolled oats
1/2 cup sugar
2 eggs – beaten
1 Cup raisins
salt

## Mama Grace's Grapefruit and Avocado Salad

*(Grace Andrews Ames)*

2 large, ripe avocados  fruit of one grapefruit
head of lettuce  3 Tbs French Dressing[52]

Peel and devein grapefruit and divide into sections, cutting each section in half and add to the salad bowl. Skin, pit, and slice avocados and intermingle with grapefruit. Core and tear lettuce into bite size pieces and add, mixing well. Toss with French dressing, and salt and pepper to taste.

## Yowell's Stew[53]

*(Margaret Ames Roehl/Helen Yowell/Eleanor "Eli" Roehl)*

Ingredients:
1 lb beef stew meat  2 potatoes, peeled and halved
2 carrots  4 stalks celery
1 medium onion  2 cloves garlic
8+ cloves  1 bay leaf
3 Tbs. brown sugar  Beef bouillon cubes or canned consommé
1 Tbs. vinegar  Tapioca [or corn starch] (optional)
1/2 stick cinnamon

Directions:
   Place stew meat in slow cooker or crockpot with bouillon cube dissolved in a cup of water.
   Add cloves, bay leaf, sugar, vinegar and cinnamon, and cook on high for 20 minutes. Add sliced onions, garlic and vegetables (amount of each is up to personal taste), and cover all with enough bouillon or consommé to fill the pot. Cook until the carrots and celery are tender and the potatoes are cooked through. Tapioca (or cornstarch) can be added if a thicker stew is desired.

Alternative method:
   Brown beef in small amount of oil in Dutch oven. Add remaining ingredients and simmer on stove for at least 5 hours.

## Pan Fried Trout

*(Frank and Margaret Ames Roehl)*

Brook trout
Bacon
Salt
Lemon wedges

*Preparation is truly everything here. The brook trout should be no larger than eight or nine inches. There are two reasons: The smaller the fish the better the taste and larger fish are too valuable to be caught only once. They can be released and re-caught many times and the pleasure grows with their size.*

Immediately upon bringing the trout to hand, have the kindness and respect to stun it (terminally) with a blow to its head. The trout must be kept cool and moist. I prefer an Arcticreel which is bag woven from Scottish flax which is soaked in water to cool by evaporation. Clean the fish as soon as practicable–the next lull in the fishing for instance.

At the end of the day sprinkle a little salt inside each trout and let them "rest" over night in the refrigerator or in the creel in the shade if you are camping. If you try to cook the fish right after catching them, they curl and twist in the pan making it a difficult job.

Take a skillet of suitable size (cast iron if you have it) and fry enough bacon to produce a good amount of bacon grease. Reserve the bacon and lay the whole trout in the pan to cook. If you lay the trout with their bellies all facing the same way, you can gently rock the skillet to slosh the hot grease into the fish to cook them from the inside out. The trout are done when their eyes turn white.

Serve the trout with the bacon and fillet them on the plate. Squeeze on fresh lemon juice and salt to taste.[54]

*Jessie Moore Sanders, c. 1946, in front of the cabin's massive fireplace.*
Photo courtesy of the author

## Fred and Jessie Sanders

Frederick Morris Sanders (1877–1962) and his wife, Jessie Moore (1881–1964), of Lincoln, Nebraska, purchased property on the Twin Sisters Peaks from Fred's business associate at Bankers Life, Colonel Ernest C. Ames, in about 1916. The Sanders family's first summers on the Hill were spent in a tent cabin on the site, consisting of a wooden platform with half walls and a "tented" canvas roof. It was Edwin Gillette who built the couple a permanent two-story log house in 1918, and Charlie Hewes, of Hewes-Kirkwood Inn, who put on the cabin's original roof.

*The dining room of the Sanders' cabin as it looked in the 1940s.*
Photo courtesy of the author

Fred and Jessie Sanders were drawn to the mountains not only because of the business association and personal friendship with the Ameses, but also because their son John (b. 1908) suffered from childhood asthma. Although Jessie was an accomplished cook in her own right, the family also depended on the extraordinary culinary skills of Freda Lee Songer (1893–1970),[55] who kept house for the family in their Lincoln home and traveled with them to the mountains every summer. Freda demonstrated her mastery of cooking and baking tasks on the cabin's wood-burning, cast-iron "Kalamazoo" stove, adapting old recipes for use at the cabin's altitude (9,000 ft.), and creating new ones as well.

At the Sanderses' cabin, food that required refrigeration was kept in a cave located off the back porch. The cave was fitted with a pulley system so that the massive door and stone weight, meant to discourage bears, could be easily opened when necessary to store or retrieve food. Bacon and ham, however, were kept in the house at night to prevent bears from coming down out of the mountain and pillaging the larder.

*Freda Lee Songer cooked for Jessie and Fred Sanders at their home in Lincoln and at their summer cabin on the Twin Sisters (photo c. 1949).*
**Photo courtesy of Jeff E. Songer**

Although their cabin was some little distance from the village of Estes Park, Fred and Jessie Sanders were, with the Ameses, charter members (1941) of the Estes Park Summer Residents

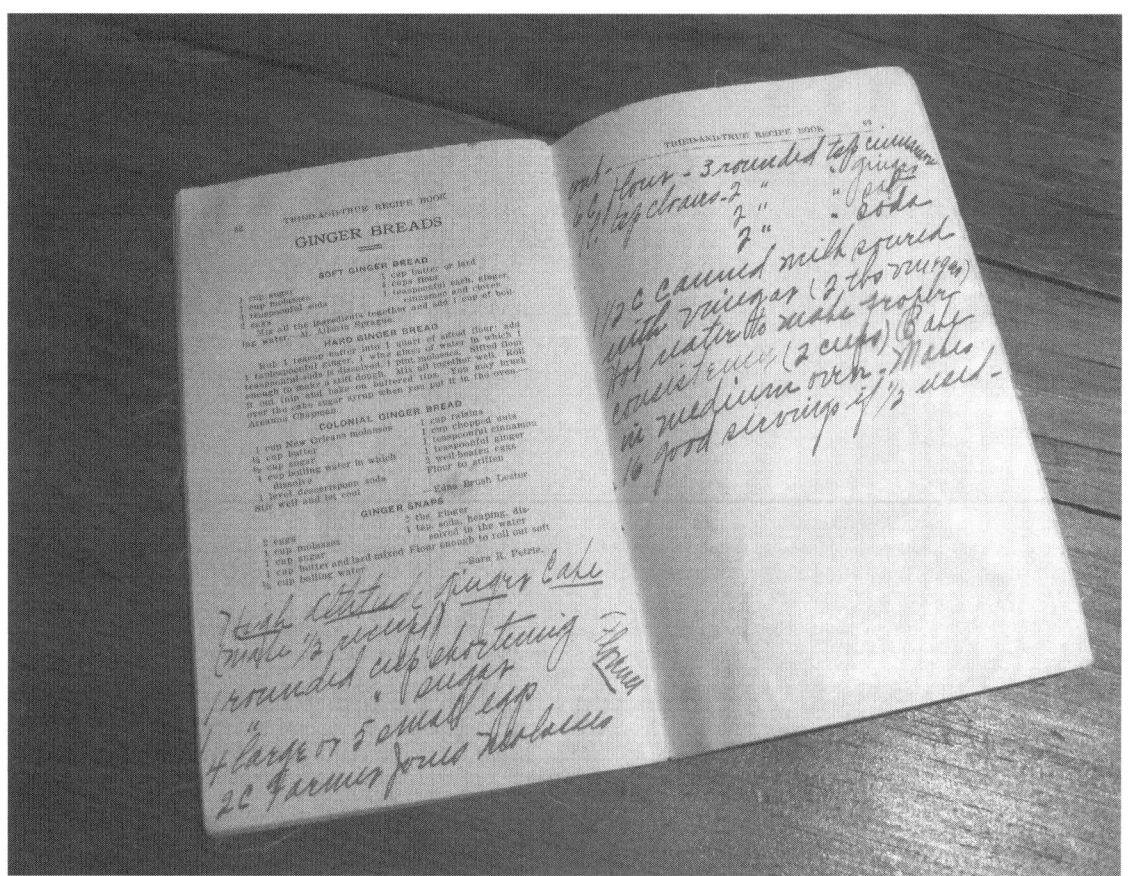

*Recipe for High Altitude Ginger Cake, recorded by Jessie Sanders.*
Artifact courtesy of the Sanders family

Association. Along with their neighbors on the Hill and across the Valley, Jessie and Fred were, initially at least, very suspicious of the National Park Service's efforts to expand the perimeters of the Park. Nevertheless, the couple was drawn to return to their Tahosa Valley cabin year after year, entertaining their son, daughter-in-law, and grandchildren; and hosting many friends, who were invited many times over the years to enjoy the cabin, the pines, and the spectacular view. In the 1960s, health issues precluded Fred and Jessie from further visits to their mountain home, but their grandchildren and great-grandchildren continue to enjoy summer visits there.

The recipes below were handwritten by Jessie Sanders in her copy of the *Tried and True Recipe Book* (1920).

## Freda's Longs Peak Cake
*(Freda Lee Songer)*

1 1/2 C sugar  
3 C flour  
3 tsp baking powder  
1/2 C butter  
1 1/2 C ice water  
4 egg whites

---

## High Altitude Chocolate Cookies
*(Jessie Moore Sanders)*

1 Cup butter  
1 Cup packed brown sugar  
1 tsp vanilla  
1 tsp baking soda  
1 Cup semisweet chocolate chips  
1 Cup white sugar  
3 eggs  
1/2 tsp salt  
3 1/2 Cups all purpose flour

---

## Boiled Halibut
*(Jessie Moore Sanders)*

3 pound piece of halibut  
1 Tb flour  
1 C fish liquor  
1/2 tsp black pepper  
2 Tbs butter  
1/2 tsp dry mustard  
1/4 tsp salt

Simmer fish about 1/2 hour in water to which has been added salt, a little lemon juice, 2 sprigs of parsley, a small cut carrot. Remove fish to hot platter, remove skin.

### *Mustard Sauce*

Melt butter, blend in flour and mustard, add gradually a cup of liquor in which fish was cooked

Bring to boiling let simmer 2 minutes. Add salt (if needed) and freshly ground black pepper.

*"I add a pound of fresh shrimp to sauce for special occasions. Follow this recipe for all boiled fish."*

## Whole Wheat Bread
*(Jessie Moore Sanders)*

1 med. potato boiled in 2 c. water
2 tbs. whole wheat flour in mixing pan—pour hot mashed potato and liquid—stir and cool.

Add    2 c. milk, warm
1/2 c. honey
2 tbs. shortening
2 tbs. salt
2 c. whole wheat flour *("I add 3")*

Rest white flour to make a kneeding dough.
Let rise twice its size. Knead down. Let bread rise again, make into loaves *("2 or 3 according to size you like; I make 3")* rise again double size.
Bake in oven 400 degrees for 15 minutes then 350 degrees for rest of hour (a little less for smaller loaves).

*Katherine Garetson and Annie Adele Shreve at the Big Owl Tea Place, c. 1915.*

Photo courtesy of the Estes Park Museum

## Katherine Garetson

For many years, Katherine Garetson "gladdened the hearts and stomachs of her friends and visitors [at her Big Owl Tea Place] with homemade cookies and cupcakes on plates in a large cheery room with tables dressed up with checkered coverings."[56] Although her prices were considered high by some of her customers, the Tea Place soon became a social center for her neighbors as well as visitors summering in the Tahosa Valley.

Born in Indiana to James S. and Caroline Griffith Garetson, Katherine (1877–1963) moved to St. Louis at the turn of the century to live with her sister, (Ella) Helen (Mrs. William W.) Dings, and her family. In 1909, the Dingses and Katherine traveled to Colorado, hoping that the trip would improve the health of one of James and Caroline's two young sons. The family stayed at Longs Peak Inn that summer and for several summers thereafter. So captivated by the mountains were the Dingses that they purchased from Enos Mills property two miles south of Longs Peak Inn and built a log cabin there that is still in the Dings family.

Having spent the summer of 1914 at the Dings' cabin, and reluctant to return to her life in St. Louis, Katherine determined to file on a claim on property located on Big Owl Road.[57] She then returned briefly to St. Louis to convince her best friend,

*Katherine Garetson's Big Owl Tea Place offered a lending library as well as a meeting place for visitors and residents of the Tahosa Valley.*
Photo courtesy of the Estes Park Museum

Annie Adele Shreve, to stay the winter with her in her new cabin. Together the pair braved the freezing temperatures and loneliness of Katherine's first high-country winter.

In 1915, Katherine enlarged her homestead cabin to accommodate a small business: a gift shop and tearoom. During the first years, the "gifts" were actually hand-embroidered items and dolls that Katherine herself had made during the previous winter. Over time, Katherine made many improvements to the cabin and managed finally to prove up on the claim in spite of efforts of the National Forestry Service to thwart her. She also had many good friends among her neighbors, and managed to maintain good relationships with both Charlie Hewes and Enos Mills, who were on opposite sides of the National Park question.

Katherine also enjoyed a close relationship with Esther Burnell (1890–1964),[58] the young woman who would eventually marry Enos Mills. When Esther determined to homestead her own claim in the Estes Valley, Katherine gave her the benefit of her

*Katherine Garetson's dog, Gypsy, on the porch of the Big Owl Tea Place, a gathering spot for cottagers in the early twentieth century.*
Photo courtesy of the Estes Park Museum

own first experiences in surviving a Rocky Mountain winter. One Christmas the two friends snowshoed miles to meet halfway between their cabins; their holiday picnic consisted of hot bacon sandwiches, tomato soup, and coffee.

Katherine Garetson continued to run the Tea Place every summer until 1935. She wrote of her Tahosa Valley experiences in *Homesteading Big Owl*, which was not published until 1989, twenty-six years after her death. Her family adored her and remembered her as an "exceptionally sparkly and interesting woman," "vivacious and full of stories," with an "enthusiasm for life and [an] intense interest in nature."[59]

*A formal portrait of Kitty Lindsey Perkins, owner/manager of the WhatNot Inn, which she built on Highway 7 in Allenspark.*
Photo courtesy of the Dayton Rabin family

## WhatNot Inn: Perkins Trading Post

Katherine W. "Addie"/"Kitty" Lindsey, a Kansas-born artist who taught china painting at Washburn University, teamed up with another artist, Marie W. "Maria" Witwer, to establish an art gallery and later a gift shop in Topeka. During the summers, the pair also ran a seasonal business in Estes Park, a curio and gift shop on Elkhorn Avenue called the WhatNot Shop. Although Kitty (1870–1965) married Oscar S. Perkins (1865–1938) in Missouri in January 1914, she and Maria (1864–1942) continued their business partnership, building the WhatNot Inn in 1924 in the town of

Hewes-Kirkwood, just one block north of the Don-Jon Market on what is now Highway 7.

The Inn, a frame building with a spacious porch, resembled a Kansas farmhouse. Kitty and Maria sold antiques and bric-a-brac, and managed to run a tearoom there as well. After a few years, Kitty's husband bought out Witwer's interest, and soon thereafter the business became known as Perkins Trading Post. Thanks to a fortuitous windfall in the form of a trunk full of priceless Indian artifacts that the couple found in Kansas, the shop began to specialize in Indian arts and crafts.

About 1927, Kitty and Oscar began offering summer work to Charles F. Burkhart (1908–1992), later a University of Colorado graduate (1932) and World War II veteran, who first came to Estes Park in 1919. Adopting the name Charles (Charlie) Eagle Plume, Burkhart became a promoter and collector of Native American arts and culture, giving interpretive Indian shows and dances at local resorts in the 1940s and 1950s. Oscar died in 1938, and after that Kitty came to rely more and more on Burkhart's assistance in running the store. Then in 1946/1947, her own health failing, Kitty turned the store over to Burkhart in recognition of his twenty years of "volunteer" service. In the years that followed, Katherine continued as a summer resident of Estes Park and was for a time a member of the Summer Residents Association. She died in 1965 at the age of ninety-four.

The Trading Post, which became known as Charlie Eagle Plume's, was for decades an icon of the Tahosa Valley until Burkhardt's own death in 1992. Today, the shop continues to offer Indian jewelry and artifacts to summer visitors and residents, under the ownership of Dayton Rabin, his wife Ann Strange Owl, and their daughter Nico.

## Ginger Cake
*(Katherine Lindsey Perkins)*

2 cups of molasses
1 cup of water
1 table spoon of ginger
1 cup butter
1 cup sweet milk
2 teaspoonfuls baking powder

1 cup of lard
1 table spoon of soda
4 cups flour
2 cups sugar
4 eggs or 7 whites
1 teaspoonful vanilla.

## Aunt Zervia's Receipt for Chow Chow
*(Katherine Lindsey Perkins)*

12 large cucumbers  12 large onions
1 head cabbage  1/4 peck of green tomatoes
6 green peppers  2 red peppers
Spices: 1 ounce tumeric [sic]  1 ounce celery seed
brown sugar  1 ounce mustard
vinigar [sic]  Pare cucumbers,
    take out seeds and chop.

Pare onions and chop cabbage and all very fine. Take seeds out of peppers and chop. Put all in a crock and let stand 24 hours (after sprinkling with salt).

Then drain it and put on some weak vinigar and let stand 2 days. Put in a vessel, put in 1 oz. of tumeric seed, 1 oz of celery seed, 1 oz of brown sugar, 1/2 pint of grated horse-radish, 1 oz of mustard seed

Disolve [sic] 1/4 lb of mustard in a little vinigar and put in. Put about 1/2 gallon of vinigar put on stove and boil for 1 hour. Then put in bottles while hot.

## Ribbon Cake
*(Katherine Lindsey Perkins)*

1 1/3 cup sugar
4 eggs
1/2 cup butter
1/2 cup sweet milk
2 cups flour
2 teaspoonfuls of baking powder

Divide batter in three parts.

Jelly in between [layers].

## The Steiner Family

Dr. Edward Alfred Steiner (1866–1956), a theologian and professor of Applied Christianity at Grinnell College in Iowa, traveled to Estes Park for the first time in 1917, to teach a summer school course at Colorado State University. An eminent scholar and theologian who held a doctorate from Heidelberg University, he had been ordained as a minister after immigrating to the United States in 1886.

During that first trip to the mountains, Steiner stayed at Columbine Lodge, located behind Longs Peak Inn at the foot of Longs Peak. While at the Lodge, a waiter told him of a 160-acre homestead for sale "down the road." Steiner walked the three miles to the site and fell in love with the property. The sale price was $600. Located on Big Owl Road, the property was improved by the Steiners, who eventually added a number of small cabins to the homestead cabin that had been built by the property's original owner, John Grant. The professor named his holdings "Steiners' Acres."

The John Cabin, as the Grant homestead cabin was known, proved to be too small for a family of four[60] and quickly grew by two bedrooms, a fireplace, kitchen annex, bathroom and a long, screened porch with several beds. A magnificent one-room cabin, which became Edward Steiner's study, was erected soon thereafter. Like other property owners in the area, Dr. Steiner sold pieces of his land to friends, including an acre near the John Cabin on which a Rev. Leroy Warren built his cabin "Skyline" in 1919. This cabin and another built in the 1920s by a Dr. Sheve have since returned to the Steiner family. Later, additional cabins were built to accommodate the Steiners' children and grandchildren.

From the beginning, Edward and his wife Sara loved to show friends their charming summer home. The Steiners' guest book contains signatures of the many local and national celebrities that visited the couple in the 1920s: the William Allen Whites, A.A. and Mrs. Hyde, Otis Skinner and his daughter Cornelia Otis Skinner, Jane Addams, Edna Ferber, Enos Mills, Dorr Yeager, and more. Edward and Sara brought their maid with them from Iowa to assist them in fulfilling their social obligations and entertaining.

Although the Edward Steiners employed a cook to handle meal preparation for the family, their grandson David, who lives year-round at Steiners' Acres, shared his mother's recipe for a dessert, which "as far as I know, is her own invention. I have never seen it anywhere. It is a legend in our family. It's quite a bit of work but the result usually astonishes and delights."[61]

## Fluffy Duffy with Foamy Sauce
*(Deborah L. Steiner)*

3 eggs
6 T sugar
3 T orange marmalade, preferably bitter
1/2 t cream of tartar
1/4 t orange extract
1/2 cup whipping cream
2 T sugar
1/4 cup slivered almonds, toasted
1/8 t almond extract

Good timing for this dish is crucial; it will not tolerate delay.
    Beat egg whites with cream of tartar until foamy.
    Add 6 T sugar gradually until stiff. Fold in marmalade and orange extract.
    Place in upper part of greased double boiler, cover, cook over gently boiling water, one hour without lifting lid.

### *Foamy Sauce*

A few minutes before the Fluffy Duffy is done, beat egg yolks with remaining 2 T sugar and almond extract, fold gently into whipped cream.
    Just before serving add almond slivers. Turn the double boiler over to release the contents on a dinner plate.
    Serve portions on smaller plates or bowls and cover each with the Foamy Sauce.
    Serve immediately.

*The Reece family c. 1883. From left, Ernest Reece, Eva Mary Reece, Mildred Reece, James Reece, and Eva Jane Reece Price.*

Photo courtesy of Cynthia Price Reedy

## Cottagers Along Devil's Gulch Road: The Price/Reedy Family

Another little cottager community in Estes Park developed on land that had once been homesteaded by William H. McCreery in the 1870s. Located along the Devil's Gulch road, tent cabins and other small log structures began to appear soon after the turn of the twentieth century, although in the early years more permanent dwellings were few and far between.

The Reedy family was among those who chose this area as a summer home. Their cabin had originally been a tent cabin, built in 1877, that belonged to the Warnocks of Loveland. David (1847–1923) and Jenny (1855–1925) Warnock had been married in Illinois in 1873 and, by the time they purchased the property for a summer home from the McCreerys in 1907, were the parents of seven children.

The property next passed to the Warnocks' daughter, Sadie Mae (1872–1959), an artist and art teacher who married Charles Emery Evett (1882–1953). The couple wintered in Loveland, where Evett worked as a traveling salesman for the Donaldson Fruit Company. In 1939, Sadie and Charlie Evett sold their tent cabin to Margaret Price and her mother Eva Jane Reece Price[62] for $100. The one-

*Margaret Price Reedy on Chief at the Arrow Livery she owned and ran in the 1940s.*

**Photo courtesy of the Reedy family**

room cabin had been moved to an adjacent lot in the mid-1930s and fully enclosed. At that time, the little building was expanded to include two bedrooms. Because in the early days, the cabin did not have indoor plumbing, the Prices shared a privy with two of their neighbors.

When Margaret Price (later, Mrs. Clyde Richard Reedy) bought the property from the Evetts, she also purchased the Arrow Livery, which was located on the Evett property and included a barn and a bunkhouse. At that time, she convinced C.E. Sholty, Evett's sometime partner, to continue to manage the business for her.

Today, the Reedy Cabin, as the Warnocks' original tent cabin is now known, is summer home to three Reedy sisters, all of whom are artists: Cynthia Price Reedy (of Estes Park); Paula Reedy Cunningham (of Greeley); and Jane Reedy Schulz (of Paonia).

## Journey Cakes (Johnny Cakes)
*(Margaret Price Reedy)*

Beat 1 egg  
1 tsp. salt  
Add 2 c. corn meal  
1 1/2 c. milk

Drop by spoonfuls onto a greased griddle or skillet. Stir batter before dropping. Cook until golden brown and serve with butter and syrup. Makes 12 to 15 cakes.

## Hunter's Stew
*(Clyde Richard Reedy)*

*I prefer to cook this in a large, cast iron Dutch oven.*

3 pounds meat, cubed. Any wild meat will do, but elk is a good choice. Generally unable to get wild meat, I use a combination of beef and pork.

2–3 large onions, chopped  
4 carrots, peeled and sliced or 1 1/2 c. baby carrots  
4 stalks celery, sliced in one inch pieces  
2 T. chopped garlic  
1 1/2 tsp. chopped ginger  
1 T. salt  
1/2 tsp. pepper  
3 quarts beef stock  
water to cover  
5–6 potatoes, peeled and cubed  
1–2 bell peppers, chunked (optional)  
splashes of Worcestershire sauce, if desired

Sear meat on all sides. Lightly sauté onions. Add beef stock, carrots, celery, garlic, ginger, salt, pepper, and water to cover and cook at a low boil, covered, for about an hour. Add potatoes and cook another 30 minutes or until potatoes are done and meat is tender. If bell pepper is desired, add 15 minutes before the stew is done. Adjust for seasonings. *This makes a large pot.*

## Saffron Bread
*(Margaret Price Reedy)*

*"Mother always made this bread at Christmas and Easter. She made both loaves and hot cross buns. It is delicious hot out of the oven."*

(Makes 2 large loaves or 3 smaller loaves)

2 c. hot water (partially milk, if desired). Add 1/2 to 1 t. saffron. Brew.

Cool mixture to tepid, add 2 packages active dry yeast. Let bubble.

Mix: 1/2 to 1 c. sugar, 2 t. salt, 2 eggs, 1/2 c. butter, 7 to 7 1/2 c. flour (start with 4).

Coat fruit with some flour before adding. 1 c. raisins, 1 c. mixed dry fruit or citron.

Add more if desired. Dried apricots may be substituted for citron.

Dough should be sticky (wet dough, to be moist).

Knead. Don't over knead.

Let rise in bowl, covered with tea towel, until doubled.

Knead a little to get air bubbles out. Form buns or loaves (snip for hot cross buns).

Let rise again to double.

350 degrees for 45 to 55 minutes, middle rack. Check at 45 minutes if making three loaves

Sugar glaze if desired.

Glaze: butter, vanilla, milk, powdered sugar – drippy. Dribble over while warm.

# Notes

1. *Estes Park Trail* (July 6, 1912).

2. William Allen White. *The Autobiography of William Allen White*. (New York: Macmillan, 1946), p. 461.

3. Both Scott and White were registered Republicans but belonged to different "wings" of the party. White was a progressive whose friends included both President Theodore Roosevelt and President Franklin Delano Roosevelt, while Scott was politically much more conservative.

4. W. A. White. *Autobiography*, p. 54.

5. The White cabins were sold to Rocky Mountain National Park in 1972 and now house the Park's Artists-in-Residence Program award recipients every summer.

6. James H. Pickering and Nancy P. Thomas. *If I Ever Grew Up and Became a Man: William Allen White's Moraine Park Years*. (Estes Park: Estes Park Museum Friends & Foundation, Inc. Press, 2010).

7. Interestingly, it was Dr. Snow who was also responsible for introducing fellow Kansan William Allen White to Estes Park, on a similar Kansas University excursion some seven or eight years later. For more information, see J. H. Pickering and N. P. Thomas. *If I Ever Grew Up and Became a Man*: *William Allen White's Moraine Park Years*. Estes Park: Estes Park Museum Friends & Foundation, Inc. Press, 2010).

8. According to the late D. Ferrel Atkins, before designing the Scottage, Chapman had never built more than a single-story cabin. For this reason, space to accommodate a stairway to the second floor was not provided; the result was that access to the loft above the main living level had to be managed by means of an almost vertical ladder.

9. "Foreward." Emerson Lynn, Carruth Scott, Angelo Scott, Dorothy Carnine Scott, and William Lindsey White, *The Scottage, A Medley* (unpublished manuscript, n.d.), p. 1.

10. Ewing was a Phi Beta Kappa scholar, as were a number of other members of the Scott family include Ewing's wife, Dorothy Carnine Scott, and his daughter, Dorothy Scott Gibbs.

11. E. Lynn, et al., *The Scottage*, p. 22.

12. According to Dorothy Gibbs, her father "was always the cook in our family, though my mother had her specialties too. Daddy always said that cooking was just a branch of chemistry." Dorothy Scott Gibbs (personal communication, 2012).

13. "My father learned this from his mother, but his version is much simpler, easier, and better—I think it's the best bread pudding I've ever eaten anywhere. The secret is in using bread crumbs instead of cubes." Dorothy Scott Gibbs (personal communication, 2012).

14. "After the soup had been served, there were always enough beans left to make baked beans for Sunday night supper." Dorothy Scott Gibbs (personal communication, 2012).

15. *Trail Talk* (July 2, 1920).

16. William E. Connelley, *A Standard History of Kansas and Kansans* (Chicago: Lewis Publishing Co., 1919), p. 155.

17. " Inholder" is the term for anyone who continues to own private property within the confines of Rocky Mountain National Park. Although the Park would welcome the donation of these properties, the owners have the right to sell or will their holdings to anyone they like. D. Ferrel Atkins (personal communication, 2008).

18. Bissell was the president of the J. R. Bissell Dry Goods Co. in St. Louis.

19. Russ Bissell (personal communication, March 2012).

20. Sanborn and his family divided their time between Greeley and Estes Park. In 1884 he married Carrie Bassett (1858–1926), who was a member of Chapter AV of the PEO sisterhood in Estes Park.

21. Justin Morrill served in Congress as Representative and Senator from Vermont from 1855 to 1898.

22. In 1971, the Boone cabin was sold to descendents of Joel and Patsey Estes, the first year-round residents of the Estes Valley.

23. The cabins most likely date from the late 1910s, as in the summer of 1914 the sisters were still staying at Hewes-Kirkwood, where they took part in group outings and amateur theatricals. In a performance of *A Midsummer Night's Dream*, Mariel had the role of Pyramus, Frances was the Moon, and Ellen "favored the guests with some . . . classic dancing . . . between the acts." *Estes Park Trail*, August 29, 1914.

24. Ida also had an older sister, Harriet Robbins Anderson, born in 1866.

25. Wyuka Cemetery tour brochure, Lincoln, Nebraska.

26. Day Heusner McLaughlin (personal communication, June 19, 2013).

27. Larry Day (personal communication, May 23, 2013).

28. Joyeuse was named after Joyeuse Plantation, on Saint-Dominique (Haiti), from which her French ancestors fled during a slave revolt (1799–1804), relocating in New Orleans in 1803.

29. See Channing F. Sweet's autobiography, *A Princeton Cowboy* (Colorado Springs: Dentan Berkeland, 1967).

30. At one time, the Sweets owned 260 acres.

31. C. F. Sweet, *A Princeton Cowboy*.

32. It is interesting to note that this was the name used by Steven King in his book, *The Shining*, and a movie of that same title, inspired by Estes' famous landmark, The Stanley Hotel.

33. Alexander A. Hyde (1847–1935); Ida Elizabeth Todd Hyde (1855–1933).

34. Laura Taylor (personnel communication, 2010).

35. Donna Clark (personal communication, 2012).

36. *Estes Park Trail* (August 17, 1923).

37. In fact, there was at least one Methodist family to whom Stone sold property: Dr. Ernest Tremont Tittle (1885–1950) and his wife Glenna, of Evanston, Illinois. An early champion of racial justice and civil rights, Tittle worked to integrate his own church in Evanston and advocated for social equality within the Methodist Episcopal Church as a whole. A prolific writer, his books included *Christians in an UnChristian Society* (1845), *We Need Religion* (1931), and *A Way of Life* (1935).

38. Donna Clark (personal communication, 2012).

39. Melanie Shellenbarger (2008). *High Country Summers: The Emergence and Development of the Second Home in Colorado, 1880–1940*. Dissertation, University of Colorado, pp. 166–167.

40. The legal name of the original organization was *The Cliffs Association;* later, it was known as *The John Timothy Stone Cliffs Association.*

41. Map published in the *Estes Park Trail-Gazette*, August 21, 1969.

42. Jerry Miller, unpublished essay, 2011 (based on *One Hundred Eleven Trees: A Compilation of Biographies* by The Memorial Tree Planting Committee of the Fort Morgan Heritage Foundation, Inc.).

43. *Idem.* And, as Jerry Miller noted, the early date for the community predates the incorporation of the town, making it "one of the older subdivisions in the area"; and, while Rocky Mountain National Park and the Town of Estes Park are starting to plan for celebrations honoring their 100-year anniversaries in 2015 and 2017 respectively, "the Fort Morgan Colony unassumingly passed its 100 years of existence in April 2011."

44. Henry C. Giese (b. 1878) was the manager of the Great Western Sugar Company's Fort Morgan factory. At the time, Henry and Nettie Giese had two school-age daughters, Helen and Ada.

45. Perry's cherry dessert won first place in a *Rocky Mountain News* recipe contest in 1948. The prize: a Sunbeam Mixmaster electric mixer.

46. *Trail Talk*, 1920.

47. Alberta Virginia Olsen Rutledge (1907–1999); Lyle Eugene Rutledge (1907–1958). After Lyle's death, Alberta married Lawrence L. Keever (1905–1987), who was from Fort Morgan.

48. M. Shellenbarger. *High Country Summers*, p. 170.

49. Enos Mills, "the Father of Rocky Mountain National Park," shared the Tahosa Valley with both permanent and summer residents, not all of whom shared his enthusiasm for creation of the "Estes National Park." One of his fiercest critics in this endeavor was Charlie Hewes of Hewes-Kirkwood Ranch and Inn, who, with Charles and Agnes Levings at "Graystone," located on the Twin Sisters Peaks to the north of Mills's own homestead cabin; Edwin and Mabel Gillette, of "Lodge Pole;" and Dean Babcock and his mother, Josie Babcock, of "the Ledges"; formed the Front Range Settlers Association in response to a perceived threat to private ownership of land and cabins posed by the creation of a national park on their doorsteps. Fears that the government would condemn private property persisted even after the Park's dedication in 1915. In fact, the National Park Service successfully sought to extend the Park's original borders, particularly on Twin Sisters, where the expansion made possible the establishment of a fire lookout. In addition to Hewes and his neighbors, who called themselves "The Brigands," the group likely included the Colonel and Grace Ames and Fred and Jessie Sanders. In the end, of course, Mills's vision for Rocky Mountain National Park won out. For a complete account of the dispute, see James H. Pickering. *In the Vale of Elkanah: The Tahosa Valley World of Charles Edwin Hewes*. (Estes Park: Estes Park Area Historical Museum, 2003).

50. Colonel Ames, as he was affectionately known, was an attorney and an actuary at Bankers Life Insurance Company. Grace was originally from Fairbury, Nebraska.

51. The Levings had strong and highly personal connections to Estes Park. Agnes Levings' sister, Josephine Babcock, was mother to Dean Babcock, who also owned a Tahosa Valley cabin. In addition, the Levings' elder son Louis had lost his life in a tragic climbing accident on Mt. Ypsilon during the summer of 1905. Located on 160 acres, Graystone was unusual not only in the originality of Leving's design (which combined Romanesque Revival and Swiss chalet architectural elements) but in the choice of materials (granite collected from the building site).

52. Commercially prepared French dressing was available from the Kraft company beginning in the late 1930s. For purists who want to make their own dressings from scratch, a 1939 cookbook provides the following recipe: *"Ingredients: 3 tablespoons sugar 4 tablespoons ketchup 2 tablespoons vinegar or lemon juice 1 teaspoon Worcestershire sauce 1/2 teaspoon salt 3/4 cup oil 1 clove garlic (peeled and sliced in two). 1. Place ingredients in order given in a pint jar; shake thoroughly or beat with spoon until consistency of maple syrup. 2. Keep in cooler and shake or beat well before using. Makes 1 1/2 cups dressing."* —Prudence Penny. *Prudence Penny's Cook Book*. New York: Prentice Hall, 1939), p. 208.

53. "My mother, Margaret Ames Roehl, collected this recipe from Helen Yowell, a summer resident neighbor on Twin Sisters Mountain. John Yowell, a Chicago attorney, and his wife Helen bought a cabin near ours in 1946. They were the third owners of the cabin, which was built in 1922, quite likely by Charles Levings from whom the first owners, Fred T. Moseley and his wife Gussie H. Moseley, acquired the land. The second owner, Herman Hoch, bought the cabin in 1931. The Yowell

family still owns the property, which is known as 'Ye Owls' Nest.' The Yowells were also active in the Summer Residents Association." John Roehl (personal communication, 2012).

54. "I can't remember acquiring this recipe, no doubt from my mother or father, but I vividly remember my father, Frank E. Roehl, teaching me to catch brookies when I was very young. Our family would visit friends named Zumwinkle at their cabin on Cabin Creek east of the Meeker Park Lodge. Cabin Creek is a delightful little stream that even a young boy could almost jump across. My father would cut a willow branch from stream side and strip the leaves. He then tied on a length of monofilament fishing line equal in length to the pole and completed the outfit with an Eagle Claw Snelled Hook which at that time was made in Denver. Bait was an angle worm dug from our land. I began catching fish my first time out and became an avid fisherman that day. My mother, who had a tenderness for all living things, taught me to be kind and respectful to my catch." John Roehl (personal communication, 2012).

55. Freda, the youngest of seven children of Charles (1842–1892) and Rachel Porter Songer (b. 1853), was born in Wytheville, Wythe County, Virginia. Sometime in the 1920s, she and her young son moved to Lincoln, Nebraska, where she went to work for Fred and Jessie Sanders. Their association was a very close one and spanned almost forty years.

56. H. F. Pedersen, *Castles*, p. 223.

57. According to Jack Zumwinkle, writing in the introduction to Garetson's *Homesteading Big Owl*, it was Katherine herself who came up with the name for the road, "after she had flushed a great horned owl near a craggy hill on her site." Katherine Garetson, *Homesteading Big Owl*. (Allenspark, CO: Allenspark Wind, 1989), p. i.

58. Esther Burnell had been working as an interior designer in Cleveland, Ohio, when she first came to the mountains of Colorado in 1916. Enos Mills hired her as his personal secretary and taught her nature guiding. In fact, Esther was the first woman to be licensed as a Nature Guide by the National Park Service. The couple was married in 1918 at Mills's homestead cabin, and became the parents of one child, a daughter Enda, born in 1919.

59. Elizabeth G. Dings. In K. Garetson, *Homesteading Big Owl*, p. iii.

60. The family consisted of his wife Sara Levy Steiner (1868–1940) and two children, Gretchen H. Steiner Hightshoe (1893–1980) and Richard M. Steiner (1901–1975).

61. David Steiner (personal communication, 2010).

62. Margaret Price Reedy (1920–1996); Eva Jane Reece (Mrs. Howard W.) Price (1885–1942).

# Bibliography of Estes Park Cookbooks

Cookbooks are among the most popular genre of literary works in the United States, and Estes Park has seen its share of locally produced volumes. Dating from 1920, collections of recipes have been published by local social clubs, civic organizations, inns and resorts, churches, businesses and shops, and radio stations, as well as individuals and family groups. A number of cookbooks are "hybrids" in the sense that they contain recipes contributed by individuals as well as sections with recipes from local inns and restaurants. Recipes for local specialties have also appeared in anthologies, compilations of signature dishes and favorites from Colorado restaurants and resorts. Then, too, recipes from historic lodges and old Estes families have also appeared, if irregularly, in the local newspapers.

While every effort has been made to create a comprehensive list of locally produced cookbooks, we feel confident that there are other collections of Estes Park recipes of which we are currently unaware. We apologize for any inadvertent omissions and hope to add to our list as additional cookbooks come to our attention.

## Individual and Family Cookbooks

Baldwin, Ralph, and Baldwin, Linda. *Kitchen Keepsakes from the Baldwin Family & Friends: A Collection of Recipes from Ralph and Linda Baldwin and Family and Friends.* Estes Park, CO: Morris Press, 2002.

Lynn, Judy. *From Lake to Plate*. Estes Park, CO: Morris Press, n.d.
*Rocky Mountain Cookery: Favorite Vegetarian and Fish Recipes*. n.d.

## Church Cookbooks

Bethel Academy. *Feeding His Flock: A Colorado Cookbook*. Estes Park, CO: Morris Press, 1991.

Community Church of the Rockies. *Good Foods for Good Friends*. Estes Park, CO, 1994.

Community Church of the Rockies. *Sweet Things from High Places—A Collection of Recipes Inspired by the Community Church of the Rockies Preschool and Enrichment*. Estes Park, CO, 2003.

Estes Park Ladies Aid Society. *High Altitude Cook Book*. Estes Park, CO: *Estes Park Trail*, 1936.

*Sharing Our Best: Episcopal Church Women of St. Bartholomew's*. Estes Park, CO, n.d.

*United Methodist Cookbook*. Estes Park, CO, 1999.

## Lodges, Resorts, and Inns

Groicher, Herman, & Groicher, Mieke. *The Fawn Brook Inn Cookbook: Allenspark, Colorado*. Boulder, CO: Johnson Books, 2008.

Smith, Lois. *The Collections of the Baldpate Inn*. Estes Park, CO, 1990.

———. *The Baldpate Collections*, 2000.

YMCA of the Rockies. *Wood Stones to Microwaves: A Collection of Recipes by YMCA of the Rockies Members and Guests*. Kearney, NE: Morris Press Cookbooks, 2006.

## Estes Valley Businesses and Shops

Broman, Jennifer, and Broman, Dennis. *Heart-Healthy Cookbook*. Estes Park, CO: Heart Center of the Rockies, n.d.

Calico Kate's, Inc. *Calico Kate's Own Cook Book*. Glen Haven, CO, 1962.

———. *Calico Kate's Holiday Cookbook*. Glen Haven, CO, 1964.

———. *Calico Kate's 3 Days Before Pay Day*. Glen Haven, CO, 1969.

———. *Calico Kate's "In Case of Emergency" Cook Book*. Glen Haven, CO, 1981.

*Coldwell Banker-Estes Village Properties Lifestyles Cookery*, n.d. Sponsored by Wayne Newsom.

Jeffrey, L., & Grace, M. *Estes Park's Unconventional One & Only Souvenir Recipe Book*. Estes Park, CO: Mountain Printery, n.d.

## Radio Stations

KLMO 1060. *Sweet Things from High Places: A Collection of Recipes Inspired by the Grandeur of Rocky Mountain National Park*, 2003.

Lynn, Merrie. *Hello Neighbor Cookbook: A Service of KOA*, 1964.

———. *Hello Neighbor Cookbook: A Service of KOA*, 1965.

———. *Hello Neighbor: 1966 Cook Book* [sometimes *Cookbook*]: *A Service of KOA Radio*. Denver, CO: KOA Radio, 1966.

———. *Hello Neighbor: 1967 Cook Book* [sometimes *Cookbook*]: *A Service of KOA Radio*. Denver, CO: KOA Radio, 1967.

———. *Hello Neighbor: 1968 Cook Book* [sometimes *Cookbook*]: *A Service of KOA Radio*. Denver, CO: KOA Radio, 1968.

Stewart, Lila Jean. *Happy Talk KLMO 1060 Cook Books*, 1973–1979.

## Social, Service, and Civic Clubs and Sororities

*All Roads Lead Home: Fine Home Cooking from Glen Haven, CO*, 2008.

*Associated Women for Circle C Camp*, Estes Park, CO, n.d.

Big Elk Meadows Volunteer Fire Department. *What's Cookin' in Big Elk*. Greeley, CO: Copy Right Printing, 1997.

Chapter AV, PEO Sisterhood. *Tried and True Recipe Book: From the Kitchens of Estes Park Pioneer Women*, 1920.

———. *Tried and True Recipe Book: From the Kitchens of Estes Park Pioneer Women*. 2nd edition, 1925.

———. *Tried and True Recipe Book: From the Kitchens of Estes Park Pioneer Women*, 1925. A facsimile copy of the 2nd edition, 1985.

Chapter HZ PEO. *Christmas Cookbook*. Estes Park, CO, 1988.

———. *Our Sisters' Recipes*. Estes Park, CO, 1998.

Elizabeth Knutsson Memorial Hospital. *From Our Kitchen to Yours: The Elizabeth Guild Cook Book*. Iowa Falls, Iowa: General Publishing and Binding, 1974.

Epsilon Sigma Alpha: Eta Omega Chapter (comp). *A Taste of Estes Park*. Iowa Falls, Iowa: General Publishing and Binding, 1976.

———. *A Treasury of Famous Recipes from Estes Park, Colorado*. 1978.

Estes Park Elementary School. *The Presidents' Cookbook*. Fourth and Fifth grades, 1984.

Estes Park Newcomers. *Estes Park Favorites: A Collection of Recipes from the Estes Park Newcomers Club, Estes Park, CO*, 2005.

Estes Park [CO] Woman's Club. *Estes Park Woman's Club Cook Book*, n.d. *(perhaps various.)*

*Family Fare "Kitchen Tested" Cookbook*. 2nd edition. Denver, Colorado, n.d.

*Glen Haven [CO] Community Cookbook*, 1999.

Hidden Valley [Estes Park, CO] Ski Patrol. *Nibbles Vittles and Drips*, 1986.

Keefe, Sue, and Barth, Ardene. *Ardene and Sue's "Science Fair Project" Collection of Recipes*, 2007. (For the benefit of the Glen Haven [CO] Area Volunteer Fire Department.)

Pinewood Springs Women's Auxiliary for Pinewood Springs. *Volunteer Fire Department Cookbook*, 1977.

SHYF. *Cookie Recipe Book, 1990*.

Town of Estes Park [CO]. *Here's What's Cooking at Town Hall*, Estes Park, CO, 1989.

## Anthologies with Estes Park B & B, Lodge, and Restaurant Recipes

Bauer, Linda, & Bauer, Steve. *Recipes from Historic Colorado: A Restaurant Guide and Cookbook*. Lanham, MD: Taylor Trade Publishing, 2008. [Featured from the Estes Park area are recipes from The Stanley Hotel, Twin Owls Steakhouse at the Black Canyon Inn, and Sylvan Dale Guest Ranch in Loveland, CO.]

Bennis, Benjamin James. *Colorado Restaurants: Off the Beaten Path*, 1988. [Featured are recipes from the Fawn Brook Inn in Allenspark.]

Faino, Carol, & Hazledine, Doreen. *Colorado Bed & Breakfast Cookbook: From the Warmth and Hospitality of 88 Colorado B & Bs and Country Inns*. 2nd edition. Denver, CO: 3D Press, Inc., 2000. [Featured from the Estes Park area are recipes from Allenspark Lodge, Barbara's, Black Dog Inn, Dripping Springs Inn, Eagle Cliff House, Romantic Riversong Inn, and Taharaa Mountain Lodge.]

Gruber, David. *Colorado's Finest Small-Town Restaurants and Their Recipes*. Golden, CO: Fulcrum Pub., 2002. [Featured from the Estes Park area are recipes from the Cascades at The Stanley Hotel, the Grumpy Gringo, Orlando's Steak House, The Other Side, Silverado at Lake Shore Lodge, Sweet Basilico Cafe, the Twin Owls Steakhouse at the Black Canyon Inn, and the Woodlands Restaurant.]

———. *Colorado Restaurants and Recipes from Small Towns*, 1996. [Featured from the Estes Park area are recipes from the Dunraven Inn, Andrea's Homestead Café (Lyons), and the Country Side Inn.]

———. *Colorado Favorites Cook Book: A Cornucopia of Colorado Cooking*, 1992/6 [Featured are recipes from the McGraw Ranch.]

Richardson, Javana M., & Richardson, David J. *Best of the Historic West*. Greenwood Village, CO: Pantry Press, 2000. [Featured are recipes from The Stanley Hotel in Estes Park.]

Walter, Claire. *Culinary Colorado: The Ultimate Food Lover's Guide*. Golden CO: Fulcrum Publishing, 2003. [Featured from the Estes Park area are recipes from Grandmaison's Chalet Room at Marys Lake Lodge, and Romantic Riversong.]

# Appendix A:
# Isabella Bird's Thanksgiving Recipes

Unfortunately Isabella Bird did not write down the specifics of the dishes she prepared for Thanksgiving dinner at the Estes Park home of Griff Evans in 1873. However, anyone wishing to try some authentic English recipes may find those printed below acceptable substitutes.

## *Rich Bread and Butter Pudding*
*(Nineteenth-century recipe)*

Give a good flavour of lemon-rind and bitter almonds, or of cinnamon, if preferred to a pint of new milk, and when it has simmered a sufficient time for this, strain and mix it with a quarter of a pint of rich cream; sweeten it with four ounces of sugar in lumps, and stir it while still hot to five well-beaten eggs; throw in a few grains of salt, and move the mixture briskly with a spoon as a glass of brandy is added to it. Have ready a thickly-buttered dish three layers of thick bread and butter cut from a half-quarter loaf, with four ounces of currants, and one and a half of finely shred candied peel, strewed between and over them; pour the eggs and milk on them by degrees, letting the bread absorb one portion before another is added; it should soak for a couple of hours before the pudding is taken to the oven, which should be a moderate one. Half an hour will bake it. It is very good when made with new

milk only; and some persons use no more than a pint of liquid in all, but part of the whites of the eggs may then be omitted. Cream may be substituted for the entire quantity of milk at pleasure. New milk, 1 pint; rind of small lemon, and 6 bitter almonds bruised (or 1/2 drachma [dram] of cinnamon); simmered 10 to 20 minutes. Cream, 1/4 pint; sugar, 4 oz.; eggs, 6; brandy, 1 wineglassful. Bread and butter, 3 layers; currants, 4 oz.; candied orange or lemon-rind, 1 oz.; to stand 2 hours, and to be baked 30 minutes in a moderate oven."—*Modern Cookery for Private Families*, Eliza Acton, 1845 facsimile reprint with an introduction by Elizabeth Ray [Southover Press: East Sussex, 1993] (p. 359).

## Sweet Biscuits

**Ingredients:**
Teacup of medium oatmeal
Teacup of plain flour
Half teacup of milk
Tablespoon of soft brown sugar
3 oz butter or margarine
Level teaspoon salt
Level teaspoon bicarbonate of soda (baking soda)

**Method:** Sieve the flour, salt and bicarbonate of soda into a bowl, add the oatmeal and mix. Cut the butter or margarine into small portions and rub into the mixture with your fingers. Add the sugar and mix well. Pour in the milk and mix until you have a stiff but workable dough.

Shake some flour on a worktop, turn the dough onto it and shake a little flour on the top. Roll out thinly (about half an inch thick) and prick over with a fork. Cut into rounds with a scone cutter and place on an oiled baking tray. Bake in a pre-heated oven for 15/20 minutes at 350F/180C/Gas Mark 4. Use a palette knife to lift the biscuits onto a wire coming rack. Store in an airtight tin.

From Traditional Scottish Recipes: available online at http://www.rampantscotland.com/recipes/blrecipe_oatbiscuits.htm

# Gingerbread Cake

*(A 2 lb version. For a 4 lb cake, double the recipe and the pan size).*

**Ingredients:**
4 oz (100g or 1 stick) butter
4 oz (100g or half cup) soft brown sugar
1 tablespoon molasses
6 oz (150g or 1½ cups) plain flour
2 oz (50g or half cup) oatmeal
1 oz (25g or quarter cup) bran
3 level teaspoons of ground ginger
1 level teaspoon mixed spice (allspice)
1 level teaspoon bicarbonate of soda (baking soda)
2 eggs
2 fluid ounces (50ml or quarter cup) [buttermilk] milk
4 fluid ounces (100ml or half cup) orange juice

**Method:** Preheat the oven to 160C/320F/Gas Mark 3 (reduce the temperature by 10C or equivalent if a fan assisted oven).

Mix the flour, bran, spices and soda together in a bowl. Put the milk and orange juice in another container and lightly beat in the eggs. Put the margarine, sugar and treacle/molasses in a saucepan on a low heat and stir until the sugar has dissolved. Remove from the heat and stir in the dry ingredients and then add the eggs/milk/juice mixture.

Pour the mixture into a 2 lb loaf tin lined with baking parchment and bake for around 40 minutes.

From Traditional Scottish Recipes: available online at http://www.rampantscotland.com/recipes/blrecipe_gingerbread.htm

## Roly-Poly Pudding
*(Nineteenth-century recipe)*

The pastry for this favourite pudding may be made in three or four ways, according to the degree of richness required. For a superior pudding mix a pound of flour with a half pound of very finely-shred suet, freed from skin and fibre. Add a good pinch of salt, an egg, and nearly half a pint of milk. Roll it out three or four times. For a plainer pudding, mix five or six ounces of suet with a pound of flour, add a pinch of salt, and make a paste by stirring in a half a pint of water. When suet is objected to, rub six ounces of butter or six ounces of sweet dripping into a pound of flour, and proceed as before. When a similar quantity of dripping is used, the addition of a spoonful of baking-powder will help to make the pastry light. Roll out the pastry to a long thin form, a quarter of an inch thick, and of a width to suit the size of the saucepan in which it is to be boiled. Spread over it a layer of any kind of jam, and be careful that it does not reach the edges of the pastry. Begin at one end, and roll it up to fasten the jam inside, moisten the edges and press them securely together. Dip a cloth in boiling water, flour it well, and tie the pudding tightly in it. Plunge it into a saucepan of boiling water, at the bottom of which a plate has been laid to keep the pudding from burning, and boil quickly until done enough. If it is necessary to add more water, let it be put in boiling. Marmalade, treacle, sliced lemon and sugar, lemon-juice and sugar, chopped apples and currants, either separately or together, may be used instead of jam for a change. Time to boil the pudding, one hour and a half to two hours, according to the size."—*Cassell's Dictionary of Cookery with Numerous Illustrations* [Cassell, Petter, Galpin & Co: London] 1875 (p. 769).

# Appendix B: Recipes from the Old Plantation Restaurant

## Cock-A-Leekie Soup
*(Robert E. Burgess)*

| | |
|---|---|
| 1 5 lb. roaster chicken (about) | 6 quarts water (about) |
| 2 pounds leeks, washed, trimmed, and sliced thin. White and yellow part only. | 1 16-ounce jar prepared prunes |
| | Chopped parsley |
| | Salt to taste |

Wash chicken and place in large pot with the neck and giblets. Discard the liver because it will darken the stock.

Cover with water. Bring to a boil. Cover and simmer until the chicken is tender, about two hours at our altitude.

When tender, remove the chicken and let cool. Reduce the stock to about three quarts. Remove the meat from the breasts. Chop fine and set aside. Reserve the dark meat for another dish.

When stock is reduced, add leeks and cook until tender, about 40 minutes. Add chopped white meat to soup. Add salt to taste. Skim.

To Serve:

Place prunes in strainer and pour over boiling water to wash off syrup and heat prunes. Place prunes in large soup tureen. Add soup and top with chopped parsley. This is a rich and delicious soup and not too many calories.

## Black Bean Soup
*(Robert E. Burgess)*

3 cups black turtle beans
2 quarts chicken stock or water
8 ounces bacon, diced
1 medium onion (8 oz) chopped
1 large green pepper, cored, seeded and chopped
3-4 stalks celery (8 oz) chopped
3 garlic cloves, diced
2 teaspoons salt
1 teaspoon ground basil
1 teaspoon ground oregano
1/2 teaspoon thyme
1/4 cup wine vinegar
1/2 pound tiny cooked shrimp
Sour cream.

Wash, pick, and soak beans overnight. Drain.
Add other ingredients, except the shrimp and sour cream. Bring to a boil.
Lower heat to low and cover. Beans should barely turn.
Stir from time to time and add more liquid if necessary.
When the beans are very tender, take an old-fashioned potato masher and mash the hell
out of those beans!
Check salt, add shrimp and serve.
Place a generous dollop of sour cream on top of each bowl of soup.

## Cucumber, Watercress, and Cream Cheese Sandwich
*(Robert E. Burgess)*

12 slices whole-grain bread
8 ounces cream cheese at room temperature
2 tablespoons mayonnaise
1 bunch watercress, washed and stemmed (there is no substitute)
1 cucumber, peeled, sliced thin, and salted.
Let cucumbers rest for an hour to draw off juice, then drain off liquid.

Cream cheese and mayonnaise are mixed until smooth.
Spread the cream cheese mixture on the 12 slices of bread. Cover six slices of bread with sliced cucumbers.
Next, a nice covering of watercress. Cover with the other 6 slices of bread. Trim the crust off and cut on diagonal and serve.

## Jalapeño Cornbread
*(Robert E. Burgess)*

1 Cup flour
3/4 Cup corn meal
1 teaspoon salt
3 teaspoons baking powder
1 tablespoon sugar
1 large egg
1 cup buttermilk
3 tablespoons melted shortening
1/2 cup whole-kernel corn, drained
1/4 cup diced chilies

Mix flour, corn meal, salt, baking powder and sugar together. Add unbeaten egg and buttermilk. Stir till lightly mixed.
Add corn, shortening, and chilies and pour into a greased 8 x 8 x 2 inch pan.
Bake at 400 degrees for 30 minutes or until golden brown.

# References

Acton, Eliza. *Modern Cookery for Private Families*. (1845). (Southover Press: East Sussex, 1993.)

Barnes, Sybil. *Estes Park (Images of America)*. (Charleston, SC: Arcadia Publishing, 2010.)

Bird, Isabella L. *A Lady's Life in the Rocky Mountains*. (New York: G. P. Putnam's Sons, 1888.)

Burgess, Harriet Rose. *Then The Women Took Over: A Hundred Years of the Estes Park Woman's Club*. (Estes Park, CO: Estes Park Museum Friends & Foundation, Inc. Press: 2012.)

Chapter AV PEO Sisterhood: *Tried and True Recipe Book*. (Estes Park, CO: 1920.)

Cassell. Colleen E. *The Golden Pioneer. Biography of Joel Estes, The Man Who Discovered Estes Park*. (Colorado: Peanut Butter Publishing, 1999.)

*Cassell's Dictionary of Cookery with Numerous Illustrations*. (London: Cassell, Petter, Galpin & Co., 1875).

Chubbuck, Kay, ed. *Letters to Henrietta*. (Boston: Northeastern University Press, 2002.)

Connelley, William E. *A Standard History of Kansas and Kansans*. (Chicago: Lewis Publishing Co., 1919.)

Crump. Robert L. *The Prints of Lyman Byxbe (1886-1980), A Catalog Raisonné: In Competition with Souvenirs, Photos, Postcards and the Like*. (Wayzata, MN: Studio K, 2002.)

Crump. Robert L. *The Prints of Lyman Byxbe, Omaha to Estes Park: An Artist's Legacy and Catalog Raisonné.* David Tanton, ed. (Estes Park, CO: Estes Park Museum Friends & Foundation Inc. Press, 2011.)

Drummond, Alexander. *Enos Mills: Citizen of Nature.* (Niwot, CO: University of Colorado Press, 1995.)

Estes, Milton. "Memoirs of Estes Park." *Colorado Magazine* (July, 1939). (Fort Collins: Friends of the Colorado State College Library.)

Estes Park Ladies Aid Society. *High Altitude Cook Book.* (Estes Park, CO: Estes Park Trail, 1936.)

Garetson, Katherine. *Homesteading Big Owl.* (Allenspark, CO: Allenspark Wind, 1989.)

Groicher, Herman, and Groicher, Mieke. *The Fawn Brook Inn Cookbook.* (Allenspark, Colorado. Boulder, CO: Johnson Books, 2008.)

Hix, Beulah Clauser. *Some Early Lineages of Berks County, PA.* (Boulder, CO: 1959.)

Hondius, Eleanor E. *Memoirs of Eleanor E. Hondius of Elkhorn Lodge.* (Estes Park, Colorado: Estes Park Museum Friends & Foundation, Inc. Press, 2010.)

Knapp, Joseph G. *The Glen Haven Story.* (Boulder: Johnson Publishing Co., 1967.)

Mills, Joe. *Joe Mills: A Mountain Boyhood.* (Lincoln, NE: University of Nebraska Press, 1988.)

Pedersen Jr., Henry F. *"Rough It with Ease": The Story of The McGraw Ranch.* (Estes Park, CO: 1990.)

———. *Those Castles of Wood.* (Estes Park, CO: 1993.)

Penny, Prudence. *Prudence Penny's Cook Book.* (New York: Prentice Hall, 1939.)

Pickering, James H. *America's Switzerland: Estes Park and Rocky Mountain National Park, The Growth Years.* (Boulder, CO: University Press of Colorado, 2005).

———. *In the Vale of Elkanah: The Tahosa Valley World of Charles Edwin Hewes.* (Estes Park, CO: Estes Park Area Historical Museum, 2003.)

———. *Joe Mills of Estes Park: A Colorado Life.* (Estes Park, CO: Estes Park Museum Friends & Foundation Inc. Press, 2013.)

———. *"This Blue Hollow." Estes Park, the Early Years, 1859–1915.* (Boulder: University Press of Colorado, 1999.)

Pickering, James H. and Thomas, Nancy P. *If I Ever Grew Up and Became a Man: William Allen White's Moraine Park Years.* (Estes Park, CO: Estes Park Museum Friends & Foundation, Inc. Press, 2010.)

Pickering, James H., Stevanus, Carey, and Clinger, Mic. *Estes Park and Rocky Mountain National Park Then & Now*. (Englewood, CO: Westcliff Publishers, 2006.)

Reed, Sally Ferguson. "Family Reminiscences of a Real Pioneer of Estes Park." In *A Pictorial History of Estes Park, Colorado*. (Estes Park, CO, 1968.)

Shellenbarger, Melanie. *High Country Summers: The Early Second Homes of Colorado, 1880–1940*. (Tucson, AZ: University of Arizona Press, 2012.)

Sprague, Abner E. *My Pioneer Life: The Memoirs of Abner E. Sprague*. (Estes Park, CO: Rocky Mountain Nature Association, 1999.)

Sweet. Channing F. *A Princeton Cowboy*. (Colorado Springs, CO: Dentan Berkeland, 1967.)

## Unpublished interviews/programs/dissertations/memoirs etc.

Transcipt of interview with Rex Roth, 2005. Estes Valley [CO] Public Library.

Transcript of interview with Duke Sumonia, 1990. Estes Valley [CO] Public Library.

"Plantation Restaurant history and the art of Richard Tallant." Presented by Bob Burgess and Rhoda Service Tallant, April 23, 1981. Estes Valley Library.

Shellenbarger, Melanie (2008). High Country Summers: The Emergence and Development of the Second Home in Colorado, 1880–1940. Dissertation, University of Colorado, Boulder, Colorado.

Lynn, Emerson; Scott, Carruth; Scott, Angelo; Scott, Dorothy Carnine; White, William Lindsey. *The Scottage, A Medley* (unpublished manuscript, n.d.).

# Index

## A

Akins, Robert and Virginia, 174
Alexander, Charles H. and Anna, 119
Alford, Dick and Mary Beth, 294
American Legion, 63, 225, 256
American Legion, Ladies Auxiliary of the. *See* American Legion Auxiliary
American Legion Auxiliary, 205, 225
American Plan, 10, 104, 117, 127, 159; defined, 17(n11)
Ames, Ernest Capron and Grace A., 346, 348–351, 373(n49–50)
Ames, John H. "Jack," 348
Anderson, Alfred "Fred," 148, 320
Anderson, Harriet Robbins, 372(n24)
Anderson's Wonder View, 261
Andrews, Ed, 75
Anspauch, Alice Byxbe, 228–232
Anspauch, Rudolph F. "Rudy," 229
Arrow Livery, 252, 368
Ashton, Grace E. Jones, 121, 180(n43)
Ashton, Willard Herbert, 121–123
Atkins, D. Ferrel, 17(n5), 371(nn8, 17)
Autochrome Lumière, 195, 196, 295(n4)
AV Chapter of PEO. *See* PEO, AV Chapter of

## B

Babcock, Dean and Josephine "Josie," 373(n49)
baking, high altitude, 6; challenges of, 3, 5
Baldpate Inn, 89, 141–143
Bankers Life Insurance Company (Lincoln, NE), 353, 373(n50)
Barclay, Houston and Mary Jane "Patti," 329–330
Barrett, Elizabeth Hunt, 308
Beaver Point, 148, 261
beaver tail, Native American, use of, 22–23
Bechtel, Orville W., 216
Berryhill, Albert Clyde, 340
Berryhill, Doris F. Perrenoud "Perry," 340, 341
Berryhill, John R. "Jack," 340
Berryhill, Mildred Bessie Vermazen (Mrs. Albert Clyde) "Mother," xiii, 340
Bible, Dana X., 320
Biggers, Earl Derr, 143
Big Owl Tea Place, 347, 359–361, 374(n57)
Big Thompson Hotel, 148–150
Birch, Albert George, 199–201, 295(n9)

Birch, Briana, 201
Birch, Phoebe Katherine Phillips (Mrs. Albert G.), 201
Bird, Henrietta (Henny), letters to, 24
Bird, Isabella Lucy, 24, 83, 85; cooking activities of, xiv, 25–26; Evans baby named for, 25, 81(n10); recipes, xv, 81(n15), 379–382
Bison Museum (Scottsdale, AZ), 298(n74)
Bissell, James Russell and Catherine Gibson "Ky," 314, 317–319, 371(n18)
Bissell, Russell, 317
Bitner, Albert, 117, 180(n40)
Bitner, Catherine, 117
Bitner, Edna Evangeline Sperry, 117–119, 180(n40)
Bitner, Harry W., 116–118, 180(n41)
Bitner, Melville, 117
Bitner's Cabins, 119
Black Canyon, settlement of, 27, 37
Blakeway family, 159
Bliss, Jack E., 119
Bliss, Ruth Eugenie Harms, 119, 120
Blue Ribbon Livery. *See* Arrow Livery
Blue Spruce Cabins. *See* Workshire Lodge
Bond, Alma E. Sanborn, 68, 234
Bond, Cornelius H., 19, 68–69, 183, 186
Bond, Frank C., 244
Bond Park, naming of, 68; library in, 129, 233; skating rink, 206, 214
Bookshop, Macdonald. *See* Macdonald Book Shop
Boone, Elliott W. and Isabelle Noyes, 321
Boone Cabin, 372(n22)
Bourk, Charles Oscar, 321
brand names and branding, 6, 7, 16
Brillat-Savarin, Jean Anthelme, 1, 17(n1)
Brinkley Drug Co., 297(n53)
Brinkley, Bert, 186, 205
Brinkley, George Earl, 205
Brinkley, Mary M. Redman, 205
Brinwood Hotel. *See* Brinwood Ranch and Hotel
Brinwood Ranch and Hotel, 75, 89, 112–115, 339
Brodie's Market, 205

Brownfield, Jerry and Vera, 272–273, 298(n65)
Brownfield's Trading Post, 272
Brigands, The, 373(n49)
Brush, Jared Lemar, 103
buffet at Stead's Ranch, 109
Burgess, Harriet Rose Bittner, 239, 242
Burgess, Janet Bovee (Mrs. Robert), 240
Burgess, Robert E. "Bob," 237, 238, 239, 241, 242–243, 383–385
Burgess, Thelma Porter. *See* Chapman, Thelma Porter Burgess
Burgess, William Endsley "Bill," 237, 239
Burkhart, Charles F. (Charles Eagle Plume), 217–218, 363
Burroughs, J. C., 196
Burroughs, John, 196
butchering process, 5
Byxbe, Geneva Mildred Blackwell "Ma," xv, 228, 229–230
Byxbe, Henry Lyman "Byx," xv, 228, 229–230; Stanley Menu, 88
Byxbe Art Gallery, 228

# C

Calico Kate. *See* Ferguson, Dorothy Elizabeth Walters
Calico Kate's Gift Shop, 285–286
Carnine, Oma Josella Langellier, 310
Carr, Ora L. Mabie, 234–236
Carruth, Fred W., 337
Carruth family, 337
Cassell, Colleen Estes, 22, 23
Chalets, Estes Park, 14, 15
Chalets, Lewiston, 137, 179(n8)
Chamber of Commerce. *See* Estes Park Chamber of Commerce
Chapin, Frederick, 51–52, 179(nn10, 11)
Chapin, Howard C. and Louisa, 190, 191
Chapin, Jessica. *See* Macdonald, Jessica Chapin
Chapman, Alson, 48
Chapman, Alson Jr., 20, 48
Chapman, Areanna "Arah" Sprague, 19, 20, 46, 47, 48, 52, 55, 82(n29)

Chapman, Charles A., 20, 181(n68), 305, 371(n8)
Chapman, Clay Warren "Chappie," 239
Chapman, Elizabeth "Libby" Buchanan, 52
Chapman, Lena, 48
Chapman, Thelma Porter Burgess, 237–239, 241, 297(n47)
Chapman family, 45
Cheney, Hazel E., 78, 80
Chez Jay Café and Lounge, 185
Christmas picnic, Burnell and Garetson's, 12, 361
chuckwagon dinners, 15
Church of the United Brethren. *See* United Brethren Church of Christ
Clapp, Raymond Gustavus and Anne Louise Barr, 320, 321
Clarendon House Hotel (Leadville, CO), 190
Clark, Donna, 333, 334
Clark, Helen, 334
Clark, Harry Martin and Marie M. Van Malsen, 334
Clatworthy, Emma Payne, 196
Clatworthy, Fred Payne, 195–197
Clatworthy, Sarah Mabel Leonard, 196–197, 198
Clauser, Ann Hettinger, 63
Clauser, Florence Yochum, 63, 66, 67
Clauser, Milton, 62, 63
Clauser, Winnie Alvida Wells, 62, 63
Cleave, John and Margaret, 57, 183, 184
Cliffs Association, The, 331, 372(n40)
Coat of Arms Tavern, Old Plantation, 297(n47)
Cobb, Alfred Lewis "Al," 82(n22), 191, 255, 297(n55)
Cobb, Edna B. *See* James, Edna B. Cobb Arnold Gray
Cobb Cabin. *See* Macdonald/Cobb Cabin
Coleman, William Coffin "W.C." and Fannie Lucinda Sheldon, 333
Coleman Lamp and Stove Company, 333
Coles, Florence Dye, 320
"Colorado," poem by Clement Yore, 150

Colorado Dude & Guest Ranch Association, 166
Colorado Mountain Club, 71
Colorado Ski Club, 76, 215
Colorado State Register of Historic Properties, 295(n9)
Columbine Lodge (The Columbines, Columbines Lodge), 116–120, 365
commercial canning, 9
Community Church of the Rockies. *See* Presbyterian Community Church of the Rockies
cookbooks, community, xiii; Estes Park, xi–xiv, 2, 6, 9–10, 28, 68, 71, 87, 294. *See also* Bibliography of Estes Park Cookbooks, 375–378
cooking schools (Boston), 3; standardization of measurements by, 3
cooking techniques, high country, 3, 5
Coolidge's Café, 186
Copeland Lodge. *See* Wild Basin Lodge
Country Club community, Estes Park, 300
Covered Wagon Dining Room. *See* Deer Ridge Chalet
Cowboy Dinner menus. *See* Stead's Ranch and Hotel
Crags Lodge, v, xiv, 89, 124–125, 127–129, 180(n49)
Crowley, J. Harold, 269
Crowley, Joseph W. "Joe," 269
Crowley, Mrs. Joe, 270
Crowley, Nell, 298(n62)
Crowley, Peggy J. Hackleman, 269, 298(n64)
Crowley's Café, 186
Crowley's High Country Restaurant 269
Crowley's Restaurant, 269, 270, 271, 298(n63)
Cunningham, Paula Reedy, 368

# D

Dairy Bar Delicatessen, 269
Dairy Dream, 275
dairying and dairy herds in early Estes Park, 6, 17(n5), 29, 33, 46, 83, 103, 104, 114
Daniels, Fisher & Company Dry Goods, 209, 296(n22)
Dark Horse Tavern, 185, 244–246
Day, Warren French and Edith Lillian Robbins, 322–325
Day family, 322–325
Deer Mountain, berry picking on, 94
Deer Ridge Chalet, 169, 216–220
dessert recipes, preponderance of, 6
Dever, Crete Mildred Childers, 161–162
Dever, Owen Leroy "Roy," 160–162
Devil's Gulch, settlement of, 280
Devil's Gulch Tea Room, 288, 289–290
Dick's Harbor. *See* Loveland Heights Court
Dings, Elizabeth G., 374(n59)
Dings, (Ella) Helen (Mrs. William W.), 359
Dinner Bell Restaurant, 269
Don-Jon Market, 347, 363
Dorsey, (Thomas) Henry, 335
Dorsey, Henry Jr., 335
Dorsey, Lulu Ward, 335
Dorsey Museum. *See* Lulu W. Dorsey Museum (YMCA of the Rockies)
Double Bar=X Ranch. *See* McGraw Guest Ranch
Double Bar=Y Ranch. *See* McGraw Guest Ranch
Drake Hotel (Chicago), 333–334
Drake, Tracy Corey and Annie D., 334
dude ranches. *See* McGraw Ranch; Stead's Ranch and Hotel; Wind River Ranch
Dunbier, Augustus William, 293
Duncan Hines Award, 143. *See also* Hines, Duncan
Dunraven, Earl of. *See* Wyndam-Quin, Windham Thomas, Fourth Earl of Dunraven
Dunraven Heights, community of, 300, 319–321, 322
Dunraven Inn, 247–249, 378
Dutch ovens, 22, 47

# E

E. D. Lindley & Son, Plumbers, 122, 225
Eagle Plume, Charles. *See* Burkhart, Charles F.
Eagle Plume's Trading Post, 363
Eastwood, Ronnie, 290
Ed's Cantina, 298(n63)
Edwards. W. G., 103
Elkhorn Lodge, 14–15, 37–41
English Hotel. *See* Estes Park Hotel
Epsilon Sigma Alpha, (Eta Omega), 170, 272, 317
Estes, Charles Francis, 22
Estes, Joel and Martha Ann "Patsey" Stollings, 19, 21–23, 81(n4), 83, 372(n22)
Estes, Mary Louise Fleming, 22
Estes, Milton, 21
Estes, Sarah, 21
Estes homestead, 22
Estes Park Area Historical Museum, Inc. *See* Estes Park Museum
Estes Park Bank, 63, 76, 107, 135
Estes Park Beer Parlor. *See* Wheel Bar
Estes Park (Town) Board of Trustees, 257
Estes Park Chamber of Commerce, 71, 139, 203, 210, 223, 257
Estes Park Drug Company, 70
Estes Park Golf and Country Club, 76, 129
Estes Park Horse Show. *See* Rooftop Rodeo
Estes Park Hotel, The (The English Hotel), 83–84, 103, 113, 179(n4), 321, 326
Estes Park Hotel Association, The, 166
Estes Park Ladies Aid Society, The, xii, 107; annual bazaar, 104; cookbook of, xiii, 2; members of, 71, 79, 197, 104, 107, 204, 210, 213, 223, 235, 252. *See also High Altitude Cook Book*
Estes Park Laundry, The, 295(n3)
Estes Park Lions Club, 252, 256, 257
Estes Park Motor Club, 76
Estes Park Museum, 255, 295(n9), 317
Estes Park Outdoor Club, 214
Estes Park Plumbers. *See* E. D. Lindley & Son, Estes Park Plumbers

Estes Park Protective and Improvement Association (EPPIA), 51, 76, 107, 233
Estes Park Public Library, 233; and the Estes Park Woman's Club, 225, 233–235; founding of, 234; funding support for, 90, 124, 204, 205, 210
Estes Park Rotary (group photo), 186
Estes Park Stage Line, 202
*Estes Park Trail*, early office of at Godfrey's, 222
Estes Park Transportation Company, 78
Estes Park Woman's Club, 90, 128, 129, 166, 170, 233, 295(n7); founding of, 11, 41, 63; members or founding members of, 29, 41, 51, 63, 68, 71, 76, 192, 197, 204, 205, 214, 223, 225, 234–235, 265, 304, 317
Estes Valley Recreation District, 257
European cuisine in Estes Park, 250
European Plan, 17(n11)
Evans, Griffith J. and Jane Owen, 19, 24–25
Evans family, 81(n9)
Evans ranch, xv, 24, 379
Evett, Charles Emery and Sadie Mae Warnock, 252, 367

# F

F. C. Adams Bakery, 7
Fagan, Robert Loren and Irmel, 172
Fall River Hand Laundry, 62–63
Fall River Hydroelectric Plant, 78; creation of, 9, 86
Fall River Lodge, 89, 144–146
Farmer, Fannie Merritt, 3
Fawn Brook Inn, 292–294
Ferber, Edna, 96, 99, 365
Ferguson, Dorothy Elizabeth Walters "Dottie" (Calico Kate) and Frank, 285–286
Ferguson, Horace V., 179(n9)
Ferguson, Horace Willis, 19, 91–93, 112, 179(n11)
Ferguson, James, 113
Ferguson, Mary L., 179(n9)
Ferguson, Mildred Frances. *See* Seaton, Mildred Frances Ferguson (Mrs. Walter)

Ferguson, Sallie E. *See* Reed, Sallie (Sally) E. Ferguson
Ferguson, Sarah "Sallie" Louise Thomson, 91–93, 112
Ferguson, William Hunter, 93, 112, 113, 179(n9)
Ferguson's Hotel. *See* Highlands, The
Fern Lake Lodge, 94; building of, 89, 212, 313, 314; "Modern Eve" at, 201; round room table in, 213
fires, destruction of early hotels and resorts from, 84, 96, 100, 103, 113, 137–138, 146, 172
Fischer, Paul, 175
Fischer brothers, 172–173
fish fries in Estes Park, 14, 15, 39, 106, 129, 331
Flagg, Monte, 290, 298(n74)
Fleshuts, Joseph, 153
foodways, 1, 6, 10; definition of, xi
Forks Hotel, The (Drake, CO), 125–127
Fort Morgan Colony, 337, 339
Fort Morgan Colony Addition, 337
Fort Morgan (CO) Outing Club, 337, 338
fox farming in Estes Park, 203
Front Range Settlers Association, 373(n49)

# G

Garetson, James S. and Caroline Griffith, 359
Garetson, Katherine G., 12, 347, 359–361, 374(n57)
garden, kitchen. *See* kitchen garden
garden, roof, 136
Gartner, Hans and Catherine Schaffer, 250–251
Gartner Haus Restaurant, 250–251
Gates, Helen, 180(n34)
Gay, Robert James and Bessie A. Henderson, 158, 182(n80)
General Federation of Women's Clubs, 158
Gere, Charles H., 321
Gere, Ellen, 321, 372(n23)
Gere, Frances, 321, 372(n23)
Gere, Mariel, 319, 321, 372(n23)

Gere family, 320, 324
Gibbs, Dorothy Scott, 305, 306, 308, 309, 310, 371(nn10, 12, 13, 14)
Giese, Henry G., 339, 372(n44)
Gillette, Edwin and Mabel, 118, 119, 353, 373(n49)
Gish, Barbara Louise "Bobbie" Clatworthy, 197, 198
Glen Comfort, 300, 343
Glen Haven, village of, 280–283, 285–286, 288, 289, 290; founding of, 280
Glen Haven, Inn of, 282–283
Glen Haven Lodge, 282
Godfrey, Dugald F. "D. F.," 185, 221, 222–223, 255
Godfrey, Lora Lee Bryant, 185, 221, 222–223, 224, 255
Godfrey's DeLuxe Store, 222–223, 296(n35)
Golden Rule Store (Loveland, CO), 209
Gooch, Alma K. Mulvaney, 209, 210, 211
Gooch, Carl Frederick, 208, 296(n21)
Gooch, Edna Morgan, 211
Gooch, Edward Augustus, 208, 209, 295(n20)
Gooch, Ernest "Ern" Clifford, 186, 208–210, 255
Gooch, Harry Augustus, 185, 208, 209, 295(n19)
Gooch, Julia Fincham, 185, 208, 209, 255, 295(n19)
Gooch, June Elizabeth, 209, 210, 296(n23)
Gooch family, 295(n19), 295–296(n20), 296(n21)
Gooch's Ready-to-Wear Shop (Gooch's Sports Wear), 208, 209, 210
Good View Ranch, 160
Gookins, Robert, quoted, 95, 98, 179(n16)
gourmet cuisine in Estes Park, 127, 136, 159, 283
Grand Central Hotel (Denver, CO), 190
Grant, John. *See* Steiner's Acres
Gray, Jeanne M. *See* Seybold, Jeanne M. Gray

Griffith, Albin, 56, 57, 82(n42), 82(n43), 188, 202
Griffith, Mary Margaret Grim, 56, 58
Griffith, Dan Braxton, 56, 57, 58, 82(nn42, 43)
Griffith, John Nolan, 56, 57
Griffith, Louise Ellen Jesser, 19, 57, 58, 59–61, 82(n43)
Griffith, Mary Lois, 56, 57–58, 61, 82(n43)
Griffith, Mary Margaret Grim, 56, 58
Griffith, Nellie, 56
Griffith, Oma Katherine, 56
Griffith, Virginia Cleave, 56
Griffith's Lumber Yard, 56
Griffith's sawmill, 56
grocery stores, local, 4, 161, 252, 269, 281, 345
Groicher, Hermann and Mieka, 294
Grooters, Fran McGraw, 164, 165
Grooters, Jay, 15, 17(n15), 164, 165

# H

Hackett, Claude H., 285
Hackett, Coyt, 230
Hackett & Walters Bakery, 285
Hall, Charles Byron, 78–79
Hall, George B. and Madge L. and family, 79
Hall, John Bigland and Hannah Roberts, 78–79
Hall, Josephine Cheney, 19, 78, 79, 80
Hallett, William H., 93, 179(n11)
Hand Laundry, Estes Park. *See* Fall River Hand Laundry
*Handbook of Rocky Mountain Plants* (Nelson), 123
Hap's Glorified Hamburger Haven. *See* Sundeck Restaurant
Harmony Guest Ranch, 266–267
Hart, Dave, 277
Hart's Cottage Inn Restaurant/Buffeteria, 277
Harvest Moon party (Elkhorn Lodge), 41
Hatcher, Dale and Laurel, 249
Hayden, Albert Jr., 74, 76, 82(n48), 186
Hayden, Albert Sr., 74

Hayden, Anna Louise Reed, 75, 77
Hayden, Emma Cornelia Howe, 74, 75, 76, 77
Hayden, Julian 74, 75, 76, 82(n48)
Hayden, Julian Reed, 76
Hayden, Sally Cornelia, 76
Hayes, Scott Wilbur and Matilda E. "Tillie," 266, 267, 268
Haynes, Ted and Karen, 283
Hays, Ethel, 177
Hellstern, Florence and Edward, 340
Herzog, Charles Lewis, 255, 256–257
Herzog, Doris Hope Romig, 256–257, 259
Herzog, Dianne Doris. *See* Seybold, Dianne Doris Herzog
Herzog's Gift Corral, 256, 257
Hewes, Charles Edwin, 346–347
Hewes-Kirkwood, town of, 347
Hewes-Kirkwood Ranch and Inn, 346, 347
Hidden Valley Ski Area, 256
Higby Clifford Starr, 212, 213, 214, 296(nn24, 29)
Higby, Edward DeVol, 214
Higby, Eunice, 215
Higby, Frances DeVol Wood, 214, 296(n31)
Higby, Harry LeRoy, 212, 213, 296(nn24, 26)
Higby, Lester Wright, 296(nn24, 25)
Higby, Nina Harris, 296(n25)
Higby, Nina Wright, 212, 213, 215, 296(nn24, 26, 27)
Higby, Reed Andrews, 212, 213, 215, 296(n24)
Higgins, Dr., 303
*High Altitude Cook Book*, xii, 2, 82(n40), 235, 252
*High Altitude Recipes* (Estes Park Trail), 296(n39)
Highlands Cabins. *See* Highlands Presbyterian Camp (Allenspark)
Highlands Hotel, The, 56, 91–94, 179(n2)
Highlands Presbyterian Camp (Allenspark), 294
Hilton, James, 185
Hilton, Mr. and Mrs. Warren, 74
Hines, Deborah, 316
Hines, Donald, 316

Hines, Duncan, 181(n62)
Hines, Frederick H. and Hilda O. Nelson, 314–316
Hines, Walter Frederick and Rachel Marie Donabauer 316
Hines-Park Foods, 181(n62)
Hix, Beulah, 63
Hix, Charles Franklin Jr., 63, 209
Hix, Charles Franklin Sr., 62–63, 186
Hix, Elizabeth Esther Clauser (Mrs. Franklin S.), 62, 63, 64–65
Hix, Elsie Claire Johnson (Mrs. Charles Franklin Sr.), 63, 65, 66
Hix, Franklin S., 62
Hix, George Franklin Johnson, 63
Hobby Horse Dude Ranch, 289
Hoch, Herman, 373
Hodder, Dr., 303
Hodson, George C., 182(n82)
Hoerner, Fred and Marian, 261–262
Hoerner, Vick, 262
Holland Inn (Holland Tavern), 247–248, 249, 297(n51)
Holy Hill (Preacher's Hill), 331–332
Holzwarth, Johann Gottlob and Sophia/Sophie Lebfromm "Mama," 152–156
Holzwarth family, 152, 181(n75)
Holzwarth's Trout Lodge, 89, 152–156, 181(n74)
Homestead Ranch. *See* Knapp, Ira Owen
*Homesteading Big Owl* (Garetson), 374(n57)
Hondius, Eleanor Estes James, 14, 19, 38–43, 81(n19), 233, 239, 295(n7)
Hondius, Peter Jr., 139
Hondius, Pieter Sr., 39, 146, 303
Hondius family, 37. *See also* Elkhorn Lodge
Hornbaker, Franklin L., 160, 161
Horseshoe Inn, 88, 121–123
Horseshoe Park, 14
"House on the Hill." *See* Crags Lodge
housekeeping and homemaking talents and tasks, 2, 24, 26, 28, 31, 49, 154, 340
housekeeping (self-catering) cabins 90, 154, 162
Hubbell, Anna Ferguson and Richard, 179(n13)

hucksters in Moraine Park, 7, 310
Hupp, Josephine, 183
Hupp Hotel, 88, 183, 212, 295(n7)
Husted, Shepherd Newcombe and Clara, 102–103
Hutchinson, Robert B. and Helen Cornish, 157–159, 182(n81)
Hyde, Alexander A. and Ida Elizabeth Todd, 328–329, 365, 372(n33)
Hyde Chapel (YMCA of the Rockies), 335
hydroelectric plant. *See* Fall River Hydroelectric Plant

# I

iceboxes and refrigerators, 8, 9, 97, 161
Irvin, Robert and Nan, 159

# J

Jackson, Burton W., 337
Jacob's Ladder, 199–201, 295(n9)
James, Charles, 37, 81(n18)
James, Edna B. Cobb Arnold Gray, 82(n22), 297,(nn55, 56), 257
James, Eleanor Estes. *See* Hondius, Eleanor Estes James
James, Homer E., 37, 39, 41, 81(n18)
James, Howard Perry, 37, 39, 43, 81(n18), 82(n22)
James, Jennie L., 41
James, William Edwin and Ella McCabe, 20, 37–39
Japanese Tea Room (The Lewiston Hotel), 136
Jelsema, Theodore Charles "Ted," 244–245. *See also* Dark Horse Tavern
Joe Mills Mountain, 129
John Cabin. *See* Steiner's Acres
Josephine Hotel, 183, 222, 264
Joslyn Art Museum (Omaha, NE), 298(n75)

# K

Keever, Lawrence L., 373(n47)
Keever, Myrtle, 345
Kelly & Sholty Grocery and Meat Market, 252
Kiley, Enda Mills, 99, 100, 180(n27), 374(n58)
Kiley, Robert, 180(n27)
kitchen equipment and utensils, early, 3
kitchen gardens, 5, 28, 93, 114, 115, 122
Knapp, Delia Dunkelberg, 280
Knapp, Ira Owen, 280–283
Knapp, Mae, 281
Knapp, Mason and Florence, 280
Knapp, Orrin Smith and Elizabeth Catherine Althouse, 280
Knapp's Homestead Ranch, 282
Knappville, 280. *See also* Glen Haven

# L

LaCoste, Guy, 328, 331
Ladies Auxiliary of the American Legion. *See* American Legion Auxiliary
Lamb, Carlyle, 96, 158, 182(n79)
Lamb, Elkanah J., 57, 96, 157, 158, 182(n79), 188
Lamb, Jemima Jane Spencer, 96, 157, 182(n79)
Lamb, Welta Jane "Hattie," 157, 182(n79)
Lamb's Notch, 158
Landon, Alfred Mossman "Al," 163, 164
Leadville, Colorado, 190, 192; boom times and silver mines, 190
Leonard, Harsey King and Ada C. Starkweather, 196
Lester, Charles E., 103, 373(n53)
Lester, Edna May Brush, 103, 104
Lester Hotel and Cottages, 103, 104
Levings, Agnes, 324, 348, 373(n51)
Levings, Charles, 324, 346, 348, 373(n49)
Levings, Louis, death of, 373(n49)
Lewis, Aneta Fannie Jackson, 135, 136, 137, 138–140
Lewis, Augustus Denby "Gus," 135, 137, 179(n8), 186
Lewis, Dorothy, 135
Lewis, Leora, 135
Lewis, Maurine, 135
Lewis, Myra Wolaver, 107, 108
Lewis, William, 107, 108
Lewiston Café, 137
Lewiston Chalets, 137, 179(n8)
Lewiston Hotel, 86–87, 88, 100, 135–137, 146, 179(n4)
Lindley, Elmer D., 225
Lindley, Mary R. Piel, 225–227
Lindley, Robert Henry, 186, 225
Lindley & Son, Estes Park Plumbers. *See* E. D. Lindley & Son, Estes Park Plumbers
Lindsey, Katherine W. *See* Perkins, Katherine W. "Addie"/ "Kittie"
Livingston, Julian M., 104
Longs Peak House, 96, 158
Longs Peak Inn, 95–100, 117, 158, 172, 173, 174, 179(n16), 180(n25), 346, 348, 359, 365
*Lost Horizon* (Hilton), 185
*Lost Trappers* (Coyner), 23
Loveland–Estes Park Auto Company, 202
Loveland Heights, community of, 343–345
Loveland Heights Cottages. *See* Loveland Heights Court
Loveland Heights Court, 344, 345
Lulu W. Dorsey Museum (YMCA of the Rockies), 335
Lundberg, Minnie, 10
Lynn, Ruth Merriam Scott. *See* Scott, Ruth Merriam

# M

Macdonald, Betty Marguerite Abildgaard, 194, 295(n3)
Macdonald, Jessica Chapin, 190, 191–193
Macdonald, Julius Edward, 186, 190, 191–192
Macdonald, Louise, 192
Macdonald, Maria, 192
Macdonald, Ralph Russell, 186, 192, 295(n3)
Macdonald Bookshop, 192
Macdonald/Cobb Cabin, 4
Macdonald family, xv, 185, 212, 255, 295(n7)
Macdonald's General Store, 190, 191–192
Mace, Charles Eric, 142

Mace, Gordon McLeod and Mary Ethel Prickett, 142, 143, 181(n59)
Mace, Stuart Garfield, 142, 181(n59)
Mace, William and Mina Aitken, 141, 181(n59), 181(n60)
MacGregor, Alexander Quiner, 27–28
MacGregor, Donald, 27–28, 30
MacGregor, George H., 27–28
MacGregor, Halbert P., 27–28
MacGregor, Maria Clara Heeney, 27–28, 30–32
MacGregor, Minnie Maude Koontz, 28–29, 30–32
MacGregor, Muriel Lurilla, 30
MacGregor family, xiv, 19, 20, 27, 37, 212
Machin, Marge Pierce, 169–171
Machin, Ralph E., 169
Machin's Cabins in the Pines, 169–170
Manford Hotel, 88, 183
March, Daniel J., 144–146, 181(n65)
March, Minnie E. Brown, 144–147, 181(nn65, 67)
March of Dimes, 265
McConnell, Bert J., 252, 297(n53)
McConnell, Helen, 252
McConnell's Pharmacy, 297(n53)
McCreery, Anna Belle, 35
McCreery, Elbert L., 33–34
McCreery, Hannah Caroline McLean, 19, 33–35
McCreery, Linda, 36
McCreery, Martha Marshall, 33
McCreery, Ruth Elberta, 33, 81(n17)
McCreery, William H., 20, 37, 38, 81(n16)
McCreery, William M., 33, 35
McCreery family, 20, 33, 35
McGraw, Frank, 164–166
McGraw, Irene McGlathery, 163
McGraw, John J., 163–164
McGraw, Ruth Hodson, 164–168
McGraw Guest Ranch, 15, 163, 164–166
McKelvey, Florence Mason, 146
McKelvey, John Russell "Russ," 146
McLaughlin, Day Heusner, 322–323, 325
McPherson, Imogene Green "Mother," 303

Meeker Park Lodge, 89, 160–162, 374(n54)
Melton, Jack, 335
Melton, Lulubeth "Lulie" Dorsey, 335–336
Melvin, George K., 303
Mengedoht, Augusta "Gussie," 292
Mengedoht, Frederick and Augusta Wilhelmine, 292–294
Mike's Tavern. See Wheel Bar
Miller, Hugo and Mary, 163–164
Miller, Jerry, xiv, 338, 372(n42), 372(n43)
Miller, Millie, 338
Mills, Eleanor Ann. See Yeager, Eleanor Ann Mills
Mills, Enoch Josiah "Joe," 124–129
Mills, Enos Abijah, 12, 95–101, 103, 117, 119, 124, 158, 172, 173, 179(n17)
Mills, Esther Burnell, 12, 99, 124, 172
Mills, Ethel Steere, v, 124–134
Mills, Mark Muir "Bud," 128
Mission 66, (National Park Service), 115
Missouri Pacific Railroad, 48
"Modern Eve" hoax, 201
Mohr, Mr. and Mrs. C. H., 248
Moraine (Willow) Park, settlement of, 300–301, 313, 314; cottagers of, 301–303, 304, 305, 315, 316, 317
Moraine Lodge, 89, 90, 215, 303
Moraine Park Post Office, 28, 52, 181(n68)
Morgan, Edna. See Gooch, Edna Morgan
Morrill, Abraham, 321
Morrill, Charles Henry and Harriet Currier, 321
Morrill, Edgar Miner and Catherine Barr Clapp, 321
Morrill, Edgar Miner Jr., 320
Morrill, Edward Lamprey, 320
Morrill, Justin Smith, 321, 372(n21)
Morrill Act (1862), 321
Morris, Michael, 208, 209, 210
Moseley, Fred T. and Gussie, 373(n53)
Mountain Home (Lamb homestead), 158
Mountain Home Plumbing and Heating Company, 177
"Mountainside" (home of John Timothy Stone), 331, 332, 333

Mulvaney, Daniel and Maria McCarthy, 209
Muriel L. MacGregor Charitable Trust, 30
Myers, John Russell, 297(n56)

# N

Nagl, Leola Byrnes "Lee," 264–265
Nagl, Linus, 297(n59)
Nagl, Margaret Ann Brannan, 264
Nagl, Orlando Michael, 264–265
Nagl, Steve and Gay, 265, 298(n61)
National Outing Company, 212
National Park Service, 56, 129, 154, 214, 247, 373(n49), 374(n58); expansion of RMNP, 356, 373(n49); historic sites, 154; personnel of, 182; photos courtesy of, v, 11, 12, 27, 28, 30, 37, 45, 47, 49, 52, 76, 102, 121, 152, 156, 157, 217, 302; Big Thompson entrance to RMNP, 247; removal of commercial inholdings by, 52, 109, 115, 146, 219
National Park Service headquarters in Estes Park, 234
National Park Village, 219. See also Deer Ridge Chalet
National Register of Historic Places, 143, 166, 332
Nature Conservancy, The, 154
Never Summer Ranch, 153, 154. See also Holzwarth Trout Lodge
Nowels, Harry Gaylord "Gay," 160–162. See also Meeker Park Lodge
Nowels, Hattie Leota Alter, 161

# O

Old Plantation Restaurant, 237–240, 296(n43), 297(n49), 383–385
Old University of Chicago, 196, 295(n5)
Olson family, 321
open-hearth cooking, 3, 22
Orlando's Steakhouse, 265
Osborn, Bessie Alberta Charter, 203, 204–5
Osborn, Daniel Obediah, 202
Osborn, Lawrence Estes, 202, 203
Osborn, Otto, 202

Osborn, Sarah C. Haley, 202
Osborn, Sarah "Sadie" Murchland, 202
Osborn, William, 202
Osborn's Garage, 202–203, 205
Overlook, The (YMCA), 328–329
Owaissa Lodge, 320

# P

pantry staples, 5–6
Parent Teacher's Association (Estes Park), 214
Pauley, Peter J., 164
Peg's Drive-in, 269
Penney, James Cash (J. C. Penney), 209
PEO, Chapter AV of, 2, 371(n20); early members of, 41, 51, 58, 63, 68, 71, 76, 166, 192, 204, 206, 223, 225
Perkins, Katherine W. "Addie" / "Kitty" Lindsey, 362–364
Perkins, Oscar S., 362–363
Perkins Trading Post, 347, 362–363. *See also* WhatNot Inn
Phillips, Phoebe Katherine, 201
photographs, hand-coloring of, 229, 230
photography processes. *See* Autochrome Lumière
Pierce, Chester E. and Bertha G., 170
Piltz, Carl, 199
Pinecone Inn. *See* Old Plantation Restaurant
Popular Shop, The. *See* Macdonald's General Store
Porter, Carl, 239, 297(n45)
Porter, Curran Rutilious and Sarah Elizabeth "Lizzie" Tadlock, 237
poultry, dressing of, 5
Preacher's Hill. *See* Holy Hill
Presbyterian Assembly Association, 280–281
Presbyterian Community Church of the Rockies, 187–189, 239; Missionary Society of, 71, 76, 225; Members of, 58, 63, 71, 76, 213; photos courtesy of, 188
preservation of food in early Estes Park, 5, 8–9
Preston, Ada Mary Ream, 205

Preston, Glenard Harry, 205
Preston, Harry Cornelius, 186, 205
Preston, Leora A. Lewis, 206
Preston, Mary M. Redman Brinkley, 205–206
Preston's Garage, 205
Prewett, John T., 22
Price, Eva Jane Reece (Mrs. Howard), 252, 367, 374(n61)
Price, Margaret . *See* Reedy, Margaret Price
processed foods, availability of, 6, 7
Prohibition, 17(n4), 245
Prospect Inn, 183
Public Works Administration (WPA), 229

# Q

Quirk, Neil, 248

# R

Rabin, Dayton, 363
ranges, kitchen: complexity of, 3; wood-burning and coal fire, 4, 97, 114, 127, 154, 177, 285, 307
Red Stallion Inn, 288, 289, 290
Redmond, Peter and Connie, 344, 345
Reece, Eva Jane. *See* Price, Eva Jane Reece
Reece family, 367
Reed, Belle Brandt, 75
Reed, Charles Lowry, 6, 75, 93–94, 112–115
Reed, Anna Louise. *See* Hayden, Anna Louise Reed
Reed, Sallie (Sally) E. Ferguson, 75, 93–94, 112–115, 179(n9)
Reedy, Clyde Richard, 369
Reedy, Cynthia Price, 368
Reedy, Margaret Price, 367, 368, 369–370, 374(n61)
Reinhold, John and Rose, 294
Richards, John and Kathy, 294
Riker, George B., 337
Riverside Amusement Park, 185, 244–245
Riverside Hotel, 265
Robbins, Edith Lillian. *See* Day, Edith Lillian Robbins

Robbins, Ida Lewis, 319, 322, 323
Robbins, Lewis "Lute" and Harriet, 322
Robbins family, 321, 322–323
Robinson, Fred E. and Harriet Lucinda "Hattie," 160–161
Rockdale Hotel, 89, 179(n8)
Rockmount Cottages, 58, 82(n43)
Rockside, 10, 84
Rocky Mountain Boys Club, 214
Rocky Mountain Jim Nugent, 24
Rocky Mountain National Park, 1, 15, 129, 164, 166, 179(n17), 182, 197, 201, 203, 214, 216, 230, 247, 256, 371(n5); dedication of (1915), 88, 146, 372(n43); Enos Mills and, 373(n49); entrances to, 247, 266; inholders within, 169–170, 371(n17). *See also* National Park Service
Rocky Mountain National Park Radio Club, 70
Rocky Mountain Nature Association, 180(n35)
Rocky Mountain Parks Transportation Company, 203
Roehl, Diane, 348, 349, 350
Roehl, Eleanor "Eli," 349, 351
Roehl, Frank, 352
Roehl, John, 347, 349, 350, 373(n53), 374(n54)
Roehl, Margaret "Peg" Ames (Mrs. Frank), 348, 351, 352
Rogers, Henry C., 103
Rome of the Rockies, The. *See* Dunraven Inn
Rooftop Rodeo, 166, 272
Roth, Rex and Shirlee Ann Kendle, 274–276, 298(n67)
Roth Family Restaurant, 186, 274–275. *See also* Wild Basin Lodge
Round-Up Grocery and Delicatessen, 269
Rustic Hotel and Cottages, 102–103, 326
Rustic Hotel Company, 103
Rutledge, Alberta Virginia Olsen, 344, 345, 373(n47)
Rutledge, Ernest and Mildred, 344
Rutledge, Jerry, 345
Rutledge, Lyle Eugene, 344, 345, 373(n47)

# S

Salvation Army, The, 100, 119, 174
Sanborn, Burton D. and Carrie Bassett, 319, 320, 321, 371(n20)
Sand Creek Massacre (1864), 202
Sanders, Frederick Morris, 346, 353–356, 373(n49), 374(n55)
Sanders, Jessie Moore, 346, 353–358, 373(n49), 374(n55)
Sanders, John, 354
Schneidkraut, Julius and Marcia, 248–249. *See also* Dunraven Inn
Schubert, Adele "Toots," 217–218
Schubert, Bertha "Bert," 217, 218
Schubert, Edward and Eleanor, 218, 219
Schubert, Emma " Bomma," 216–217. *See also* Deer Ridge Chalet
Schubert family, 218, 219
Schulz, Jane Reedy, 368
Schureman, Rev. William H., 280
"Scotch" (Enos Mills's dog), 95, 100
Scotch-Irish and English roots of early Estes Park settlers, 6
Scott, Angelo C., 13
Scott, Callie (Mrs. Ira D.), 118
Scott, Charles Frederick, 13, 180(n29), 305, 307, 308
Scott, Charles F. Jr, 307
Scott, Dorothy. *See* Gibbs, Dorothy Scott
Scott, Dorothy Carnine, 7, 307, 308, 309, 371(n10)
Scott, Ewing Carruth, 307, 308, 309, 310–311, 371(nn10, 12, 13)
Scott, Ira D., 117, 118, 180(n40)
Scott, May Brevard Ewing, 3, 305–307, 308, 311
Scott, Ruth Merriam, 307, 308
*Scottage: A Medley, The*, 7, 13, 101
Scottage, The, 180(n29), 305–307, 371(n8)
Seaton, Mildred Frances Ferguson (Mrs. Walter), 75, 93
Sellers, Tom and Sheila, 283
servants, household, 10, 75, 326, 354, 355, 365
Servey, Albert Benjamin, 247–248
Servey, Kathryn, 247–248

Service, Minnie E. Brown March. *See* March, Minnie E. Brown
Service, Rhoda, 181(n68)
Service, Samuel M. "Sam," 146, 184, 203, 256
*Seven Keys to Baldpate, The*, 143
Seybold, Dianne Doris Herzog, 257, 258, 259, 260
Seybold, James S. "Jim" 256, 257
Seybold, Jeanne M. Gray, 255, 258
Seybold, John Ross Jr. "Jack," 255–256
Seybold, John Ross Sr. "Ross" and Loua N. Steinmetz, 255
Seybold, Jeanne M. Gray, 255, 258
Seybold family, 297(n55)
Seybold's Gifts, 257
Sherman, John Dickinson, 158
Sherman, Mary Belle King, 158
Sherwood Hotel, 183
Shoffner, Elizabeth Ames, 350
Sholty, Chloe S. Berry Wurfel, 252, 253–254
Sholty, Clarence Earl "C.E.," 252, 368
Sholty family, 252
Sholty Food Market, 252
Shreve, Annie Adele, 359, 360
Smith, Lois, 143
Smithsonian Institution, 229
Snow, Francis Huntington, 305, 371(n7)
Songer, Freda, 354, 355, 357, 374(n55)
Songer family, 374(n55)
Sparks, Mr. and Mrs. J. B., 282
Sprague, Abner Erwin, 12, 20, 45–47, 48–52, 82(n29), 87, 105–106, 108, 181(n68), 212, 302, 305, 313
Sprague, Areanna. *See* Chapman, Areanna "Arah" Sprague
Sprague, Mary Alberta "Bert" Morrison, 11, 19, 45, 47, 48, 49–54, 82(n40), 105–106, 302
Sprague, Mary Margaret Wolaver "Grandma," 20, 45–47, 48, 108
Sprague, Thomas, 45–46, 48, 50, 82(n36), 108
Sprague's Hotel and Ranch, 48, 51, 82(n36), 105.
Sprague's House (1878), 45–49, 50, 82(n36)

Sprague's Lodge (1914), 46, 50–52, 82(n31), 89, 109
Sprague's Lodge pottery, 50
stagecoach, travel to Estes Park by, 184, 203
Stanley, Flora Jane Record Tileston, 10, 14, 84–85, 86
Stanley, Frances Edgar, 84
Stanley, Freelan Oscar "F. O.," 9, 10, 56, 78, 79, 84–85, 86, 102, 107, 179(nn3, 6)
Stanley Hotel, The, 14, 56, 68, 79, 84, 86–88, 89, 137, 179(n3), 180(n35)
Stanley Hydroelectric Plant. *See* Fall River Hydroelectric Plant
Stanley Steamers and Mountain Wagons, 63
Stead, James D., 105–107, 108
Stead, Mary Eudora Wolaver, 105, 107, 108, 111
Stead's Ranch and Hotel, 45, 52, 88, 105–110, 111, 180(n37)
Steige, Paula Laing, 192
Steiner, David, 365
Steiner, Deborah L., 365, 366
Steiner, Edward Alfred and Sara Levy, 365
Steiner's Acres, 347, 365
Stone, John Timothy, 214, 331–332, 334, 472(n37)
Stopher, Alberta, 50
Stopher, Dorothy Eleanor Hansen, 108, 109, 180(n37)
Stopher, Edgar M. "Ed," 50, 51, 52, 108–109, 111, 180(n35)
Stopher, Elizabeth W. "Libby," 111, 180(n37)
Stopher, John Samuel, 50
Stopher, Mabel Morrison, 50, 51, 55, 82(n38)
Strange Owl, Ann, 363
Strange Owl, Nico, 363
Summer Residents Association, 301, 315, 317, 349, 355–356, 363, 373(n53)
Sun Shine Inn, 33
Sundeck Restaurant, 261–262. *See also* Hoerner, Fred and Marian
Sweet, Channing Fullerton, 326
Sweet, Joyeuse Lennig Fullerton, 326–327

Sweet, Nancy, 327
Sweet, William Ellery, 326
Swiss Village Resort, 100, 172–175

# T

Tabor, Augusta, 192
Tabor, Elizabeth McCourt "Baby" Doe, 295(n2)
Tabor, Horace A. W., 190, 192, 295(n2)
Tabor Opera House (Leadville), 190, 295(n2)
Tallant, Helen, 237
Tallant, Leland, 181(n68)
Tallant, Louise, 237
Tallant, Reginald H., 237
Tanton, David and Carol, 85, 185, 277
Taylor, Edward, 320
Taylor, Florence Dye Coles, 320
Taylor, Laura, 328–329
Taylor, Marcia, 16, 329
Taylor, Frances "Fannie" Chamberlin Brown, 320
Taylor, William George Langworthy, 319, 320
Thanksgiving Day dinner, Isabella Bird's, 26, 379–382
Thompson, Kathleen Woodward, 340, 342
Thompson, Mr. and Mrs., 74
Timberline (Timber Line) Hotel/Cabin, 98, 99
tipping policies at resorts and restaurants, 98, 126, 127–128
Tresnor, Leon Worthington, 33
*Tried and True Recipe Book*, xi, xii, 2, 63, 76, 82(n40), 206, 356

# U

United Brethren Church of Christ, 56, 157, 202
U.S. Olympic Team, 320
U.S. Olympic Wrestling Committee, 320

# V

Van Horn, George N. and Mariah Belle C., 288–289
Van Horn, Mary Jo Janosec, 288
Van Horn, Paul H., 288–290
Van Horn, William "Bill", 289, 290
Van Valkenburgh, Horace B. "Van," 119
Vance, Ben, 264
Vick, Leanne Mace, 143

# W

waitstaff, 98, 159, 219, 240, 297(n48)
Walters, Herman and Henrietta Erdbruegger, 285, 287
Warnock, David and Jenny, 367
Warren, Rev. Leroy, 365
Washburn, Patricia Yeager, 124, 125, 126, 127, 129
Way, Lewis Claude, 201
Webermeier, John and Pat Schubert, 219
Wells, Doris Evans, 282–283
Wells, Wilbur Lavern, 282–283, 284
Wetig, Charles and Ann, 294
WhatNot Inn. *See* Perkins Trading Post
WhatNot Shop, 362
Wheel Bar, 264–265
Wheeler Inn, 262
White, Mary, 302–304
White, Sallie Lindsey, 302, 304
White, William Allen, 303–304, 371(nn3, 5, 7)
White, William Lindsey "Bill," 304
Wiest, Dr. Roy Francis, 70–71, 186, 256
Wiest, Sara Armstrong, 19, 70–73
Wiest, Dr. Sard, 70
Wigwam Cottages, 196
Wild Basin Lodge, 89
Wilson, Dick, 344
Wind River Lodge (YMCA), 328, 335
Wind River Ranch, 89, 157, 158–159
Witwer, Marie W. "Maria," 362–363
Woodward, Merrill H., 340
Woodward, Paul, 340
Women's Christian Temperance Union (WCTU), 17(n4), 129
Woman's Missionary Society, 71, 76, 205–206, 213, 225
Work, Donna, 177
Work, Jim, 176–177
Work, Virginia R. Hays "Pep," 176–177
Workman, Dorothy J., 314
Workman, Emma Wells Howard, 313
Workman, Florence Jane Mount, 314
Workman, Florence Wilma, 414
Workman, Julia Lulu Ripley Oliphant, 314
Workman, Katherine Jane Elbert, 313
Workman, Dr. William J., 212, 303, 313–314
Workshire Lodge, 176–177
Wright, Frank Lloyd, 121–122, 180(nn25, 44)
Wurfel, Grace Mildred, 252
Wyndam-Quin, Windham Thomas, Fourth Earl of Dunraven, 83, 103, 113, 141, 142. *See also* Estes Park Hotel

# Y

Ye Lyttel Shop, 195–196
Yeager, Dorr, 365
Yeager, Eleanor Ann Mills, v, 124, 125, 126
Yelm, Mrs., 317
Yore, Alberta Evelyn McAuley Plonke, 149, 150, 151
Yore, Clement, 148–149, 151, 181(n70)
Yowell, Helen, 351, 373–374(n53)

# Z

Zumwinkle, Jack, 374(nn54, 57)

# Recipe Index

## A

*Aebleskiver* (Calico Kate's Applesauce Pancakes), 286

**Almond Caramel Ice Cream** (Elsie Hix), 66

**Angel Cookies** (Seybold), 260

**Appetizers**
  Canapé, Byxbe (Byxbe), 231
  Crab Dip, Hot (Bissell), 317
  Cream Cheese Ball (Dianne Seybold), 258
  Pastete (Ethel Mills), 133

**Apple Custard** (Lindley), 227

**Apple Fritters, Dutch** (Hondius), 43

**Apple Pudding** (Berryhill), 340

**Apple Roll** (Ethel Mills), 132

**Applesauce Pancakes**. *See Aebleskiver*

**Apricot and Cheese Molded Salad** (Gooch), 211

**Asparagus with Cheese Sauce** (Godfrey), 224

**Aunt Zervia's Chow Chow** (Perkins), 364

**Avocado Ring with Lobster or Crabmeat Salad** (Hutchinson), 159

## B

**Baked Chicken** (Roth), 276

**Baking Powder Biscuits** (Osborn), 204

**Barbecue.** *See* **Columbine Chicken in Sherry Barbecue**

**Barbecue Beef** (Work), 178

*Baroks, Kraut*. *See* **Cabbage Pockets**

**Batter Bread / Coffee Can Bread** (Seybold), 258

**Bean Soup, Company** (Scott), 312

**Beaver Tail** (Estes), 23

**Beef**
  Beef, Barbecue (Work), 178
  Beef Bourguignon (Dianne Seybold), 259

Beef Brisket, Roast, or Veal (MacGregor), 32
Beef Loaf (Wiest), 73
Flank Steak, McGraw (McGraw), 167
Meat Loaf, Chappie's (Harriet Burgess), 242
Meatloaf with Mustard Sauce (Ethel Mills), 131

**Beets, Harvard** (Preston), 207

**Berry Pie** (Scott), 312

**Beverages: Alcoholic**
Cider Cocktail, Harmony Ranch Special (Matilda Hayes), 268
Dark Horse Special, 246
Mint Julep (Thelma Chapman), 241
Special Glog, Harmony's (Scott Hayes), 268
Wheel Cocktail (Nagl), 265

**Beverages: Nonalcoholic**
Iced Chocolate (Elsie Hix), 65
Punch—Six Quarts (Bond), 68
Punch (Lester), 104
Raspberry Shrub (Macdonald), 193

**Biscuits**
Baking Powder Biscuits (Osborn), 204
Sweet Biscuits (Traditional), 380
See also **Rolls**

**Black Bean Soup** (Burgess), 384

**Blueberry Tea Cake With Crumb Topping** (Ethel Mills), 133

**Breads**
Batter Bread/Coffee Can Bread (Seybold), 258
Brown Bread (Elizabeth Hix), 64
Dilly Bread, Grandpa Barclay's (Barclay), 330
Italian Bread, Red Stallion (Van Horn), 291
Nut Bread (Gooch), 211
Raisin Graham Bread (Clauser), 67
Saffron Bread (Reedy), 370
White Bread (Sprague), 53
White Bread, Mother's Wonderful (Henrietta Walters), 287
Whole Wheat Bread (Sanders), 358
See also **Biscuits**; **Rolls**

**Bread and Butter Pickles, Grandmother Day's Favorite** (Day), 325

**Bread Boat** (Bissell), 318

**Bread Jug or Soft Yeast** (Sprague), 53

**Bread Pudding** (Scott), 311

**Brisket, Beef Roast or Veal** (MacGregor), 32

**Brown Bread** (Elizabeth Hix), 64

**Brown Sugar Candy** (Bond), 69

**Brownies, Fudge** (Machin), 171

**Butterscotch Pie** (Wiest), 71

# C

**Cabbage**
Cabbage. See **Sauerkraut**
Cabbage Pockets (*Kraut Baroks*) (Thompson), 342

**Cake**
Cheese cake. See **Cheese Cake**
Chocolate Cake (Bay), 36
Chocolate Cake (Chocolate Fudge Frosting) (Mary Lois Griffith), 61
Chocolate Cake (*Schokoladenkuchen*) (Holzwarth), 156
Coffee Cake. See **Coffee Cake**
Devil's Food Cake, High Altitude (Anspauch), 231
Eggless, Butterless, Milkless Cake (Wiest), 72
Fruitcake, Boiled (Carnine), 310
Fudge Cake, Wellesley (Lewis), 139
Ginger Cake (Perkins), 363
Gingerbread Cake (Traditional Scottish), 381
Ice Water Cake and Boiled Frosting (Dever), 162
Longs Peak Cake, Freda's (Songer), 357
Pineapple Upside Down Cake (Carr), 236
Potato Cake (Wiest), 72
Ribbon Cake (Perkins), 364
Spice Cake (*Gewurzkuchen*) and Icing (Holzwarth), 155
Sponge Cake for Jelly Roll (Hall), 80
**Cake, Cheese**. See **Cheese Cake**
**Cake, Coffee**. See **Coffee Cake**

**Canapé, Byxbe** (Byxbe), 231

**Candy and Fudge**
Brown Sugar Candy (Bond), 69
Fudge (Louise Griffith), 59
Mexican Orange Candy (Carr), 235
Molasses Taffy (Hondius), 42
Peanut Brittle (Wiest), 73
Walnut Brittle (Byxbe), 231

**Caramel Flavoring** (Elsie Hix), 66

**Casseroles**
    Community Church of the Rockies Scalloped Chicken, 189
    Crunchy Chicken Casserole (Ames/Shoffner), 350
    Ham en Casserole (Lindley), 226
    Preacher's Casserole (Clark), 334
    Smothered Sausage (Lewis), 140
    Wild Rice Casserole (Brownfield), 273

**Cauliflower, French** (Lewis), 138

**Cheese Cake**, **German** (*Kaese Kuchen*) (Hart), 279

**Cheese Cream** (Lewis), 139

**Cheese Soufflé** (Lewis), 140

**Cheese Soup, Crowley's Famous** (Crowley), 270

**Cheese, Scalloped** (Hall), 80

**Cherry Dessert, Lickin' Good** (Berryhill), 341

**Chicken**
    Chicken, Rex's Baked (Roth), 276
    Chicken, Scalloped (Community Church of the Rockies), 189
    Chicken Curry (Macdonald), 193
    Chicken in Sherry Barbecue, Columbine (Bliss), 120
    (Chicken) Pot Pie, York County (Ethel Mills), 130
    Chicken Soup. *See* **Rochester Soup**
    Crunchy Chicken Casserole (Ames/Shoffner), 350

**Chili, Hines** (Hines), 316

**Chocolate, Iced** (Elsie Hix), 65

**Chocolate Cake** (Bay), 36

**Chocolate Cake (Chocolate Fudge Frosting)** (Mary Lois Griffith), 61

**Chocolate Cake** (*Schokoladenkuchen*) (Holzwarth), 156

**Chocolate Cookies, High Altitude** (Sanders), 357

**Chop-Suey** (Hondius), 42

**Chow Chow, Aunt Zervia's** (Perkins), 364

**Christmas Star Salad** (Clauser), 66

**Cider Cocktail, Harmony Ranch Special** (Matilda Hayes), 268

**Cinnamon Rolls**
    McGraw Guest Ranch Cinnamon Rolls (McGraw), 168
    Sweet Bread Dough Cinnamon Rolls (Schubert), 220

**Clem Yore's Own Pudding** (Yore), 151

**Coffee Cake**
    Blueberry Tea Cake with Crumb Topping (Ethel Mills), 133
    Coffee Cake (Anna Louise Reed Hayden), 77
    Coffee Cake, German (Lewis), 139

**Coffee Can Bread**. *See* Batter Bread / Coffee Can Bread

**Company Bean Soup** (Scott), 312

**Cookies and Bars**
    Angel Cookies (Seybold), 260
    Chocolate Cookies, High Altitude (Sanders), 357
    Cowboy Cookies, McGraw Guest Ranch (McGraw), 167
    Date Cookies (Clauser), 67
    English Toffee Squares (McGraw Ranch), 166
    Ginger Cream Cookies (Herzog), 259
    Lemon Freeze (Schubert), 219
    Molasses Cookies (Higby), 215
    Molasses Drop Cookies (Mabel Stopher), 55
    Oatmeal Cookies (Ames), 350
    Pinwheel Icebox Cookies (Carr), 236
    Raisin Drop Cookies (Griffith), 60
    Rich Cookies (Preston), 207
    Sugar Cookies, Grandma Carlson's (Machin), 171

**Corn, Scalloped** (Work), 177

**Corn Bread**
    Corn Bread (Griffith), 61
    Corn Bread, Golden (Lindley), 226
    *See also* **Cornbread, Jalapeño**

**Cornbread, Jalapeño** (Burgess), 385

**Corn Relish** (Carnine), 310

**Cowboy Cookies, McGraw Guest Ranch**, 167

**Crab Dip** (Bissell), 317

**Crabmeat Salad**. *See* **Avocado Ring with Lobster or Crabmeat Salad**

**Cream Cheese Ball** (Dianne Seybold), 258

**Crullers, Mother's** (Bond), 69

**Crust**. *See* **Pie Crust**

**Cucumber, Watercress, and Cream Cheese Sandwich** (Burgess), 385

**Curry, (Chicken, Veal or Pork)** (Jessica Macdonald), 193
**Custard, Apple** (Lindley), 227

## D

**Danish Rolls, Crowley's Restaurant** (Crowley), 271
**Dark Horse Special**, 246
**Date Cookies** (Clauser), 67
**Date Pudding** (Reed), 94
**Desserts**
    Apple Custard (Lindley), 227
    Apple Pudding (Berryhill), 340
    Apple Roll (Ethel Mills), 132
    Cherry Dessert, Lickin' Good (Berryhill), 341
    Date Pudding (Reed), 94
    Dutch Apple Fritters (Hondius), 43
    Fig Delight (Sugared Figs and Whipped Cream) (Hondius), 42
    Fluffy Duffy and Foamy Sauce (Steiner), 366
    Lemon Freeze (Schubert), 219
    See also **Cakes, Cookies and Bars, Pies, Puddings**
**Devil's Food Cake, High Altitude** (Anspauch), 231
**Dilly Bread, Grandpa Barclay's** (Barclay), 330
**Doughnuts**
    Ice Box Doughnuts (Stead), 111
    Sweet Milk Doughnuts (Griffith), 59
    See also **Crullers, Mother's**
**Dressing, Poultry**
    Goose or Duck, Dressing for (MacGregor), 31
**Dressing, Salad**
    McCreery Family Salad Dressing (McCreery), 35
    Poppyseed Dressing, Columbine (Bliss), 120
    Salad Dressing (Bond), 69
**Dumplings, Drop** (Elixabeth Hix), 64
**Dutch Apple Fritters** (Hondius), 43

## E

**Eggless, Butterless, Milkless Cake** (Wiest), 72
**Eggs, Scotch** (Bob Burgess), 243
**English Toffee Squares (McGraw Ranch)**, 166

## F

**Fig Delight (Sugared Figs and Whipped Cream)** (Hondius), 42
**Filling, Lemon Cream** (Reed), 115
**Fish**
    Halibut in Mustard Sauce, Boiled (Sanders), 357
    Salmon Mousse (Lewis), 140
    Trout, Forelle Blau/Blue Trout (Truite au Bleu) (Sundeck), 263
    Trout, Pan Fried (Bird), 26
    Trout, Pan Fried (Roehl), 352
    Trout, Poached. See **Trout, Forelle Blau**
    Trout, Smoked (Bissell), 318
**Flank Steak, McGraw**, 167
**Floating Islands (*Île Flottante*)** (Sweet), 327
**Fluffy Duffy with Foamy Sauce** (Steiner), 366
**Freda's Longs Peak Cake** (Songer), 357
**French Toast, Stead's Ranch Ice Cream** (Stopher), 111
**Frosting**
    Boiled Frosting (Dever), 162
    Chocolate Fudge Frosting (Mary Lois Griffith), 61
    Fluffy White Frosting (Anspauch), 232
    Lemon Cream Filling (Reed), 115
    See also **Icings**
**Fruit Salad** (March Service), 147
**Fruitcake, Boiled** (Carnine), 310
**Fudge.** See **Candy and Fudge**
**Fudge Brownies** (Machin), 171
**Fudge Cake, Wellesley** (Lewis), 139

## G

**Game.** See **Pheasant Dinner; Venison Roast**
**German Coffee Cake** (Lewis), 139
**German *Kaese Kuchen* (Cheese Cake)** (Hart), 279
*Gewurzkuchen.* See **Spice Cake**
**Ginger Bread**
    Ginger Bread, Hard (Chapman), 55
    Ginger Bread, Soft (Sholty), 253
    Ginger Bread, Soft (Sprague), 54

**Ginger Cake** (Perkins), 363
**Ginger Cream Cookies** (Herzog), 259
**Gingerbread Cake (Traditional Scottish)**, 381
**Glog, Harmony's Special** (Scott Hayes), 268
**Golden Corn Bread** (Lindley), 226
**Gooseberry Pie Filling** (Burgess), 241
**Goulash, Hungarian For Seven Persons** (Macdonald), 193
**Goulash**
    Hungarian (Gartner), 251
    Hungarian For Seven Persons (Macdonald), 193
**Grandma Carlson's Sugar Cookies** (Machin), 171
**Grandpa Barclay's Dilly Bread**, 330
**Grapefruit and Avocado Salad, Mama Grace's**, 351

# H

**Halibut, Boiled** (Sanders), 357
**Ham and Beet Salad** (Elizabeth Hix), 65
**Ham en Casserole** (Lindley), 226
**Hard Sauce** (Louise Griffth), 60
**Hard Sauce for Steamed Pudding** (Sholty), 253
**Harvard Beets** (Preston), 207
**Hot Cakes**. *See* **Pancakes**
**Hungarian Goulash**. *See* **Goulash, Hungarian**
**Hunters' Stew** (Reedy), 369

# I

**Ice Cream**
    Almond Caramel Ice Cream (Elsie Hix), 66
    Ice Cream (Vanilla) (Machin), 171
**Ice Cream French Toast, Stead's Ranch**, 111
**Ice Water Cake and Boiled Frosting** (Dever), 162
**Icings**. *See* **Frosting**
**(Île Flottante)**. See **Floating Island (*Île Flottante*)**
**Italian Bread, Red Stallion** (Van Horn), 291

# J

**Jams, Jellies, and Preserves**
    Orange Marmalade (Sprague), 54
    Preserved Strawberries (Cheney), 80
    Strawberry Jam (Anspauch), 232
**Journey Cakes (Johnny Cakes)** (Reedy), 369
    *See also* **Pancakes**

# K

**Kraut**. *See* **Cabbage**; **Sauerkraut**
*Kraut Barocks*. See **Cabbage Pockets (*Kraut Barocks*)**

# L

**(Lamb) Curry** (Macdonald), 193
**Lemon Apple Pie** (Sholty), 254
**Lemon Chiffon Pie, Annie's (Turner)** (Ethel Mills), 134
**Lemon Cream Filling** (Reed), 115
**Lemon Freeze** (Schubert), 219
**Lemon Pie** (Elizabeth Hix), 64
**Lemon Pudding** (Hall), 79
**Lemon Sauce (For Plumb Pudding)** (Thelma Chapman), 241
**Lemon Sponge Pudding, Aunt Blanche's** (Keever), 345
**Liver and Bacon/Onions** (Burgess), 243
**Longs Peak Cake, Freda's** (Songer), 357

# M

**Macaroni and Cheese** (MacGregor), 32
**McCreery Family Salad Dressing** (McCreery), 31
**Marge's Rolls** (Machin), 170
**Marmalade, Orange** (Sprague), 54
**Mayonnaise, Cooked Oil** (Carr), 235
**Meat Loaf (Meatloaf)**
    Beef Loaf (Wiest), 73
    Meat Loaf, Chappie's (Harriet Burgess), 242
    Meatloaf with Mustard Sauce (Ethel Mills), 131
**Mexican Orange Candy** (Carr), 235

**Minestrone Soup, Red Stallion** (Van Horn), 291
**Mint Julep** (Thelma Chapman), 241
**Mint Sauce** (Godfrey), 223
**Molasses Cookies** (Higby), 215
**Molasses Drop Cookies** (Mabel Stopher), 55
**Molasses Taffy** (Hondius), 42
**Mousse, Salmon** (Lewis), 140
**Muffins**
   Twin Mountain Muffins (Sprague), 53
   Whole Wheat Muffins (Osborn), 204

# N

**Never Fail Pie Crust** (Byxbe), 231
**Noodles, Byxbe** (Byxbe), 232
**Nut Bread** (Gooch), 211
**Nutmeg Sauce** (McCreery), 35

# O

**Oatmeal Cookies** (Ames), 350
**Orange Candy, Mexican** (Carr), 235
**Orange Marmalade** (Sprague), 54
**Oyster Soup** (Cornelia Hayden), 77

# P

**Pancakes**
   Apple Pancakes (*Aebleskiver*) (Calico Kate's), 286
   Delicate Fluffy Pancakes (Byxbe), 232
   *See also* **Journey Cakes**
**Parker House Rolls** (James), 44
**Pastete** (Ethel Mills), 133
**Peach Salad, Spiced** (Ethel Mills), 132
**Peanut Brittle** (Wiest), 73
**Pecan Pie, Edna James' Texas** (Dianne Seybold), 257
**Pheasant Dinner** (Brownfield), 273
**Pickles**
   12-Day Chunk (Louise Griffith), 59
   Bread and Butter, Grandmother Day's Favorite (Day), 325
   Chopped (Bond), 69

**Pies**
   Berry Pie (Scott), 312
   Butterscotch (Wiest), 71
   Lemon Apple Pie (Sholty), 254
   Lemon Chiffon Pie, Annie's (Turner) (Ethel Mills), 134
   Lemon Pie (Elizabeth Hix), 64
   Pecan Pie, Edna James' Texas (Dianne Seybold), 257
   Pumpkin Pie (Elizabeth Hix), 65
   Raisin Pie (Lester), 104
   Rhubarb Pie (Clatworthy), 198
**Pie Crust**
   Pie Crust, Boiling Water (Clatworthy), 198
   Pie Crust, Never Fail (Byxbe), 231
**Pie Filling**
   Gooseberry (Burgess), 241
**Pineapple Upside Down Cake** (Carr), 236
**Pinwheel Icebox Cookies** (Carr), 236
**Plantation Sauce Robert** (Burgess), 242
**Poppyseed Dressing, Columbine** (Bliss), 120
**(Pork) Curry** (Macdonald), 193
**Potato Cake** (Wiest), 72
**Potato Salad, Good Ol' Mrs. Work's** (Work), 178
**Potatoes**
   Devil's Gulch Potatoes (Melton), 336
   Scalloped Potatoes (Betty Macdonald), 194
   Sweet Potatoes Southern Style (Osborn), 204
**Poultry**. *See* **Chicken**
**Preacher's Casserole** (Clark), 334
**Preserves**
   Marmalade, Orange (Sprague), 54
   Preserved Strawberries (Cheney), 80
   Strawberry Jam (Anspauch), 232
**Puddings**
   Apple Pudding (Berryhill), 340
   Bread Pudding (Scott), 311
   Bread and Butter Pudding, Rich, 379
   Clem Yore's Own Pudding (Yore), 151
   Date Pudding (Reed), 94
   Lemon Pudding (Hall), 79
   Lemon Sponge Pudding, Aunt Blanche's (Keever), 345
   Roly-Poly Pudding, 382

Steamed Pudding and Hard Sauce (Sholty), 253
Steamed Suet Pudding for Christmas (McCreery), 35
Suet Pudding (Louise Griffith), 60
Yorkshire Pudding (Macdonald), 194

**Pumpkin Pie** (Elizabeth Hix), 65

**Punches**
Punch—Six Quart (Bond), 68
Punch (Lester), 104

# R

**Raisin Drop Cookies** (Griffith), 60
**Raisin Graham Bread** (Clauser), 67
**Raisin Pie** (Lester), 104
**Raspberry Shrub** (Macdonald), 193
**Red Stallion Italian Bread** (Van Horn), 291
**Red Stallion Minestrone Soup** (Van Horn), 291
**Relish, Corn** (Carnine), 310
**Rex's Baked Chicken** (Roth), 276
**Rhubarb Pie** (Clatworthy), 198
**Ribbon Cake** (Perkins), 364
**Rich Cookies** (Preston), 207
**Rochester Soup** (Lewis), 138

**Rolls**
Cinnamon Rolls, McGraw Ranch (McGraw), 168
Danish Rolls, Crowley's Restaurant (Crowley), 271
Marge's Rolls (Machin), 170
Parker House (James), 44
Sweet Bread Dough Cinnamon Rolls (Schubert), 220
*See also* **Muffins**

**Roly-Poly Pudding**, 382

# S

**Saffron Bread** (Reedy), 370

**Salads**
Apricot and Cheese Molded Salad (Gooch), 211
Avocado Ring with Lobster or Crabmeat (Hutchinson), 159
Christmas Star Salad (Clauser), 66
Fruit Salad (March-Service), 147
Grapefruit and Avocado Salad, Mama Grace's (Ames), 351
Ham and Beet Salad (Elizabeth Hix), 65
Potato Salad, Good Ol' Mrs. Work's (Work), 178
Spiced Peach Salad (Ethel Mills), 132
Tomato Salad (March-Service), 147
Wilted lettuce and Bacon (*Kopfsalat mit Speck*) (Swiss Village), 175

**Salad Dressing**. *See* **Dressings, Salad**

**Salmon Mousse** (Lewis), 140

**Sandwich, Cucumber, Watercress, and Cream Cheese** (Bob Burgess), 385

**Sauce Robert, Plantation** (Bob Burgess), 242

**Sauces**
Foamy Sauce (Steiner), 366
Hard Sauce for Steamed Pudding, (Sholty), 253
Lemon Sauce (For Plumb Pudding) (Thelma Chapman), 241
Mint Sauce (Godfrey), 223
Mustard Sauce (for fish) (Sanders), 357
Mustard Sauce (for meat) (Mills), 131
Nutmeg Sauce (McCreery), 35
Plantation Sauce Robert (Bob Burgess), 242

**Sauerkraut** (Holzwarth), 154

**Sausage**. *See* **Smothered Sausage**

**Scalloped Chicken, Community Church of the Rockies**, 189

**Scalloped Cheese** (Hall), 80
**Scalloped Corn** (Work), 177
**Scalloped Potatoes** (Macdonald), 194
**Scones, Scottish** (Reed), 94
**Scotch Eggs** (Bob Burgess), 243
**Scottish Scones**. *See* **Scones, Scottish**
**Smothered Sausage** (Lewis), 140
**Snacks**. *See* **Trail Mix**
**Soufflé, Cheese** (Lewis), 140

**Soups**
Bean Soup, Company (Scott), 312
Black Bean Soup (Bob Burgess), 384
Cheese Soup, Crowley's Famous (Crowley), 270
Cock-a-Leekie Soup (Bob Burgess), 383
Minestrone, Red Stallion (Van Horn), 291

Oyster Soup (Cornelia Hayden), 77
Rochester Soup (Lewis), 138
Spanish Soup (Reed), 115
Vegetable, Inn of Glen Haven (Wells), 284

**Spanish Soup** (Reed), 115

**Spice Cake (Gewurzkuchen) and Icing** (Holzwarth), 155

**Spiced Peach Salad** (Ethel Mills), 132

**Sponge Cake for Jelly Roll** (Hall), 80

**Steak, Flank, McGraw** (McGraw), 167

**Steak Sauce.** *See* **Sauce Robert**

**Stews**
Hunters' Stew (Reedy), 369
Yowell Stew (Roehl/Yowell), 351

**Strawberries, Preserved** (Cheney), 80

**Strawberry Jam** (Anspauch), 232

**Stuffing or Dressing**
Stuffing for Roast Brisket or Veal (MacGregor), 32
Stuffing for Goose or Duck (MacGregor), 31

**Succotash** (Birch), 201

**Suet Pudding.** *See* **Puddings**

**Sugar Cookies, Grandma Carlson's** (Machin), 171

**Sweet Biscuits** (Traditional), 380

**Sweet Potatoes Southern Style** (Osborn), 204

# T

**Taffy, Molasses** (Hondius), 42

**Tea Cake, Blueberry** (Mills), 133

**Tomato Salad** (March-Service), 147

**Tomatoes, Baked** (Ethel Mills), 131

**Trail Mix** (Enos Mills), 101

**Trout**
Forelle Blau (Blue Trout; Truite au Bleu) (Hoerner), 263
Pan Fried (Bird), 26
Pan Fried (Roehl), 352
Smoked Trout (Bissell), 318

**Twin Mountain Muffins** (Sprague), 53

# U

**Upside Down Cake, Pineapple** (Carr), 236

# V

**(Vanilla) Ice Cream** (Machin), 171

**Veal.** *See* **Roast Beef Brisket or Veal**

**(Veal) Curry** (Macdonald), 193

**Vegetable Soup, Inn of Glen Haven** (Wells), 284

**Vegetables**
Asparagus with Cheese Sauce (Godfrey), 224
Cauliflower, French (Lewis), 138
Harvard Beets (Preston), 207
Succotash (Birch), 201
Tomatoes, Baked (Ethel Mills), 131

**Venison Roast** (Day family), 325

# W

**Waffles, Sour Milk** (Godfrey), 224. *See also* **Pancakes**

**Walnut Brittle** (Byxbe), 231

**Welsh Rarebit, Elkhorn Lodge** (Hondius), 41

**Wheel Cocktail** (Nagl), 265

**White Bread** (Sprague), 53

**White Bread, Mother's Wonderful** (Walters), 287

**Whole Wheat Bread** (Sanders), 358

**Whole Wheat Muffins** (Osborn), 204

**Wild Rice Casserole** (Brownfield), 273

**Wilted Lettuce Salad, Swiss Village** (Fischer), 175

# Y

**Yeast, Soft (Bread Jug)** (Sprague), 53

**York County (Chicken) Pot Pie** (Ethel Mills), 130

**Yorkshire Pudding** (Macdonald), 194

**Yowell's Stew** (Roehl/Yowell), 351

Made in the USA
San Bernardino, CA
27 March 2014